A MANAGEMENT SOURCEBOOK

A MANAGEMENT SOURCEBOOK

edited by
Franklin G. Moore
University of Michigan

HARPER & ROW, PUBLISHERS
NEW YORK, EVANSTON, AND LONDON

CONTENTS

Preface

vii

LIST OF AUTHORS

BARKDULL, C. W. Former Organization Counsel, *Lockheed Aircraft Company;* Management Consultant, *Management Services Division, Ernst and Ernst.*

BENEDICT, ROGER W. Staff Reporter, *The Wall Street Journal.*

BENGE, EUGENE J. Management Consultant.

CHAMBERLAIN, JOHN. Staff Writer, *Fortune.*

COUGHLAN, JOHN. CPA; Lecturer, *CPA School of Washington.*

DRUCKER, PETER F. Consultant and Professor of Management, *New York University.*

FISCH, GERALD G. Director of Management Services, *Touche, Ross, Bailey & Smart; Senior Partner P. S. Ross & Partners.*

FISH, LOUNSBURY S. Assistant to the Chairman of the Board, *Standard-Vacuum Oil Company.*

FOX, HARLAND. Staff Writer, *National Industrial Conference Board.*

FRIEDMAN, JACK J. Staff Writer, *Dun's Review and Modern Industry.*

GIBBONS, CHARLES C. *The Upjohn Company.*

GOODWIN, E. S. L. Captain (retired), U.S. Navy; former Lecturer, *University of Michigan.*

GREEN, ESTILL I. Executive Vice President, *Bell Telephone Laboratories.*

GREEN, PAUL E. Marketing Research Department, *E. I. duPont de Nemours & Company;* Lecturer in Statistics, *University of Pennsylvania.*

GREER, HOWARD C. Former Vice President *Chemistrand Corporation* and *Monon Railroad.* Currently part-time management consultant for several business concerns.

HABERSTROH, CHADWICK J. Assistant Professor of Industrial Management, *Massachusetts Institute of Technology.*

HARRISON, JAMES C., JR. Sales Manager, *Claussen Bakeries, Inc.*

HENNING, DALE A. Associate Professor of Policy and Personnel Relations, *University of Washington.*

IRWIN, PATRICK H. CPA.

JARMAN, W. MAXEY. Chairman of the Board of Directors, *Genesco Company.*

JOHNSON, RICHARD A. Professor of Business Administration, *University of Washington.*

KAST, FREMONT E. Professor of Business Administration, *University of Washington.*

KOLB, HARRY D. Manager, Employee Relations Research, *Esso Standard Division, Humble Oil & Refining Company.*

KOONTZ, HAROLD. Professor of Business Philosophy, *University of California at Los Angeles.*

KURSHAN, DANIEL L. Director of Administration, *The Port of New York Authority.*

LEAVITT, HAROLD J. Professor of Industrial Administration and Psychology, *Carnegie Institute of Technology.*

LEBRETON, PRESTON P. Professor of Policy, Personnel Relations and Production, *University of Washington.*

LIKERT, RENSIS. Director of Survey Research Center and Professor of Psychology and Sociology, *University of Michigan.*

LOVEWELL, PAUL J. Director of Economic Research, *Stanford Research Institute.*

MARCH, JAMES G. Associate Professor of Industrial Management, *Carnegie Institute of Technology.*

MC GREGOR, DOUGLAS. Professor of Industrial Management, *Massachusetts Institute of Technology.*

MEYER, MITCHELL. Staff Writer, *National Industrial Conference Board.*

MILLER, NORMAN C., JR. Staff Reporter, *The Wall Street Journal.*

NEWMAN, WILLIAM H. Samuel Brontman Professor of Democratic Business Enterprise, *Columbia University.*

NICHOLSON, SCOTT. Staff Writer, *Dun's Review and Modern Industry.*

PFIFFNER, JOHN M. Professor of Public Administration, *University of Southern California.*

ROSENZWEIG, JAMES E. Associate Professor of Business Administration, *University of Washington.*

RUBENSTEIN, ALBERT H. Professor of Industrial Engineering, *Northwestern University.*

SCHLEH, EDWARD C. President, *Edward Schleh & Associates.*

SCOUTTEN, E. F. Vice President, Personnel, *Maytag Company.*

SHERWOOD, FRANK P. Professor of Public Administration, *University of Southern California.*

SHILLINGLAW, GORDON. Associate Professor of Accounting, *New York University.*

SIMON, HERBERT A. Professor of Administration, *Carnegie Institute of Technology.*

SMITH, GEORGE A., JR. Professor of Business Administration, *Harvard Business School.*

SMYTH, RICHARD C. President, *Smyth & Murphy Associates Inc.*

STIEGLITZ, HAROLD. Assistant Director, Division of Personnel Administration, *National Industrial Conference Board.*

SUMMER, CHARLES E., JR. Associate Professor of Business Administration, *Columbia University.*

SUNDERLIN, DONALD H. Managing Partner, *Sunderlin Organization, Consultants.*

THOMPSON, STEWART. *General Products Mfg. Company.*

TILLES, SEYMOUR. Consultant and Lecturer on Business Administration, *Harvard Business School.*

TOMB, JOHN O. *McKinsey & Company.*

URIS, AUREN. *Research Institute of America.*

WARD, LEWIS B. Professor of Business Research, *Harvard Business School.*

WHITE, K. K. Staff Researcher, *American Management Association.*

WILLINGHAM, B. H. President, *Genesco Company.*

YOUNG, ROBERT B. Industrial Economist, *Stanford Research Institute.*

PREFACE

The literature on management has gotten to be so voluminous that it is nearly impossible to read or synthesize it all. Not only has the number of publications reached staggering proportions but frequently authors put forth many, even occasionally conflicting views. There are today several well-done books — usually textbooks — in which an author tries to present an overview of total thinking on management. Obviously, he has a difficult job both in selecting the ideas to represent and — even more difficult — in weaving them together into a coherent book. And even when he has succeeded, he must put before his readers material that reflects his own thinking and views on the subjects he is writing about.

Not surprisingly, teachers and students sometimes like to hear other writers on these same subjects, and to meet this need books of readings have become common in recent years. Such books bring together in one place the views of many different authors and authorities: they allow whole groups of readers ready access to those views without their having to do extensive research in libraries or having to rely on the one or two copies of primary sources kept on reserve shelves.

A Management Sourcebook contains 56 readings from original sources. It differs from other books like it, however, in that it is not narrowly confined. The subjects covered range more widely and more completely represent the whole subject of business management. A good many of the selections were written by business men; they tell how these men view and how they have solved the management problems they faced. But in addition to such ideas from men on the "firing line," A Management Sourcebook includes many of the more important ones of researchers and theoreticians.

Both the sequence of subjects and the space devoted to each subject, as it is taken up, parallel my textbook, Management: Organization and Practice; but this does not preclude A Management Sourcebook's being used as a companion to other books. To facilitate such use, the readings are grouped into parts according to topics commonly discussed in them.

F.G.M.

PART ONE:

THE MANAGERIAL JOB

1 THE IMPORTANCE OF ENVIRONMENT IN COMPANY GROWTH

by Paul J. Lovewell and Robert B. Young

Stanford Research Institute has long been interested in the subject of corporate growth. For the past six years the Institute has sponsored a continuing study of various aspects of the causes of growth. The more clearly the underlying causes of growth are understood, the more dynamic, efficient, and prosperous our democratic economy can become. Our research has taught us that predicting growth situations is difficult indeed but not necessarily impossible if the right tools are used in the right way.

In our comparative analysis of the characteristics and tactics of large groups of companies, several discernible differences have been noted that appear to distinguish the fast growing from the slowly growing or declining companies. In the future there will surely be other, _different_ characteristics that will mark the distinction. For example, the specific growth products of the sixties — perhaps new fuel cells — may bear little resemblance to those characteristics of the fast growers of the fifties.

The business world is dynamic and its specific needs and opportunities are constantly changing. But the nature of the environment that fosters growth can be examined. Growth inducing stimuli in this environment _can_ be identified, and the types of responses to these stimuli most often promoting growth _can_ be studied.

Our studies have shown that companies with high rates of growth usually . . .

First, have an affinity for growth products or fields;

Excerpts from two lectures on "The Importance of Environment in Company Growth," presented by Paul J. Lovewell and Robert B. Young to the Financial Analysts Seminar of the National Federation of Financial Analysts Societies, at Beloit College, Beloit, Wisc., August 22, 1960. Used by permission.

Second, have organized programs to seek and promote new business opportunities;

Third, possess proven competitive abilities in their present lines of business; and

Fourth, have courageous and energetic managements, willing to take carefully studied risks.

The first of these — a high correlation indicated between growth companies and growth industries — deserves more consideration than a statement of the obvious, because the ways in which industries become "growth fields" and the ways in which companies become involved in growth fields are not so obvious. If growth product fields do provide a vital source of stimuli for corporate growth, it will behoove us to examine in more detail what it is that makes an industry a "growth field," and how the potential for future growth can be recognized.

Our current research, therefore, has been focused on the influence of changes in the business environment on the growth of product fields, and, in turn, on the growth of companies. By examination of the environmental causes that appear to generate growth situations, we have sought to determine if the major forces in our society, economy, government, technology are measurably reflected in the growth of companies. And if so, in what ways do companies recognize and respond to these forces? What is the nature of the impact of these forces that enables growth situations to emerge, and specific companies to grow?

Our conclusions may be summarized by stating that we do find evidence to support a belief that changing environment plays a most significant role in corporate growth. It provides the opportunities that growth companies are able to capitalize on, and the threats that account for the relative decline of other companies less aware of the changing requirements of a changing world. Company growth seldom occurs without the helping stimulus of environmental change. Once the environmental stimulus is present, management is the intermediary link able to translate the potential into actual growth. Proper timing of action in response to the stimulus, effective long-range strategy, and a courage and willingness to shift to product fields of greater potential are important steps along the way.

Symptoms of forthcoming environmental changes can be recognized in their early stages by application of scientific research methods. Once the potential for change is recognized, companies and investors alike can build a base for growth by sensing where the impact of change will be the greatest and by shifting their product or investment emphasis to those areas where potential opportunity is the greatest.

First, let us examine in more detail just what we mean by "environment" and to discuss our theory of the impact of changing environment on company growth. Later we will consider some of the more specific characteristics of growth companies and of environmental impact that have been noted in our research.

The business environment, broadly, is the summation of all the factors outside the control of company management that have an influence on a company's sales, profits, markets, products, competition — or, on its growth. This environment is in constant flux. The character of its recognizable symptoms and colorations, the nature of its impact on companies, and the source of its influence change with time. It represents in sum a complex of shifts in the structure of our society, economy, and government; in the state of our technology; in the needs and tastes of our national market; and in our creative ability to master these shifts. These types of changes surround every business management.

In our research into company growth at the Institute it has been found useful to divide environmental changes into four categories for ease of discussion and analysis: social changes, economic changes, political changes, and technological changes.

FIG. 1. Examples of Environmental Changes of the 1950's.

Social	Economic	Political	Technological
● More older persons	● Higher family incomes	● Higher military expenditures	● Accelerating innovation rate
● More young children	● Increasing foreign competition	● Shifts in military budget expenditures	● Increased research spending
● Growth of suburbia	● Higher advertising budgets	● Increased farm supports	● Advanced state of technology
● More leisure time	● Rising labor costs	● Tighter business regulation	● Birth of company laboratories
● Higher educational levels	● Bull stock market	● Increased state and local government spending	● Increased need for scientific manpower

It is not necessary to comment on each of these changes, because most are well known and self-evident. You are probably noticing that many of these changes are of extremely broad description and of widely diffused influence. The broad, almost overpowering character of environmental changes is a notable descriptive characteristic. These trends seem so remote, so almost incomprehensible to the average businessman that they frequently are ignored in favor of smaller influences much closer to a company's recognizable daily business problems. But the influence of these broad changes on the prosperity and growth of companies, however disguised and diffused, is substantial, is measurable, and, in the last analysis, is the real key to the growth process.

Environmental changes are beyond the control of individual corporate management — they can be neither stopped nor accelerated. But even slow moving environmental changes, such as our lengthening life spans, resulting in greater numbers of the aged, eventually build up sufficient momentum to have a significant impact on the sales and profits of hundreds of companies.

All too often environmental changes progress so subtly that it is difficult to isolate or describe them. Numerous cases are found where managements are faced with reversals of long standing trends of sales and earnings, because they did not recognize a threatening change until too late. The problems of the big three auto makers since 1955 are a case in point. Surely those of you who placed your investment bets on George Romney's compact car preference back before 1957 can justly thumb your noses at Ford, GM, and Chrysler stockholders today.

Occasionally, the impact of change is a benign one — by coincidence a company happens to have products, capabilities, and capacities that fit perfectly in with the environmental changes, and with no particular effort on its part, experiences a rapid expansion in sales. This has been somewhat the experience of Outboard Marine and such cement companies as Ideal and Penn-Dixie, although even these companies that happened to be in the right place at the right time have had to improve their products and substantially expand their facilities. Growing pains are usually felt, because seldom can employment and output be quadrupled, for instance, without some waste along the way.

The result of unawareness of changes in the business environment is much more often crisis management, declining sales, and even losses on the profit and loss statement. Additional unrealized losses occur with a decline in the worth of assets used for the production of products unfavorably affected by changing times.

One of two things usually happens — first, some environmental change may cause the market for a company's products to stop growing or to decline. This condition frequently can be detected by observing that a company's sales are following a trend of a declining industry, pressed tighter and tighter by a cost-price squeeze. But the cause of the trouble is very often environment; only the symptoms of the cause appear on the P&L.

Examples taken from our research would include such rayon producers as American Viscose, Celanese, and Industrial Rayon, which seem to have been unable to keep abreast of the advancing state of synthetic fiber technology.

Second, the impact of an unplanned-for environmental change may be a significant expansion in the market for goods in which a company has excelled in the past — but the company is unable to capitalize on the growth potential. The reason is often that competitors have recognized a forthcoming change some time earlier and made necessary technological improvements in their products and processes. A company caught by surprise by the increased market potential may find itself several years behind firms that were formerly considered inferior competition. It may take as long as a decade to make up for one or two years' lag in a growth industry, and some companies are never able to regain their lost position.

Underwood, one of the declining companies we have used for comparison with some exceptionally rapid growers, is a good case in point. Underwood's business office machinery industry has grown right around it, but the company's unfortunate timing in recognizing the changing conditions that accounted for the industry growth have hurt Underwood's position severely.

There appears to be a critical time when potential opportunities must be seized. This time is different with nearly every change, and there may be as much danger from too early response to a change as well as from delayed action. But usually the "right time" to act upon a belief that the company can capitalize on an expected change is well before the change gains sufficient momentum to be either measured or generally publicized.

Can methods be adopted for creatively and objectively monitoring the buildup of future changes, for anticipating their impact on specific industries, products, and companies, and for choosing the optimum time for action? Figure 2 shows how a company might do this.

This diagram of the process of growth...has been designed as a method of illustrating the relationship of environmental change to corporate growth, and of demonstrating the critical importance of the timing of strategic company planning. Both of these concepts are reduced, of course, to their simplest fundamentals.

Neither a company nor its environment are ever static. In the diagram time is shown as progressing from left to right. Company management is shown in the lower left, surrounded by its environment. Management can recognize its present environment, most usually, by identifying and watching those factors which affect its familiar operations — the state of technology in its industry, for example, or the markets for its own products and for those of its competitors, suppliers, and customers. That is to say, today's environment filters to a company through its products, markets, and processes.

The importance of the products of a company as a determinant of growth is obvious. A company can grow only if it can sell more

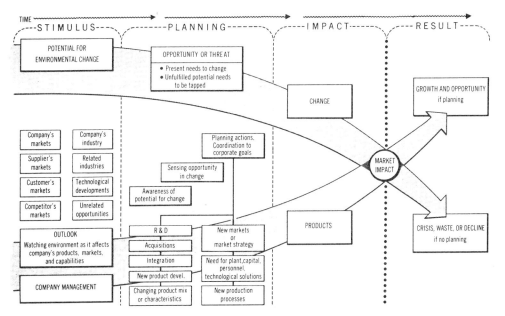

FIG. 2. Environment & Corporate Strategy.

of its products and increase its earnings from these products. Despite the effectiveness of advertising, sales promotional methods, and the like, if the over-all market potential for a product is not rapidly expanding, the growth of the company that produces this product will of necessity be limited and temporary. One can only increase his market penetration to a certain practical limit determined by such factors as the pressures of competition and the restraining hand of the Justice Department.

The product also is perhaps most important as the vital link between environmental change and growth. A company cannot come in contact with an environmental change unless it is in a position to produce a product that will benefit from a change. No company's products are inviolate — they can be changed.

It is important that sufficient emphasis be given to a company's outlook of what may happen in its environment, in contrast to what is happening. This is because environment, we know, is dynamic — many factors not in action today may very significantly affect the company at some future date. The coming to life of a new element in the environment is represented in the diagram as beginning in the upper left corner and progressing, through time, closer and closer to impact with the company's operations.

The potential for a forthcoming change can often be recognized by examining what sometimes seem to be remote symptoms. The general requirements for new metals to meet exacting specifications, for high energy fuel substances, or for microminiature electronic control assemblies could have been recognized several years ago by analyzing the inevitable needs of an expanding program of missile and space development.

Some companies did recognize the potential for these forth-coming changes in the government's procurement requirements, planned their research and product development capabilities in these areas, and today are leaders in three of the most envied current growth fields. Minneapolis-Honeywell, Thiokol Chemical, and Fansteel Metallurgical are examples. None of these companies owes its recent outstanding growth to luck or to good internal operations. The managements of each worked energetically and courageously to plan the growth that is now history, based on a recognition of opportunities that they were convinced would yield profitable business, and a willingness to commit their corporate destiny to their convictions.

As time progresses, the environmental change and the company's operations draw closer and closer together, until there is finally an interaction between the two. The characteristics of the change and its potential effect become more and more apparent as the change nears the point of impact.

There are three recognizable steps in the progression of planning for change that are found upon analysis of the tactics of growth companies. First, top management must be aware of the potential for a change. An open mind — a willingness to acknowledge that the future may be different from the present — is a prerequisite.

Second, the changes must be identified. A full time organized program of monitoring present and potential changes is the best method we have found of making early identification of opportunities and of insuring the company against being caught unprepared by environment-caused threats. [Later] I will discuss a method of applying formal scientific techniques to the enormous task of reviewing potential changes in the almost infinite total scope of business environment.

Third, consideration must be given to determining what opportunities or threats are inherent in the change that could fit in with the company's capabilities and goals. Here, an inventive ability is needed to translate potential trends into tangible products. The initial concept of specific product opportunities in pioneer fields can often be "sensed" by a creative mind.

Once the opportunities are recognized, it then becomes management's job to develop and implement a strategic long-range plan to capitalize on the opportunity or avoid the threat. The importance of this function in the growth process — long-range planning, and the development of corporate strategy to implement the plan — cannot be over-emphasized. Company growth without some sort of a strategic plan to capitalize on opportunities of a long-term nature is rare and usually coincidental. . . .

2 THE ENTREPRENEURIAL TASK AND ITS ELEMENTS

by Peter F. Drucker

It is the task of entrepreneurship to impart new and greater economic resources — as measured in the capacity of the resources to yield new and greater economic results.

*   *   *   *   *

1. OPTIMISING BUSINESS EFFECTIVENESS

The normal business situation is not the one the textbooks like to talk about: the start of a new business from scratch. The normal business situation in which the entrepreneurial task has to be performed is that of a going business. Here products and markets exist. Facilities and equipment are in place. Capital has been invested and has to be serviced. People are employed and are in specific jobs, and so on.

In this situation management, we are usually told, should concern itself with efficiency, that is with doing better what is already being done. It should, therefore, focus on costs. But the entrepreneurial approach focuses on effectiveness, that is, on the decisions what to do. It focuses on opportunities to produce revenue, to create markets and to change the economic characteristics of existing products and markets. It asks not: how do we do this or

---

Excerpts from a paper entitled "Entrepreneurship in Business Enterprise," presented by Peter F. Drucker to the Conference on Business Policy at the Harvard Business School, Cambridge, Mass., April 9, 1963; reprinted by permission of the author. A fuller exposition of the ideas in this paper can be found in Mr. Drucker's book, Managing for Results (New York: Harper & Row, 1964).

that? It asks: which of the products really produce extraordinary economic results or are capable of producing them? Which of the markets and/or uses are capable of producing extraordinary results? It then asks: to what results should therefore the resources and efforts of the business be allocated so as to produce extraordinary results rather than the "ordinary" ones which is all efficiency possibly can produce.

Efficiency concerns itself with the input of effort into all areas of activity. Effectiveness, however, starts out with the realization that in business, as in any other social unit, 10 or 15% of the phenomena — such as products, orders, customers, markets or people — produce 80 to 90% of the results. The other 85 to 90% of the phenomena, no matter how efficiently taken care of, produce, however, nothing but costs (which are always proportionate to transactions, that is to busy-ness).

The entrepreneurial job in the going business is therefore one of making effective the very small core of worthwhile activities which is capable of being effective. At the same time the entrepreneur neutralizes (if he does not abandon) the very large penumbra of transactions: products or staff activities, research work or sales efforts, which, no matter how well done, will not yield extraordinarily high economic results (whether they represent the opportunities of the past, mere busy-ness or unfulfilled hopes and expectations of the past, that is, the mistakes of yesterday).

2. IDENTIFYING AND REALIZING BUSINESS POTENTIAL

The second entrepreneurial task is to bring the business all the time a little closer to the full realization of its potential. Even the most successful business works at a low coefficient of performance as measured against its potential, that is, against the economic results that could be obtained were efforts and resources to produce the maximum yield they are inherently capable of.

This is not "innovation"; it actually takes the business as it is today and asks: what is its theoretical optimum? What inhibits attainment thereof? Where, in other words, are the limiting and restraining factors that hold back the business and deprive it of the full return on its resources and efforts?

*   *   *   *   *

In steel, these vulnerabilities, that is, the factors that hold the economic results of the steel industry way below the theoretical potential of industry and process, might, for instance, be the need, in present steel technology, to create high heats three times, only to quench them three times. Yet the most expensive thing to produce are temperatures, whether heat or cold. In the electrical apparatus business one vulnerability might well be the habit of the public utility customers to have each generating turbine designed as if it were a unique product rather than assembled as one of a large number and according to standard performance specifications. Another vulnerability might be the habit of the public utility customers to order turbines when money-market rates are low which then creates expensive fluctuations in demand and production schedules. If these two habits could be changed, large generating turbines might well come down 40 to 50% in cost. In life insurance, to give one more example, a central vulnerability might be the high cost of the individual sale. A way to overcome this vulnerability and to realize the potential of the business somewhat more fully might be either statistical selling — that is, elimination of the expensive personal selling efforts — or enrichment of the sales channel, for instance, by selling financial planning (including all other investment instruments such as investment trust shares) rather than life insurance.

These examples are cited to show that a "relatively minor change" does not necessarily have to be easy to make. In fact, we may not know how to do it. But it is still "minor," that is, the business would remain essentially as it is now, yet would have different economic characteristics. And while the illustrations show clearly that these changes may require "innovation," they are not, in themselves, "innovations." They are primarily modifications of the existing business.

Another basic approach to the identification and realization of business potential starts with the question: what are we in this business afraid of?

It is the characteristic task of the entrepreneur to convert into opportunity what everybody else in industry or market considers dangers.

The pharmaceutical industry today is, for instance, scared stiff of a trend towards generic names for drugs. The entrepreneurial approach would ask: can we use this trend as an opportunity? The company which first looks upon this "threat" as an opportunity might well emerge as the giant of tomorrow's pharmaceutical business.

Or one asks the question: what are the areas everybody neglects today, including ourselves? Profits — as well as productivity — are the result of differential rather than of absolute capability. This means that the bandwagon climber cannot be profitable, cannot obtain extraordinary economic results. Those lie in the areas which are not pursued by everyone.

* * * * *

3. MAKING THE BUSINESS OF TOMORROW

This is the area which is usually meant when people talk of "entrepreneurship." But unless it is connected organically to entrepreneurship in today's going business, work here cannot be effective. The approach towards making the business of tomorrow starts out with the conviction that the business of tomorrow will be and must be different, but it also starts out — of necessity — with the business of today. For Making the Business of Tomorrow cannot just be "flash of genius." It requires not only systematic analysis but hard, rigorous work today — and that means by people in today's business and operating within it.

It may indeed be said to be the specific job of entrepreneurship in business enterprise to make today's business capable of making the future, that is, of making itself into a different business. It is the specific job of entrepreneurship in the going business to enable today's already existing — and especially today's already successful — business to remain existing and to remain successful in the future.

* * * * *

Here are some approaches to the task:

First, there is projection. The question is asked: what has already happened in economy and in society, in technology and in organization, in our business and in the great world outside, that has fundamentally changed the basic assumptions that underlie our behavior, but which has not yet had full impact? (One way to find such development is to look at the popular "forecasts" of what is likely to happen in the future. For what is being forecast as likely to happen in the future, has often already happened. If it has not yet happened, it rarely seems "plausible"; few of us can imagine what we have not already seen.)

Here is an example, now past history.

* * * * *

[Late in] the twenties, Sears Roebuck shifted
from mail-order business to retail stores. This
reflected an understanding that Sears' customers, the farmers, had changed both economically and sociologically. The automobile
had made them mobile; they could now come to
a store where, formerly, the merchant and his
merchandise had to come to the farmer. And
the farmer was no longer a distinct and separate
customer but, increasingly, became one with the
low and low-middle income customers in American society.

A second approach is combination: combining two major
developments, each of which has already happened and has already
had major impact.

IBM, within the last fifteen years, brought
together two separate developments into one new
business: the emergence of "professional" management with its emphasis on figures and analysis; and the new data-processing capacity which
was developed for different (partly military,
partly scientific) purposes.

The third approach is, unlike the first two, focused on the
future rather than on the future impact of past or present events.
It is what could be called genuine Innovation. What can and should
we do to make a different future — for the economy and for the
society, for technology and for the market, for ourselves in this
business and for an entire industry?
Innovation so conceived, is not a "thing," indeed, it is not
necessarily technological. It need not come out of research; on
the contrary, it often precedes research. Nontechnological, social
innovation has, throughout history, been at least as important
as technological innovation; only the other day somebody said,
and with considerable justice, that the supermarket has changed
the American economy and society (as well as other economies
and societies) a great deal more drastically than all of atomic
energy.

* * * * *

The fourth approach, though by far the best known and the most
popular one, should really be considered marginal: Anticipation —
that is, the attempt to answer what is likely to happen that would
or could have fundamental impact on the business.
People usually mean anticipation when they talk about "planning" today. And the term is popular precisely because it imputes

to the process a degree of reliability, if not certainty. Actually, this is the least certain and most speculative one of all the approaches — and the one least likely to succeed. It is not given to human beings to predict the future. Yet this is what "Anticipation" attempts.

Nevertheless, this is one of the approaches; and in the systematic attempt at Making the Future of a Business it should be included and should be used, if only as a control and as a check on the other three, less speculative and more satisfactory approaches.

* * * * *

3 THE PRESIDENT LOOKS AT HIS JOB

A company president's job is too big to be fully explored in a two- or three-hour discussion. This was more than evident a year ago when six company presidents — in January, 1962 — engaged in such a discussion. (See "The President Looks at His Job," Management Record, May, 1962.)

It was evident then that at least two aspects of the chief executive's job — his accountability and his control — warranted much further analysis. Accordingly, this year, another six presidents agreed to engage in an unrehearsed discussion of these subjects.

Both concepts are difficult to pinpoint. And dictionary definitions of the terms don't seem to fully satisfy chief executives. To them, the terms are meaningful only when personalized. This is especially true of accountability. For in the discussion it was clear that "responsibility" very often was used instead of "accountability." Is there any difference between the two? One chief executive volunteered that, to him, responsibility is a "subjective" term, accountability an "objective" term; his accountability is flavored by his feeling of responsibility.

Whatever the nuances between the two terms, during the discussion they were used interchangeably. While the semanticist may bemoan this lack of precision, it in no way deterred the

Excerpts, reprinted from Management Record, March, 1963, pages 2-11, by permission of the National Industrial Conference Board.

chief executives from stating what they felt accountable and/or responsible for.

What follows is a portion of their candid, off-the-record remarks at the January, 1963, meeting, including some questions from audience participants.

The chief executives were: Chairman, J. Wilson Newman, Chairman of the Board, Dun & Bradstreet, Inc.; William E. Blewett, Jr., Chairman of the Board and President, Newport News Shipbuilding & Dry Dock Co.; Richard P. Chapman, President, New England Merchants National Bank; Charles L. Huston, Jr., President, Lukens Steel; C. Virgil Martin, President, Carson Pirie Scott & Company; Robert B. Semple, President, Wyandotte Chemicals Corporation; Austin J. Tobin, Executive Director, The Port of New York Authority.

Chairman Newman: Last year, when a group of us sat before a similar audience and talked about the job of the president, Jack Holman made this telling comment: "When a fish dies it smells first at the head." Terrible language, but perhaps it is à propos of the situation when an organization dies. The decay starts at the head. If we are going to measure slippage or progress or stagnation, maybe some tests should be applied. And from that we get into areas of accountability and areas of control.

If you look up the definition of control in the dictionary, you will find two or three words that are repeated rather frequently. One is "check," another is "regulation," and a third is "restraint." I hope that some of the comments will indicate how "control" is used in the management sense — whether, in this battle of semantics that we engage in every day, we are using "control" to mean "restraint"; and, if it is "restraint," should it be?

Many of you probably saw a statement made by Jack Rathbone recently, which intrigued me greatly. It was published under the heading "The Antennae of Corporate Management."[1] One of the sentences that appeared was this:

"Now, just to whom do we listen?" Mr. Rathbone listed six groups. Four of these were : stockholders; customers; employees;

---

[1] Talk by M. J. Rathbone, Chairman of the Board, Standard Oil Company (New Jersey) at annual dinner of Wharton School Alumni Society of the University of Pennsylvania, October 31, 1962.

governments — federal, state, local, and, now, international. His fifth group was "the people as a whole" — this certainly is a group we must consider in plumbing accountability. His sixth point, to me, was interesting and penetrating: "Management's conscience that searches its soul, this self-judging quality, which is the source of management's self-respect."

I offer that thought as a preface to our own evaluations. Now let's get on with it.

ACCOUNTABILITY

Chuck Huston, let me start with you. What do you know now about accountability and control that you have learned from experience, that you wish someone had told you before you took your office?

Mr. Huston: In the president's job, as well as during executive experience prior to that appointment, all of us probably learn that accountability requires a target for a standard. It may be a quality standard or an expense standard. It can be a standard in terms of performance, or profit, or anything else. But, nevertheless, accountability has to be based on something to account for or against. A target or a standard is fundamental, and it's important that the target be established with good judgment.

Chairman Newman: Let's try to look at accountability in a very practical way. Bill Blewitt, among the small craft that your company has manufactured is the liner, the United States. If on the next voyage she sprung eight rivets in the forward plate, would you be accountable for that?

Mr. Blewett: In the first place, she hasn't eight rivets in the forward plate, she's welded.

Chairman Newman: Are you accountable for the fact that she doesn't have rivets, but is welded?

Mr. Blewett: Yes, very probably; and to an extent, of course, the design agent is also accountable.

Chairman Newman: Can we tie the rivets and welding to accountability in a different way? Billions of dollars have been spent in research and development in this country. As a result, technology has advanced tremendously. New techniques will have to be tested.

When a new product or a new technique comes out, such as welding rather than riveting, where does the chief executive's responsibility start and end? What is his accountability for putting the product on the market, where people are betting their lives on its use?

Mr. Blewett: It's all management's accountability, if that is what you are driving at.

Mr. Semple: If you are trying to fix the responsibility for

moving ahead on product development, I think that is just one of those things in a creative business about which you use your best judgment in trying to make progress. It seems to me impossible to get into new fields of activity of any significance without taking some risk.

Mr. Martin: I think perhaps we put our finger directly on one of the biggest accountabilities of the chief executive officer of the company. Our main accountability is for what the business will be ten years from now.

In other words, if there is any one area of accountability that a chief executive officer has to accept, it is in answering the question: "Where are we going to be ten years from now?"

In Bill Blewett's situation, the risk they took on the welding was a real risk. But it was a risk they had to take. The experimentation had to go on or they would not be in business today.

Chairman Newman: All right. We have probed the subject of accountability; and in answer to the question, "For what?" we'll say, "For the future of our enterprise."

Mr. Tobin: I would agree with that as a prime responsibility but I think there's far more to it. Certainly the correctness or incorrectness of his judgment about future development of the company is something for which the chief must be fully accountable because he is — in large part — the image of the company. Fairly or unfairly, the policies of the company and where the company was going ten years ago, where it will be ten years from now, as well as the blunders of today, are what he is paid to take responsibility for.

*　*　*　*　*

I also believe that the chief executive has an additional job of accountability in leadership. He's got to be out front, setting the tone of the corporation and moving the corporation forward. When things go wrong, he ought to be in the first line of defense, accepting his accountability and bolstering the morale of everybody in his whole organization by reassuring them that he is not in the back line some place, but out where the going is tough.

Of course, he's accountable for profits, for growth; but I would submit that he is much more accountable for many intangibles such as tone, morale, and leadership.

Chairman Newman: This is a very interesting point. You are saying that, whatever area is in question, it is the chief executive's obligation to identify himself with the things that do not go right, just as it is his pleasure to identify himself with the things that do go well.

Mr. Huston: We are probing on the basis that presidents are accountable — and accountable for the future. But the average life, I think, of a chief executive officer in his job is only about ten years, isn't it?

Accountable for What?

Mr. Chapman: I don't think any of us meant to define the accountability summarily as just for the future or the ten-year picture. Of course you are accountable for the direction and the progress of your corporation and the climate in which it labors: geographic, economic, and so on. You are responsible, not merely for where it is going to be, but for its progress along the way and how it gets there. Never mind whether you are going to be around to have the tag pinned on you, ten or fifteen years from now. I'd say that I won't be. My mistakes or failures will be assessed in memoriam, more or less. I think that is true of most chief executives.

Mr. Martin: I think I said that the future is one of the chief areas of accountability. We are accountable for return on invested capital. This is one of our principal responsibilities. And we are accountable for selecting people who can be held accountable for certain aspects of the business. To me, selecting accountable people is one of the real tests of a chief executive.

Chairman Newman: I think it's rather significant that so far, in our discussion of accountability, the word profit has hardly been stressed.

Mr. Huston: Yes, it is profit that we're accountable for. But I'd like to emphasize that it is not just this year's profits — it's next year's profits and continuing profits in the years ahead. When we think of our job, it's the many things that result in a profit to which we direct our attention. It's like trying to reach a state of happiness. If you just suddenly try to be happy, it doesn't happen.

I think this same thing is true of profitability. If we are doing a tremendous job of marketing and sales, of manufacturing, a really imaginative job of methods, new equipment, and new processes to produce the product — if our attention is given to these things and we use good judgment — profit happens, like happiness happens. I suppose that is the reason we didn't just stress profit, per se.

Chairman Newman: How does your conception of the public, of the government, of the stockholders, and of the employees affect your views of what a chief executive officer should be accountable for, what he is accountable for, and what he can reasonably be expected to be accountable for? Maybe that question would be simpler if I reversed it. Do you think that some people believe that you are accountable for things that you don't think you should really be held accountable for?

Mr. Semple: You have set forth a rather broad format of accountability. Certainly, the views of the general public, the views of one's employees, and the views of the government are very important in the conduct of business. However, the essence of accountability is that which I am accountable for to my board of directors. If you satisfy your board, I think your actions would be such that the other groups would more or less think you are doing the job right.

In our industry, chemicals, for example, the problem of air and steam pollution is an increasing one. The industry is making serious efforts to control it. If we don't, we are going to get into trouble with the public. It will hold us accountable for running, let's say, a pollution-free shop. But top management in that situation should really be aware of its accountability before the public comes into the picture. If you do not do the job right, you will be held more accountable by the public than if you do do it right.

Chairman Newman: Now if, by design or accident, the stream is polluted below one of your plants and it is traceable to some activity in that plant, do you feel any personal accountability because of that fact?

Mr. Semple: Surely.

* * * * *

What Cannot Be Delegated

Participant: It is very brave for the president of a company to be accountable for everything. I wonder, however, whether part of it couldn't be delegated rather effectively: whether accountability can't be given meaningfully to other people? If you give it to a vice-president and he disagrees with you on a certain program, isn't that the time you separate the ways? In other words, the vice-president should be accountable for the project because, even if it is your idea, he implemented it and is responsible for it and he should stand up and answer for it.

My question is, can't accountability be delegated, and isn't it wise to do so?

Chairman Newman: As far as delegating accountability — and I'm going to use responsibility as being synonymous — in my judgment that cannot be delegated. I believe the chief executive officer can delegate authority, not responsibility. When he delegates authority, his responsibility is just as great as it was before he did that.

* * * * *

Mr. Semple: Don't you think you could postulate, really, two kinds of responsibility? Certainly, in a reasonably delegated industrial operation, the vice-presidents and, in turn, their own key fellows, are all carrying a tremendous load of responsibility. A president may approach his total responsibility as he would a pie. He cuts it up so that there are a lot of pieces to the pie. Some pieces work out better than the others. The measure of a president is the average performance of his key people in carrying out their responsibility.

I don't think our hypothesis is that the president is the only one who has responsibility in the company.

Who Gets the Blame?

Chairman Newman: If I conveyed that impression, I would like to correct it very quickly. I think everyone in an organization bears responsibility. But I don't think that anyone in an organization, regardless of his level, can delegate his responsibility. A superintendent can delegate authority to do a job to a foreman, but the responsibility for seeing that the job gets done remains with him. That stands, from the lowest-level supervisor right up the line. I didn't mean to say that one man carries the entire responsibility.

* * * * *

CONTROL

Chairman Newman: Let's shift our attention to the control or controls the chief executive relies upon.

Mr. Tobin: As we move into the area of control, we all start thinking about "standards" or the textbook controls we all use in our companies. I think it's a perfectly obvious fact that if these controls — the reports, audits, projections whether automated or not — were 100% successful, you would not need presidents of corporations. I am suggesting that the more significant area of control is the decisions the chief executive makes that go beyond the "control" data available to him. Actually, his only period of usefullness may be when he has to make a decision without all the necessary facts. This may be a "Yes" or "No" decision, or a decision that he has made a mistake and must take action to cut his losses. These are frightfully hard decisions that we all have to face from time to time. They go beyond the machine and into the factors of judgment and responsibility that are the basis of the chief executive's control.

Mr. Semple: I would agree that there is a point where the control of a chief executive depends a great deal on the methods by which he approaches his job and the way he runs his business.

Some fellows do a great deal of delegation, without too much follow-up. Some go about it sort of half-and-half. I think I am in that category. Some don't delegate very much at all, and I can't agree with that approach. But there is certainly a wide swath in the approaches to control and the methods that any individual chief executive relies upon. In certain areas, I depend upon reports; in others, I depend upon meetings. We have capital forecasting, analysis of capital expenditures, and post-audits on the performance of our investments. There are about twenty-five separate methods that I use.

Mr. Martin: To be an effective chief executive officer, you have to drive with a loose rein, knowing when to gee or haw.

In this area of controls, you have the same variables that you have in this whole discussion of accountability. I don't think the chief executive officer can devote too much attention to what I would call the precise departmental controls; these are for the operating department heads.

There are functional controls that he has to be more concerned with. These tie together the various elements of the different departments that either have the same function or an interrelated function.

The chief executive's most important controls — those he has to devote most of his time to — are what I would call directional or policy controls.

You have to establish how far you will go with these controls by knowing the people with whom you work. That determination gets you into the whole motivational field. There are some executives with whom you use a hard bit instead of a loose rein. With other executives, you have to adjust this control; it's encouragement, rather than the whip, that you use.

A lot of people make the mistake of thinking that by throwing some precise information into a computer they can control the business. These precise machine controls belong down the line and the men who have them must understand that they have them. But when I think of the chief executive and control, I think of functional, or directional and policy, control.

Mr. Huston: I agree with that, but I would like to take a little different slant. When I got this job a number of years ago, I found I had to dig out a lot of the information to get a basis from which to develop control. The answer for us was to try to get some fellows who were good controllers. I don't mean maintainers; I mean really good fellows who get things done. It has been a great satisfaction that in virtually all our major areas, we have a bunch of positive executives who are so much on top of their jobs, doing their own controlling, that I find myself a sort of radar screen, more or less scanning. I have a few sleepless nights now and then when a couple of these positive executives get at each other, but it is my job to see that there is some sort of balance.

So I think one of my major controls is getting the right sort of people — those who understand the objectives, who can interpret the goals not only to me but to their own people, and who can get ideas and actions from their people which can move a company.

Mr. Chapman: I don't think that any business can get anywhere today unless the chief executive practices the art of delegation. Of course, you delegate responsibility to selected, trusted people. They are accountable to you, and they have their accountabilities also. You measure performance, to some extent, by working with them and studying the reports they make, and, to some extent, by the objectivity of factual reports from your control group.

But a lot of these areas don't lend themselves to precise measuring, as was already said. For example, in the banking business some of the most expensive services you perform produce no income. To set a standard of performance for these services is hard, if not impossible. But even if you have determined that a function is being provided very efficiently and economically, there are further questions: Should that function be provided at all? Why not abolish it and save the money? Could the bank do its business and serve its customers as well without that function? Could you halve the department — never mind whether it is run sufficiently — just reduce the size of it? Of course, no one that you delegate that kind of function to is going to slit his own throat. It's the kind of a decision that an executive simply cannot delegate. It is nothing that you can objectively decide.

* * * * *

Principal Tools of Control

Mr. Blewett: The principal control in my company would be the ability to continue to get work. In other words, are we building? Can I make a bid at a price that will give us a profit?

Mr. Chapman: I would simply say that the principal tool was to see how we are doing in our environment; in relation to our competitors; in growth, profits, and public standing.

Chairman Newman: Aren't we talking about the end result here? As I understand the question, it has to do with the mechanics. What are the tools?

Mr. Tobin: What is the principal tool? In my line of business, it's what we call our net revenue control, which indicates whether the department is meeting the necessary net revenue coverage that we have to have if we are to continue to sell bonds.

Chairman Newman: Budget — that's the major control tool for me.

Mr. Martin: In our instance, I think it is the rate of return on the net capital investment in comparison to others in the same business, and whether it is healthy.

Mr. Blewett: In other words, in relation to competitors?

Chairman Newman: The answer to the question, "How are we doing relative to what can be expected?"

* * * * *

THE PEOPLE PROBLEM

Participant: One of the areas that you have indicated you are accountable for is people — concern for people, development of people, and so on. How much time do you give to this area of concern?

Mr. Tobin: A tremendous amount of time — in one sense, almost all my time. But, pulling a figure out of the air, certainly 10% or 15% of my time has to do with my accountability, responsibility, or concern for people. I have all the mechanical and technical controls we can work out. Since what you ultimately accomplish depends upon your judgment in developing and handling people — that can make or break you faster than anything else — a tremendous amount of this executive's time is put on that.

Mr. Semple: If I had to pick a figure out of the air, I would pick 25%. In my own experience, however, it varies, depending upon the state of health in my company. At one time, I believe I devoted as much as 50% or more of my time to the development of the management group and the problems connected with that. I think 50% is quite a lot of time, because there is so much else to do. Simply reading the mail takes up quite a lot of time.

Mr. Martin: I always disliked the term, "concern for people." Too often, it's construed to mean concern for individuals. For example, if you release an executive after you have had a good deal of discussion about him and with him, he immediately says, "You have no concern for people." As president, I have to have concern for 9,000 people and not only one individual. So I translate the phrase to mean concern for the effectiveness of people within the organization. In that sense, I would say it averages out to about 25% or 30% of my time. Sometimes, when you are expanding or reorganizing, it could go to 90%. But I still dislike the term, "concern for people."

Mr. Huston: A few minutes ago, someone said, "Know thyself." Relating that to "concern for people," I have found there are so many smarter people in the world than me that I try to find all the smartest guys in a particular area, whether it is capital expenditures or methods change or buying a new outfit, and go with them. In arriving at my own judgments, I rely heavily upon their recommendations and their supporting information.

I don't want to give the impression that I am, or any other chief executive is, merely a polltaker whose job is to lead by consensus. It's the judgment and experience factor of the chief executive, which oftentimes causes him, and has to cause him, to override the individual or concerted judgment of the second-line people.

* * * * *

Chairman Newman: The question, as I understand it, concerns people. It seems to me that the chief executive does hardly anything in the business that does not have some relation to appraising the accomplishments of people or their lack of accomplishments, their strengths or their weaknesses. You read and appraise every memorandum you get in reference to not only who signed it, but who wrote it; you appraise it in terms of, not merely what it says, but also how it is said.

From an organizational standpoint, one of the haunting concerns of the chief executive officer — I believe it's his primary obligation — is who is the person who is going to succeed him, and what is he doing about getting him ready. The chief executive officer, I believe, gives a whole lot more thought to this than the public, the stockholders, or even the board realize. It is not easy, because there are not many businesses that can run around with a stable of four, five, or six men, any one of whom could do the top job. Other companies buy them away very quickly.

Mr. Huston: As a quick way of putting the "people concern" into perspective, you might say a company is known by the men it keeps. It's these men — and women — who produce and sell the ideas, the products, and the services, and that is what makes up your company.

Participant: In connection with your comment that a chief executive spends lots of time thinking about his successor, I would like to know what it is the chief executive looks for — what kinds of qualities — in the choice of a successor?

Chairman Newman: That's easy. He looks for the best man he can find, and, certainly, he looks for one who is better than himself.

THE "BIG" PROBLEM AHEAD

Participant: I am concerned with the fact that through the lack of self-control, management is losing the ability to control the over-all actions. I came down here from Canada. I don't suggest that we are any better, because we have the same problem. We get worse to the extent that you get worse.

We see more and more laws being introduced at the state and federal levels to limit the freedom of action of management in their corporations. What is the attitude of management in this country with regard to this matter of the gradual loss of your ability to control your own business?

Chairman Newman: I cannot answer your question, but I think you have put your finger on something that is of greater overriding importance than anything we have mentioned here so far. I mentioned it before, but I feel strongly enough about it to repeat it: The profit motive is on trial in this country. It is on trial in your country. These controls come because the constituents of the people elected to the legislative bodies do not identify profits with human welfare. To the extent that leaders in business, big or small, do not do their part to make this identification obvious, we are going to get more and more controls. It seems that it would be appropriate to close this discussion by again referring to my opening question: "Now, just to whom do we listen?"

The answer, you'll recall, is stockholders, customers, employees, governments, the people as a whole — and our own conscience.

4 ARKANSAS LOUISIANA GAS' WITT STEPHENS

by Roger W. Benedict

How can a company bolster its profits? How can it meet new competition? Should it expand into new areas? Many men have faced up to such problems in recent years as they have moved into top corporated posts. This is one of a series of stories on the management methods of some of these new bosses.

LITTLE ROCK, Ark. — One blustery day recently a tall, stoop-shouldered man hurried along a residential street here, ringing doorbells and chatting with housewives. In a short time he accomplished his mission: He lined up a customer for a $1,250 central gas air-conditioning unit.

The hustling salesman was no ordinary peddler. Wilton Robert (Witt) Stephens, former belt buckle salesman and small town stockbroker, is chairman and president of fast-growing Arkansas Louisiana Gas Co. Though it's a bit irregular for a utility chief executive to promote his business door-to-door, Mr. Stephens' associates have grown accustomed to the practice in the eight years since he joined the firm. Every few weeks he forsakes his busy downtown office for such a personal sales effort — one of the tactics he employs to spur subordinates to greater achievements and boost the fortunes of Arkla, as his utility is known.

This flair for selling, coupled with an imaginative eye for offbeat opportunities for profit, has enabled Witt Stephens in

---

Reprinted from The Wall Street Journal, Wednesday, January 17, 1962, page 1, by permission of the publisher.

recent years to bring about a dramatic improvement in the affairs of Arkansas Louisiana Gas. Formerly a conservative utility with one of the industry's worst earnings records, it now ranks as one of the most aggressive and successful organizations in the business.

For 1961, Arkla expects to report profits more than six times the $2.7 million earned in 1954, the year Mr. Stephens entered the picture. Total sales have tripled over the same span, and the company now boasts some 500,000 customers, more than twice the number seven years ago.

The cigar-puffing Mr. Stephens, now 54 years old, has deftly reshaped his company from one almost wholly dependent on sales of natural gas to a widely diversified corporation with income from a score of sources. The diversification moves, which make Arkla's business much less subject to the whims of the weather than is the case with most utilities, have involved both the purchase of going concerns and the undertaking of ventures from scratch. Arkla's activities now include the making of appliances, boats, cement, chemicals, and rocking chairs and the operation of a restaurant and a bowling alley.

All these businesses have proved profitable in themselves; but other motives underly the utility's diversification program: To stimulate the economy of the area served by Arkla — most of Arkansas, northwest Louisiana, east Texas and sections of Oklahoma and Kansas — and, thus, boost gas sales. "Too many utility executives just sit back and collect bills, think up snappy slogans, make flowery speeches and wait for their service areas to grow," rasps Mr. Stephens, a six-foot, three-inch, 230-pound self-styled "country boy." "I believe in getting out and aggressively selling the product and doing what I can to make our territory grow."

Arkla was in a troubled state when Mr. Stephens arrived on the scene in 1954. Earnings had dropped to about half the level of five years earlier, despite a 69% rise in revenues. Utilities are dependent on area growth, and population in the Arkla service area was declining. Because of a short winter heating season, the company used its full capacity only four days a year. During four summer months it didn't earn enough to meet payroll and maintenance costs.

TRIMMING THE PAYROLL

Mr. Stephens immediately set out to bolster profits. A study by his investment firm's staff indicated widespread inefficiency in the company's operations; among other things, it was found a senior clerk was reading meters and an engineer was operating a boiler. A thorough revamping of the organization was undertaken, and 500 employes — 22% of the payroll — were dismissed.

To cut costs further, the company stopped paying for country club memberships for executives, curtailed personal use of company cars and pared expense accounts.

"We now run a lean and hungry organization in which we try to get the maximum effort out of the minimum number of people," says Mr. Stephens. A typical Stephens innovation: A vice president was put in charge of both buying and selling gas "so he'll know just what the gas he's selling costs."

A look at the utility's books showed the company's retail appliance department was not selling enough to pay its $300,000-a-year operating cost; one salesman hadn't sold anything for six months. Mr. Stephens abolished the elaborate department. In its place he created a small but active sales force and made every Arkla employe — including himself — responsible for turning up sales. "Do you think my vice presidents, managers and other employes would get out and sell if I didn't do the same thing?" he asks. Arkansas Louisiana claims it sells more gas appliances than any other utility in the country, and the concern's average residential customer burns 50% more gas than he did seven years ago.

RAISING RATES

Another study by Mr. Stephens' investment firm's staff indicated the company was charging unprofitable prices for its gas sales to industrial concerns, which accounted for more than 80% of the utility's total gas volume. Mr. Stephens successfully sought rate increases from state commissions in Arkansas, Texas and Louisiana. He also began negotiating long-term contracts with industrial firms, gaining higher rates in exchange for priority service and firmer supply. Result: Arkla now gets about 40% more for industrial gas than it did seven years ago.

Though these initial moves by Mr. Stephens were important, the most spectacular aspect of Arkla's transformation unquestionably is the series of diversification steps he has taken. Mr. Stephens places no limits on diversification areas, and some of his moves have been startling. But nothing is done by whim. Mr. Stephens scrutinized each possibility with a securities expert's cold eye for profits, painstakingly studying pertinent facts and figures his Arkla staff, in his words, "coons down" for him.

The first diversification step came in 1957. Mr. Stephens figured the best way to boost the summer gas load was to increase the use of gas air conditioning. But Servel, Inc., then the only manufacturer of gas air conditioners, wanted to quit the appliance business. After a study of Servel and the air conditioner market and negotiations with Servel, Mr. Stephens went to his board with a proposal.

BUYING A FAILURE

Mr. Rebsamen of the Arkla board recalls the session: "He was challenging us to buy a plant that had been a failure, to make a product no one had been able to sell. He was asking this of a utility that had no experience in manufacturing operations. And the plant was well outside our service area, in Evansville, Ind. But he's the greatest salesman in the world, and he sold us on the project in a tremendous talk. He closed by saying that if we didn't want to buy the plant, he wanted permission to do so with his own money. That convinced us to go ahead with the purchase."

Arkansas Louisiana Gas bought Servel's air conditioner division for $4.6 million. Mr. Stephens stepped up the plant's research and development program, producing in one year air conditioners that could compete in performance and price with electric units. Arkla's sales force went to work, and at the end of 1961 enough gas air-conditioning units had been installed in the company's territory to cancel out a significant part of the usual summer slump in demand. The Arkla subsidiary making the air conditioners contributed over $1.1 million to the utility's earnings last year.

Other diversification moves followed quickly. On a trip to New Orleans, Mr. Stephens saw two old-fashioned gas lights in a restaurant. His salesman's instinct told him the lights would appeal to many people, and the air conditioner subsidiary was put to work making them. The company sold 80,000 of the units in 1961, and more than 64,000 gas lights have been installed on Arkansas Louisiana Gas' own system, mainly by home owners.

THE BUGGY BUSINESS

A visit by Mr. Stephens to Indiana resulted in an even more unusual venture. He got Arkla to buy a buggy manufacturing firm in Huntington for $27,000 after his researchers decided 1,000 buggies a year could be sold for use in television and advertising and to people who simply wanted to own a buggy. He shifted the buggy works to Emmett, Ark., a dying rural community. Arkla also has opened a factory turning out rocking chairs, bedroom furniture and saddles at Emmett and by the addition of a "sarsaparilla bar," the Chuck Wagon restaurant and a bowling alley has made the town into a tourist attraction. All this has revitalized the community and sharply boosted local gas consumption.

Other new Arkla enterprises are less bizarre but even more profitable. Arkansas Cement Co., a cement-producing subsidiary established in western Arkansas, can't keep up with demand, despite the fact large cement companies had insisted no market for additional cement existed in the area; Arkansas Cement also burns about $1 million worth of gas a year. By leasing an idle plant from the Federal Government at Pine Bluff, Ark., Arkla entered the chemical business. It got into boat production by buying a maker of fiber glass boats and building a new $600,000 plant at Malvern, Ark.

The steady expansion of Arkla's industrial business, both through its own ventures and through the addition of other industrial customers, has had one unsatisfactory aspect: It's meant the company has continued to be sensitive to the vicissitudes of the general economy. Though 1961 earnings appear to have rebounded to record or near-record levels, the most recent recession dropped 1960 net income $880,559 below 1959's $17.3 million, the highest yearly profit reported by the company to date.

SOFTENING SLUMPS' IMPACT

To lessen the impact of economic downturns in the future, Arkansas Louisiana this year extended its gas lines into 62 additional residential communities. It also negotiated mergers with Southwest Natural Gas Co. and Mid-South Gas Co., adding 94,000 customers who are mainly in the residential and commercial category. Arkansas Louisiana Gas' monthly revenues from residential and commercial customers now about equal industrial volume.

Mr. Stephens, whose Arkla salary is $67,116 a year, picks up many of the ideas for new ventures for his company from the stream of visitors who parade through his unpretentious office on the third floor of the Stephens Building here every morning between eight and noon. Associates say he literally will see anybody about anything. The variety of subjects covered in a typical morning is astonishing. On a recent morning he talked with farmers about cattle, cotton and possible construction of a sorghum mill, with lumbermen about a new process for treating wood, with bankers about loans and economic conditions and with a committee from a small Arkansas community seeking help on an industrial development program.

Between visitors he scans reports from division and department heads and dashes off occasional needling telegrams, such as the following: "Noted in the weekly report you were considerably behind quota on gas dryer sales. Do you need any help? Call on us if we can assist. Witt Stephens, assistant sales manager."

Though Mr. Stephens gives his executives and local managers considerable authority to act independently, one subordinate says on major decisions he "pretty much flies by the seat of his pants," often going against the advice of associates. Mr. Stephens himself notes he told none of his assistants or executives about the gas light idea "because they probably would have talked me out of it."

At noon on many business days, Mr. Stephens breaks away from his office for four or five hours. With an assistant or two and perhaps a visitor, he heads for his 2,500-acre farm 40 miles south of Little Rock in his Cadillac. En route the party eats a picnic lunch prepared by the company kitchen.

Once at the farm, talk of Arkansas Louisiana Gas affairs ends. Mr. Stephens may direct land-clearing operations or oversee the building of a fence; a guest may drive a tractor or help round up cattle.

The group is rolling back to Little Rock by 5 p.m. for the second half of Mr. Stephens' business day. Typically, Mr. Stephens holds a business conference over steaks at the Coachman's Inn, a plush Little Rock motel in which he owns an interest. After dinner he often returns alone to his office to dictate letters to a dictating machine till midnight.

5 LETTER TO AN ASPIRING VP

by Charles C. Gibbons

> It isn't always easy for a middle- or lower-
> level manager to know what the job of a top
> executive really comprises — or to judge whether
> he is qualified, by nature and by training, to
> move into a top spot himself. Here, in the form
> of a letter to a subordinate with his eye on a
> bigger job, is a fresh look at some of the ques-
> tions a would-be top manager should take into
> consideration.

Many men who aspire to executive positions do not have the
necessary qualifications — and others, who have reached a high
level in the organization, find to their dismay that the job isn't
quite what they thought it would be. Before deciding to strive for an
executive position, you should take a long, objective look at your
potential and qualifications for the job — and give some sober
thought to whether or not you really want to take on the problems
of top management.

You can appraise your own executive potential by answering
ten specific questions. The first, and in some ways the most basic,
is this: <u>Are you willing to pay the price of becoming a top executive?</u>

A young man, just graduated from college, went to a friend of
the family who was a successful businessman and asked for some
advice about how to get along in the world. The businessman thought
for a few minutes, then said, "Son, the most important thing that

Reprinted from Management Review, August, 1963, pages 4-12,
by permission of the American Management Association.

I have learned, and the most important thing for you to learn, is this: There's no such thing as free lunch."

You don't get anything for nothing. If you want to be an executive, with the privileges, rewards, and prestige of being an officer of a company or a member of the higher management group, you must pay a price. It is a very real price, so the first thing you have to decide is: Do I want to pay the price? Do I really want to be an executive?

WHAT PRICE GLORY?

What is the price that an executive must pay? Naturally, it varies from one company to another and from one executive to another. All executives, however, bear heavy responsibilities that require them to commit their energies and resources fully to their jobs. Unlike the lower-level employee whose hours are nine to five, the executive is always on call, even after he has put in a longer day than his subordinates. In most cases, his job must come first — and personal and family considerations necessarily suffer. In addition to the sheer amount of time a top job consumes, the stress of a position of responsibility taxes the psychological and physical resources of the executive. Even men who are eminently well suited for the task feel the burden of their responsibility for the welfare of the company and its employees. In spite of constant interaction with others, the man who makes the decisions is essentially alone.

The second question is: Do you know your own strengths and weaknesses? An essential part of a management-development program is for you to know where you stand. Without an objective look at your strengths and weaknesses, you can be either overconfident or overly humble. Some people who deprecate their abilities — "I'm not very bright in this area," or "I'm not a good speaker," or "I'm not good in getting along with people" — use such modesty as an excuse to themselves and to others for failure to make the effort. This is one thing you have to weigh in your own mind with regard to yourself. Are you underselling yourself so you won't have to make the effort to achieve?

Another approach to self-appraisal is to ask yourself this question: Am I part of the problem or part of the solution? Every company has individuals who create problems and other individuals who help solve them. Which are you?

PULLING YOUR WEIGHT

Every employee should be worth at least twice his salary. If you're worth only as much as you are being paid, you are not making any money for your company. If you have real executive potential, your contribution to the company should be equivalent to three or four times your present salary. Think about the things you accomplish. Are you really accomplishing enough to pay for your salary and your office space? Can your company pay for these items and have some money left over? The only way a company can prosper is to have people who contribute more than they are paid.

The third question is: <u>Can you think creatively?</u> What we might call "managerial creativity" is the ability to diagnose problems, to evaluate alternative solutions, and to come up with the right decision. If you aren't strong in this area, you probably don't have much executive potential.

Can you distinguish between the important and the unimportant problems? If you spend your time and effort on comparatively trivial problems and neglect problems of greater importance to the company, your managerial creativity is low.

Your ability to create a climate that encourages creativity in other people is even more inportant than your ability to think creatively yourself. In your supervision of other people, the atmosphere you create will determine to a great extent whether or not they will be willing and able to come up with the new ideas that are the future strength of the organization.

Question four is closely related to managerial creativity: <u>Can you make decisions?</u> The men at the top have a great many decisions to make. This is their stock in trade. President Truman had a sign on his desk that read, "The buck stops here." To a great extent, this is true of most top-executive positions. If you become an executive, you will have many difficult decisions to make. Do you like to make decisions? Do you feel that you procrastinate too much? Do you ask for more information simply to postpone the necessity of making the decision? Are you likely to consider two solutions and compromise on one that is not so good as either? How do you appraise yourself on decision-making? Saying that you want to become an executive but are poor at making decisions would be like saying you want to be a pilot but don't enjoy flying.

Making decisions is related to the matter of delegation. The most important thing you have to delegate is the authority to make decisions. Are you able to let the people under you make decisions without interfering? If you insist on making all the decisions yourself, you are probably a bottleneck. Along with the ability to make decisions goes the willingness to delegate.

Question number five is: <u>Do you know how to establish and maintain good relationships with other people?</u> Obviously, this is an important part of an executive's work. The first person you want to have good relations with is your boss. Your ability to establish good relations with him will probably have a lot to do with whether you ever have a chance to be an executive. Your boss doesn't have time to do all the work himself; he needs your support to get the job done, to accomplish his objectives. He doesn't need someone to bring problems to him; he needs someone to bring solutions. Evaluate your relationship to your boss in these terms.

AS OTHERS SEE US

In establishing and maintaining good relations with others, you have to put yourself in the other person's place. In thinking about your relations with your boss, for example, try to imagine that you have his job. What would you want from the person in the job you now hold if you were the boss! Similarly, put yourself in the place of your subordinates. There is no better way to improve your relationships with people.

Above all, try to keep from questioning the motives of people. It's one thing to tell an individual you don't think he is doing a very good job, but it is quite another thing, and much more serious, to tell him that you don't think he wants to do a good job. You have to start by assuming that the other fellow is trying as hard as you are. He may not be doing the job the way you would do it, but if you want to have good relations with him you will not question his motives.

Question number six: Are you an effective leader? You may be high on the organization chart, but unless someone is following you, you are not really a leader. Do people follow you willingly? Do they follow you reluctantly or with enthusiasm?

A leader must set goals for himself and his group, and must be able to get his men to make these goals their own. The primary skills of a leader are the techniques of motivating people and communicating with them. A leader is forward looking, dynamic, and respected by his group.

Question number seven: Do you know how to motivate yourself and others? The first question to ask on the matter of motives is: Why do you want to be an executive? What are your motives for wanting to be a member of the top-management group — money, prestige, bigger office, or the respect of others in the organization? Unless you have motivation and plenty of it, your chances of becoming a top executive are not very great.

You may be familiar with Douglas McGregor's theory of motivation. Briefly, this theory holds that people must be motivated by higher-level motives, such as self-realization, recognition, and self-fulfillment. The satisfaction of hunger, thirst, and sex, although necessary, is not sufficient to a high level of accomplishment, for once these primary motives are satisfied they cease to act as motives. Everyone needs air, but unless he is deprived of it, this need does not operate as a motive.

Consider whether your motives go beyond the satisfaction of basic needs, or beyond the needs for security and acceptance. Would you work hard even if you had a lot of money, or do you feel that you would relax if your salary were doubled? To be effective, the executive must be motivated by the need for achievement, self-fulfillment, and the satisfaction of knowing that he is doing an important job and doing it well.

The eighth question is: <u>Can you communicate effectively</u>? Communication in business primarily involves communicating with your boss and with your subordinates — understanding what they have to say and getting your ideas across to them. How effective are you in this? An executive who can't communicate with his boss and with his subordinates is almost totally ineffective.

Can you sell your ideas in a reasonable percentage of the cases? No one expects to sell his ideas all the time. You can strike out two times out of three and still play baseball on any baseball club in America. Do you feel that you have an above-average ability to sell your ideas?

Communicating, of course, requires some skill in speaking, in listening, in writing, and in reading. We are tempted to speak more than we listen. There is a tendency to emphasize the active part of communication rather than the passive part; but you will never be a good communicator until you learn to do both — listening as well as speaking, reading as well as writing. If you feel that you have a deficiency here, you can do something about it.

Do you react to the feelings that people are expressing as well as to the content of their remarks? We often react to the intellectual content of a conversation, even when the most significant aspect is the emotion or feeling conveyed.

If an employee comes into your office to complain that he didn't get a certain memo and that he isn't being kept up to date on things, the content of his remarks is less important than the feeling he is expressing: "I feel that I am being pushed around here, and I'm not fully appreciated. Maybe you don't like me as well as you like someone else in your organization, and I feel threatened by the fact that I didn't receive this memo."

Question number nine: <u>Do you know how to live with stress</u>? The higher you go in the management hierarchy, the more stress you will encounter. Can you cope with stress, or does it tear you apart? Can you be in a situation that demands everything you have for eight or nine hours a day and still be a person your wife and children can enjoy? Do your wife and children just live for the weekends, because then "Daddy's in a better mood"? If this is the case, you may be a person who cannot handle stress. If you can't you would be foolish to aspire to an executive position. It would be the worst possible thing for you — and for your company.

THANK GOD IT'S FRIDAY

There is a constitutional difference in the ability of people to handle stress. Perhaps your wife should rate you on this point. She may know more than you do about the effect that stress has on your health. Be honest with yourself. If you find that you feel much better on weekends and vacations than you usually do when you are working, it probably means that you are carrying about as much of a load as you should expect yourself to carry, and you would be ill-advised to seek an executive position.

Poor management of time is a source of unnecessary stress. Is every day hectic and fragmented, and a series of crises, or are you reasonably effective in managing your time? All of us must deal with emergencies, but life shouldn't be just one emergency after another. There should be some continuity and order to your day, so you are doing the things that you want to do. Remember, the important things are seldom urgent, and the urgent things are seldom important.

CAN YOU RELAX?

Do you know how to reward yourself for a job well done, or do you just keep on driving yourself without any respite? Some people have ways of rewarding themselves and thoroughly enjoy periods of release from tension. They can work hard and they can play hard, and their recreation is truly "re-creation." Are you able to reward yourself, or do you find that your work is so demanding that you spend all your time and all your energy and all your thinking in trying to keep up with the job? If so, then your job is as big as it should be, and it would be a mistake to aspire to a bigger one.

The final question is: Do you have a program for your own development? You can't really be serious in thinking that you want to be an executive unless you have a program for your own development. You should realize that no one is really interested in your development but you. You're just kidding yourself if you think that the president of the company or anyone else is lying awake nights thinking about how to develop you.

The program you plan for yourself should be built around the points we have just been considering. Decide where you are strong, where you are weak, and what you want to do about improving your weaknesses.

AN INDIVIDUAL PROGRAM

One program won't fit everyone, any more than the same suit of clothes would fit everyone. Tailor-make your program to fit your own interests and capacities. There is a good chance, for instance, that you need to do something about your speaking, writing, or reading; few of us would say that we are as effective as we would like to be in these communications skills.

Reading articles and books on business subjects can contribute to your development. But don't set an excessively high goal. Don't tell yourself that you are going to read a book every night or a book every week — set a reasonable goal, like reading one book a month.

Have you gained leadership experience by participating in community activities? If you want to gain additional experience in leadership, be the chairman of the board of trustees at your church, seek election to your school board, or be active in the Junior Chamber of Commerce. If you are really interested in your own development, you will do some of this community work, not only because you think it helps the organizations in the community, but because you recognize that it helps you.

What are you doing to improve your management skills? If you want to be an executive, you need to improve your work habits, your management of time, your communications skills, and your ability to motivate people. You need to develop these skills in the same sense that a man who wants to be an Olympic swimmer will give attention to his stroke, his breathing, and his kick. If you do not have a program for your own development, then I would question your interest and your potential for higher management.

YOUR EXECUTIVE POTENTIAL

If you appraise yourself realistically on these ten points, you will know what your executive potential is. If you decide that your potential is low, do not aspire to promotion, but be content to discharge well your present responsibilities. If, on the other hand, you honestly feel that your executive potential is high, that you have what it takes to do well and be happy in an executive position, then do all you can to gain recognition and promotion. You owe it to yourself and your company to be a leader.

6 YOUR BOARD CAN BE AN ASSET

by Donald H. Sunderlin

The fact that a company is making money is not, of itself, convincing proof the board of directors is effective. Better yardsticks are (1) whether the profits are all they could be; (2) whether the company occupies a respected position in its industry; and (3) whether continued good earnings are assured.

Criticism of the board is scarcely avoidable when markets are unexpectedly lost, when the sudden departure of a key individual creates confusion, when strikes are frequent, when bank loans are denied, or when similar administrative maladies beset management. During business recessions the strength or weakness of a board becomes clearly visible. Seeing red ink puts the nerves of stockholders on edge, while large earnings and dividends palliate and soothe those who risk their capital.

Corporations or companies noted for management excellence, such as General Motors, IBM, Minnesota Mining, Du Pont, and others of towering stature, make maximal use of their directorates' exceptional talent. Smaller companies do not often tap this potent reservoir, and when they do they seldom draw more than a trickle.

One compelling reason for this latter situation is that many medium-sized businesses emerged from small ones so recently the individuals who contributed to the successful growth are still in dominant positions. Originally these founding executives had little need for help from a truly constructive board. Thus, they filled board seats with friends, relatives, or employees to meet legal requirements.

By perpetuating a practice, satisfactory during the infantile stage of their companies, these founders deny themselves the forward thinking, the balanced viewpoint, and the specialized

Reprinted from Advanced Management — Office Executive, April, 1962, pages 6-9, by permission of the publisher.

abilities that are so helpful during the adolescent and early adulthood periods of corporate life.

Another, although less generally recognized, reason for this phenomenon is that radically different executive profiles are required for the various stages of corporate development. The founding type must be a promoter, an independent thinker who dares to venture when the odds are poor — an entrepreneur. The professional executive, wholly competent to manage an established business, is usually ill-equipped to start a new enterprise. It is natural, therefore, for the entrepreneur to tend toward self-reliance, leading to a one-man show, instead of group action.

COMMITTEE VERSUS JUDICIAL AGENCY

A board, composed solely of management members, functions more as a committee and less as the contemplative, judicial agency it is intended to be. The chance of a fresh viewpoint being brought to bear on the corporate problems is somewhat slim if the view is contrary to the ideas of a well-respected, but opinionated and strong-willed boss. Self-reliant outside directors can afford independence, while the security of inside directors could be jeopardized.

In four medium-sized corporations where the board was dominated by chairmen or presidents who held financial control, these untoward events occurred:

In corporation A, the profits accruing from one product line were dissipated on the promotion of another line having poor potential. Over-all, there was a loss until a bank's realistic thinking led to termination of the loss venture.

In corporation B, overly generous salaries, bonuses, and dividends, during an extended period of prosperity, left a dearth of working capital to face lean times, despite the long-felt need of plant modernization to meet choking competition.

In corporation C, fear that large-scale expansion would result in the loss of his entire investment caused a minority stockholder, who was also an officer, to take his life.

In corporation D, the corporation expired after the management group had deteriorated so much that rebuilding would have been difficult and favorable liquidation was impossible.

Not all outsiders are innocent of politicking, of course, and the "system," mutual back-scratching, causes their number to be disappointingly large. Gratifying though it is for anyone to be associated with successful institutions and respected executives, board membership should be accepted with full cognizance of attendant moral and legal responsibilities.

The primary function of the board is to look forward to and take full advantage of favorable business conditions while avoiding possible pitfalls. In this respect the chairman corresponds with yesterday's battleship captain whose foremost duty was coordination of his ship's firepower with other units of the fleet. He looks "out."

BOARD'S SECONDARY FUNCTION

The board's secondary function is to ensure proper managing of the corporation's regular, day-to-day operations. Reverting to the naval analogy, this part of the chairman's job is similar to yesterday's battleship commander who "looked in" and concentrated on "managing" his ship's company.

Primarily, then, the chairman plans for the future while secondarily he controls the routine business operations. The board is simply an extension of the chairman's personality, giving him the benefit of more heads and hands. Judgment reaches a fine balance when the needed collective experience is available, and the directors, inside and outside, are free to concentrate objective and fresh thinking on policy decisions.

Separating forward planning from operating permits the management staff to function more as an administrative body, and the board becomes more the deliberative body it should be. The first puts into action the plans made by the second, which makes for sounder planning and better execution.

COMPELS HIM TO THINK LOGICALLY

A strong board compels the chairman to think logically before putting his proposals before those who are his peers. Regardless of his democratic tendencies the chief executive has no corporate equals except for the outside directors and his management consultant. In exchange for this restraint, which no broad-minded individual resents, his effort to achieve greater profits and growth receives tremendous impetus.

The chief executive need have no qualms about his control being weakened if he adds outside directors. Functioning as balance wheels, with influence proportionate to their contribution, outsiders can prevail only through sheer weight of logic. In the final analysis, the chief executive continues to be boss, for he can sack them if he chooses.

Independent directors support the officers' wishes that are in the company's best interests, yet act as a check-rein on excesses. For example, the board that fixes the officers' compensation, a subject on which they themselves should not vote. The American Institute of Management cited Bethlehem Steel Corp., with all inside directors, as a case in which fifteen members voted themselves bonuses of more than $5 million despite a $19-million dip in profits.

James M. Skinner, Jr., formerly President of Philco Corp., was quoted as saying, "We don't want the officers auditing their own work and admiring what they do as administrators."

The board stipulates the portion of earnings to be distributed as dividends. Again the principal stockholder who is also chairman controls the situation and can do as he desires, but, with outsiders to contend with, the action taken is likely to be more sound in terms of his objectives.

LARGE ENOUGH — YET SMALL ENOUGH

As regards size, a board of seven to nine members, for a medium-sized company, is large enough to provide complementary points of view and yet small enough to act intimately and efficiently.

Any company benefits by peppering its board with men whose specialties tie in with its business — banking, engineering, law, science, marketing. A residential hardware manufacturer put a famous architect on its board for prestige purposes. Outsiders definitely help solidify relations with the public and the stockholders of publicly held corporations.

The heads of large, successful companies readily accept membership on the boards of companies in their own league. Here are a few examples selected at random.

Eastman Kodak Co.
> Frederick C. Crawford
>> Former Chairman, Thompson Ramo Wooldridge Inc.
> Gwilym A. Price
>> Chairman, Westinghouse Electric Corp.

Warner & Swasey Co.
> Francis H. Beam
>> Chairman, National City Bank (Cleveland)
> George S. Dively
>> Chairman, Harris Intertype Corp.

Socony Mobil Oil Co.
> Albert L. Williams
>> Executive Vice President, I. B. M. Corp.

Gladding Mc Bean & Co.
> Benjamin C. Carter
>> Executive Vice President, Food Machinery and Chemical Corp.

Many fully capable but perhaps less prominent men are available to medium-sized companies. After the kinds of talents and personalities needed have been firmed up, suggestions for candidates may be obtained from banks, trade associations, law firms, and management consultants.

Not long ago it was customary to reward each outside director of a small- to medium-size company with a crisp, new $100 bill for his services at the meeting. But the trend in compensation has been upward. Recently a chemical company with net assets of $50 million raised the pay of its ten outside directors more than three fold — from $3,000 to $10,000 per year. A much larger chemical company pays a yearly retainer of $3,000 plus $300 per meeting, while a small drug company pays $200 per meeting.

And to insure continued personal interest, fees are placed in a deferred account from which common stock may be purchased at the option of the owner.

The Chairman of the International Minerals and Chemical Corp. was recently quoted as saying, "We want to attract not only good names but also men who will spend time on the problems of growth and risk, and we expect to get our money's worth."

CAN OFTEN BE SIMPLIFIED

Problems requiring director's opinions and recommendations can often be simplified or expedited by providing proper operating statements and other data. The right information, in the right amount, enables the directors to exercise reasonable care and prudence in the discharge of their duties. Irrelevant data are worthless. Too much of the right information is needlessly time-consuming, and too little creates a mental vacuum.

The minimum, as a general rule, are balance sheet, profit and loss, analysis of cost of sales, comparative sales analysis, and the operating budget with variances. Reports on specific areas are supplied when problems in those areas arise.

The working relationship between the officers and the board should permit ordinary or regular administrative matters to be handled expeditiously by the line executives.

COUNSELS THE CHIEF EXECUTIVE

The classic board sets goals and formulates major policies beyond the ordinary routine of daily business and sees that these policies are properly implemented. It continuously watches the operating results and counsels the chief executive to improve the caliber of the executive group. The board appoints competent officers, fixes officers' salaries, declares dividends, and passes on stock options. It does these things by supplementing the operating management without usurping its rightful prerogatives or authority.

The task of a forthright director can be difficult since acquiescence and subservience are more prevalent than constructive candor. The late Thomas H. White exhibited a refreshing attitude when asked if he would accept membership on a client's board. "Yes," he said and then added, "if I can be constructive." The most helpful directors are usually the ones whose competence and success in their chosen fields make axe-grinding in any form abhorrent to them.

A good director devotes time to his work in addition to that spent in board meetings. Supplied with pertinent information before decisions are called for, he prepares for the meeting itself. If he is not an officer, he develops informal contacts with the company's executives and his fellow directors so that his opinions may be oriented to the existing climatic circumstances. He is realistic and thorough.

A good director considers the humanitarian aspects of top-level decisions. A Canadian corporation with scattered lumber mills found it necessary to reduce output and decided to focus its attention on the highest-cost mill. But since a small community was largely dependent upon this operation, the corporation decided to shut down another mill.

At the other extreme is the company that gave its employees so many benefits it could not compete with companies in similar lines. Fringe benefits costing twice the national average caused such severe losses that jobbing contracts had to be canceled. The workers lost their jobs. A good director recognizes labor and community obligations, but he does not allow paternalistic generosity or union pressure to backfire.

Freely asking questions designed to broaden his knowledge of details or to test the strength of a specific proposal, a good director greatly concerns himself with the progress of new projects and the profitability of current operations.

HOW TO UTILIZE BOARD TALENT

How can medium-size companies build cooperation between the line executives and the directors while fully utilizing board talent? Here are a few suggestions.

1. Supply the directors with agenda in advance of the meetings and copies of the minutes after it. Thus, attending directors can have given advance thought to the matters to be discussed, and the absent ones may learn what transpired.

2. Hold monthly meetings on regularly scheduled dates.

3. Present a new plan, goal, or policy as something tentative rather than as an action for ex post facto approval.

4. Invite the corporation counsel and the comptroller to attend every board meeting, irrespective of whether they are directors, so that advice on the legal or financial aspects of proposals is available without delay.

5. Empower an executive committee to transact the "ordinary and administrative" business during the interval between board meetings. Ratify decisions on matters outside the ordinary course of business at the next meeting or at a special board meeting, before they are adopted.

6. (a) Provide the directors with monthly and year-to-date figures of sales, profits, balance sheet changes, etc.. . . . The possible objections to disseminating confidential information fail to recognize the contributions informed members can make. Hand complete figures to those in attendance and mail copies to those absent. (b) Make available to the directors the detailed reports of

independent auditors — not merely the condensed statements released to stockholders.

7. Require that loans by the corporation to officers, directors, or stockholders be made only with board approval and only when such action is legal.

8. Give each outside director opportunity to know the younger executives so they can intelligently assist in making future promotions from within. If inside talent is unavailable, the director will then know the kind of man who must be found outside.

Knowledgeable chief executives realize that the board contributes more and costs less than any expenditure their corporations could possibly make. A good board is, literally, a priceless asset.

7 WHY IT'S HARDER AND HARDER TO GET A GOOD BOARD

by John Chamberlain

*   *   *   *   *

Some of the more troublesome facts about [the] recent economic life   [of board members] would seem to bear out the "painful duty" aspects. Hardly a day passes without reports in the newspaper financial pages that some board, somewhere, is having the devil of a time trying to pick up the pieces because of managerial inability to breast the profit squeeze. One day it is the Chrysler Corp. board engaged in tortured contemplation of the fact that the old 22 per cent market penetration of Chrysler cars has dwindled to 9.6 per cent in eleven years. Another day it is the Twentieth Century-Fox board trying to cope with the changes that have turned the movie industry upside down. Still another day it is the Fairbanks Whitney Corp., besieged by certain directors because of alleged unwillingness to provide the information requisite to keeping an eye on what management is doing in its attempts to restore health to the stock.

There is more to it, of course, than the profit squeeze. The ever widening influence of government on the ancient prerogatives of business — in pricing, labor settlements, antitrust, etc. — inevitably involves the board in basic policy decisions of a critical nature. The evolving internal complications of big companies, enhanced by the augmented drift to geographical decentralization and diversification of product, pose their own intricate problems for board members. Taxes are another trouble, for as the founders' sons and grandsons are being taxed out of their industrial inheritances, strong proprietary control is fading from the industrial scene, forcing bereft companies to look to board members for guidance.

Reprinted from the November 1962 issue of Fortune magazine by Special Permission; © 1962 Time Inc.

As the responsibilities of boards mount, another trend is apparent. With owner-manager control giving way to widely diffused holdings, the so-called "outside board," with its non-proprietary, non-management members, tends more and more to become the rule in modern business. Out of 600 corporations replying to a _Fortune_ questionnaire, two-thirds have a majority of outside board members and all but fourteen have some outside board members. . . . The old textbook argument of outside vs. inside boards is no longer a central issue because the outside board seems destined to carry the day. What needs to be asked today is how outside boards (or the increasing outside minorities on inside boards) can fulfill their responsibilities under modern business conditions.

In approaching such a question the first step is to recognize the serious disadvantages under which outside directors labor as compared with inside directors, who are managers wearing other hats. Of course, there have been a number of recent instances where outside directors became the rallying point for a corporate turnaround after (in most cases long after) serious trouble developed. For this reason alone many stockholders prefer to have boards with a minority, at least, of directors who are independent of management. Nevertheless the outside director often finds himself in a role something akin to that of the interplanetary traveler, who doesn't know how fast he is going until he knows where he is, and can't know where he is until he knows how fast he is going. The outside director, in a sense, is required to exercise responsibility without timely knowledge of what he really should know — which, of course, is something of a contradiction in terms. (It could even be said to be a definition of irresponsibility.)

The problem, given both the need for knowledgeability and a trend away from the inside board, is how to endow the outsiders with the best qualities of an inside board. To discover what those qualities are, it will be useful to look at some inside boards that function efficiently.

THE COMMANDING VIEW FROM INSIDE

Adaptations of the inside idea, usually involving the use of powerful insider or insider-dominated operating or financial committees, are more numerous than might be supposed. And the success of certain companies that have hung onto wholly or at least predominantly inside boards even in the face of diffused ownership is proof that the inside-directed corporation is still very much alive and kicking. Certain of these "old-fashioned" models, in fact, still stand out for possible behavioral emulation.

Standard Oil Co. (New Jersey) is still the prime example of the advantages of the undiluted inside board. In fact, it is difficult to see, even at this late date, how Standard could have any other board than it has. To begin with, its tight "line and staff" tradition of officer directors goes back to the 1880's, and to uproot it would be like trying to uproot a century-old oak. Then, too, the Jersey company is a holding company charged with keeping a multibillion-dollar worldwide congeries of 250-odd operating companies both profitable and sociologically decent, and if its directors weren't busy every day in the week relating general policy to special problems of a most intricate and demanding nature, the giant would indeed by headless. Theoretically, an outside board could be imposed over Standard's inside board, but whenever the proposal is made it is answered by a question: What would be the point of flying in the face of performance? Any significant change at Standard would be a case of a competent caretaker hiring a less competent man to take care of him.

Standard Oil might be dismissed as a special instance. But actually, many boards that qualify statistically as "outside" operate in fact with inside style. E. I. du Pont de Nemours and General Motors are interesting cases in point. Du Pont has on its board of thirty-odd members several who have had little active connection with the company. But on close inspection it becomes apparent that du Pont is set up to get all the benefits of inside, or full-time working, direction. Two big committees of the board — the finance committee and the executive or operating committee, each consisting of nine men — work constantly at the business of keeping profits high through constructive industrial innovation. Though it meets only twice a month, the finance committee, consisting of elder statesmen not all of whom have operating responsibilities, can spend as much time on the problems of finding the capital to support progressive innovation as is deemed necessary. Beyond this, du Pont still has the flavor of a proprietary company, for an important number of its "outside" directors are du Pont family members who have a substantial stock interest in the business. Not counting indirect Christiana holding-company interest, 4.1 per cent of the du Pont stock is voted by owner-directors. There being no retirement limit for a du Pont director, an owner-member of the du Pont family can stay on the board as long as he likes.

Crawford H. Greenewalt, who recently relinquished the presidency of the du Pont company to become board chairman, is strong on the value of the "owners concept around the board table." Though an owner-director is technically an "outside" director if he holds no company job, he is really an "inside" man in Greenewalt's definition of substance. The inside or proprietor director is the more effective, to the du Pont way of thinking, if he doesn't spread himself thin by taking on tutelary jobs for other companies. Greenewalt himself gave up his membership on a bank board (the Bank of Delaware) when he became a du Pont director, and he felt it inadvisable to go on the General Motors board. Though he admires Sidney Weinberg, of the Wall Street investment house of Goldman, Sachs, who has been on many boards, he notes that Weinberg's investment-bank position is really a license to spend time on keeping up with many businesses. The men in an industrial company usually can't spread themselves around in that way.

* * * * *

A GENERAL PROBLEM FOR THE GENERALS

The transition of the corporation from the proprietary to the "public" stage has its many perils, which may or may not be sidestepped. This is suggestively demonstrated by the natural history of, among others, certain big companies with the word "general" in their titles. The "general" companies — General Electric, General Motors, General Foods, General Mills, General Dynamics — have all been formed by merger and/or acquisition as well as by inside promotion of a variegated style mix or product mix. Where mergers tend to bring strong men together on boards, it sometimes takes the strongest of the strong to enforce a unified policy. It is when the strongest of the strong relaxes his grip, through death or retirement, that the problem of unity may demand the mediation of the outside interest to prevent a barons' war. But the existing "outside" board that has been dominated by a strong man may have hidden weaknesses. The outsiders, having been chosen by Napoleon, may be yes-men. Or they may have been kept from acquiring the amount of information about the parts of a company that is necessary to make valid policy decisions.

The trouble General Dynamics encountered when it struck its "dangerous age" is recent history (see "How a Great Corporation Got Out of Control," Fortune, January and February, 1962). With the huge Convair aircraft division tacitly reverting to an extreme autonomy after the death from cancer of the General Dynamics strong man, John Jay Hopkins, the communications of the big defense company broke down and disaster ensued. Certainly no outsider on the General Dynamics board even conceived that the Convair program was going to involve the corporation in the biggest product loss ever sustained by any company in U.S. history. Indeed, such a hazard was not clear even to the inside members.

In contrast to General Dynamics, General Foods Corp. survived its dangerous-age ordeal by correctly diagnosing the perils involved in welding a number of hitherto independent units together. While the comparison between a corporation that makes jet planes and atomic submarines and a corporation that merchandises cereals, dog food, and Sanka coffee may seem a trifle forced, it is noteworthy that when General Foods was created in the 1920's, special care was taken to provide it with a board that

-49-

would be equal to establishing an overview. The local satraps of the individual companies that were merged with the original Postum Co. (Grape Nuts) were not permitted indiscriminately to assume seats on the board of General Foods when that corporation was organized; instead, the board was set up with an eye to forestalling divisional Napoleons and with full attention to establishing good communications. Its "outsiders" were chosen with a shrewd view toward getting merchandising and financial know-how for the modest cost of the director's fee.

Quite apart from its recent troubles in the price-fixing case, in which both top management and the board of directors had to plead ignorance of what was going on in the lower company echelons, General Electric had a moment of shakiness when its founders — Thomas Edison, the inventor of the incandescent electric bulb, and Henry Villard of Northern Pacific Railroad fame — were relinquishing their hold on the original Edison General Electric Co. But the strong hand of the elder J. P. Morgan and the arrival on the scene of the strong-minded Charles A. Coffin via the merger route carried G.E. through its dangerous age. Morgan and Coffin insisted on a responsibly knowledgeable governing body for G.E. and, while the present-day outsider-dominated board of the big Schenectady company obviously has a hard time keeping up with a heterogeneity that ranges from the manufacture of electric toasters to the making of jet engines and great turbogenerators, it has still managed to ensure the corporation a continuity of good management.

General Mills, which grew via the acquisition of Washburn Crosby Co. and several smaller milling companies, has only recently been faced with the departure of its second-generation strong man, James Ford Bell, son of the "predecessor" company's president. As for General Motors, it has, as we have already noted, just reached the threshhold of its dangerous age. Since G.M.'s Alfred P. Sloan has always been an organizational genius, one can be sure that the company has been insured against any weakness that might possibly ensue from the disappearance of the old proprietary interests. Nevertheless, the failure of the Chrysler Corp. to avoid trouble in bridging the gap between the departure of the great Walter P. Chrysler, who thought he had chosen good lieutenants, and the emergence of the modern "public" Chrysler company suggests that transitions in the automobile business are not easy.

AN OATH OF DISALLEGIANCE?

Just what can be done to shorten the time lag in forcing management to consider the right questions is something that requires brainstorming. Is it frivolous to suggest that every new board member should be required to take an oath of disallegiance to any personality in management before taking his seat at the directors' table? Friendship for the president may be a reason for going on a board. But it should be understood between friends that there may come a moment of truth, to use the bullfighter's term, when past ties must be cut. The Biblical injunction about "greater love hath no man than . . . [he] lay down his life for his friend" should be waived in connection with directors. The neophyte director should, like the monk or like the drama critic who knows all the playwrights, be prepared to take vows. He should have a strain of austerity, of ultimate coldness, deep inside him. For the issue between friend and duty may, at the moment of truth, become extremely painful. Such a moment came to banker Fred F. Florence of Dallas, who chose to resign from the Metro-Goldwyn-Mayer board rather than turn on his old benefactor Louis B. Mayer. Since banker Florence was in precarious health, resignation was obviously the only sensible way of dealing with his dilemma. But when a man is young and healthy, and the issue is between friend and duty to question that friend's policies or favored choice of successor, the moment of truth requires a stern willingness to be unpleasant.

* * * * *

AN EYE FOR THE ROYAL SUCCESSION

Professional students of management, noting that the outside board is more often than not stacked with friends of the president, tend to throw up their hands when they hear, for the nth time, that the board "represents the stockholders." To Peter Drucker, for example, the board is a "tired fiction," a "shadow king," a "showcase," and "a place to inject distinguished names." Yet Drucker himself thinks a board is still needed, not as a governing organ but as an organ of review, appraisal, and appeal. It is something for management, through its officer-directors, to bounce its ideas against. It is useful as a source of information and advice and it can be a valuable lever when new financing is indicated. Because an outside board is generally recruited from among men with a wide range of experience, it can help solve the problem of isolation in a company. So Drucker, though he scoffs at the definition of the board that is to be found in the legal textbooks, is really saying that the board has evolved from "king" to king's cabinet and, as such, is certainly no "tired fiction." The cabinet is doubly necessary in that it provides a medium for choosing a departing king's successor. In a well-managed company, junior executives will appear periodically before the board to outline proposals and to serve as experts "on tap." Thus, when the time comes to "make provision for tomorrow's managers" (Drucker's phrase), the outside directors will have some idea about the ability of men whom the retiring president has slated to take over when he moves up to become board chairman. Since the corporation, while only a fictitious "person," is nonetheless "immortal," the problem of the royal succession is extremely important. It takes a board to settle it legitimately.

* * * * *

HOMEWORK IS MORE FUN THAN GOLF

The good man, meditating upon his directorial experiences, may find himself formulating a personal philosophy of board service. Sidney Weinberg, who has been a director of as many as thirty-five companies at one time (he is now down to seven), regards his board service as an "avocation." He prefers spending weekends on company "homework" to golf. His investment-banker position as a partner of Goldman, Sachs actually requires that he give much of his time to thinking about business-in-general, but Weinberg has obviously long since outgrown that stage in life when a man has to think primarily of his own interests. He finds the relation of general principles to specific problems mentally exhilarating — and, though he has said that men should be automatically retired from board activities at seventy, Weinberg — now seventy-one — will miss the work if he shucks off all of his directorates. He prides himself on his independence, and in case of continuing malfeasance or misfeasance on management's part, he would not hesitate to resign from a board and call a press conference to force a change. But Weinberg draws a line that is clear in his own mind between independence and professional dissidence. Because of his feeling for independence he refuses to go on boards that are proprietor-controlled. "I wouldn't," he says, "be a captive director for a million dollars." Though he concedes that corporations with inside and proprietary boards can be competently run, he doesn't think it healthy for officer-directors to pass on things that affect their own self-interest. True enough, the president of an inside-board corporation will leave the room when his own salary and bonus are up for review. But the "inside" men who are left behind to discuss the figure are all dependent on the president for advancement. When the salary committee of an outside board is charged with settling questions of rewards and perquisites, no comparable inhibitory factors need operate.

* * * * *

GOOD MEN ARE HARD ENOUGH TO FIND

The problem of getting good men to serve on the boards of companies is complicated by the human animal's increasing unwillingness to let voluntary judgment serve as the basis for its choices. One-third of the 600 companies reporting in <u>Fortune's</u>

survey have automatic retirement ages for board members, ranging from sixty-five to seventy-seven. While compulsory retirement may force a company to bring in younger blood to keep a good board balance between experience and energy, it is obvious that men frequently retain their business acumen into old age. So some good men are lost by arbitrary age limitation. It may be true in certain businesses that a board member tends to lose his feel for the realities of shop and marketplace within a few years of his retirement from active company management. But this is not true for all businesses — and if a board chairman needs an automatic rule to help him get rid of senility it could be a sign that he isn't sufficiently skillful as a diplomat to warrant holding his job. Why, after all, should the vigorous oldster be deprived of scope merely because others in his age bracket lack biological resilience? Some companies get the best of two worlds by retaining their retired board members as consultants — and then proceed to consult only those who still have something to contribute.

In addition to narrowing the choice of good board men by arbitrary retirement rules, corporations find themselves hobbled by the legal prohibitions on "conflicts of interest." No railroad director, for example, can be the owner of a "substantial" interest in another company if the railroad does more than $50,000 worth of business with that company in a given year. Board members of railroads which live up to the letter of the law complain ruefully that they cannot buy G.M. stock without running a risk if their railroads decide to buy a G.M. diesel. The laws enumerating conflict-of-interest situations are not so severe when it comes to companies that are not regulated by government commissions. But the fact that the SEC is now raising questions about the desirability of letting brokers or investment bankers join the boards of corporations may portend a further shrinkage in the area of board recruitment.

*   *   *   *   *

Back of everything there lies the problem of clarity of purpose. What is a board for? If the definition is not plain to both managers and directors, management is likely to make only the most bumbling use of board members. Hence Edward H. Litchfield, who doubles in brass as chancellor of the University of Pittsburgh and chairman of the board of Smith-Corona Marchant Inc., insists that his board revise a six or seven-page "general propositions" statement every year for distribution to board members and company officers. The statement, a model of terseness and clear exposition, covers both general board functions and specific activities (relating to selection of personnel, budget review, approval of foundation appropriations, changes in product line, mergers, information-to-be-received-from-the-company, and so on). It stands both as a guide to action and as a prod to self-discipline — and as a reminder to management that a board has a functional reason for being.

In the U.S., home of the big decentralized corporation, the science of management has plumbed all the topics that have relevance to the business of making boards of directors responsive to their manifest duties. There have been conferences, symposiums, books, and articles without end. The science of management begins with clarity of purpose, and rays out from there into problems of measurement, forecasting, communications, decisions based on knowledge, the use of follow-through, and the final act of review and appraisal. The job of picking a good outside director is, theoretically, the job of finding the man who is capable of taking scientific management at its textbook word.

But when all the books have been read, business, including the business of picking a board (of directors), still remains an art. Scientific management has its rules, but to make a profit in the still problematical future involves intuitive judgment as well as the ability to hire pollsters and to read the Harvard Business Review. This intuitive judgment must extend to the choice of men for the board. When it comes to choosing a board, one can throw all the books away. A good man is hard to find. Nevertheless, good men must be found. Between the challenge and the opportunity falls the shadow. But the corporation that has succeeded in solving — provisionally — its problems of employee relations, customer relations, dealer relations, and public relations can always hope to solve its director relations as well.

PART TWO:

OBJECTIVES AND POLICIES

8 THE MANAGEMENT CREED AND PHILOSOPHY OF WHIRLPOOL CORPORATION

by Stewart Thompson

Whirlpool Corporation, makers of household appliances and a company of 19,000 employees, has no written creed. It has a "climate" and an implicit philosophy — parts of which have been written down from time to time — but as yet no fully developed statement has been formulated.

THE DECISION FOR A WRITTEN CREED

Asked whether the absence of a written philosophy was the result of a considered decision, Juel Ranum, assistant to the president and director of public relations, answered: "No, it is not the result of any decision. The need for a written creed has never been discussed formally by our management. But I believe the need has been felt and that someday in the future we will at least attempt to put part of our philosophy into writing. In telling you that we do not have a written creed, it is important to point out that we do have an employee handbook and a visitor's handbook which is distributed to the public, and that we direct written communications to employees at various times. All of these booklets and letters spell out many of the things that one might expect to find in a company creed. Until recently, the company was small enough so that everyone within the organization had a 'feel' of what the company wants to be. They all knew that quality ranks first in all our decisions, that integrity is unquestionable."

Mr. Ranum stated the firm's tacit philosophy as follows: "All who come in contact with the company ought to have some opportunity to benefit from that contact — prospective employees,

Reprinted from Management Creeds and Philosophies, Research Study, No. 32 (New York: American Management Association, 1958), pages 66-73, by permission of the publisher.

employees, vendors, customers, stockholders, or anyone else. The company has grown from a small organization to quite a large one in a very short time. When I joined it seven years ago, it had 970 employees, and it has 19,000 now. The greatest increases took place within the last three years. I think we will eventually develop a written creed, for the same reasons behind our development of more and more written procedures and policies. We know that the chain of command is getting so long that we can't trust everyone to be aware of the particular philosophy guiding our operations. Until September of 1955, we operated in three small communities; now we are in seven or eight major cities. I believe that our rapid expansion makes it necessary for us to sit down and spell out our creed. It will only express in writing those things that, prior to our sudden growth, we were able to understand almost without conscious thought."

Mr. Ranum was next asked whether the firm's creed would be published and widely distributed after it had been formulated. "No," he replied, "I don't see any reason for publicizing the creed intensively. I expect this will happen, though: It will probably be distributed to employees, and perhaps, by its own momentum, it will appear in various company publications, statements of policy, and the like. There will be no determined effort to publicize it. Our creed will be mostly for the guidance of management and employees."

The next query attempted to discover whether Mr. Ranum thought that a written statement of the company's philosophy or beliefs would actually achieve the type of guidance needed by the firm. "Not at all," he answered. "I think that a creed can only be effective if it is written to express the kind of spirit that has always prevailed within the company. In documenting our creed we will merely put into words what has actually been the 'spirit' and the unwritten 'attitude' of us all."

"If the attitude and the spirit prevailing in your firm are satisfactory, why bother to write it out?" he was asked. "At present," Mr. Ranum answered, "we are still relying on key management people to reflect their beliefs and attitudes. As I said before, we are growing so rapidly that this automatic transference of ideas and beliefs is not so sure as it formerly was. If we do put our creed into written form, it will have to be done at a time when our special spirit is still felt strongly within the firm. Unless our people actually experience the effect of the beliefs that are spelled out in writing, the creed will be, in my opinion, a hollow and meaningless document."

THE RESPONSIBILITY FOR FORMULATION

"Who will actually propose writing out the creed?" This question was asked to shed further light on the data gathered in the survey, which showed that the president or the chairman of the board most often initiates the idea. The answer: "Perhaps either the director of personnel or myself as director of public relations and assistant to the president. One of us will probably call the attention of the firm's officers to the fact that writing a creed is one way of preserving and enhancing the spirit of the company. When it has been made, this recommendation will probably go to an officers' meeting and be discussed and voted on there. The decision to develop a creed would require a unanimous vote of this group. Once a decision is made to develop a company creed, personnel in our communications department — those who have been here long enough to have actually experienced the spirit of the company — will be called upon to put it into writing. Their draft will probably be discussed and refined several times before the final draft is presented to the officer group again for adoption."

THE "SPIRIT" OF THE COMPANY

Question: "Mr. Ranum, you have referred several times to the 'spirit' of your company. What do you mean by this word? Is it different from your previous outline of your firm's 'philosophy'?" Answer: "Well, we believe that we have a company that has earned the right to exist; we feel we can do the impossible. Without this spirit, our company — or any other company — could not have experienced the growth that has come about within the last few years. I suppose that 'spirit' means the basic energy behind our firm. Certainly, it should be expressed in the creed."

Question: "Are there any factors operative in your firm which make this spirit possible?" Answer: "I personally believe that it reflects the top management of Whirlpool. The kind of leadership and positive direction the company has had has helped us to preserve the basic energy or spirit behind our entire operation. This has always been coupled with a recognition that proper rewards should go to all those who have had any part in the development of the company. Just to cite a few examples: We have a very liberal bonus plan for all those in supervisory capacities. We enourage — rather than direct — all supervisors in every level of management to discuss with each of his people just where that individual stands with respect to his own performance and his future with the firm. In other words, we try to engender individual communication between supervisor and employee on all levels. We constantly encourage the awareness that each individual has a vital stake and a vital share in the growth of the company and that he or she will benefit directly from this growth. This appears to be a major part of the spirit of the firm. You know, it's rather hard to find exact language to describe things like this. But I suppose we're doing some of the basic spadework. . . ."

Mr. Ranum went on to describe how this group of ideas or beliefs influences company practice in one or two specific ways:

"In personnel selection and training we try to find or to develop the kind of people who are like us — that is, people who are interested in growth and interested in extending themselves beyond just what the job calls for. The fact that we are dedicated to growth has done a great deal to create our spirit. Perhaps it's something like the feeling that prevailed during the war years when people did almost superhuman things in order to get the job done. Time and time again it was demonstrated that the impossible can be done. Willingness on the part of all to make an attempt at accomplishing the impossible is perhaps the best definition of our spirit here at Whirlpool."

Mr. Ranum was then asked whether group decision making plays a part in developing or enhancing the spirit of the company. This was asked in order to see how Whirlpool's management feels about the frequent references to "teamwork" found in many company creeds. Mr. Ranum's description of the climate obtaining at Whirlpool indicated, to some extent, that the firm encourages a great deal of individual action and personal development, with only a minimum of direct control from superiors. "We believe," he said, "it is best for a manager or supervisor to avoid going ahead with a project until all who are involved in that project understand it and are willing to shoulder their load. But we do not encourage a manager to make every decision by means of a group discussion. We believe that all decisions should be made at the lowest possible level in the organization — by the individual directly concerned. Though our officers do meet regularly to review company activities and to vote on the over-all direction of the company, we have no other groups that could be called 'committees,' except for a few temporary ones appointed from time to time to study broad problems. These temporary committees have no operating authority. We do not conduct day-to-day operations through committee action. The top management group is the only place in the organization where committee action is a regular procedure and where decisions are taken by means of a vote. The top management group, however, concerns itself with a general policy making affecting all divisions of the company, and, in actuality, it acts as a coordinating group to see that all parts of the firm are functioning together. It makes few specific operating decisions. In this group, and in this group alone, committee action and decision by voting are appropriate. Outside of this group, when the manager returns to his own office, and among other individuals throughout the firm, it's the individual action which we feel actually maintains the spirit of the firm. Each single person is responsible for doing things according to his best judgment. We all feel that this is the way to operate. If somebody tries to impose group decision making on us, the reaction is such that the usefulness of that individual either comes to an end or is really limited."

The interview brought out earlier that Mr. Ranum believes the firm will probably write a creed at an early date, for the same or similar reasons it is developing more and more written procedures and policies. He also indicated that individual action is greatly valued. Since working according to established policy and procedure statements seems to be the opposite of individualized effort, Mr. Ranum was asked to clarify the point. "We have no program for writing policies," he replied. "In fact, I think there is a genuine feeling that we should avoid written policies or procedures. But you can't avoid them entirely, and sudden expansion seems to create at least some legitimate need for them. Written policy on the amount of sick leave and paid vacation to be granted are examples of the few written policy statements that we have developed. In order to operate effectively and efficiently, we believe we should be flexible enough to take action as it is indicated from time to time. We do not want to be bound by published and documented organization charts and written policies. But some things are more effective in written form. For instance, our pay structure is carefully formalized. We have a set of carefully prepared job descriptions. But even in these written job descriptions, we attempt to avoid limiting a person's field of initiative to an overly circumscribed area."

PROFIT AS AN OBJECTIVE

Question: "According to many of the replies we received in response to our survey of company creeds, many of them were written to de-emphasize profit and emphasize other objectives such as quality, teamwork, and the like. At Whirlpool, Mr. Ranum, how does profit fit in with the other objectives of the company?" Answer: "Profit is a primary objective of Whirlpool. In making a profit, however, we adhere strictly to standards of quality and integrity. We never sacrifice either of them to make a profit, but we do have definite profit goals."

THE PHILOSOPHY OF "BENEFIT"

Mr. Ranum had previously stated that the philosophy of Whirlpool Corporation allows anyone in contact with the firm to benefit from that contact. He was next asked what specific attempts were being made to create a uniform understanding and application of this concept. "At various stages in our growth," he replied, "two or three persons were brought in from the outside to take positions with management responsibility. These new people had no real understanding of our basic beliefs. Usually, when they attended their first meeting of the officer group, the president or some other officer would begin the meeting by saying, 'Let's review how we operate.' A discussion of the whole subject would ensue among people with a great deal of experience, so that the newcomers could imbibe our basic climate, our beliefs, and our philosophy (or whatever else you want to call it) quite naturally. Our philosophy of 'benefit' is something that comes up again and again in meetings as well as in informal conversations. Our officers and managerial people refer to it quite often when speaking to employees. I recognize that all of us do not reflect this philosophy to the same degree at all times. For example, after our last merger we brought in all employees of the firm we had acquired and spoke to them in small groups. At these meetings we discussed the philosophy of Whirlpool. We took care to point out that when a person joins our company he is expected to carry out his responsibilities in keeping with our philosophy. We felt it was important to emphasize this right after the merger, since we were, in effect, acquiring a large number of new people who were not familiar with our outlook. They were told that if a new employee's past experience can benefit the company, his ideas should be brought to the attention of the appropriate people in our firm. But we also stated that the new employee is not at liberty to inject new policies or a new outlook into our organization until such new thoughts are discussed with us. We have one direction in which we are going. Any person who is not in agreement with this does not belong in this company. Sooner or later, he will be in conflict and he will be unhappy and ineffective. He will either be invited to leave or will leave voluntarily. Occasionally, precisely this situation develops. It happens rarely, but it does happen — even within our management group. We have had people who came in from the outside and were not made aware of or did not find out our attitude, or who just assumed that we didn't mean all the things we said; they have been 'hard nosed' in their managerial function and have alienated themselves from the rest of the management group."

"Do you recall," Mr. Ranum was asked, "some of the questions which were asked after you presented the philosophy of Whirlpool to meetings of new employees?" He answered, "Well, one of the questions was: 'Do you actually believe you can operate a company with this philosophy of benefit to others and still make a profit? It sounds as if you are trying to be a do-gooder.' Our answer to this question was that our whole philosophy is based on what we believe is sound business practice. Another question that was asked was: 'What do we do when our superior does not act in accordance with the expressed philosophy of Whirlpool?' To answer this question, we frankly emphasized the fact that even though we do have a well-understood spirit or philosophy, we are not so naive as to believe that there are not variances in the application of this philosophy. It would be really naive to expect a new employee to enter into a controversy with his superior about the superior's variation from our expressed philosophy. How we deal with conflicts of this type is an important question. I have no ready answer to it. Each case must be dealt with as it arises, considering all of the circumstances at the particular time."

Many management creeds appear to use similar language, even identical phrases. For example, it is not uncommon to see references made to the importance of "teamwork" or to the "development of people." Mr. Ranum was asked whether Whirlpool's creed would be likely to make similar statements. His answer: "We believe that the success of the company depends on our philosophy of mutual benefit. If we can express this adequately in our creed, I think it will be enough. Part of our philosophy is expressed in a booklet entitled 'Welcome to Our Administrative Center,' which is given to visitors. We mention that we are 'deeply interested in a philosophy that places the success of people and community citizenship right along with profits as primary company goals.' We cannot be a growth company unless we encourage people to be leaders and managers and provide the proper atmosphere for the development of the talent of our employees. We try not to write our statements in a platitudinous vein, nor do we adopt such statements because they are currently in vogue. We do not make such statements because of suggestions made by public relations consultants or management consultants, who sometimes advise that a company can get its point across if it only 'talks it up.' Statements of our management are made with the intention of definitely committing the company as a whole to act in a certain way. Unfortunately, there is no way to control the insincere statements being made by some companies in order to impress the public or prospective employees. Any such statements that we make are made because we believe them and because they represent sound business practice which we intend to follow."

9   CAN IBM KEEP UP THE PACE?

Just 13 years ago, electronic computers were a curiosity to most mathematicians, statisticians, and scientists. Most predicted that eight or 10 of the big electronic brains — which then had about a hundredth of the power of one large-scale computer of today — would satisfy the needs of the entire scientific community and the few businesses that might be able to use their strange talents.

This market miscalculation — one of the worst, yet most important, ever made — was accepted by most businessmen in 1950, including the top echelon at International Business Machines Corp. The worldwide market that has grown to about $3-billion a year for electronic computers and other equipment associated with automatic data processing was not recognized by most of the companies then qualified to develop the new technology.

The resulting hiatus gave just time enough for IBM to spot its error, learn some of the fanciest new skills in the technological world, take off on [a] growth spurt . . . and pull into a lead that even its toughest and largest competitors are privately inclined to admit is so commanding it may never be overtaken.

Last week, IBM took another leap forward with the announcement in its annual report that worldwide sales for 1962 passed the $2.5-billion mark ($2,578,337,070, to be exact) — more than three and a half times what they were when Thomas J. Watson, Jr. . . . took full command seven years ago.

Pervasive

IBM, in fact, has become almost a phenomenon as well as a company. It has installed more than three-fourths of the computers in the world — an estimated 13,000 to 14,000 — or more

---

Reprinted from the February 2, 1963 issue of Business Week, pages 92-98, by special permission. Copyrighted ©̧ by the McGraw-Hill Publishing Company, Inc.

than 10 times the tally of its nearest competitor, Univac Div. of Sperry Rand Corp. It has over 19,000 data-processing customers, more than 125,000 employees. Though some five decades old, its stock has been one of the darlings of the growth stock fanciers of the past decade.

As a company, IBM is probably more pervasive in its influence on the way business is done than any in history. Its products, preceded by squads of salesmen and flanked by corps of educators, are changing the whole fabric of management structure in business and altering the basic methods used in science and engineering.

Its growth pattern — a threefold increase in assets, 3.6-fold increase in sales, and more than fourfold increase in net since 1955 to this year's $241-million — is more typical of a new company in a growing industry than of one that has been a bona fide member of the billion-dollar-a-year sales club for half a decade. And it keeps pushing along at a $12\frac{1}{2}\%$ per year increase in domestic sales, a 25% increase in foreign revenues.

The question is: Can it keep up this speedy pace?

Driver

Much depends, of course, on the man in the driver's seat. Thomas Watson, Jr., a tall, spare man of 49 — and an accomplished skier, sailor, and airplane pilot — joined IBM shortly after his graduation from Brown University in 1937.

Like his father, Thomas J. Watson, long-time IBM head, he is a political liberal (and ardent New Frontiersman), and speculates that some conservatives "must think I'm something of a radical." His egalitarian streak led him in 1958 to abolish hourly wages at IBM and put all employees on salary, thus eliminating a distinction in treatment of blue and white collars.

In performance of jobs, however, he demands excellence — "superiority." He manages the big company by cannily delegating authority to capable lieutenants, having taken hold of it when it was beginning to run into serious management problems and turned it around before there was even a jog in its sales growth rate.

'New' Company

It's that change, as much as anything else, that explains IBM's continued growth — that, and the fact that applications for data processing are still growing by leaps and bounds in many new fields. IBM isn't an "old" company any more. It's vastly different from what it was in 1955.

There are many outward signs of the change. Eyebrows of some veterans of the sales division, with its tradition of sartorial neatness, still rise at the sight of a mathematician in checked shirt and baggy pants. But the transformation goes deep down, too — the company is vastly different today in product mix, in production technology, in management structure.

I. PRELUDE TO GROWTH

In 1950 IBM was, as it is now, the dominant company in the data processing industry. But then it was dominant in electro-mechanical equipment, based on the Hollerithtype punched cards known as unit record systems — with only a smattering of electronic equipment attached to the punch card sorters.

The company had its first warning of the coming electronic transformation of the industry in 1948, when the Bureau of the Census in Washington ordered a UNIVAC electronic computer from a new and struggling company called Eckert Mauchly Computer Co. (later bought by Remington Rand). The warning had little immediate effect; IBM went its electro-mechanical way and did not grasp the chance to get in early by embarking on all-out computer development. The younger Watson blames the oversight on his own and others' complacency.

Dissension

Eventually, though, dissension about computers came into the open in IBM. The argument put the younger Watson (who became executive vice-president in 1940) in the unenviable position of leader of the progressive element that wanted to plunge into computers — with his father, Thomas Watson, Sr., then chairman and chief executive officer, counseling caution and refusing to put the bulk of the company's resources behind a major computer development program.

In those days IBM was a monolith, the creation of the elder Watson's business genius and the reflection of his personality — with some 35 lines of management command leading directly to his office. Inevitably the chairman, then in his 70s, gradually turned over more authority to his sons. Thomas, Jr., became president in 1952; his younger brother Arthur took over the IBM World Trade Corp., the subsidiary for foreign operations. But the elder Watson remained chief executive officer until 1956.

First Ventures

During that period, more than a little because of Thomas Jr's enthusiasm and support, IBM did indeed get into computers. The tremendous success of the first UNIVAC at the Census Bureau left little doubt that technological leadership and prestige would follow the electronic calculators.

IBM had already had some computer experience. In 1944 it financed and helped build the first big stored-program machine — Harvard's largely electro-mechanical Mark I. Its punch card equipment had calculators that worked electronically.

So it was able to come up fast with its first large computers of a type that could compete with UNIVACs — the 701 and 702 — and follow these up with its first really successful machines, the 704 and 705. With these, it quickly caught and passed the UNIVACs in number and units installed — and began learning the tricks of the trade in selling million-dollar systems and the new skills required for maintaining computers. When the elder Watson stepped down in 1956, IBM was already clearly out in front in computers.

Outside Push

Between 1952 and 1956, another major irritant was pushing IBM — the Dept. of Justice was pressing an antitrust action against IBM's domination of the punch card machine business. The action, settled by consent decree early in 1956, required among other things that IBM divest itself within seven years of enough of its card-making capacity to get down to 50% of industry capacity, and that it license competitors under its patents at reasonable royalties.

Again, son and father disagreed — much more, it's said, than they had over computers. The elder Watson considered the decree an admission of guilt and was ready to fight a long and expensive court battle. Thomas, Jr., considers the decree a device to protect the public interest — a method of correcting an imbalance, even though that imbalance arose, as he insists, from just all-round excellent performance.

"It never seemed to me," he says, "that this action (the consent decree) gave me grounds to criticize the government. I have no quarrel at all with the decision in relation to IBM."

Just last month, the Justice Dept. prodded IBM to complete by Sept. 1 compliance with the consent decree. . . .

Turning Point

Many consider the signing of the consent decree by Thomas Watson, Jr., as the actual turning point in company control. Shortly afterward, the senior Watson resigned as chief executive officer and the son took full command.

The timing was fortunate. The elder Watson had carried the company to what may have been its maximum size under centralized, monolithic management. It needed new blood to reorganize it for handling the even bigger jobs then pressing.

II. DIVIDING A MONOLITH

Once he had full authority, Thomas Watson, Jr., wasted little time in making changes in IBM. In the spring of 1956 he began a series of meetings with Albert L. Williams, now president, and Louis H. La Motte, now chairman of the executive and finance committee. The three redesigned the corporation between the spring and the fall.

"We had a superb sales organization," says Watson, "but lacked expert management organization in almost everything else."

He recalls that when IBM was coming up from behind with the 701, 25 or 30 people would meet every day in his office. "When I'd ask who was responsible for something, either a lot of hands would go up, or no hands at all." About the only cross-check the company had on its activities, he says, was "letters from customers."

It wasn't just that IBM had grown up under a single dominant founder. With the computer advance, its whole technological base was out of balance. It had to make the leap from electro-mechanical equipment — basically, the slowly changing world of the machine shop — to the galloping technology of electronics.

The older unit record equipment had been used mainly in accounting functions that changed but little. Now the big computers were going into scientific and engineering labs, where problems were of a wholly different nature and changed at bewildering speed.

Voice of Experience

In this swift-moving new world, IBM did have one advantage. "Our biggest benefit," says Watson, "was that we did have some knowledge of how to design, install, and service systems." Because IBM's sales staff had that experience, it turned out to be a gold mine of executive talent.

Says ex-salesman T. V. Learson, now vice-president and group executive of IBM's manufacturing divisions: "Most of us had seen among our customers just about every way there was to manage a company."

So, for the big reorganization Watson decided to stick to an old IBM tradition — promotion from within.

In One Sweep

The new setup was worked out in a series of meetings between Watson, Williams, and La Motte, together with John L. Burns, then with Booz, Allen & Hamilton, Inc., management consultants. Watson had met Burns socially and asked him to help set up the new organization. When Brig. Gen. David Sarnoff later hired Burns as president of Radio Corp. of America, largely to establish RCA's commercial computer operation, this came as something of a shock to IBM, and the wrench it felt still serves to spice the competition between IBM and RCA.

IBM Pres. Williams tells the results of the planning sessions: "We ended up with about 110 empty boxes in a new line-and-staff structured management chart. And Tom decided to go ahead and do the whole thing at once."

"We just about had to do it all at once," Watson puts in. "For one thing, I couldn't figure out how to do it gradually."

The "all at once" came at a three-day session at Williamsburg, Va., to which Watson, Learson, and La Motte invited the 110 IBM executives they had picked to fill the 110 empty boxes in the chart. Says Watson: "We went in a monolith, and we emerged three days later as a modern, reasonably decentralized organization, with divisions with profit responsibility and clear lines of authority."

Experts in a Hurry

Necessarily, men were put into jobs they weren't thoroughly prepared for; the switch from an operating job to a staff position is a difficult one at best. A number of executives had to become experts in a hurry, says Williams: "Quite a few were stretched, and found out what they could do." For six months, things were pretty confused, he adds, then started to get better. "I think we've been improving ever since."

Watson and Williams say that 80% to 85% of their choices for the new jobs turned out successful.

Split

Even after this subdivision of the monolith, the reorganization was not complete. Going into 1957 IBM had one large and four small divisions. The small ones were Federal Systems Div. for military and government, Electric Typewriter Div., Time Equipment Div. (sold in 1958), and the Service Bureau Corp. The big one, Data Processing Div., which made and sold unit record systems and computers, was doing a $700-million-a-year business by 1958 — larger than IBM itself before the reorganization.

The monster Data Processing Div. now had to be split — though DP people insisted it couldn't be done logically. Watson and his top aides labored at it a whole summer, tried various methods, found none that worked. Eventually, they did find a way — and out of the split came IBM's present form.

The split isn't along ordinary product or market lines, yet it's relatively simple: three (now four) autonomous manufacturing or "hardware" divisions and one independent sales division. Data Systems Div. produces large-scale computer systems and the 1410 series, General Products Div. the smaller computers and unit record equipment. Advanced Systems Development Div. looks into wholly new products and applications, then turns them over to the other divisions.

Last year the Components Div. was added to make and buy electronic components for all divisions. It moves this spring into a new plant at East Fishkill, N. Y. — the first stage in a $30-million components program.

The sales division, still called Data Processing Div., sells, installs, and services all IBM data processing equipment and provides special programming and systems engineering for customers. With about 28,000 employees, it's still the biggest hunk of IBM.

Peak

The corporate staff of specialists set up in the 1956 reorganization transmits corporate policy and advises operating management. It has more power than most corporate staff organizations.

If line and staff disagree, each files a report to IBM's ultimate authority, the Corporate Management Committee, with Watson as chairman. This committee also includes Pres. Williams, five group executives, and Dr. E. R. Piore, vice-president of research and engineering.

Problems of Size

Though this management and divisional revamping provides IBM with Watson's "modern, reasonably decentralized organization," the company's steady growth still piles up problems of sheer size. Some practices left over from small business days have a hard road.

With over 125,000 employees, and the top office insulated by nine management levels from the production line and eight from salesmen, the time-honored "open door policy" that permits any employee to bring grievances to the chairman's office is difficult to keep up. Yet Watson's door still remains open.

But the worst problem, says Watson, is complacency — the tendency of men in a large company that dominates its field to relax in overconfidence. To fight it IBM imposes tough standards. Though it seldom fires nonperformers outright, its practices of moving them sideways or demoting them with a cut in salary is well known. "It's a tough blow to a man's pride to be demoted," says Williams. "Some resign, but a surprising number buckle down and make a good comeback."

Carrots

There are also tasty carrots. Commissions and salaries run high, and a "tiger" in the sales division can soon afford luxuries.

As IBM has become more and more populated by scientists, engineers, and mathematicians, it has set up a ladder of professional development to parallel the management ladder. Williams likes to tell of a young systems engineer who complained a couple of years ago that IBM was all wrong in handling its "SE's" (who help customers organize and set up computer and data processing systems). SE's, he said, didn't always want to become salesmen or branch managers, which was the incentive the company held out. They were often more interested in rising in their new profession.

Management liked his idea, and put him on the corporate staff in charge of systems engineering.

III. JUST BEGINNING

Now that the "modern, relatively decentralized" management machinery is humming along in high gear, what is IBM going to do with it?

Perhaps one of the strangest things about IBM, when you consider its growth and its $2.5-billion annual revenues, is the widespread feeling among its employees that they are in on something that is just beginning. Changes come so fast, in fact, that a favorite inside saw is that IBM means "I've Been Moved."

Exactly where IBM is moving to isn't easy to say, even for IBM executives with access to its five-year plans. But the company definitely sees its future as involving a much broader range of systems and services. Says Pres. Williams: "We are in the business of increasing productivity, and I don't see any particular limits."

Drastic Change

As Williams describes it, the business IBM is in has undergone just as drastic a change as IBM itself. That means new goals for the company, new sophistication in its products, a new place for IBM in the U. S. business picture.

IBM's business, Williams points out, was built on handling historical data — as the name, unit record systems, indicates. It produced systems to count things after they happened. Williams figures that about one out of seven in the total work force is engaged in this paper-shuffling work — and except for scientific computers, IBM's market was limited to this one out of seven.

Today, computers can be dispersed through business and hooked up to communications networks to keep track of what is happening as it happens. Management no longer has to wait for data to make decisions.

To Williams, this step from record keeping to handling current operating events is the most significant market trend. It puts IBM in a position to increase productivity not just in handling historical data, but in "almost all aspects of business" — in a position, that is, to offer its services to production, sales, and management, or, as Williams puts it, "the other six out of every seven employed people."

Keyspot

That's not all. Designing and installing so-called "integrated" or "real time" data processing systems that tie in production, sales, and accounting is vastly difficult. It means, IBM management feels, that IBM sales and systems men have to know in depth how all other businesses operate.

It's a formidable task and an expensive one, but it's about what IBM has decided it takes to stay on top of the computer heap.

IV. SOFTWARE PUSH

That situation, which will demand of IBM that it have men who are experts in almost every\ kind of business in the country, arises because of the special relation that exists between a computer maker and his customer.

Data processing machines put unique demands on the ability and knowledge of the people who set them up. A computer is a helpless tangle of wires, and won't do a single thing until you educate it, or put in the complex, detailed program that makes it flick its flip-flop circuits properly and fill its memory with the right bits in all of the right places.

In effect, when you buy or rent a computer, you get a general purpose machine. By educating — or programming — it you make it a special purpose calculator for your own business or scientific needs.

Essentially, programming a computer means putting into its memory a long series of numbers that must ultimately be in binary form — nothing but ones and zeros. Most computers will automatically convert alphanumeric information into binary numbers; and they have certain built-in responses — addition, multiplication, and so on. Over-all, though, programming means assembling instructions in seemingly endless rows and columns of numbers.

But before you can educate the computer for your purposes, you have to organize your record systems rigorously. And to educate the computer, you have to know not only the technical procedures, but the business needs the computer was hired to answer.

Block

Had IBM and other companies decided just to sell computers and let customers do all the work of programming them, they would live in a much simpler world. But the market for computers would have lagged until there were enough people around who knew how to program them.

So IBM, which has had a long tradition of educating its customers, took on the job of educating their computers, too. Right now, in the view of many IBM executives, it's programming — or "software," in industry parlance — rather than new developments in electronic hardware, that has become one of the major limitations on computer applications.

IBM, therefore, is shifting much of its effort and money toward breaking through that roadblock. A large share of its $60-million-a-year educational budget goes for educating its own programmers and systems men, and some $26-million to $28-million of the total goes for educating its customers.

Shortcuts

There are other ways to cut the cost of programming besides educating customers — and IBM is headed in this direction along various paths.

Computers are supplied with generalized master programs, or compilers, that enable the computer to program itself from shorthand or even English language instructions. These cost millions to develop but, once complete, can be recorded on reels of tape . . . and distributed inexpensively. IBM considers such programming shortcuts as much a part of the system as the hardware itself. Manufacturing divisions are responsible for supplying the major ones, such as COBOL, the business language compiler, and FORTRAN, a scientific or mathematical compiler.

For certain industries with reasonably standardized practices, it's possible to assemble special shortcut programs, on jobs such as utility billings or production scheduling problems. IBM calls these applications programs, and its Data Processing Div. produces them as part of the marketing package. But since no two companies even have the same payroll system, there's a limit to such pre-programming.

Looking farther ahead, IBM's Advanced Systems Development Div. is concentrating on even more complex and costly compilers to cut costs of programming networks of computers, schedule operations, and set up priority systems where computers are connected to direct inputs such as production line monitoring devices.

There's one overpowering reason why the problem of software is a serious one at IBM's high policy levels: The company has a tremendous amount of equipment out with customers that eventually will be replaced.

"The problem," says Watson, "is to give customers mobility from one system to the next, without obsoleting all the expensive programming they've done."

So important is the software problem, in Watson's view, that to make sure top management can make knowledgeable policy decisions about programming, he invited the entire Corporate Management Committee to spend three days in Vermont recently working on everything from binary and octal numbers to FORTRAN AND COBOL.

"By the time we got through," he says, "I think all of us had a better understanding of why some of our customers have as much as $3-million invested in computer programs."

V. WIRED FOR SPEED

IBM executives are fully convinced that the biggest effect on the future market for data processing will come from software developments rather than new hardware. But that doesn't mean they feel computers have evolved to their electronic best.

Though no one in the company will tip his hand on what's coming up next in hardware, some recent activities point up the general trends.

One is the way IBM itself has put computers to work designing and manufacturing other computers. Another indicator is the company's recent decision to produce a good proportion of its own electronic components.

*　*　*　*　*

VI. HOW FAST AND HOW FAR?

With all these fast-moving changes in both software and hardware, IBM executives look forward confidently to an exciting future of continued growth. For 1963, total sales will approach $3-billion. And IBM World Trade's sales are growing so fast that Pres. Williams predicts they'll exceed domestic revenues "in a reasonable number of years." If, as a mathematical exercise, you project IBM's current growth rates for foreign and domestic revenues, the two sales curves cross in 1973 at about $6-billion each. But IBM management itself refuses comment on such projections.

The one specter that darkens any optimistic forecast for IBM is the possibility of antitrust action. And last month's reminder from the Justice Dept. that time is running out on the 1956 consent decree serves to give it more vivid outlines.

IBM is making a lot of money in the computer business. Its competitors, on the other hand, are having a hard time. It has something like 70% or 80% of the market — only the company itself knows for sure. IBM got into trouble before on charges of dominating the punch card tabulating business. Will antitrust history repeat itself?

Conundrum

As far as share of the market goes, the question has to be raised. But there are major differences between IBM's position in computers and the domination it had over tabulating equipment.

For one thing, its competitors now are a lot stronger, and two of them — General Electric Co. and Ford Motor Co., which owns Philco Corp. — are much bigger. Highly diversified and only slightly smaller competitors, such as RCA, Sperry Rand Corp., and Litton have exceptional staying power. Both National Cash Register Co. and Burroughs Corp. have good marketing positions to work from and are increasing their sales. Control Data Corp., one of the few independents in the field, is a profitable company.

Without the collapse of several of these competitors — which no one in or out of IBM thinks very likely — it is hard to imagine an antitrust action against IBM alone that would not be extremely punitive.

Besides, how would you divide IBM up? Even its own executives confess they had a nearly impossible time cutting it up into reasonable divisions.

10 HOW TO EVALUATE CORPORATE STRATEGY

by Seymour Tilles

No good military officer would undertake even a small-scale attack on a limited objective without a clear concept of his strategy. No seasoned politician would undertake a campaign for a major office without an equally clear concept of his strategy. In the field of business management, however, we frequently find men deploying resources on a large scale without any clear notion of what their strategy is. And yet a company's strategy is a vital ingredient in determining its future. A valid strategy will yield growth, profit, or whatever other objectives the managers have established. An inappropriate strategy not only will fail to yield benefits, but also may result in disaster.

In this article I will try to demonstrate the truth of these contentions by examining the experiences of a number of companies. I shall discuss what strategy is, how it can be evaluated, and how, by evaluating its strategy, a management can do much to assure the future of the enterprise.

DECISIVE IMPACT

The influence of strategy can be seen in every age and in every area of industry. Here are some examples:

1. From the time it was started in 1911 as the Computing-Tabulating-Recording Co., International Business Machines Corporation has demonstrated the significance of a soundly conceived strategy. Seeing itself in the data-sys-

Reprinted from Harvard Business Review, July-August, 1963, pages 111-121, by permission of the publisher.

tem business at a time when most manufacturers were still preoccupied with individual pieces of equipment, IBM developed a set of policies which resulted in its dominating the office equipment industry.

2. By contrast, Packard in the 1930's was to the automobile industry everything that IBM is today to the office machine industry. In 1937, it sold over 109,000 cars, compared with about 11,000 for Cadillac. By 1954 it had disappeared as an independent producer.

Strategy is, of course, not the only factor determining a company's success or failure. The competence of its managerial leadership is significant as well. Luck can be a factor, too (although often what people call good luck is really the product of good strategy). But a valid strategy can gain extraordinary results for the company whose general level of competence is only average. And, conversely, the most inspiring leaders who are locked into an inappropriate strategy will have to exert their full competence and energy merely in order to keep from losing ground.

When Hannibal inflicted the humiliating defeat on the Roman army at Cannae in 216 B.C., he led a ragged band against soldiers who were in possession of superior arms, better training, and competent "noncoms." His strategy, however, was so superior that all of those advantages proved to be relatively insignificant. Similarly, when Jacob Borowsky made Lestoil the hottest-selling detergent in New England some years ago, he was performing a similar feat — relying on strategy to battle competition with superior resources.

Strategy is important not only for aspiring Davids who need an offensive device to combat corporate Goliaths. It is significant also for the large organization faced with a wide range of choice in domestic and international operations. For instance, the following corporations are all in the midst of strategic changes, the implications of which are worldwide in scope:

1. Massey-Ferguson, Ltd., with 26 factories located around the world, and vying for leadership in the farm-equipment industry.
2. General Electric Company and Westinghouse Electric Corporation, the giant producers of electrical equipment who are recasting their competitive policies.
3. Singer Sewing Machine Company, trying to make its vast assets yield a greater return.

A strategy is a set of goals and major policies. The definition is as simple as that. But while the notion of a strategy is extremely easy to grasp, working out an agreed-upon statement for a given company can be a fundamental contribution to the organization's future success.

In order to develop such a statement, managers must be able to identify precisely what is meant by a goal and what is meant by a major policy. Otherwise, the process of strategy determination may degenerate into what it so often becomes — the solemn recording of platitudes, useless for either the clarification of direction or the achievement of consensus.

Identifying Goals

Corporate goals are an indication of what the company as a whole is trying to achieve and to become. Both parts — the achieving and the becoming — are important for a full understanding of what a company hopes to attain. For example:

> 1. Under the leadership of Alfred Sloan, General Motors achieved a considerable degree of external success; this was accomplished because Sloan worked out a pattern for the kind of company he wanted it to be internally.
> 2. Similarly, the remarkable record of Du Pont in the twentieth century and the growth of Sears, Roebuck under Julius Rosenwald were as much a tribute to their modified structure as to their external strategy.[1]

Achieving. In order to state what a company expects to achieve, it is important to state what it hopes to do with respect to its environment. For instance:

> Ernest Breech, chairman of the board of the Ford Motor Company, said that the strategy formulated by his company in 1946 was based on a desire "to hold our own in what we foresaw would be a rich but hotly competitive market."[2] The view of the environment implicit in

---

1 For an interesting discussion of this relationship, see A. D. Chandler, Jr., Strategy and Structure (Cambridge: Massachusetts Institute of Technology Press, 1962), pages 1-17.

2 See Edward C. Bursk and Dan H. Fenn, Jr., Planning the Future Strategy of Your Business (New York: McGraw-Hill Book Company, Inc., 1956), page 8.

this statement is unmistakable: an expanding over-all demand, increasing competition, and emphasis on market share as a measure of performance against competitors.

Clearly, a statement of what a company hopes to achieve may be much more varied and complex than can be contained in a single sentence. This will be especially true for those managers who are sophisticated enough to perceive that a company operates in more external "systems" than the market. The firm is part not only of a market but also of an industry, the community, the economy, and other systems. In each case there are unique relationships to observe (e.g., with competitors, municipal leaders, Congress, and so on). A more complete discussion of this point is contained in a previous H[arvard] B[usiness] R[eview] article.3

Becoming. If you ask young men what they want to accomplish by the time they are 40, the answers you get fall into two distinct categories. There are those — the great majority — who will respond in terms of what they want to have. This is especially true of graduate students of business administration. There are some men, however, who will answer in terms of the kind of men they hope to be. These are the only ones who have a clear idea of where they are going.

The same is true of companies. For far too many companies, what little thinking goes on about the future is done primarily in money terms. There is nothing wrong with financial planning. Most companies should do more of it. But there is a basic fallacy in confusing a financial plan with thinking about the kind of company you want yours to become. It is like saying, "When I'm 40, I'm going to be rich." It leaves too many basic questions unanswered. Rich in what way? Rich doing what?

The other major fallacy in stating what you want to become is to say it only in terms of a product. The number of companies who have got themselves into trouble by falling in love with a particular product is distressingly great.4 Perhaps the saddest examples are those giants of American industry who defined their future in terms of continuing to be the major suppliers of steam locomotives to the nation's railroads. In fact, these companies were so wedded to this concept of their future that they formed a cartel in order to keep General Motors out of the steam locomotive business. When the diesel locomotive proved its superiority to steam, these companies all but disappeared.

---

3 Seymour Tilles, "The Manager's Job — A Systems Approach," HBR, January-February, 1963, page 73.
4 See Theodore Levitt, "Marketing Myopia," HBR, July-August, 1960, page 45.

The lesson of these experiences is that a key element of setting goals is the ability to see them in terms of more than a single dimension. Both money and product policy are part of a statement of objectives; but it is essential that these be viewed as the concrete expressions of a more abstract set of goals — the satisfaction of the needs of significant groups which cooperate to ensure the company's continued existence.

Who are these groups? There are many — customers, managers, employees, stockholders, to mention just the major ones. The key to corporate success is the company's ability to identify the important needs of each of these groups, to establish some balance among them, and to work out a set of operating policies which permits their satisfaction. This set of policies, as a pattern, identifies what the company is trying to be.

The Growth Fad

Many managers have a view of their company's future which is strikingly analogous to the child's view of himself. When asked what they want their companies to become over the next few years, they reply, "bigger."

There are a great many rationalizations for this preoccupation with growth. Probably the one most frequently voiced is that which says, "You have to grow or die." What must be appreciated, however, is that "bigger" for a company has enormous implications for management. It involves a different way of life, and one which many managers may not be suited for — either in terms of temperament or skills.

Moreover, whether for a large company or a small one, "bigger," by itself, may not make economic sense. Companies which are highly profitable at their present size may grow into bankruptcy very easily; witness the case of Grayson-Robinson Stores, Inc., a chain of retail stores. Starting out as a small but profitable chain, it grew rapidly into receivership. Conversely, a company which is not now profitable may more successfully seek its survival in cost reduction than in sales growth. Chrysler is a striking example of this approach.

There is, in the United States, a business philosophy which reflects the frontier heritage of the country. It is one which places a high value on growth, in physical terms. The manager whose corporate sales are not increasing, the number of whose subordinates is not growing, whose plants are not expanding, feels that he is not successful. But there is a dangerous trap in this kind of thinking. More of the same is not necessarily progress. In addition, few managers are capable of running units several times larger than the ones they now head. The great danger of wholehearted consumer acceptance or an astute program of corporate acquisition is that it frequently propels managers into situations that are beyond their present competence.

Such cases — and they are legion — emphasize that in stating corporate objectives bigger is not always better. A dramatic example is that of the Ampex Corporation:

> From 1950 to 1960 Ampex's annual sales went from less than $1000,000 to more than $73,000,000. Its earnings went from $115,000 to nearly $4,000,000. The following year, the company reported a decline in sales to $70,000,000, and a net loss of $3,900,000. The Wall Street Journal reported: "As one source close to the company put it, Ampex's former management 'was intelligent and well-educated, but simply lacked the experience necessary to control' the company's rapid development."[5]

Role of Policy

A policy says something about how goals will be attained. It is what statisticians would call a "decision rule," and what systems engineers would call a "standing plan." It tells people what they should and should not do in order to contribute to achievement of corporate goals.

A policy should be more than just a platitude. It should be a helpful guide to making strategy explicit, and providing direction to subordinates. Consequently, the more definite it is, the more helpful it can be. "We will provide our stockholders with a fair return," is a policy no one could possibly disagree with — or be helped by. What is a fair return? This is the type of question that must be answered before the company's intentions become clear.

The job of management is not merely the preparation of valid policies for a standard set of activities; it is the much more challenging one of first deciding what activities are so strategically significant that explicit decision-rules in that area are mandatory. No standard set of policies can be considered major for all companies. Each company is a unique situation. It must decide for itself which aspects of corporate life are more relevant to its own aspirations and work out policy statements for them. For example, advertising may be insignificant to a company which provides research services to the Defense Department, but critical to a firm trying to mass-merchandise luxury goods.

It is difficult to generalize about which policies are major, even within a particular industry, because a number of extraor-

5 "R for Ampex: Drastic Changes Help Solve Big Headache of Fast Corporate Growth," Wall Street Journal, September 17, 1962, page 1.

dinarily successful companies appear to violate all the rules. To illustrate:

> 1. In the candy industry it would seem safe to generalize that advertising should be a major policy area. However, the Hershey Company, which is so successful that its name is practically the generic term for the produce, has persistently followed a policy of no advertising.
> 2. Similarly, in the field of high-fidelity components, one would expect that dealer relations would be a critical policy area. But Acoustics Research, Inc., has built an enviable record of sales growth and of profitability by relying entirely on consumer pull.

Need to Be Explicit

The first thing to be said about corporate strategy is that having one is a step forward. Any strategy, once made explicit, can quickly be evaluated and improved. But if no attempt is ever made to commit it to paper, there is always the danger that the strategy is either incomplete or misunderstood.

Many successful companies are not aware of the strategy that underlies their success. It is quite possible for a company to achieve initial success without real awareness of its causes. However, it is much more difficult to successfully branch out into new ventures without a precise appreciation of their strategic significance. This is why many established companies fail miserably when they attempt a program of corporate acquisition, product diversification, or market expansion. One illustration of this is cited by Myles L. Mace and George G. Montgomery in their recent study of corporate acquisitions:

> "A basic resin company . . . bought a plastic boat manufacturer because this seemed to present a controlled market for a portion of the resin it produced. It soon found that the boat business was considerably different from the manufacture and sale of basic chemicals. After a short but unpleasant experience in manufacturing and trying to market what was essentially a consumer's item, the management concluded that its experience and abilities lay essentially in industrial rather than consumer-type products."[6]

---

6 Management Problems of Corporate Acquisitions (Boston: Division of Research, Harvard Business School, 1962), page 60.

Another reason for making strategy explicit is the assistance it provides for delegation and for coordination. To an ever-increasing extent, management is a team activity, whereby groups of executives contribute to corporate success. Making strategy explicit makes it far easier for each executive to appreciate what the over-all goals are, and what his own contribution to them must be.

MAKING AN EVALUATION

Is your strategy right for you? There are six criteria on which to base an answer. These are:

1. Internal consistency.
2. Consistency with the environment.
3. Appropriateness in the light of available resources.
4. Satisfactory degree of risk.
5. Appropriate time horizon.
6. Workability.

If all of these criteria are met, you have a strategy that is right for you. This is as much as can be asked. There is no such thing as a good strategy in any absolute, objective sense. In the remainder of this article I shall discuss the criteria in some detail.

1. Is the Strategy Internally Consistent?

Internal consistency refers to the cumulative impact of individual policies on corporate goals. In a well-worked-out strategy, each policy fits into an integrated pattern. It should be judged not only in terms of itself, but also in terms of how it relates to other policies which the company has established and to the goals it is pursuing.

In a dynamic company consistency can never be taken for granted. For example:

> Many family-owned organizations pursue a pair of policies which soon become inconsistent: rapid expansion and retention of exclusive family control of the firm. If they are successful in expanding, the need for additional financing soon raises major problems concerning the extent to which exclusive family control can be maintained.
>
> While this pair of policies is especially prevalent among smaller firms, it is by no means limited to them. The Ford Motor Company after World War II and the New York

Times today are examples of quite large, family-controlled organizations that have had to reconcile the two conflicting aims.

The criterion of internal consistency is an especially important one for evaluating strategies because it identifies those areas where strategic choices will eventually have to be made. An inconsistent strategy does not necessarily mean that the company is currently in difficulty. But it does mean that unless management keeps its eye on a particular area of operation, it may well find itself forced to make a choice without enough time either to search for or to prepare attractive alternatives.

2. Is the Strategy Consistent with the Environment?

A firm which has a certain product policy, price policy, or advertising policy is saying that it has chosen to relate itself to its customers — actual and potential — in a certain way. Similarly, its policies with respect to government contracts, collective bargaining, foreign investment, and so forth are expressions of relationship with other groups and forces. Hence an important test of strategy is whether the chosen policies are consistent with the environment — whether they really make sense with respect to what is going on outside.

Consistency with the environment has both a static and a dynamic aspect. In a static sense, it implies judging the efficacy of policies with respect to the environment as it exists now. In a dynamic sense, it means judging the efficacy of policies with respect to the environment as it appears to be changing. One purpose of a viable strategy is to ensure the long-run success of an organization. Since the environment of a company is constantly changing, ensuring success over the long run means that management must constantly be assessing the degree to which policies previously established are consistent with the environment as it exists now; and whether current policies take into account the environment as it will be in the future. In one sense, therefore, establishing a strategy is like aiming at a moving target: you have to be concerned not only with present position but also with the speed and direction of movement.

Failure to have a strategy consistent with the environment can be costly to the organization. Ford's sad experience with the Edsel is by now a textbook example of such failure. Certainly, had Ford pushed the Falcon at the time when it was pushing the Edsel, and with the same resources, it would have a far stronger position in the world automobile market today.

Illustrations of strategies that have not been consistent with the environment are easy to find by using hindsight. But the reason that such examples are plentiful is not that foresight is difficult to apply. It is because even today few companies are seriously engaged in analyzing environment trends and using this intelligence as a basis for managing their own futures.

3. Is the Strategy Appropriate in View of the Available Resources?

Resources are those things that a company _is_ or _has_ and that help it to achieve its corporate objectives. Included are money, competence, and facilities; but these by no means complete the list. In companies selling consumer goods, for example, the major resource may be the name of the product. In any case, there are two basic issues which management must decide in relating strategy and resources. These are:

1. What are our critical resources?
2. Is the proposed strategy appropriate for available resources?

Let us look now at what is meant by a "critical resource" and at how the criterion of resource utilization can be used as a basis for evaluating strategy.

Critical Resources

The essential strategic attribute of resources is that they represent action potential. Taken together, a company's resources represent its capacity to respond to threats and opportunities that may be perceived in the environment. In other words, resources are the bundle of chips that the company has to play with in the serious game of business.

From an action-potential point of view, a resource may be critical in two senses: (1) as the factor limiting the achievement of corporate goals; and (2) as that which the company will exploit as the basis for its strategy. Thus, critical resources are both what the company has most of and what it has least of.

The three resources most frequently identified as critical are money, competence, and physical facilities. Let us look at the strategic significance of each.

Money. Money is a particularly valuable resource because it provides the greatest flexibility of response to events as they arise. It may be considered the "safest" resource, in that safety may be equated with the freedom to choose from among the widest variety of future alternatives. Companies that wish to reduce their short-run risk will therefore attempt to accumulate the greatest reservoir of funds they can.

However, it is important to remember that while the accumulation of funds may offer short-run security, it may place the company at a serious competitive disadvantage with respect to other companies which are following a higher-risk course.

The classical illustration of this kind of outcome is the strategy pursued by Montgomery Ward under the late Sewell Avery. As reported in _Fortune_:

> "While Sears confidently bet on a new and expanding America, Avery developed an _idée fixe_ that postwar inflation would end in a crash no less serious than that of 1929. Following this idea, he opened no new stores but rather piled up cash to the ceiling in preparation for an economic debacle that never came. In these years, Ward's balance sheet gave a somewhat misleading picture of its prospects. Net earnings remained respectably high, and were generally higher than those of Sears as a percentage of sales. In 1946, earnings after taxes were $52 million. They rose to $74 million in 1950, and then declined to $35 million in 1954. Meanwhile, however, sales remained static, and in Avery's administration profits and liquidity were maintained at the expense of growth. In 1954, Ward had $327 million in cash and securities, $147 million in receivables, and $216 million in inventory, giving it a total current-asset position of $690 million and net worth of $639 million. It was liquid, all right, but it was also the shell of a once great company."[7]

Competence. Organizations survive because they are good at doing those things which are necessary to keep them alive. However, the degree of competence of a given organization is by no means uniform across the broad range of skills necessary to stay in business. Some companies are particularly good at marketing, others especially good at engineering, still others depend primarily on their financial sophistication. Philip Selznick refers to that which a company is particularly good at as its "distinctive competence."[8]

In determining a strategy, management must carefully appraise its own skill profile in order to determine where its strengths and weaknesses lie. It must then adopt a strategy which makes the greatest use of its strengths. To illustrate:

---

7 "Montgomery Ward: Prosperity Is Still Around the Corner," _Fortune_, November, 1960, page 140.

8 _Leadership in Administration_ (Evanston, Ill.: Row, Peterson & Company, 1957), p. 42.

1. The competence of The New York Times lies primarily in giving extensive and insightful coverage of events — the ability to report "all the news that's fit to print." It is neither highly profitable (earning only 1.5% of revenues in 1960 — far less than, say, the Wall Street Journal), nor aggressively sold. Its decision to publish a West Coast and an international edition is a gamble that the strength of its "distinctive competence" will make it accepted even outside of New York.

2. Because of a declining demand for soft coal, many producers of soft coal are diversifying into other fields. All of them, however, are remaining true to some central skill that they have developed over the years. For instance:

— Consolidation Coal is moving from simply the mining of soft coal to the mining and transportation of soft coal. It is planning with Texas Eastern Transmission Corporation to build a $100-million pipeline that would carry a mixture of powdered coal and water from West Virginia to the East Coast.

— North American Coal Company, on the other hand, is moving toward becoming a chemical company. It recently joined with Strategic Materials Corporation to perfect a process for extracting aluminum sulfate from the mine shale that North American produces in its coal-running operations.

James L. Hamilton, president of the Island Creek Coal Co., has summed up the concept of distinctive competence in a colorful way:

"We are a career company dedicated to coal, and we have some very definite ideas about growth and expansion within the industry. We're not thinking of buying a cotton mill and starting to make shirts." [9]

Physical Facilities. Physical facilities are the resource whose strategic influence is perhaps most frequently misunderstood. Managers seem to be divided among those, usually technical men, who are enamored of physical facilities as the tangible

---

[9] Wall Street Journal, September 11, 1962, page 30.

symbol of the corporate entity; and those, usually financial men, who view physical facilities as an undesirable but necessary freezing of part of the company's funds. The latter group is dominant. In many companies, return on investment has emerged as virtually the sole criterion for deciding whether or not a particular facility should be acquired.

Actually, this is putting the cart before the horse. Physical facilities have significance primarily in relationship to over-all corporate strategy. It is, therefore, only in relationship to other aspects of corporate strategy that the acquisition or disposition of physical facilities can be determined. The total investment required and the projected return on it have a place in this determination — but only as an indication of the financial implications of a particular strategic decision and not as an exclusive criterion for its own sake.

Any appraisal of a company's physical facilities as a strategic resource must consider the relationship of the company to its environment. Facilities have no intrinsic value for their own sake. Their value to the company is either in their location relative to markets, to sources of labor, or to materials; or in their efficiency relative to existing or impending competitive installations. Thus, the essential considerations in any decision regarding physical facilities are a projection of changes likely to occur in the environment and a prediction about what the company's responses to these are likely to be.

Here are two examples of the necessity for relating an evaluation of facilities to environmental changes:

1. Following the end of World War II, all domestic producers of typewriters in the United States invested heavily in plant facilities in this country. They hypothesized a rapid increase of sales throughout the world. This indeed took place, but it was short-lived. The rise of vigorous overseas competitors, especially Olivetti and Olympia, went hand in hand with a booming overseas market. At home, IBM's electric typewriter took more and more of the domestic market. Squeezed between these two pressures, the rest of the U.S. typewriter industry found itself with a great deal of excess capacity following the Korean conflict. Excess capacity is today still a major problem in this field.

2. The steady decline in the number of farms in the United States and the emergence of vigorous overseas competition have forced most domestic full-line manufacturers of farm equipment to sharply curtail total plant area.

For example, in less than four years, International Harvester eliminated more than a third of its capacity (as measured in square feet of plant space) for the production of farm machinery.

The close relationship between physical facilities and environmental trends emphasizes one of the most significant attributes of fixed assets — their temporal utility. Accounting practice recognizes this in its treatment of depreciation allowances. But even when the tax laws permit generous write-offs, they should not be used as the sole basis for setting the time period over which the investment must be justified. Environmental considerations may reveal that a different time horizon is more relevant for strategy determination. To illustrate again:

As Armstrong Cork Company moved away from natural cork to synthetic materials during the early 1950's, management considered buying facilities for the production of its raw materials — particularly polyvinyl chloride. However, before doing so, it surveyed the chemical industry and concluded that producers were overbuilding. It therefore decided not to invest in facilities for the manufacture of this material. The projections were valid; since 1956 polyvinyl chloride has dropped 50% in price.

A strategic approach to facilities may not only change the time horizon; it may also change the whole basis of asset valuation:

Recently a substantial portion of Loew's theaters was acquired by the Tisch brothers, owners and operators of a number of successful hotels, including the Americana in Florida.[10] As long as the assets of Loew's theaters were viewed only as places for the projection of films, its theaters, however conservatively valued, seemed to be not much of a bargain. But to a keen appraiser of hotel properties the theater sites, on rather expensive real estate in downtown city areas, had considerable appeal. Whether this appraisal will be borne out

---

10 See "The Tisches Eye Their Next $65 Million," Fortune, January, 1960, page 140.

is as yet unknown. At any rate, the stock, which was originally purchased at $14 (with a book value of $22), was selling at $23 in October 1962.

Achieving the Right Balance

One of the most difficult issues in strategy determination is that of achieving a balance between strategic goals and available resources. This requires a set of necessarily empirical, but critical, estimates of the total resources required to achieve particular objectives, the rate at which they will have to be committed, and the likelihood that they will be available. The most common errors are either to fail to make these estimates at all or to be excessively optimistic about them.

One example of the unfortunate results of being wrong on these estimates is the case of Royal McBee and the computer market:

> In January 1956 Royal McBee and the General Precision Equipment Corporation formed a jointly owned company — the Royal Precision Corporation — to enter the market for electronic data-processing equipment. This joint operation was a logical pooling of complementary talents. General Precision had a great deal of experience in developing and producing computers. Its Librascope Division had been selling them to the government for years. However, it lacked a commercial distribution system. Royal McBee, on the other hand, had a great deal of experience in marketing data-processing equipment, but lacked the technical competence to develop and produce a computer.
>
> The joint venture was eminently successful, and within a short time the Royal Precision LPG-30 was the leader in the small-computer field. However, the very success of the computer venture caused Royal McBee some serious problems. The success of the Royal Precision subsidiary demanded that the partners put more and more money into it. This was no problem for General Precision, but it became an ever more serious problem for Royal McBee, which found itself in an increasingly critical cash bind. In March 1962 it sold its interest in Royal Precision to General Precision for $5 million — a price which represented a reported $6.9 million loss on the investment. Concluding

that it simply did not have sufficient resources to stay with the new venture, it decided to return to its traditional strengths: typewriters and simple data-processing systems.

Another place where optimistic estimates of resources frequently cause problems is in small businesses. Surveys of the causes of small-business failure reveal that a most frequent cause of bankruptcy is inadequate resources to weather either the early period of establishment or unforeseen downturns in business conditions.

It is apparent from the preceding discussion that a critical strategic decision involves deciding: (1) how much of the company's resources to commit to opportunities currently perceived, and (2) how much to keep uncommitted as a reserve against the appearance of unanticipated demands. This decision is closely related to two other criteria for the evaluation of strategy: risk and timing. I shall now discuss these.

4. Does the Strategy Involve an Acceptable Degree of Risk?

Strategy and resources, taken together, determine the degree of risk which the company is undertaking. This is a critical managerial choice. For example, when the old Underwood Corporation decided to enter the computer field, it was making what might have been an extremely astute strategic choice. However, the fact that it ran out of money before it could accomplish anything in that field turned its pursuit of opportunity into the prelude to disaster. This is not to say that the strategy was "bad." However, the course of action pursued was a high-risk strategy. Had it been successful, the payoff would have been lush. The fact that it was a stupendous failure instead does not mean that it was senseless to take the gamble.

Each company must decide for itself how much risk it wants to live with. In attempting to assess the degree of risk associated with a particular strategy, management may use a variety of techniques. For example, mathematicians have developed an elegant set of techniques for choosing among a variety of strategies where you are willing to estimate the payoffs and the probabilities associated with them. However, our concern here is not with these quantitative aspects but with the identification of some qualitative factors which may serve as a rough basis for evaluating the degree of risk inherent in a strategy. These factors are:

1. The amount of resources (on which the strategy is based) whose continued existence or value is not assured.
2. The length of the time periods to which resources are committed.

3. The proportion of resources committed to a single venture.

The greater these quantities, the greater the degree of risk that is involved.

Uncertain Term of Existence

Since a strategy is based on resources, any resource which may disappear before the payoff has been obtained may constitute a danger to the organization. Resources may disappear for various reasons. For example, they may lose their value. This frequently happens to such resources as physical facilities and product features. Again, they may be accidentally destroyed. The most vulnerable resource here is competence. The possible crash of the company plane or the blip on the president's electrocardiogram are what make many organizations essentially speculative ventures. In fact, one of the critical attributes of highly centralized organizations is that the more centralized they are, the more speculative they are. The disappearance of the top executive, or the disruption of communication with him, may wreak havoc at subordinate levels.

However, for many companies, the possibility that critical resources may lose their value stems not so much from internal developments as from shifts in the environment. Take specialized production know-how, for example. It has value only because of demand for the product by customers — and customers may change their minds. This is cause for acute concern among the increasing number of companies whose futures depend so heavily on their ability to participate in defense contracts. A familiar case is the plight of the airframe industry following World War II. Some of the companies succeeded in making the shift from aircraft to missiles, but this has only resulted in their being faced with the same problem on a larger scale.

Duration of Commitment

Financial analysts often look at the ratio of fixed assets to current assets in order to assess the extent to which resources are committed to long-term programs. This may or may not give a satisfactory answer. How important are the assets? When will they be paid for?

The reasons for the risk increasing as the time for payoff increases is, of course, the inherent uncertainty in any venture. Resources committed over long time spans make the company vulnerable to changes in the environment. Since the difficulty of predicting such changes increases as the time span increases, long-term projects are basically more risky than are short ones. This is especially true of companies whose environments are unstable. And today, either because of technological, political, or economic shifts, most companies are decidedly in the category of those that face major upheaval in their corporate environments. The company building its future around technological equipment, the company selling primarily to the government, the company investing in underdeveloped nations, the company selling to the Common Market, the company with a plant in the South — all these have this prospect in common.

The harsh dilemma of modern management is that the time span of decision is increasing at the same time as the corporate environment is becoming increasingly unstable. It is this dilemma which places such a premium on the manager's sensitivity to external trends today. Much has been written about his role as a commander and administrator. But it is no less important that he be a strategist.

Size of the Stakes

The more of its resources a company commits to a particular strategy, the more pronounced the consequences. If the strategy is successful, the payoff will be great — both to managers and investors. If the strategy fails, the consequences will be dire — both to managers and investors. Thus, a critical decision for the executive group is: What proportion of available resources should be committed to a particular course of action?

This decision may be handled in a variety of ways. For example, faced with a project that requires more of its resources than it is willing to commit, a company either may choose to refrain from undertaking the project or, alternatively, may seek to reduce the total resources required by undertaking a joint venture or by going the route of merger or acquisition in order to broaden the resource base.

The amount of resources management stands ready to commit is of particular significance where there is some likelihood that larger competitors, having greater resources, may choose to enter the company's field. Thus, those companies which entered the small-computer field in the past few years are now faced with the penetration into this area of the data-processing giants. (Both IBM and Remington Rand have recently introduced new small computers.)

I do not mean to imply that the "best" strategy is the one with the least risk. High payoffs are frequently associated with high-risk strategies. Moreover, it is a frequent but dangerous assumption to think that inaction, or lack of change, is a low-risk strategy. Failure to exploit its resources to the fullest may well be the riskiest strategy of all that an organization may pursue, as Montgomery Ward and other companies have amply demonstrated.

5. Does the Strategy Have an Appropriate Time Horizon?

A significant part of every strategy is the time horizon on which it is based. A viable strategy not only reveals what goals are to be accomplished; it says something about when the aims are to be achieved.

Goals, like resources, have time-based utility. A new product developed, a plant put on stream, a degree of market penetration, become significant strategic objectives only if accomplished by a certain time. Delay may deprive them of all strategic significance. A perfect example of this in the military sphere is the Sinai campaign of 1956. The strategic objective of the Israelis was not only to conquer the entire Sinai peninsula; it also was to do it in seven days. By contrast, the lethargic movement of the British troops made the operation a futile one for both England and France.

In choosing an appropriate time horizon, we must pay careful attention to the goals being pursued, and to the particular organization involved. Goals must be established far enough in advance to allow the organization to adjust to them. Organizations, like ships, cannot be "spun on a dime." Consequently, the larger the organization, the further its strategic time horizon must extend, since its adjustment time is longer. It is no mere managerial whim that the major contributions to long-range planning have emerged from the larger organizations — especially those large organizations such as Lockheed, North American Aviation, and RCA that traditionally have had to deal with highly unstable environments.

The observation that large corporations plan far ahead while small ones can get away without doing so has frequently been made. However, the significance of planning for the small but growing company has frequently been overlooked. As a company gets bigger, it must not only change the way it operates; it must also steadily push ahead its time horizon — and this is a difficult thing to do. The manager who has built a successful enterprise by his skill at "putting out fires" or the wheeler-dealer whose firm has grown by a quick succession of financial coups is seldom able to make the transition to the long look ahead.

In many cases, even if the executive were inclined to take a longer range view of events, the formal reward system seriously militates against doing so. In most companies the system of management rewards is closely related to currently reported profits. Where this is the case, executives may understandably be so preoccupied with reporting a profit year by year that they fail to spend as much time as they should in managing the company's long-term future. But if we seriously accept the thesis that the essence of managerial responsibility is the extended time lapse between decision and result, currently reported profits are hardly a reasonable basis on which to compensate top executives. Such a basis simply serves to shorten the time horizon with which the executive is concerned.

The importance of an extended time horizon derives not only from the fact that an organization changes slowly and needs time to work through basic modifications in its strategy; it derives also from the fact that there is a considerable advantage in a certain consistency of strategy maintained over long periods of time. The great danger to companies which do not carefully formulate strategies well in advance is that they are prone to fling themselves toward chaos by drastic changes in policy — and in personnel — at frequent intervals. A parade of presidents is a clear indication of a board that has not really decided what its strategy should be. It is a common harbinger of serious corporate difficulty as well.

The time horizon is also important because of its impact on the selection of policies. The greater the time horizon, the greater the range in choice of tactics. If, for instance, the goals desired must be achieved in a relatively short time, steps like acquisition and merger may become virtually mandatory. An interesting illustration is the decision of National Cash Register to enter the market for electronic data-processing equipment. As reported in Forbes:

> "Once committed to EDP, NCR wasted no time. To buy talent and experience in 1953 it acquired Computer Research Corp. of Hawthorne, California. . . . For speed's sake, the manufacture of the 304's central units was turned over to GE. . . . NCR's research and development outlays also began curving steeply upwards."11

6. Is the Strategy Workable?

At first glance, it would seem that the simplest way to evaluate a corporate strategy is the completely pragmatic one of asking: Does it work? However, further reflection should reveal that if we try to answer that question, we are immediately faced with a quest for criteria. What is the evidence of a strategy "working"?

Quantitative indices of performance are a good start, but they really measure the influence of two critical factors combined: the strategy selected and the skill with which it is being executed. Faced with the failure to achieve anticipated results, both of these influences must be critically examined. One interesting

---

11"NCR and the Computer Sweepstakes," Forbes, October 15, 1962, page 21.

illustration of this is a recent survey of the Chrysler Corporation after it suffered a period of serious loss:

> "In 1959, during one of the frequent reorganizations at Chrysler Corp., aimed at halting the company's slide, a management consultant concluded: 'The only thing wrong with Chrysler is people. The corporation needs some good top executives.'"[12]

By contrast, when Olivetti acquired the Underwood Corporation, it was able to reduce the cost of producing typewriters by one-third. And it did it without changing any of the top people in the production group. However, it did introduce a drastically revised set of policies.

If a strategy cannot be evaluated by results alone, there are some other indications that may be used to assess its contribution to corporate progress:

1. The degree of consensus which exists among executives concerning corporate goals and policies.

2. The extent to which major areas of managerial choice are identified in advance, while there is still time to explore a variety of alternatives.

3. The extent to which resource requirements are discovered well before the last minute, necessitating neither crash programs of cost reduction nor the elimination of planned programs. The widespread popularity of the meat-axe approach to cost reduction is a clear indication of the frequent failure of corporate strategic planning.

CONCLUSION

The modern organization must deploy expensive and complex resources in the pursuit of transitory opportunities. The time required to develop resources is so extended, and the time-scale of opportunities is so brief and fleeting, that a company which has not carefully delineated and appraised its strategy is adrift in white water.

In short, while a set of goals and major policies that meets the criteria listed above does not guarantee success, it can be of considerable value in giving management both the time and the room to maneuver.

---

12 "How Chrysler Hopes to Rebound," Business Week, October 6, 1962, page 45.

11 MAKING SENSE OF MANAGEMENT THEORY

by Harold Koontz

*　*　*　*　*

While problems of managing have existed since the dawn of organized life, the systematic examination of management problems is, with few exceptions, the product of the present century and especially of the past two decades. Moreover, until recent years, almost all of those who have attempted to analyze the management process and look for some scientific underpinnings to help the practice of management were alert and perceptive practitioners of the art who could base their speculations on many years of experience. Thus, the earliest meaningful writing came from such experienced business management practitioners as Henri Fayol, James D. Mooney, Alvin Brown, Oliver Sheldon, Chester Barnard, and Lyndall F. Urwick. Although not based on questionnaires, controlled interviews, or mathematics, the observations of such men can hardly be regarded as "armchair."

The noteworthy absence of academic writing and research in the formative years of modern management theory is now more than atoned for by a deluge of research and writing pouring from academic halls. What is interesting (but perhaps nothing more than a sign of the unsophisticated adolescence of management theory) is how the current flood has brought with it waves of differences and confusion.

*　*　*　*　*

[My] purpose here will be to avoid allying myself with this or that theoretical fad, and to shed some light on the issues and problems involved in the management theory area today. So that

Excerpts, reprinted from Harvard Business Review, July-August, 1962, pages 24-30, by permission of the publisher.

some of the more worthwhile literature on this subject may be made useful to those who manage, I will — at the risk of serious oversimplification — classify the various "schools" of management theory into six main groups:

1. The <u>Management Process School</u>. This approach to management theory perceives management as a process of getting things done by people who operate in organized groups. By analyzing the process, establishing a conceptual framework for it, and identifying the principles underlying the process, this approach builds a theory of management. It regards management as a process that is essentially the same whether in business, government, or any other enterprise, and which involves the same <u>process</u>, whether at the level of president or foreman in a given enterprise. It does, however, recognize that the environment of management differs widely between enterprises and levels. According to this school, management theory is seen as a way of summarizing and organizing experience so that practice can be improved.

*   *   *   *   *

This school bases its approach to management theory on several fundamental beliefs. Specifically:

1. Managing is a process which can best be dissected intellectually by analyzing the manager's functions.

2. Long experience with management in a variety of enterprise situations can be grounds for the distillation of certain fundamental truths or generalizations — usually referred to as principles — that have a clarifying and predictive value in the understanding and improvement of managing.

3. These fundamental beliefs can become focal points for useful research both to ascertain their validity and to improve their meaning and applicability in practice.

4. Such beliefs can furnish elements, at least until disproved, of a useful theory of management.

5. Managing is an art, but, like medicine or engineering, one which can be improved by reliance on sound underlying principles.

6. Principles in management, like principles in the biological and physical sciences, are true even if exceptions or compromises of the "rules" prove effective in a given situation.

7. While there are, of course, many factors which affect the manager's environment, management theory need not encompass <u>all</u> knowledge in order for it to serve as a scientific or theoretical foundation for management practice.

The basic approach this school takes, then, is to look first at the functions of managers — planning, organizing, staffing, directing, and controlling — and to distill from these functions certain fundamental principles that hold true in the understandably complicated practice of management.

Also, purely to make the area of management theory intellectually manageable, those who subscribe to this school do not usually attempt to include in the theory the entire areas of sociology, economics, biology, psychology, physics, chemistry, and so on.

*   *   *   *   *

2. The Empirical School. This second approach to management is taken by those scholars who identify management as a study of experience, sometimes with intent to draw generalizations but often merely as a means of transferring this experience to practitioners and students. Typical of this school are those who see management or "policy" as the study and analysis of cases, as does Ernest Dale in his "comparative approach."[1]

The empirical school seems to be founded on the premise that if we analyze the experience of successful managers, or the mistakes made in management, we will somehow learn the application of the most effective kinds of management techniques.

No one can deny the importance of studying managers' experience, or of analyzing the "how it was done" of management. But management, unlike law, is not a science based on precedent, and situations in the future which are exactly comparable to the past are exceedingly unlikely to occur. Indeed, there is a positive danger in relying too much on past experience or on the undistilled history of managerial problem solving, since a technique or approach found "right" in the past will seldom fit a situation of the future.

But this is denied by advocates of the empirical approach. As a case in point, Ernest Dale, after claiming to find "so little practical value" in the principles enunciated by the universalists, curiously drew certain "generalizations" or "criteria" from his valuable study of The Great Organizers.

*   *   *   *   *

3. The Human Behavior School. This approach to the analysis of management is based on the central thesis that, since managing involves getting things done with and through people, the study of management must be centered on interpersonal relations. Variously called the "human relations," "leadership," or "behavioral sciences" approach, this school brings to bear "existing and newly developed theories, methods, and techniques of the relevant social sciences upon the study of inter- and intrapersonal phenomena, ranging fully from the personality dynamics of

---

1 The Great Organizers (New York: McGraw-Hill Book Company, Inc., 1960), pages 11-28.

individuals at one extreme to the relations of cultures at the other."[2] In other words, this school concentrates on the "people" part of management and rests on the principle that since people work together in groups to accomplish objectives, "people should understand people," and has as its primary focus the motivation of the individual as a sociopsychological being.

Adherents of this school, as a result, have a heavy orientation toward psychology and social psychology; nevertheless, the emphasis of various groups within this school varies widely. There are those who emphasize human relations as an art that the manager should advantageously understand and practice. Some focus attention on the manager as a leader and sometimes equate managership with leadership, thus, in effect, tending to treat all group activities as "managed" situations. Still others see the study of group dynamics and interpersonal relationships as simply a study of sociopsychological relationships and seem, therefore, merely to be attaching the term management to the field of social psychology.

It can hardly be denied that management must deal with human behavior; nor can it be disputed that the study of human interactions, whether in the environment of management or in unmanaged situations, is important and useful. And it would be a serious mistake to regard good leadership as unimportant to good managership. But whether the field of human behavior is equivalent to the field of management is quite another thing. Perhaps it is like calling cardiology the study of the human body.

4. The Social System School. Closely related to the human behavior school (and often confused with it) is the school which includes those researchers who look upon management as a social system, that is, as a system of cultural interrelationships. Sometimes, as in the case of James G. March and Herbert A. Simon,[3] the system is limited to formal organizations, and the term organization is used as a synonym for enterprise, and not as the equivalent of the authority-activity concept used most often in practice. In other cases, the system is not limited to formal organizations, but rather encompasses any kind of a system of human relationships.

Heavily sociological in nature, this approach to management does essentially what any study of sociology does: identifies the nature of the cultural relationships of various social groups and attempts to show these as a related, and usually integrated system.

---

[2]See Robert Tannenbaum, Irving R. Weschler, and Fred Massarik, Leadership and Organization (New York: McGraw-Hill Book Company, Inc., 1961), page 9; see also Robert Dubin, Human Relations in Administration: The Sociology of Organization (Englewood Cliffs, N. J.: Prentice-Hall, Inc., 1961).

[3] Organizations (New York: John Wiley & Sons, Inc., 1958).

The spiritual father of this ardent and vocal school of management theorists is the late Chester Barnard.[4] In searching for an answer to fundamental explanations underlying the managing process, this thoughtful business executive developed a theory of cooperation grounded in the needs of the individual to overcome, through cooperation, the biological, physical, and social limitations of himself and his environment. Barnard then carved from the total of cooperative systems so engendered one set of interrelationships which he defined as "formal organization." His formal organization concept — quite unlike that usually held by management practitioners — consists of any cooperative system in which there are persons able to communicate with each other and willing to contribute action toward a conscious common purpose.

The Barnard concept of cooperative systems pervades the work of many contributors to the social system school of management. For example, Herbert A. Simon at one time defined the subject of organization theory and the nature of human organizations as "systems of interdependent activity, encompassing at least several primary groups and usually characterized, at the level of consciousness of participants, by a high degree of rational direction of behavior toward ends that are objects of common knowledge."[5] Simon and others subsequently have apparently expanded this concept of social systems to include any cooperative and purposeful group interrelationship or behavior.

Basic sociology, the analysis of concepts of social behavior, and the study of group behavior in the framework of social systems do have great value in the field of management. But one may well ask whether this is management. Is the field of management the same as the field of sociology? Or is sociology an important underpinning like language, psychology, physiology, mathematics, and other fields of knowledge? Must management be defined in terms of the universe of knowledge?

5. The Decision Theory School. Another approach undertaken by a growing number of scholars might be referred to as the decision theory school. This group concentrates on rational approaches to decision making — the selection of a course of action or of an idea from various possible alternatives.[6] In its approach, this school may deal with the decision itself, or with

---

4 The Functions of the Executive (Cambridge, Mass.: Harvard University Press, 1938).

5 "Comments on the Theory of Organizations," American Political Science Review, December 1952, page 1130.

6 See R. Duncan Luce and Howard Raiffa, Games and Decisions (New York: John Wiley & Sons, Inc., 1957); David W. Miller and Martin K. Starr, Executive Decisions and Operations Research (Englewood Cliffs, N. J.: Prentice-Hall, Inc., 1960).

the persons or organizational group who make the decision, or with an analysis of the decision process. Some limit themselves primarily to the economic rationale of the decision, while others regard anything that happens in an enterprise as the subject of their analysis. Still others expand decision theory so it covers the psychological and sociological aspects of decisions and decision-makers.

Thus, by expanding the horizons of decision theory well beyond the process of evaluating alternatives, many use the subject as a springboard from which to bound into an examination of the entire sphere of human activity (including the nature of the organization structure, the psychological and social reactions of individuals and groups, the development of basic information for decisions, and the analysis of value considerations with respect to goals, communications networks, and incentives). As one would expect, when the decision theorists study the small but central area of decision <u>making</u>, they are led by this keyhole look at management to consider the entire field of enterprise operation and its environment. The result is that decision theory tends to become a broad view of the enterprise as a social system, rather than merely a neat and narrow concentration on decision.

6. <u>The Mathematical School</u>. Although mathematical methods can be (and have been) used by any school of management theory, I have chosen to group under this heading those theorists who see management as a system of mathematical models and processes. Perhaps the most widely known group comprises the operations researchers or operations analysts, who have sometimes anointed themselves with the rather pretentious name of "management scientists." The abiding belief of this group is that, if management, or organization, or planning, or decision making is a logical process, it can be expressed in terms of mathematical symbols and relationships.[7]

There can be no doubt of the great usefulness of mathematical approaches to any field of inquiry. This type of approach forces upon the analyst the definition of a problem or problem area; conveniently allows the insertion of symbols for unknown data; and due to its logical methodology — developed by years of scientific application and abstraction — furnishes a powerful tool for solving or simplifying complex phenomena. But it is even harder to see mathematics as a truly separate school of management theory than it is to see it as a separate school in physics, chemistry, engineering, or medicine. I only deal with it here because

---

7 See Miller and Starr, <u>op. cit.</u>; Joseph F. McCloskey and Florence N. Trefethen, <u>Operations Research for Management</u> (Baltimore: Johns Hopkins Press, 1954); C. West Churchman, Russell L. Ackoff, and E. Leonard Arnoff, <u>Introduction to Operations Research</u> (New York: John Wiley & Sons, Inc., 1957).

a kind of cult appears to have developed around mathematical analysts who have subsumed to themselves this area of management.

In pointing out that mathematics is a tool, rather than a school, I have no intention of underestimating the impact of mathematics on the science and practice of management. By bringing to this immensely important and complex field the tools and techniques of the physical sciences, the mathematicians have already made an immense contribution to orderly thinking. They have forced on people in management the means as well as the desirability of seeing many problems more clearly; they have pressed on scholars and practitioners the need for establishing goals and measures of effectiveness; they have been extremely helpful in getting people to view the management area as a logical system of relationships; and they have caused people in management to review and occasionally reorganize information sources and systems so that mathematics can be given sensible quantitative meaning. But even with this meaningful contribution, and the greater sharpness and sophistication of planning which has resulted, I cannot see that mathematics is management theory any more than it is astronomy.

MAJOR ENTANGLEMENTS

When these various schools or approaches to management theory have been outlined, it becomes clear that these intellectual cults do not draw greatly differing inferences from the physical and cultural environment surrounding businessmen. Why, then, have there been so many disputes among them? And why such a struggle (particularly among our academic brethren) to gain a place in the sun by denying the approaches of others? Like the widely differing and often contentious denominations of Christianity, all have essentially the same goals and deal with essentially the same world.

While there are many sources of the mental entanglement in the management theory jungle, the major ones seem to me to be:

1. The Semantics Jungle. As is so often true when intelligent men argue about basic problems, much of the trouble lies in the meaning of key words. The semantics problem is particularly severe in the field of management. There are even difficulties related to the meaning of the word "management." Most people would agree that it means getting things done through and with people, but do they mean only in formal organizations or in all group activities? Do they mean by governing, leading, or teaching?

Perhaps the greatest single semantic confusion lies in the word "organization." Most members of the management process school use it to define the activity-authority structure of an enterprise. Certainly most managers think that they are "organizing" when they establish a framework of activity groupings and authority relationships. In this case, organization represents the formal framework within an enterprise that furnishes the environment in which people perform. Yet a large number of organization theorists conceive of organization as the sum total of human relationships in any group activity; they thus seem to make it equivalent to social structure. And some use organization to mean enterprise.

Other semantic entanglements might be mentioned. Decision making is regarded by some as a process of choosing from among alternatives; by others as the total managerial task and environment. Leadership, often made synonymous with managership by some, is analytically separated by others. Communications may mean anything from a written or oral report to a vast network of formal and informal relationships. Human relations can imply a psychiatric manipulation of people, or it can refer to the study and art of understanding people and their interpersonal relationships.

2. Different Views of Management. As was indicated in the discussion of semantics, management has far from a standard meaning, although most agree that it involves getting things done through and with people. But does it mean dealing with all human relationships? Is a street peddler a manager? Is a parent a manager? Is a leader of a disorganized mob a manager? Does the field of management equal the fields of sociology and social psychology combined? Is it the equivalent of the entire system of social relations?

While I recognize that sharp lines cannot be drawn in management any more than they can in medicine or engineering, surely there can be a sharper distinction drawn than at present. With the plethora of management writing and with experts calling almost everything under the sun management, can one expect management theory to be regarded as very useful or scientific by the manager on the firing line?

3. The A Priori Assumption. Confusion in management theory has also been heightened by the tendency for many newcomers in the field to cast aside significant observations and analyses of the past on the grounds that they are a priori in nature. This accusation is often made by those who wish to cast aside the work of Fayol, Mooney, Brown, Urwick, and others who are branded as "universalists." To make the assumption that the distilled experiences of men such as these represent a priori reasoning is to forget that experience in and with managing is empirical. While the conclusions arrived at by perceptive and experienced practitioners of the art of management are not infallible, they do represent an experience which is certainly real and not armchair. No one could deny, I feel sure, that the ultimate test of accuracy of management theory must be practice; management theory and science must be developed from the real life of managing.

4. Misunderstanding of Principles. Those people who feel

that they gain caste by advancing a particular notion or approach often delight in throwing away anything which smacks of management principles. Some refer to principles as platitudes, forgetting that a platitude is still a truism and a truth does not become worthless because it is familiar.

* * * * *

One of the favorite tricks of the managerial theory group is to disprove a whole framework of principles by reference to one principle which the observer sees disregarded in practice. Thus, many critics of the universalists point to the well-known cases of dual subordination in organized enterprise, coming to the erroneous conclusion that there is no substance to the principle of unity of command. But this does not prove that there is no cost to a business by designing around, or disregarding, the principle of unity of command; nor does it prove that there were not other advantages which offset the costs, as there often are in cases of establishing functional supervision in organization.

Perhaps the most hackneyed stand-by for those who would disprove the validity of all principles by referring to a single one is the misunderstanding surrounding the principle of span of management (or span of control). The usual source of authority quoted by those who criticize is Sir Ian Hamilton, who never intended stating a universal principle (but rather was attempting to make a personal observation in a book of reflections on his army experience) when he said that he found it wise to limit his span to three to six subordinates.

No modern universalist relies on this single observation, and, indeed, few can or will state an absolute or universal numerical ceiling. Even Lyndall F. Urwick's often cited limit of six subordinates (a limit which is by no means accepted as universal even by the universalists) is hedged and modified by requirements of "direct supervision" and "interlocking operations" of subordinates; in fact, these conditions tend to make the numerical limit meaningless.

What concerns those who feel that a recognition of fundamental truths, or generalizations, may help in the diagnosis and study of management, and who know from managerial experience that such truths or principles do serve an extremely valuable purpose, is the tendency for some analysts to prove the wrong things through either misstatement or misapplication of principles.

A classic case of such misunderstanding and misapplication is in Chris Argyris' otherwise interesting and valuable book, Personality and Organization. Argyris concludes that "formal organization principles make demands of relatively healthy individuals that are incongruent with their needs," and that "frustration, conflict, failure, and short-time perspective are predicted as

results of this basic incongruency."[8] I wonder whether this startling conclusion — the exact opposite of what "good" formal organization based on "sound" organization principles ought to cause —
is not explained by the fact that, of four "principles" Argyris
quotes, one is not an organization principle at all but the economic principle of specialization, three other principles are
interpreted incorrectly, and other applicable organization and
management principles are not even considered.

5. <u>Mutual Reluctance to Understand</u>. What has been said
above leads one to the conclusion that much of the management
theory jungle thrives on the unwillingness or inability of the management theorists to understand each other. Doubting that it is
inability (because one must assume that a person interested in
management theory is able to comprehend, at least in concept
and framework, the approaches of the various schools), I can
only come to the conclusion that the roadblock to understanding
is unwillingness.

Perhaps this unwillingness is an outgrowth of the professional
"walls" developed by learned disciplines. Perhaps the unwillingness stems from a fear that some new discovery will undermine
professional and academic status built upon the acceptability of
one approach or another. Or perhaps it is fear of professional or
intellectual obsolescence. Whatever the cause, it seems that
these walls will not be torn down until it is realized that they
exist, until all cultists are willing to look at the approach and
content of other schools, and until, through the exchange and understanding of ideas, some order may be brought from the present
chaos.

* * * * *

8 New York: Harper & Brothers, 1957, page 74.

12 RECENT CONCEPTS IN ADMINISTRATIVE BEHAVIOR

by Harold J. Leavitt

My purpose here, which I can not possibly achieve, is to try to organize and summarize recent theoretical developments in administration and organization. Let me start by saying that I shall use the terms "administration" and "organization" more or less interchangeably; assuming simply that we are all concerned with understanding and perhaps directing the behavior of ongoing groups of people.

We have enough perspective now on the rash of new developments in these areas so that it is feasible to set up some gross categories, and then to describe some examples of novel and stimulating activity within these categories.

My categories are four: The first is the jumping-off place in organizational thinking; i.e., the state of classical organizational theory. This category contains nothing notably new, but it is worth a quick look because it will help us spotlight what is new in the "new."

Second, we can look quickly at new descriptive approaches to organization. This category specifically includes the new March and Simon[1] book; Mason Haire's[2] use of biological analogies to organizational growth; a series of sociologically based models like those of Whyte, Sayles, Selznick, and others (which I shall not try to run through here); and the clinically based work of

---

[1] J.G. March and H. A. Simon, Organizations (New York: John Wiley & Sons, 1959).

[2] M. Haire, "Biological Models and Empirical Histories of the Growth of Organizations," in M. Haire (ed.), Modern Organization Theory (New York: John Wiley & Sons, 1959.)

Excerpt, reprinted from Personnel Psychology, Summer, 1960, pages 287-294, by permission of the publisher.

Argyris.[3] Many of the sociological models and those of Argyris are not entirely descriptive; they have strong normative elements. These are not so much normative in an analytic sense, however, as in a value sense.

The next category covers analytic-normative studies. For the most part these have their origins in economics and mathematics, with close connection to game theory, and other quantitative and rigorous attacks on decision processes. I shall cite only one example of these, the work of Jacob Marschak.[4]

The fourth and final category is the action-influence category. The question here is not about theoretical developments that show promise of future influence but on currently influential ideas. Names cannot easily be attached to ideas in this realm, but I shall argue that the sophisticated practice of "human relations training" and the impact of "information technology" are the two currently vital and partially conflicting forces on the changing organizational scene.

THE JUMPING-OFF PLACE

Until relatively recently organization theory meant Taylor and Urwick and ideas like "span of control" and the "exception principle." It seems clear that the impact of these kinds of ideas on the thinking of managers and business school academicians (and they provide a pretty good cue about trends) has lessened. As Simon has pointed out, these early formalizations about administration suffered considerably from — among other things — their hortatory qualities. In retrospect we can isolate at least three other major limitations:

1. They tended to treat only the physiological attributes of persons, ignoring the complexities of motivation and perception.

2. They began, usually, with the assumption of a known and fixed organizational task, which can then be differentiated into subparts. They thereby carry a static quality with no provision for organizational search for new tasks, or redefinition of present ones under pressure from a changing environment.

3. Traditional theory has focused almost exclusively on the individual as the unit of the enterprise, working implicitly toward a goal of functional specialization. Perhaps one reason these early theories missed the major phenomena of individual behavior is precisely because they failed to consider interaction among subparts of organizations.

---

[3] Chris Argyris, Personality and Organization (New York: Harper & Brothers, 1957).

[4] J. Marschak, "Efficient and Viable Organizational Forms," in M. Haire (ed.), Modern Organization Theory (New York: John Wiley & Sons, 1959).

The freshest ideas about organization and administration belong in this category. There are many of them, semi-independent of one another. They have in common a concern about understanding organizational phenomena and about developing a more adequate underpinning for eventual applications in the real world.

The most important aspect of these descriptive models is that they are descriptive: i.e., impersonal efforts to comprehend, analyze, and predict organizational behavior. They either draw on empirical evidence or permit empirical tests of their propositions and hypotheses.

The March and Simon book is a good example. It is an effort to state a set of interrelated propositions that will account for variation in such diverse intra-organizational phenomena as, for example, intergroup conflict, innovative activities, and compensation.

It draws very heavily upon a dynamic model of individual motivation that includes variables like satisfaction level, search behavior, expected value of reward, and level of aspiration. It offers up some stimulating new concepts, too, differentiating "satisficing" from "optimizing" behavior and points out that the behavior of individuals and organizations is probably more accurately described by the first word than the second. Satisficing means searching for a satisfactory solution to a problem, rather than the optimal one — a process which is far more parsimonious of energy and other costs than optimizing, and a class of behavior which is also far more "sympatico" with dynamic personality theory than with classical economic theorizing.

Perhaps this is enough to give you a flavor of this view of organizational phenomena. It is descriptive-predictive; it is rigorous in that its propositions appear to be empirically testable; and it makes good use of what is known about individual and group behavior.

Let me turn now to another fresh look at organizations. Mason Haire has recently introduced some D'Arcy Thompson-type biological notions into organizational thinking. He cites the square-cube law; i.e., that as the mass of an object is cubed, its surface is only squared; then goes on to show how this surface-volume relationship becomes critical in relation to the biological size of organisms. The giant, in Jack the Giant Killer, were he proportioned like Jack but ten times as big, would include a mass so great as to break his own bones.

Haire's point is that as organisms grow they much change shape, and even create new organs to perform functions not required by another size and shape. He carries the analogy to organizations and then offers data to show similar, and predictable, change phenomena during organizational growth. Using historical data from small companies, he shows consistent relationships between, for example, numbers of people on the "surface" in the organization; i.e., who deal chiefly with the outside environment — receptionists, purchasing agents, salesmen, etc. — and numbers in the inside mass. The work is intriguing, suggestive, and a little worrisome.

Now to consider briefly the most clinically oriented of recent models of organization — the one offered up by Chris Argyris. Argyris' thesis, based largely on observational studies of worker-management relationships, is essentially that organizations are restrictive of individual psychological growth. Argyris argues that people grow from dependence toward independence, from an undifferentiated state to a differentiated one, etc., while some characteristics of large organizations press people back toward dependency, toward nondifferentiation, and toward other "unhealthy," "immature" conditions. Argyris offers prescriptions for cure, but not perfectly precise ones. He seems to offer at least a palliation in the form of organizational changes that will make for greater individual health; e.g., more freedom of decision-making for individual employees, etc.

Argyris' model does not belong entirely in the descriptive category. It lies rather in the limbo between description and prescription. It is concerned with individual mental "health" and the improvement thereof, and, whether intentionally or not, it has a hortatory quality — urging administrators to show greater concern for the mental health of their people.

In one sense Argyris' work seems to me an almost necessary outcome of the last decade's studies of human relations. It draws heavily upon human relation research, and measures almost entirely against criteria of individual and group "maturity." Very little emphasis is placed on other economic or social criteria of organizational effectiveness.

A NORMATIVE-ANALYTIC MODEL

The Marschak view is based less in psychology than the others I have described, and more in the mathematical economics from which he hails. But it is not psychological nonsense (as some ideas from economics seem to be); it is a good example of the way recent mathematico-economic developments can be focused on administrative processes.

Marschak makes an effort to construct a model of organizational behavior that does not contradict empirical data, and then to show an analytic method for deciding whether one organizational form is better than another.

Let me try to give you just a flavor of the Marschak model. Marschak treats an organization simply as "several persons" who "agree to follow a certain set of rules that are supposed to further certain goals." This set of rules (Marschak equates them with the sociologists' "roles") is the organizational form. Such rules are all concerned with communication: <u>action</u> rules about communication outside the organization; <u>internal communication</u> rules, which are rules about sending and receiving of messages between members (and which include communication with one's own memory); and <u>observation</u> rules which refer to the receipt of messages from outside the organization.

Marschak then specified a simplified problem in which the issue is centralization vs. decentralization; which is to say, whether we build in a rule for intercommunication between subunits or do not. By considering three functions — a payoff function, a probability function, and a factor of the cost of communication — he demonstrates that one can analytically determine (in his little example) the efficiencies of the two alternatives. He argues that such cognitive, analytic methods can be refined for use in real organizations. I would argue further that I see no <u>fundamental</u> reason why such methods cannot be integrated into real organizations, made up of real and complicated people.

ACTION-INFLUENCE IDEAS

We can turn from these efforts to describe or improve upon the behavior of complex organizations. The models we have sketched thus far exist mostly in universities, traveling in circles among academicians via academicians.

But it is appropriate also in this quick review to examine those ideas which are in fact currently having an impact on organizational practice — on the structure of organizations, on the relationships among members of organizations, and on the practices of administrators.

It might be said, first, that classical organization theories are having almost no noticeable <u>new</u> impact. Their old impact hangs on, of course; managers still talk about an authority-responsibility balance, about span of control, et al. But I have been unable to detect any recent changes in organizational behavior that appear to be consequent to extensions of old organizational theory.

However, organizational practice is, I believe, changing under the serious and current influence of two kinds of phenomena, both of which are related to ideas we mentioned earlier. The two are "human relations" and "information technology."

By "human relations" I mean several fairly specific things: first, the techniques of human relations training; second, the related, business school-taught, business journal-promulgated, and consulting firm-carried-out techniques of "participative" management — techniques which include the use of committees, the encouragement of easy expression of feelings across status levels, etc.

These ideas are having effects, I believe, because they have been converted into technical mechanisms, and it is the technique that makes operational change possible.

These techniques are being adopted partially because they are novel, and we value the novel, but mostly because they offer promise for solving problems of social and self-esteem needs, and problems of interpersonal communication. These kinds of problems seem to have come necessarily to the fore in modern, complex organizations. They have come to the fore, I believe, mostly because some lower order problems have been resolved, and hence are less prominent; because, using Haire's analogy, the enlarged internal mass of most organizations has radically increased the need for better internal mechanisms for processing information.

Whatever the reasons, however, there is abundant evidence (numbers of consulting firms doing such work; the spread of "group dynamics" training activities into industry; the increasingly "human" views of executives about how to manage) that these ideas are changing industrial organizations, especially at the middle levels of the hierarchy.

Dr. Thomas Whisler and I[5] have elsewhere pointed out the practical conflict between this trend toward human relating middle management and the other major current trend in the technics of management — the intrusion of information technology. Information technology is a label for the amalgam of new mathematical techniques applicable to managerial problems, plus those that are growing up around the computer.

In any case, information technology is moving in on organizations. It is beginning in a very small way to cause quite agonizing reassessments of ideas about decentralization, about where creativity is needed, about what constitutes an executive job, and about the relative merits of human and organizational values. It seems to be leading in many cases to solutions to those same problems of efficient information processing that are very different to those offered by human relations techniques.

These two, the techniques of human relations and the techniques of information processing, are the sets of ideas currently finding most widespread application to the practice of management. Right now they seem to me to be causing a mild schizophrenia in organizations. It is my own opinion that the potential, short run power of information technology is, by far, the greater of the two powers; at least as long as the two technologies remain separate from one another. But it is already becoming clear, back at the theoretical level of describing organizations and building organizational models, that the two are inseparably intertwined. The computer is already a tool for psychological and organizational research. Human relaters are already going cognitive, studying with new vigor the processes of conscious thinking

---

5 H. J. Leavitt and T. L. Whisler, "Management in the 1980's," Harvard Business Review, XXXVI (1958), 41-48.

and problem solving; studies which will, I am confident, yield a general descriptive theory of organization and administration; a theory which will, in turn, bear practical fruit.

*   *   *   *   *

PART FOUR:

DECISION-MAKING

13 DECISION MAKING OR BLINDMAN'S BUFF

by Auren Uris

In 1956, Nation's Business published an article by Peter F. Drucker, an "expert's expert" widely and deservedly renowned for the practicality as well as the sophistication of his views on management. Drucker's article, "How to Make a Business Decision," suggested the following approach:

1. Defining the problem. What kind of problem is it? What is its critical factor? When do we have to solve it? Why do we want to solve it? What will solving it cost?
2. Defining expectations. What do we want to gain by solving it?
3. Developing alternative solutions. Which of several plans offers the surest way to avoid things that are unexpected?
4. Knowing what to do with the decision after it is reached.

In his article, Drucker emphasizes that most managers spend too much time looking for the answer instead of for the problem — a particularly helpful caution. But Drucker would be among the first to point out that his approach is not the general panacea that some people would like to make it.

What's more, Drucker's approach is the exception rather than the rule among the techniques that the management experts make available to the practitioner. It raises meaningful questions instead of trying to provide definitive answers. Many executives remain unpersuaded by the prescriptions of the run-of-the-mill management experts.

With help from the management expert almost as limited as that from the scientist, how does the manager manage?

* * * * *

Excerpts, reprinted with permission of The Macmillan Company from The Management Makers by Auren Uris. © 1962 by Auren Uris.

You'll find more jokes about decision making than about any other management function. One of the old saws points up the reluctance to commit oneself:

> Reporter: Do you have any difficulty making decisions?
> Executive: Yes and no.

Then there's the hoary gag that stresses the strain of decision making on the inexperienced:

> Farmer (to Hobo): Sort these apples into three piles — large, medium, and small. (He goes off, returning some time later to find the hobo in a dead faint. Finally revives him.) What's wrong?
> Hobo (mutters): Decisions, decisions! They're killing me.

A "Decision Decider" has gained considerable currency in executive circles. It's a small folder featuring a metal arrow which is spun around like a carnival wheel to land on one of 32 numbers. Depending upon which number the arrow stops at, you select one of 32 prefabricated decisions:

1. Conduct a survey.
2. Tell my wife.
3. Refer it to assistant.
4. Expand.
5. Tell them "Yes."
6. Put on expense account.
7. Hire an expert.
8. See my psychiatrist.
9. Fire the salesman.
10. Call a conference.
11. Tell them business is lousy.
12. Let them wait a week.
13. Say it was a clerical error
14. Call my bookie.
15. Check if it is deductible.
16. Brainstorm it.
17. Blame the ad agency.
18. Ask my barber.
19. Tell them "No."
20. Stall for a week.
21. Play golf
22. Retrench.
23. Leave town.
24. Don't tell my wife.
25. Blame government.
26. To committee.
27. Check competition.
28. Ask for additional funds.
29. Decide after three martinis.
30. Tell them business is excellent.
31. Blame high taxes.
32. Secretary, get me off the hook.

* * * * *

Every management area has its share of semantic confusion. In the area of decision making, semantic confusion is especially violent. Not only is the precise sense of the terms used sometimes difficult to ascertain; in some instances there's a failure to distinguish between decision making, and an entirely different function, problem solving.

At least, in the case of one authority, the situation requiring decision is referred to as "the problem," and he goes on to talk of analyzing "the problem," clarifying "the problem," and so on. Some basic differences between decision making and problem solving are touched on by the chart below.

Problem Solving	Decision Making
Situation. Given facts $\underline{A}$, $\underline{B}$, $\underline{C}$, and $\underline{D}$. (The number of significant facts is usually limited and known.)	Situation. Given facts, $\underline{A}$, $\underline{B}$, $\underline{C}$, plus assumptions $\underline{X}$, $\underline{Y}$, and $\underline{Z}$. (The number of significant facts and assumptions is usually unlimited.)
Procedure. You set about seeking an "answer" that satisfies the conditions set by the problem.	Procedure. You set about developing alternatives that promise a high probability of success in satisfying the situation.
Outcome. You end up with an "answer" or "conclusion" that you feel will "work" because of accepted facts derived from observation or experience.	Outcome. You end up with a "decision" that represents a course of action with an undetermined probability of success.
Example. What is the best type of bridge we can build at a particular point over a river? The answer you arrive at — it may be to build a suspension, cantilever, or viaduct bridge — is a combination of engineering and cost calculations. You can tell by inspection whether or not the solution is suitable.	Example. How large should we make the bridge, in view of its potential load? Here, someone must make an estimate of the amount of traffic to expect and decide on that basis — never knowing until after the bridge is built whether the decision was a good or bad one.

THE DECISION GAP

In addition to confusion over the differences between decision making and problem solving, we're beset by another difficulty that derives from the point we've reached in our thinking about decision making.

To recap what was said earlier, the decision-making art is up in the air. Go through the current management literature on the subject and you find two approaches:

1. Learned, technical articles on game theory, mathematical models, the concept of probability, and so on.
2. How-to-do-it articles, usually some version of the standard three-step approach: (a) Select the objective; (b) develop and compare alternatives; (c) select the best course.

Between the highly technical approach and the lowly oversimplification, the practical executive is left dangling. And the worst of it is, he's in mid-air over an abyss whose denizens, the serpents of failure, are particularly deadly.

Where, then, is today's manager to turn for help? It's of no use to him to know that within fifteen or twenty years scientists will formalize decision-making techniques and offer him a dependable tool. Right this minute he's beset by a dozen crises that require decision: should he retire executive A? Should he start a second shift in the branch plant? What kind of capacity will be needed for the new product? The course of action he selects can make or break him.

For practical situations, game theory and probability provide little immediate help. Even where the manager is able to follow the line of reasoning and make sense of the mathematical formulas that frequently pepper the page, translating the abstruse theory into practical terms is usually a lot more difficult than he'd like it to be. And the pat formula — as, for example, "Select the objective, develop and compare alternatives, then pick the best" — also leaves much to be desired. In the more primitive days of management, we felt we really had something in this approach. As we became more experienced, the flaws began to be evident.

To begin with, "selecting the objective" itself requires making a decision. Then, for some situations, there is almost an infinite number of alternatives: When do you stop "developing and comparing" them? Finally, "picking the best" alternative begs the question, for if you could tell by inspection which alternative is best, you wouldn't have to bother with all of this rigmarole in the first place.

An even more forceful argument against the pat procedures is that they're not followed by top decision makers. Here are some revealing statements about decision making collected by John McDonald for a Fortune article on the subject:

Charles Dickey, chairman of the Executive Committee of J. P. Morgan Company: "There are no rules."

Benjamin Fairless, ex-chairman of United States Steel: "You don't know how you do it; you just do it."

John McCaffrey, president of International Harvester: "It's

like asking a pro baseball player to define the swing that has always come naturally to him."

A FRESH TRAIL

The two extremes we've been talking about — the technical approach and the oversimplified formula — have one thing in common: They both are concerned with how decisions should be made. But there is another possibility that holds out the chance for constructive assistance. It's in investigating how decisions are actually made.

In the pages ahead, you'll find this lead developed to the end that you will be able to —

1. Identify and understand the approach you yourself use to arrive at decisions.
2. Suggest possible adjustments that may help improve your decision-making results.

↑   *   *   *   *

DECISION MAKING OBSERVED

A brief study was conducted to analyze the process by which a decision is made. A group of executives was given a sample situation and asked to come up with a decision.

The sample situation: the traffic manager of X Company has quit, and three people are available to fill the job:

Applicant A. He was the subordinate of the traffic manager. He's capable, prepared to take over at once, and sure to be able to perform to present standards.

Applicant B. He's an up-and-comer from the shipping department. Would need training, but eventually could be expected to turn in an outstanding performance, much better than applicant A.

Applicant C. He's headed for big things in the company but needs the traffic manager's job as a stepping stone for a higher position.

The objective of the study, remember, was to determine the general decision-making approach of each of the executives in the group. In order to compare the approach of each executive, five factors involved in decision making were considered: (1) situation assessment, (2) slant or bias, (3) adequacy of alternatives, (4) time tendency, and (5) control-mindedness. Although these characteristics varied from one manager to the next, they generally could be identified in some form. Here's how the five factors looked on closer analysis.

1. Situation assessment. The executives' attempts to size up the given situation set them asking such questions as these: What's the policy on promotion? What's the work record of each individual? How is his health? Age? Any other way for applicant

C to get his training? The answers to these and similar questions eventually constituted a body of facts that made possible subsequent decision-making considerations.

Observe a sufficient number of decision makers at work and you will see that this extremely important beginning of the decision-making process is subject to much variation. In some cases it seems almost nonexistent. Example: The telephone rings on an executive's desk. A subordinate says, "That shipment of plywood is going to be delayed a week. What should we do about the Jones job?" The executive must make a decision: Should he call the Jones Company and tell them their order will be delayed, have the Jones order processed with a substitute material, or call another plywood supplier to see if he can give a better delivery date? Because he knows the situation thoroughly, the executive has no trouble at all in assessing the situation at once and going on to further considerations.

But compare the almost instantaneous assessment of the above situation with a different example. Here an executive is told by his boss, "We're having trouble recruiting clerical help. What can we do about it?" Before he does anything else, the executive must determine (a) what has been done in the way of recruiting; (b) why it has been unsuccessful; (c) what the potential supply of clerical help is; and so on. It is in this first phase of decision making that the executive must arrive at a concise idea of the nature of the situation that confronts him. In the case of the executive who must decide what to do about a shortage of clerical help, he must be sure, before he concludes that the situation can indeed be labeled "a shortage of clerical help," that it isn't a matter of low pay scale, inaccurate job description, poor job recruiting methods, or a community relations policy that has made the local populace reluctant to work for the company.

The next of the five decision-making characteristics is particularly interesting because it seems to have escaped most observers' attention.

2. Slant or bias. As each manager's technique was studied, a basic fact emerged: A personal element entered the situation. Whether the executives depended on reason or intuition, each made his decision on the basis of a consistent slant. Here are some of these slants or biases — for the most part outside the awareness of the executives who demonstrated them:

a. Minimum cost. This was a common bias. Many of the managers tended to select that course of action which involved the least expenditure of money. In our experiment, this showed up as an observation by one executive that applicant A would save the company the expense of training. Another manager with this bias wanted to know what cost saving might be represented by the given fact that applicant B eventually might do the job much better than applicant A.

b. Minimum risk. A number of executives showed a preference for that course of action which promised the least harmful consequences. For example, they warned about the possible kickback if the man in line for the job, applicant A, didn't get it.
c. Maximum risk. This exceptional bias was shown by one executive. "Nothing ventured, nothing gained" was his motto, and he tended to bet on the course of action that risked the most but also promised the most gainful results. He favored applicant C.
d. The humanitarian slant. The alternative chosen in this case was the one that favored the human values implicit in the problem. This slant tended to push the executives toward Applicant A.

* * * * *

The importance of the individual orientation of each decision maker cannot be too strongly emphasized. Your own slant will almost certainly reflect your own unique ideas and values.

3. Adequacy of alternatives. This characteristic is evidenced in the phase in which the decision maker answers the question, "Is the kind of action I'm considering appropriate to the magnitude of the situation?"

At some point the managers in the test group assessed the magnitude or scope of the alternative decisions, as compared with the situation given. One of the test group asked, "If we appoint any of these three applicants, will we be taking care of all aspects of the situation?" It was this kind of question that led one manager to realize that a decision sometimes creates difficulties which in turn require decision. Thus, for example, giving the job to either B or C would necessitate giving A some sort of "consolation prize" whose nature would demand another decision.

The adequacy of the alternatives considered is an important key to the final success of the decision. Failure in this area leads to such outcomes as the classic "too little and too late" result. Consider the situation faced by one executive: The works manager of a toy factory tumbles to the fact that one of the divisions is in a mess because of poor housekeeping. "Get this place straightened out," he warns the division head, "or you'll be stuck at inventory time." The division head tells his foreman to put two men on the job of cleaning up the department. The foreman does, but inventory time comes around and the surface of the problem has barely been scratched. The adequacy of the course of action had been incorrectly judged. What had been assessed as minor really called for a remedy of heroic proportions.

* * * * *

The process of decision making, then, is a reciprocating one, in which these two evaluations — of the situation and of the possible alternatives — are compared and appropriate mental shifts made. This finding explains why "step-by-step" formulas for decision making fail. They don't take into account the necessary shuttling back and forth of your thinking as you go about the business of arriving at a decision.

4. Time tendency. Among the group whose decision making was studied, there were big differences in the actual amount of time spent in arriving at a decision.

Of course, the nature of a situation itself frequently dictates the amount of time required. Routine matters may be decided upon in seconds. More complicated situations demand large outlays of time simply to understand what's involved.

* * * * *

The speed of a decision is often a factor in its payoff. There are handicaps at both ends of the scale. The off-the-cuff answer can be as harmful as the decision reluctantly arrived at by the procrastinator.

5. Control-mindedness. In considering their decisions, some of the executives studied thought in terms of a single, decisive course of action. Others, in the process of designing alternative courses of action, tended to look for ways and means to control the implementation of the decision — typically, by breaking down the action into a sequence of moves, each dependent on the outcome of the one before. This is an important consideration because it lessens the risk.

In the experimental case, there was not too much latitude for this kind of thinking. One of the managers, however, suggested: "I'm inclined to give the job to applicant B, but I'd stipulate that there should be a three-month trial period, at the end of which he could be removed if his progress wasn't up to expectations."

* * * * *

Practical decision makers are aware that often it's not how you decide but how you implement the decision that makes or breaks you. Interestingly enough, it is frequently the executive's picture of himself as a decision maker that determines whether he designs the one-shot decision or the chain variety. Some executives like the self-image they see when they are fast, decisive. They feel a surge of power when their decisions are firm: "The die is cast, let 'er ride." For managers choosing the opposite approach, the feeling of control heightens their feeling of confidence and security. Which approach is better in terms of results? True, some situations call for taking the plunge. But, in many cases, the more flexible your implementation, the more you can use "body English" to get a beneficial outcome.

* * * * *

14 DECISIONS INVOLVING HIGH RISK

by Paul E. Green

* * * * *

It is hardly surprising that relatively little use (at least by business planners) has been made of the procedures developed under the general heading of decision theory.

First, these techniques are, for the most part, of recent origin. Moreover, many of the contributions to this subject have had rather specialized distribution, and they have been associated with areas of interest (such as the foundations of statistics) that are typically outside the purview of business planning personnel.

A notable exception, however, is the recent book by Robert Schlaifer, Probability and Statistics for Business Decisions.[1] This particular work offers one of the most provocative and complete procedures for dealing with decisions under uncertainty, namely the Bayesian approach,[2] available to the business planner.

The Bayesian approach to decision making under uncertainty provides a framework for explicitly working with the economic costs of alternative courses of action, the prior knowledge or judgments of the planner, and formal modification of these judgments as additional data are introduced into the problem.

DESCRIBING IT IN TERMS OF QUESTIONS

While the full richness of this set of techniques cannot be explored here, at least the principal aspects of Bayesian decision

---

[1] New York: McGraw-Hill Book Co., 1959.

[2] The so-called Bayesian approach owes its name to a central feature of the procedure, Bayes' theorem, named after its developer, Thomas Bayes.

Excerpt, reprinted from Advanced Management — Office Executive, October, 1962, pages 18-23, 34, by permission of the publisher.

theory might be described in terms of a series of questions with which this approach is designed to cope. These questions are:

1. Given specific alternative courses of action (such as different plant sizes or introductory price levels) whose effectiveness is dependent upon the occurrence of alternative "states of nature" (such as consumer demand or competitive retaliation), how should a decision-maker choose the "best" course of action, if he is not certain as to which state of nature will in fact prevail?

2. Given the opportunity to conduct, at a cost, some type of data-gathering activity (such as a consumer survey), should the decision-maker "purchase" more data bearing on the chances that alternative states of nature will occur and then take terminal action, or should he choose some "best" act now and forego the collection of additional data? Moreover, how should the data collection be designed?

3. Given the additional data (frequently subject to both sampling error and systematic error or bias), how can the decision-maker use the additional data to modify his initially held judgments about the occurrence of the alternative states of nature deemed relevant to the problem and then take optimal action?

FEATURES OF THE BAYESIAN APPROACH

An oversimplified planning example may illustrate some of the features of the Bayesian approach.

Assume a decision-maker is faced with the problem of choosing an appropriate plant addition for the commercialization of a modified textile yarn product (called, say, Texcel) under an uncertain future demand for the modification.

Building a plant too large, relative to demand, would result in costs associated with idle capacity. Building a plant too small, relative to demand, would result in costs associated with both profits foregone and the opportunity for competitors to increase their share of the market at the firm's expense.

If we assume the decision-maker is considering four alternative plant sizes — A, B, C, and D — ranging from large to small, then if the demand were high, payoffs would tend to favor the A plant addition, while if the demand were low, payoffs would tend to favor the D plant addition.

Assume that the firm's marketing personnel have attempted to forecast alternative levels of potential sales for the product (states of nature in Bayesian parlance) and they believe that some levels are more likely to occur than others. These alternative levels appear in Figure 1. Subjective probabilities of occurrence have been assigned to each forecast, 1 through 4.

The planner must then consider the payoffs over the whole planning period which would be associated with the combination of each plant size and sales forecast. These calculations would typically take into account the flows of revenues and costs after

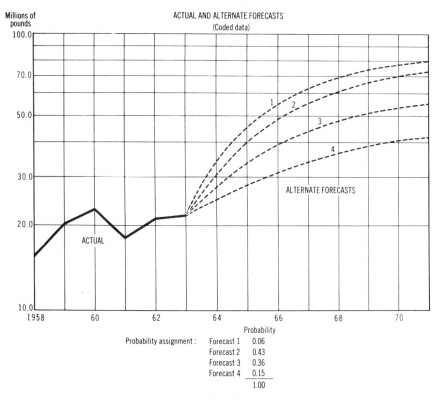

Millions of pounds

ACTUAL AND ALTERNATE FORECASTS
(Coded data)

ALTERNATE FORECASTS

ACTUAL

Probability assignment :		Probability
	Forecast 1	0.06
	Forecast 2	0.43
	Forecast 3	0.36
	Forecast 4	0.15
		1.00

FIG. 1. Texcel Fiber Forecasts.

certain assumptions have been made on competitive behavior, pricing, and similar considerations.

In this example, assume that the payoff (say, in discounted cash flow) associated with the conjunction of each alternative course of action and each alternative state of nature (potential sales) has been summarized as shown in Figure 2, Table 1. If the high sales forecast (Forecast 1 in the chart) were to occur, then strategy A (large plant) would provide the highest payoff.

APPLYING SUBJECTIVE PROBABILITIES

Under Forecast 2, strategy B would provide the highest pay-off, and so on. However, by applying the subjective probabilities associated with the occurrence of each forecast, as noted in Figure 2, Table 2, strategy B provides the highest expected monetary value, EMV, and would then be selected under the Bayesian approach.

Moreover, to test the sensitivity of the best choice to changes in the forecast probabilities, it is noted in Figure 2, Table 3, that

FIG. 2. Texcel Problem.

Table 1. Payoff Matrix — Unweighted (Entries-mm $).

Capacity Addition Strategy	Sales Forecast			
	1	2	3	4
A	30.8	21.7	(−) 2.2	(−) 29.3
B	28.3	23.6	8.3	(−) 17.8
C	14.8	14.2	10.9	(−) 9.8
D	7.3	6.5	5.1	(−) 7.2

Table 2. Originally Weighted Payoff Matrix (Entries-mm $).

Capacity Addition Strategy	Sales Forecast				EMV
	1 (P=.06)	2 (P=.43)	3 (P=.36)	4 (P=.15)	
A	1.85	9.33	(−) 0.79	(−) 4.40	5.99
B	1.70	10.15	2.99	(−) 2.67	12.17
C	.89	6.11	3.92	(−) 1.47	9.45
D	.44	2.80	1.82	(−) 1.08	4.00

Table 3. Equally Likely Weighted Payoff Matrix.

Capacity Addition Strategy	Sales Forecast				EMV
	1 (P=.25)	2 (P=.25)	3 (P=.25)	4 (P=.25)	
A	7.70	5.43	(−) 0.55	(−) 7.33	5.25
B	7.08	5.90	2.08	(−) 4.45	10.61
C	3.70	3.55	2.73	(−) 2.45	7.53
D	1.83	1.63	1.28	(−) 1.80	2.94

assignment of an equiprobable measure (0.25 probability to each forecast) would not change the decision to select the strategy listed as B.

In this example, many other features of the Bayesian approach have been omitted.[3] Still, the illustration, though brief, does demonstrate the planner's need to consider alternative environments and their associated probabilities of occurrence, flows of

_____

[3]For instance, "indifference probabilities" could have been computed. These are probabilities which would have to be associated with the occurrence of some state of nature more favorable to an inferior strategy before that strategy would break even with strategy B. Also, calculation of the costs of uncertainty

revenues and costs, and the use of sensitivity analyses to indicate how the profitability of the "best" strategy might behave with changes in the assumptions underlying the analysis.

However, as can readily be imagined, the calculational burden associated in dealing with the complexities of actual problems goes considerably beyond what is illustrated here.

IMPLEMENTING BAYESIAN APPROACH

It is hardly surprising that the use of an electronic computer can assist materially in implementing the Bayesian approach as well as in other areas of business planning activity. For instance:

1. The computer can be used in screening possible courses of action. In diversification planning, for example, the usual procedure is to set up a list of criteria, against which candidate products and/or companies are matched. In large-scale programs of this sort, the computer can provide a ready means to perform this screening function.

2. The computer can be used to explore relevant states of nature via various types of forecasting models. Not only may the usual techniques of regression analysis and related statistical procedures be employed, but also forecasting models incorporating various dynamic features can be devised and tested retrospectively on the computer.

3. After various courses of action or states of nature are screened, the computer also provides an effective way to implement the Bayesian model. For example:

a. The computer provides the capacity for expeditiously evaluating a greater number of courses of action, if relevant to the problem.
b. The computer may be used to establish the initial payoff functions — a not easy calculational task if the planning period is long.
c. The computer provides a means to perform the desired sensitivity calculations after initial outcomes have been determined.
d. The computer can be used to provide a flexible model in which field data can be entered for the calculation of revised probabilities via the Bayesian approach. In other words, this model (for example, the computer program) can be established and maintained on a reasonably current basis, for incorporating new estimates as needed and then determining the implications stemming from these revisions.

($2.63 million in this case) could have been illustrated to show the stake involved in a decision to collect more information before taking terminal action. Moreover, the modification of initial probabilities by using additional data has been omitted as well.

It would thus seem that the computer can provide a useful (and frequently necessary) device to develop the payoffs associated with the complex course of action-state of nature combinations found in actual planning problems.[4] In the two years during which this approach has been used experimentally at Du Pont, computer assistance has been decidedly useful.

In summary, the decision theory-computer approach offers provocative possibilities for dealing with the uncertainty aspects and ill-structured nature of business planning problems. Continued development of this approach might well provide the business planner with a set of techniques powerful enough to be commensurate with the complexity and importance of his functional area.

---

[4]As an illustration dealing with the complex characteristics of industrial market planning, the writer's: "An Application of Bayesian Decision Theory to a Problem in Long Range Pricing Strategy," Annual Meeting of American Statistical Assn. (New York, December 1961), might be of interest.

PART FIVE:

PLANNING

15 A NEW WAY TO MANAGE—INTEGRATED PLANNING AND CONTROL

by John O. Tomb

One way to make planning vital and effective is to let line officers make the plans they must fulfill. This not only results in more realistic goals, but in a positive, workable program of action, with room for improvisation in case of emergencies.

"We spend three months developing forecasts and budgets and disregard them after the first month's actual results are reported." "All planning does is divert the attention of operating executives from sales and production." "Planning causes a lot of hard feeling in our organization. Everyone tries to outmaneuver the controller, who keeps a tight fist on the purse strings."

These comments, and others like them, attest that something is amiss in the prodigious efforts most managements devote to planning and control. Despite many technical refinements, all too often planning and control activities still seem to be regarded as annoying interruptions to the normal course of business operations.

What has been wrong? Why is it that the thousands of man-hours that go into preparing and reviewing plans, and then measuring actual performance against them so seldom yield real improvements in profits?

The fault is certainly not in any failure to accept the idea of planning or control. No textbook on management, no executive

---

Reprinted from California Management Review, Vol. V, No. 1, Fall 1962. Copyright 1962 by The Regents of the University of California.

development program, no description of modern business practice fails to list planning and control among the central responsibilities of every manager. The fault does not lie in a lack of procedures or mechanics. There are elaborate forms, timetables, and flow charts. Nor do the difficulties stem from inadequate provision for the planning and control process in the organizational structure. Departments traditionally concerned with these two processes have grown in number and scope of responsibility. Separate groups and positions are increasingly being created to coordinate planning activities in diversified, complex enterprises. But for all the acceptance, and the mechanism, and the organization, the effort remains more often a disappointment than a triumph.

MUCH PLANNING IS UNREALISTIC

A basic difficulty is simply this — most planning and control systems are not rooted in the realities of the business. All too often they function within the straitjacket of accounting conventions. They require an estimated number for every blank space on a form, but they require little attention to the ways in which these numbers are to be achieved. As a result, they provide neither a useful guide to action nor a reliable basis for control.

So it is not really surprising that the operating manager looks upon planning as an exercise for which he must find time, rather than a useful tool to increase his own contribution to corporate goals. It is red tape that diverts his attention from the company and its objectives, rather than an activity that identifies him more closely with them.

Clearly, what is needed is a planning process that makes things happen, a planning process that provides a secure basis for control by the man who plans and by those above him, a planning process that is an integral part of the management task.

Recently, a few pioneering companies have worked out a new approach to developing such a process. It has been called "Integrated Planning and Control" (IPC) because it integrates planning and control into a single, on-going activity, which is itself the very heart of the managerial function.

Under this approach, the planning and control process is no longer a numerical exercise so separate from day-to-day operations that it appears to be pursued as an end in itself. Nor is it a procedure restricting the actions of line managers to a pattern imposed by some other part of the organization. Instead, IPC is a job-oriented approach to planning — an approach that concentrates on planning action. For example, under IPC a sales manager is required to develop his marketing program before he sets a sales target. Thus, if poor distribution has been curtailing sales, he includes in his plan a program to obtain better outlets before indicating a sales increase. Similarly, if a plant manager wants to show reduced overhead in his plan he must support this reduction by a program to cut back his staff by a specified number of people.

Obviously, a manager who plans this way develops a total operating program. Thus, IPC makes planning and control an integral part of his job rather than an appendage only remotely associated with the way he performs his job.

In the words of one executive, it represents, quite literally, a "new way to manage the business." The results of this new way of managing to date have been dramatic:

> A drug company had completed its conventional budget for the coming year when management decided to introduce IPC. The IPC approach resulted in a planned profit increase of 25 percent over the earlier budget figures. More important, the individuals in the company felt more confident of achieving these higher profits than the previous budgeted amount....
>
> A retail merchandising chain introduced IPC on a limited basis and found that expense and profit control were notably better in stores that used the IPC approach than in others that did not. . . .
>
> A multidivision capital goods producer found that IPC made its managers "aware of profit improvement opportunities they never imagined existed." The result — a profit increase in one year of 47 percent. . . .
>
> A large equipment producer planned for an increase in profits of more than 60 percent after it installed IPC — and then proceeded to achieve an increase of 70 percent.

HOW IPC WORKS

There are three distinctive characteristics of integrated planning and control that enable it to make unusual contributions to corporate profit. First, it multiplies the creative and constructive analysis of improvement opportunities by every manager who participates in the process. Second, it identifies him so closely with his work, his objectives, and his opportunities that he functions far more effectively in the pursuit of his goals. Third, it provides managers with a basis for positive control instead of merely giving them historical analysis or explanations. As a result, managers can deal imaginatively with change rather than defensively with their shortcomings.

Integrated planning and control requires three major steps:

1. Each manager identifies the activities for which he is specifically responsible.

2. Each manager selects from the entire range of his responsibilities those activities where significant improvements can be made.

3. For each of these selected activities, each manager prepares a plan to achieve clearly defined improvement. Each plan is more than a statement of an expected end result; it also indicates how that end result is to be achieved and what its profit impact will be.

A manager who goes through these steps develops plans that are realistic and reliable. Because such plans incorporate his proposed actions and are not limited to accounting forecasts, he acquires a sense of personal commitment to whatever objectives his plan states. As a result, top management can have real confidence that approved plans will be carried out. The sections that follow discuss in detail each of these major steps of an IPC action plan.

Relating Plans to Responsibilities

Before any manager can effectively develop plans, he must have a clear understanding of the activities for which he is responsible. Although this statement may seem axiomatic, any experienced organization analyst knows how few managers have a full and accurate understanding of their responsibilities.

In many companies, apparently, form is mistaken for substance. An organization manual is prepared containing detailed position descriptions. Once the manual has been distributed, everyone assumes that all members of the organization understand what they are supposed to do. The fact of the matter is that this assumption is often incorrect; for the descriptions themselves are typically incomplete, highly generalized, and frequently out of date. They are full of such words and phrases as "coordinate," "collaborate with," and "keep alert to." They are often inadequate in assigning basic responsibilities for important tasks that involve several participants. And, of course, they give almost no indication of the relative importance of major elements of performance. For example:

> When describing the allocation of marketing activities in a large multidivision company, several key managers claimed responsibility for the same tasks. The product managers, marketing research manager, and sales man-

agers each believed he had final responsibility for establishing the planned sales level. Further, the marketing research and product managers named the tasks of "determining marketing programs" and "specifying advertising media" as among their responsibilities. And there were other activities for which none of the key managers assumed responsibility. Although the company could point with pride to the manuals of position descriptions, there was an extraordinary lack of understanding of individual responsibilities among the men who filled the positions.

To ensure the understanding of individual responsibilities that is essential to developing meaningful plans, the IPC process begins by identifying all the activities that need to be performed if the business is to be successful. These activities — or "elements of performance" — are listed without attempting to assign them to a particular position.

Once these elements of performance have been defined for a functional area, responsibility for them is reviewed. This review does not embrace the larger task of an organization study. Rather, it focuses on identifying for each individual all the activities he needs to perform in order to carry out his job. The discussion of a particular element of performance with an individual manager usually helps him to think a lot more deeply about his job and to distinguish more clearly between routine, administrative tasks and those activities that can influence company profits. Because this process reveals position relationships so clearly, it identifies the critical points at which plans of individual managers have to be reconciled and consolidated to form a single, effective program for the total functional area or division.

Selecting Areas for Improvement

The second step in effective planning is to identify opportunities for improvement. This is totally different, it should be noted, from the typical budgeting approach. There, managers are preoccupied with determining what amounts should be set for such accounting categories as salaries, overtime, supplies, telephone, and travel. These figures are often arrived at by applying percentage increases or decreases to the amounts for the previous year. Rarely does a manager free himself from this preoccupation with numbers and ask the key question: "How can the activities assigned to me be performed better or at a significantly lower cost?"

IPC has been designed to overcome this critical limitation.

A manager does not start to plan until he thoroughly understands the performance elements making up his job. He starts his planning by using these performance elements as a check list. From this check list he selects those activities that present opportunities for significant improvement.

Thus, planning is a selective process that builds in an automatic bias for profit improvement. Of the 15 to 20 performance elements for which a manager may be responsible, he is likely to build improvement plans for only five or six. Of course, he might limit himself to one or two; or he might decide to tackle nine or ten.

For example, one marketing executive might soundly decide that his major efforts for the coming year should be aimed at increasing his field sales force in certain regions and improving his distribution structure in certain markets. But another marketing executive might add to these two goals improved packaging, a modified system of account coverage, revision in pricing structure, and a new type of sales promotion campaign. What is important in either case is that plans are developed to capitalize on what the manager considers to be his own best opportunities for significant improvement.

Preparing Plans

Once he has selected his improvement areas, a manager develops his detailed plan. Every such plan should indicate both the desired end result and the means for achieving it. Thus, every plan involves three key ingredients:

1. Objective — the improvement to be achieved.
2. Action program — the specific steps required to achieve the objective.
3. Profit impact — the effect of the action on company profits and resources.

Exhibit I illustrates a typical plan for the manufacturing function which includes each of the primary ingredients outlined above. It also indicates who is responsible for each action program step and the timing of each step.

The development of the "how to do it" action program illustrated encourages a manager to explore many alternatives that may be available instead of settling for the first solution that comes to mind. More often than not the first solution is the traditional one. The manager grows in his job and increases his worth to the company only when he begins increasingly to take fresh and imaginative looks at the way old problems are solved. IPC makes it difficult for a manager to continue in the same old rut; it prods him to break new ground.

EXHIBIT I. Manufacturing Plan.

Objective

Reduce the frequency and cost of faulty castings received from the XYZ Company

Action Program

Steps	Responsibility	Timing
Ensure recognition by supplier of problem with "hard spots" in castings	Purchasing Manager Production Manager	Completed
Negotiate price concession on all castings received during weeks when we return more than ten bad castings	Purchasing Manager	January 31, 1962
Set up storage area to accumulate ruined castings	Facilities Manager	January 31, 1962
Establish procedures to record machine downtime and cutter breakage with individual castings	Production Control	February 15, 1962
Submit information weekly to XYZ Company	Purchasing Manager	Begin March 1, 1962

Profit Impact		1962 Profit Increase (Decrease)
Price concessions		$ 7,000
Effect of improved quality	Scrap	8,500
	Overtime	3,500
	Expense tools	9,000
	Lost production	20,000
	Other	12,000
Modifications in storage area		(2,000)
Recording procedures		(1,000)
Other costs		(3,000)
	Total profit impact	$54,000

The completeness of this type of planning also gives a manager confidence in his ability to carry out his plans. Most managers who go through the IPC sequence begin to develop a much stronger proprietary interest in their jobs. The fact that they played a major role in identifying improvement opportunities and in determining how to capitalize on them tends to develop a spirit of dedication to make things happen. This sense of commitment and of self-discipline is an integral part of the IPC process and becomes a key factor in achieving desired end results and controlling performance against plan.

Integrated planning and control thus creates and maintains a sense of urgency and responsibility among managers that is, in many ways, its most important aspect. It literally forces a manager to take a good hard look at the activities assigned to him, evaluate each activity and determine where improvement can be made, and decide how much improvement he can achieve and how he will achieve it.

KEEPS BOSS INFORMED

A plan like the one illustrated is also of great value to a manager's superior. Because each plan details the steps to be taken to achieve its objective, the superior knows exactly what his subordinates intend to do. He can constructively appraise the soundness of their proposed actions. The superior may be able to contribute recommendations, based on his broader experience, that lead to helpful modifications in the objectives or in the action steps. He also can integrate each subordinate's objectives with those developed by other managers. In contrast, a typical budgeting system may provide a superior with little more than accounting data, but without any indication of the action programs planned by his managers.

The section on "Profit Impact" illustrated at the bottom of Exhibit I shows how the action programs contained in each manager's plans are tied into the company's accounting and budgeting system. This section translates planned actions into monetary terms. But, by its very structure, it focuses attention on what is to be done, not on expense categories.

COPING WITH CHANGING CONDITIONS

No planning process can foresee all the contingencies that may develop — either internally or externally — during the period covered by a plan. It is important, however, that unfavorable changes do not result in watering down the objectives agreed upon when plans were developed and approved. And it is equally important that managers do not use these changed conditions as an excuse for failure to achieve planned goals.

IPC fosters a commitment to achieving planned objectives in spite of change or difficulty. When unanticipated internal or external conditions prevent the achievement of an objective through the means planned in the original action program, most managers respond by developing an alternative program rather than using changed conditions as a scapegoat.

This positive approach is illustrated by the actions of the marketing director in a company using the IPC approach:

> The marketing plan for 1961 — which had been developed in depth — included the introduction of a major new product during the second month of the fiscal year. It was planned that this product would account for 10 percent of the 1961 sales volume and 12 percent of the merchandising profit. At the time the marketing plan was developed, other functional areas within the company — e.g., engineering and manufacturing — also developed specific plans to ensure availability of the new product. However, when manufacturing started to produce the product in volume, it found that a critical assembly, supplied by an outside vendor, was 95 percent defective. Investigation revealed that the problem was caused by the vendor's manufacturing process and would take six months to correct. No other suppliers were available.
>
> Rather than give up the planned additional profit, the marketing director initiated a series of revised action steps to make up for the lack of this new product. These steps involved:
>
> 1. Evaluating existing products to determine those with the highest merchandising profit.
>
> 2. Identifying segments of the market where sales of existing products could be increased; revamping the advertising and sales promotion program to reduce emphasis on the new product and divert funds to new promotions on existing products.
>
> 3. Redeploying the sales force to maximize selling effort in markets that promised immediate response.
>
> The net effect of these revised action steps was a gain just as large as the one the manager originally planned; the marketing division reached both its sales and its profit objective.

The marketing director could have used the unavailability of the new product as a good excuse for not achieving the sales and profit objectives. The unforeseen event was completely beyond his control or influence. But because of his deep sense of personal commitment, he was convinced that something could be done about the situation, and he did it.

This attitude is in sharp contrast with management's attitude in many companies using a conventional budgeting approach. In such companies, management tends to lower its sights whenever the going gets a bit rough. Managers look for scapegoats for failure to reach planned objectives. As the rather typical general manager of a construction materials company put it: "We are completely at the mercy of the level of housing starts. If they go down, our sales go down; if they go up, our sales go up." It simply never occurred to him that by imaginative management action he could control his company's destiny to a far greater degree than he, or many of his competitors, believed possible.

RETENTION OF SOME CONVENTIONAL STEPS

IPC by no means abandons conventional planning and control approaches in their entirety. Rather, it extends the usefulness of such conventional steps as:

1. The development and communication of corporate or divisional goals and planning assumptions that provide a frame of reference for the planning efforts of individual managers.

2. The review and evaluation of plans by each manager's superior.

3. The consolidation of plans from individual managers into functional plans (i.e., marketing, manufacturing, personnel, etc.), and the later translation of these functional plans into accounting terms so that conventional statements of income, costs, expenses, and cash flow can be prepared.

4. The consolidation of functional plans into divisional or corporate plans, and the review of these consolidated plans at successive levels of management.

SUMMARY

IPC is more than the substitution of new labels for old. It makes planning and control an integral part of the everyday thinking and acting of every manager. It lifts planning and control out of the systems and procedures category and provides the basis for a total operating program for every individual with management responsibility.

IPC does this by integrating the thoughts and actions of a manager in five ways. This new approach does these things:

1. Integrates planning with each manager's responsibilities by relating his plans to the performance elements in his job.
2. Integrates each manager's planning with the continuing search for ways to improve profits.
3. Integrates the objectives that each manager sets with a detailed action program for achieving each one.
4. Integrates into each individual's plans a measure of the overall purpose of the enterprise — effect on profits.
5. Integrates into each manager's planning a commitment to "make things happen" regardless of changing conditions.

Integrated planning and control is not something that can be plugged in and then left to run itself. The installation of IPC takes time and dedicated effort. More important, its success requires the unqualified and continuing support of top management. With intelligent installation and use, however, IPC injects a dynamic element into management behavior that can produce dramatic results.

As the president of a company that has pioneered in the development of IPC reported to his stockholders: "During the past year a new planning and control process to achieve maximum effectiveness was developed and is now being established in all of the company's operations. The results from this new planning and control approach have thus far exceeded all expectations."

It is instances like this that lead enthusiastic executives to refer to IPC as " a new way to manage."

16 SYSTEMS CONCEPTS IN PLANNING

by Richard A. Johnson, Fremont E. Kast,
and James E. Rosenzweig

We suggested [earlier in the chapter] that growing complexities of administration and technological advances have forced the adoption of systems concepts in business planning. This point should be reemphasized. The systems concept in business planning should start with the awareness of the need to think of several levels and the integration of these into a hierarchy. One useful way is to consider the three major systems which are paramount for any business organization:

1. The environmental system — sets forth the broad social, cultural, political, and economic parameters in which the business must operate.

2. The competitive system — describes the industrial structure, competitive relationships, and producer-customer relationships for the particular industry in which the company competes.

3. The internal organizational system — indicates the organizational structure, objectives and policies, and functional relationships which make the business a unique system.

* * * * *

Effective business planning should receive informational inputs from each of these three systems and translate them into plans of action. Increasingly, business firms are becoming aware of the growing importance of relating their plans to environmental systems. The majority of broad, long-range plans made

---

by companies are prefaced by forecasts of such environmental factors as population, gross national product, national income and expenditures, governmental receipts and expenditures, and even international considerations. Growth of interest in appraising and forecasting the environmental system is seen by the rise in the number of economists and other social scientists employed by business organizations to provide special skills in these areas.[1]

Planning must also give consideration to the competitive system. This idea is not new; the free-enterprise system has been referred to as an example of the competitive model. Planning information on volume of sales, profit levels, rate of return, share of market and pricing, and so forth, may be available, but companies frequently do not attempt to obtain this information in an orderly fashion. As Daniel says:

> Competitive information, like environmental data, is an infrequently formalized part of a company's total information system. And so there seldom is concerted effort to collect this kind of material, to process it, and to report it to management regularly.[2]

The third level of systems, the internal organization, must be given major consideration in the planning process. The functioning organization has certain strengths, skills, and specializations that are important inputs for planning. Furthermore, the organization is the source of internal information which must be communicated to decision centers. This system will be discussed in detail in the next chapters on organization, control, and communication. In general, managerial planning should give recognition to the integration of information from all three systems and should recognize the interactions among them.

Within the business system there are other important aspects of the systems concept in planning. With the advent of further mechanization and automation it is no longer possible to think of planning on a functional basis — sales, finance, manufacturing, and so forth. Rather, it is necessary to integrate planning for all functional activities into a unified system. Automation, for example, does not facilitate variations in product quantity and design, the meeting of individual customer requirements, or a number of other variables. With automation these factors become

---

[1] Clark S. Teitsworth, "Growing Role of the Company Economist," Harvard Business Review, January-February, 1959, page 97.

[2] D. Ronald Daniel, "Management Information Crisis," Harvard Business Review, September-October, 1961, page 116.

inflexible and must be standardized for an extended period. Therefore, in planning for the automated operation, the total functional efforts in marketing, finance, and manufacturing must be integrated on a systematic basis.

One idea for the integration of decision making in various functional areas is the concept of flows of information, money, orders, materials, personnel, and capital equipment in the company. Planning does not concentrate on functional performance, but on these flows. This is the concept of industrial dynamics as set forth by Forrester:

> It treats the interaction between the flows of information, money, orders, materials, personnel, and capital equipment in a company, an industry, or a national economy.
>
> Industrial dynamics provides a single framework for integrating the functional areas of management — marketing, production, accounting, research and development, and capital investment.[3]

Under this concept of planning, the organization is not a collection of separate functional activities but a system in which the flows of information, materials, manpower, capital equipment, and money are the basic forces which determine the company's growth and prosperity. It stresses the dynamic nature of these flows and their constant interaction. Many of the modern techniques of communication and decision making have utilized the concepts of flows. . . .

* * * * *

EXAMPLE OF PLANNING

An example of how the systems concept of planning might be adapted to an important area of management planning and decision making is illustrated by diversification planning. In a dynamic economy, product-line determination is one of the major planning areas, because the successful company must adapt continually to changing product-mission requirements. Many examples of this need are seen in a variety of industries, such as the product planning of the automobile companies in bringing out their various product lines, or the product-line planning of an aircraft company that is determining whether or not to move into the fields of propulsion and electronics. A framework for inte-

---

[3]Jay W. Forrester, Industrial Dynamics, MIT Press, Cambridge, Mass., and John Wiley & Sons, Inc., New York, 1961, p. 13.

grated decision making in diversification planning might be set forth as follows:

1. Appraising environmental system to determine those economic, social, and political forces that will influence decision.

2. Evaluating competitive system to appraise competitors, industrial structure, and potential customers.

3. Clearly defining and stating broad company objectives to provide guidelines for further appraisals.

4. Continually reappraising whether the company can meet these long-term objectives with its present product line and distribution channels, or whether it will need to develop a program of diversification.

5. Coordinating the diversification program with company objectives. A clear understanding of company objectives will help determine the types of programs which the company should consider. This will provide a narrowing process and will eliminate from consideration a number of marginal possibilities.

6. Continually appraising the tangible and intangible company assets and limitations for diversification. Aside from guiding objectives, the company will have certain characteristics, such as managerial skills, technological know-how, distribution channels, and facilities, which will be prime determinants of a diversification program.

7. Setting forth specific criteria for measurement of new-product ideas as related to the first six steps. Here the primary purpose is to determine the characteristics of the type of products which would meet requirements of the first six steps.

8. Establishing an environment favorable to diversification. A program of diversification is doomed to failure unless management is convinced that there is a need for this diversification and that it meets company objectives. Furthermore, top management must provide the initiative in establishing a climate in which the organization will come up with useful ideas and will channel them in for a check against established criteria.

9. Providing an established and well-recognized procedure for the evaluation of suggestions for product diversification in terms of the criteria of measurement. This will usually take the form of specific organizational adjustment, such as the creation of a product-diversification committee or department. If left to the chance that the regular line organization will perform this function, it is likely that their other duties and the constant demands for immediate results will push the longer-range consideration of product development into the background; the question will see the light of day only when the situation becomes critical.

TECHNIQUES FOR APPLICATION OF SYSTEMS CONCEPTS TO PLANNING

Within the past two decades several major developments have occurred which forecast the transformation of the managerial processes of planning and decision making. These innovations have been made possible through the development of computers, mathematical techniques, and systems concepts.

To understand the significance of this movement better, we might refer to a table by Herbert Simon which sets forth the traditional and modern decision-making methods. He breaks down all executive decisions and planning into two broad types — programmed decisions and nonprogrammed decisions — and defines them as follows:

> Decisions are programmed to the extent that they are repetitive and routine, to the extent that a definite procedure has been worked out for handling them so they won't have to be treated de novo each time they occur.
>
> Decisions are nonprogrammed to the extent that they are novel, unstructured, and consequential. There is no cut-and-dried method for handling the problem because it hasn't arisen before, or because its precise nature and structure are elusive or complex, or because it is so important that it deserves a custom-tailored treatment.[4]

The traditional techniques for decision making for programmed decisions include organizational habits, clerical routines, and the organizational structure itself. As we have seen in our previous discussion, organizational habit and clerical routine are most frequently translated into the standing plans. Policies and procedures provide the major vehicles for dealing with programmed decisions in the traditional sense. These habitual patterns of organizational behavior usually evolved through organizational adaptations to the best decision under the given circumstances. The trial-and-error aspect of this kind of programming is obvious.

For nonprogrammed decisions, the traditional means was to rely upon the development of executive judgment cultivated by selection, education, and training. There are obviously many psychological and sociological processes involved in the complex problem of nonprogrammed decision making. This is the area of uncertainty where it has been difficult for successful executives even to explain exactly how they arrive at "decisions." (An even greater difficulty often is determining whether or not the right decision has been made.)

Newer techniques for both programmed and nonprogrammed

---

[4]Herbert A. Simon, The New Science of Management Decision (New York: Harper & Brothers), pages 5-6.

decision making suggest major changes in these traditional methods of planning and decision making. The development of computers, mathematical techniques, operations research, and simulation will have important bearing upon the planning process. . . .

SUMMARY

One of the primary purposes of an integrated planning concept is to provide a hierarchy of goals and objectives based upon predetermined premises about the external environment and internal organizational resources. This approach ensures that the planning decisions made in one functional area are related to those in other areas. As the operational departments in our modern organizations become more specialized and the changing environment requires more complex planning, the need for this integrative concept becomes even more apparent.

With application of systems concepts to planning based upon a hierarchy of goals and objectives, alternative courses of action can be evaluated. Without integrative planning it is difficult to ensure that the proposed courses of action will aid the organization in moving toward its established goal. With an integrated decision system, proposals can be evaluated within the framework of objectives and plans. . . .

17 PROFIT PLANNING

THE PROS AND CONS OF PROFIT PLANNING

Before beginning a profit-planning program, you should first have a clear idea of what it can do for you, and what, if any, are its limitations.

There are many benefits and advantages. Some of these are:[1]

1. Profit planning provides a disciplined approach to business problems. A profit plan requires the whole organization to undertake certain regular and systematic actions in the development of operating plans. It requires the expression of operating plans in the form of budgets. It requires the pursuit of the goals established in the plan and measurement of actual performance against planned performance, with explanations of why performance varied, whether it exceeded or fell short of the established goals. In short, a profit plan creates the necessity for further planning. It also necessitates coordination, teamwork, and improved communication among all elements of the business, in that every element is required to contribute significantly to the development and pursuit of the plan.

2. Profit planning helps to distinguish between actual needs and wants. As we all know

---

[1]Vincent D. Donahue (Comptroller, Continental Can Company), "Financial Planning for Greater Profits," Research Report, No.44 New York, American Management Association, Pages 35-37.

Excerpts, reprinted from How to Make a Profit Plan, by Patrick H. Irwin (Hamilton, Ont.: The Society of Industrial & Cost Accountants of Canada, 1961), pages 13-15, 35-37, 47-50, by permission of the publisher.

from personal experience with our family budgets, there is no limit to our wants. We also know that there is a limit to our needs, as well as to our income and other resources. In many respects the budgeting problems of a business are similar to those of the family: Its wants are virtually endless, its needs are ascertainable, and there is a definite limit to the amount of funds available. A good part of the capital-budgeting process, for example, consists in weeding out those things which would be nice to have but are not essential, and allotting available funds against a descending order of priorities. Any order of priorities must, of course, reflect some balancing of the long- and short-term requirements of the business. . . .

3. Profit planning encourages an atmosphere of profit-consciousness, cost-consciousness, and thrift throughout the organization. Since every supervisor and manager throughout the company is obliged to participate in the development of the profit plan and to explain variations between actual performance and budget objectives, they must all be aware of the factors making for good or bad performance. This breeds profit-consciousness and lends impetus to the search for profit opportunities. Also, the people who are responsible for expenditures are bound to exercise care because they know that their performance is subject to measurement against a budget.

4. The budgetary aspects of profit planning should simplify the comparative analysis and interpretation of financial statements. Financial analysis frequently requires comparison between a given period of the current year and the corresponding period of the preceding year. In such comparisons, adjustments must constantly be made for changes in material costs, labor rates, the opening and closing of plants, unusual one-time transactions, and other such factors. The current year's budget is usually adjusted to reflect these changes, and the impact of each change on current income is made readily identifiable, thus simplifying the comparative analysis and interpretation of financial statements.

5. Profit planning provides an excellent vehicle for management development. Every

level of supervision and management is required to participate in the development of the profit plan and in explaining variations between actual performance budget objectives. This is excellent training since in effect every member of management is obliged to look at his area of responsibility just as though he were an independent business man. This is what we frequently refer to as 'planning in depth'; it is also a method of developing management in depth.

6. Profit planning supports the practice of 'management by exception.' Accounting systems which do not include budgetary controls have certain pronounced limitations. Frequently the reports represent transcriptions of the bookkeeping system and contain more facts than any reasonably busy executive could hope to shake a stick at. They may also lack a reporting style based on simplicity, significance, and brevity — qualities essential to the conservation of the readers' time and attention. It is not unusual to find that the major job of digestion, selection, and analysis is left to management. To expect management to devote its valuable time to this chore is about as economically sound as using a cannon to shoot fleas.

* * * * *

7. Profit planning necessitates periodic critical appraisal of every element of the business. The planning process requires a periodic review of every facet of the business and of every operating and staff function. The review naturally raises questions as to the necessity and cost of each such function. This annual critical appraisal is comparable to the annual medical examination that people undergo in order to assure themselves that they are reasonably healthy and to gain forewarning of possible serious trouble ahead.

8. Profit planning projects accounting into the future. Prior to the advent of the modern concept of profit planning with budgetary controls, accounting was largely devoted to a recitation of history and was of relatively little assistance in guiding future action. Profit planning with budgetary controls recognized the fact

that conducting a business is, in a way, analogous to driving a car: Although a rear-view mirror is necessary, the driver's attention must bear mainly on the road ahead. One of the very real values of a profit planning program is that it permits accounting to reflect the pattern of a plan directed toward the future.

To be sure, there are also some apparent limitations in profit planning. Some of these arise from misconception. They can, for the most part, be resolved by recognizing these simple truths:[2]

1. A profit-planning program is not a substitute for sound operating programs or good business judgement. It is a normal reaction of people inexperienced with profit planning to assume that the budget is the plan. Actually, the relationship between the budget and the basic planning process is somewhat similar to that between the visible portion of an iceberg and the total mass, of which the visible portion is only about one-tenth. The process of planning involves months of hard work and the development of alternative plans based on a variety of possibilities. Several plans may be proposed; the one that is selected and approved becomes the program, which is then expressed in fiscal terms as the official budget. The budget itself does not reflect any of the alternative possibilities, nor is it an assurance that the program represents the best possible selection among the different proposed plans. These are matters of business judgment for which no budgeting device can substitute.

2. A profit plan is not a guarantee of success. Few of us are gifted with the powers of Merlin, nor are many of us infallible forecasters of the future. In business there is nothing more certain than change. It is entirely possible that a man might miss his budget by a wide margin but still perform in a superior manner in adapting to changes beyond his control.

3. The profit plan, as evidenced in the budget, must be based on a sound understanding of

[2]Ibid., pp. 38, 39.

human nature. Budgets may not represent the best way to make friends, but they generally influence people. They furnish guidelines and impose restraints, and most of us have a tendency to dislike restraints. Budgets are a basic instrument of human motivation, especially when tied in with compensation plans. . . .

4. A profit-planning program must be based on a soundly balanced view of the relative importance of the various elements of the over-all enterprise. Probably one of the principal difficulties experienced in the installation and early use of a profit planning program is failure to maintain a sense of balance. For example, it is understandable that a budget should be regarded as a device aimed primarily at expense control and overhead reduction. Important as these matters are, however, they can be overdone. . . .

5. Care must be exercised to avoid over-planning. It is possible to try so hard for perfection that a program never gets off the ground.

* * * * *

MAKING PLANS

The objectives establish the course your business should follow and its ultimate goal. In sports parlance, the objectives state the game you are going to play, the league you will play in, and the size of your desired score. To do these things, you must plan; plan when and how you are going to do it.

This means spelling out what must be done each year in each activity to move from your present position towards achieving your long-range goals.[3]

The plans should constitute an integrated program directed towards securing your objectives. They should reinforce one another; they should mesh. Perhaps the best illustration of a complete program of plans is the budget produced by a well-conceived budgetary procedure. Typically, the sales department furnishes estimates of sales volumes and selling expenses, both broken down to show component

---

[3]Adapted from Ernest Dale and Lyndall Urwick, Staff in Organization, Chapter 3 and Appendix E (New York: McGraw-Hill Book Company, 1960).

elements. On the basis of these sales estimates, the planning department plans inventories and production. These plans serve as a basis for estimates of purchases of materials, of employment of labour, and of needs for machinery and equipment. These estimates, in turn, supply a basis for forecasting purchasing and employment department activities and thus for estimating the expense of these two departments. Data concerning machinery needs and aggregate personnel requirements furnish the starting point for calculations of floor-space, locker and wash-room facilities, heating, electricity, etc., required to maintain over-all operations. All these plans are reduced to anticipated cash revenues and expenditures, leads and lags are estimated, and a cash budget calculated. Finally, estimated financial statements are prepared. The whole procedure provides a complete, internally consistent, integrated program of enterprise operations.

This illustration is appropriate. Many businessmen are likely to get into profit planning after they have adopted budgetary control. The planning is similar except that under profit planning a longer time period is covered and every element of operations should be dealt with in the plans.

Start by forecasting sales for existing operations — the products now made in the markets now sold. At the fact-finding stage, the trends of sales of individual products, of the company, of the industry, and of the economy are plotted and their relationships determined. Now it is necessary to project this information into the future.

This calls for participation by all key executives. Each must later plan his own operations to fit the forecast and so he has a stake in its accuracy. Moreover a group approach to forecasting tends to counteract the over-optimism or excessive conservatism of one individual. If all participate, none can disclaim responsibility for failing to secure planned results.

The steps to prepare the sales forecast are described below. In preparing the forecast, consideration should be given to consulting an independent research organization or economists to obtain additional statistical data and to check conclusions on expected trends in the industry and the economy.

1. Make a projection of future industry sales based on previous years' trends and relationships. This indicates what industry sales will be, assuming past behaviour will continue. The sales department should make this projection with the help of the planning officer.

2. Consider the effect of known or likely changes to the economy and the industry. This should be based on the collective knowledge and judgment of company executives.
3. From 1 and 2, develop the expected industry sales, according to executive opinion.
4. Obtain a consensus of executive opinion concerning the expected trend of sales of each of the company's lines bearing in mind:

   a. Past performance of each line.
   b. Expected industry sales.
   c. Share of market.
   d. Competitors' likely plans.
   e. Specific company programs contemplated.

The last two items, 4d and 4e, obviously have a significant bearing on the sales forecast. It is implied that the sales forecast cannot be completed without first considering the company's over-all marketing strategy. This means that broad marketing plans must be made in conjunction with the sales forecast, and these should take into consideration such factors as —

1. Quality of products (What is the probable effect on sales volume of upgrading or downgrading quality?)
2. Type of customers (What is the probable effect on sales volume of directing our selling to a broader class of customer?)
3. Channels of distribution (What is the probable effect on sales volume of changing our methods of distribution — selling direct vs. through jobbers, etc.?)
4. Pricing and credit (What is the probable effect on sales volume of changing our prices up or down? of altering terms of sale?)
5. Advertising and sales promotion (Which products should we push? What do we need to spend to keep our share of the market? to increase it?)

Various alternatives under each of these headings must be considered and assessed in relation to their effect on sales and costs as well as in relation to competitors' expected moves. The strategy and related plans to be adopted will, of course, be those which have the greatest impact on profits over the long term and most closely meet objectives.

Having made a forecast and drafted plans for sales in existing markets, a forecast should now be prepared for selling existing products in new markets, for new uses, and in new territories (both national and foreign). This may present difficulty because information on which to forecast may be relatively scanty, but an attempt must be made. This will become easier in future years as experience is gained.

Next, plans must be made to introduce new products or activities needed to meet the effect of expected technological, social, and economic changes. These too must be based on the facts previously gathered and the objectives set in recognition of internal weaknesses or external influences. These are the plans for innovation and diversification.

Where the course is clear and the decision firm, indicate the year the project starts, then forecast sales year by year. However, where thorough studies have not been made to choose a new activity, where the timing is vague, then all that can be planned is to carry out the proper studies in sufficient depth which will lead to action in accordance with objectives.

Up to this point, no mention has been made of the term of the profit plan. This will depend mainly on the industry. Those involved in natural resources should plan 15 to 20 years ahead. Rapidly changing industries such as electronics often find it difficult or impractical to plan as long as five years. As a general guide, however, five years is suggested. Where possible, the first profit-plan period should coincide with a "break point" in the company's activities — when sales demands match production capacity, when long-term debt is extinguished, or when diversification is completed. This permits concentration on primary objectives; as these come to be realized, new "primaries" should be set and the revised profit-plan period extended to their time of fulfilment.

*   *   *   *   *

PUTTING THE PROFIT PLAN TO WORK

Much time and effort has been spent to this point in preparing the profit plan. So far, good value should have been obtained merely by crystallizing ideas as to future courses of action. But most of the value will have been lost if it is abandoned after issue or looked upon only as an exercise in arithmetic.

The profit plan is not merely a prediction to be revised if things do not work out. It is a plan of intended action and result. Therefore its real worth is derived from controlling actual performance towards reaching the desired goals. [Here,] the means of controlling day-by-day action so as to reach our objectives will be discussed.

The importance of balancing long- and short-range plans was pointed out [earlier.] Our profit plan has set out long-range goals and the year-by-year planned movement to secure them working from our company's present position. Having completed and issued the profit plan, our next concern is to make sure that the first year's goals will be secured. So we must now plan for the year ahead, by preparation of the annual budget.

The annual budget should be prepared in a very similar manner to the profit plan, the main difference being that the budget is in greater detail and is broken into more time periods, usually one month's duration. Annual objectives and plans should be based on detailed sales forecasts and costs based on correct physical conditions and realistic standards of performance.

The budget should tie in with the first year of the profit plan in every important respect — earnings, return on assets, return on investment, share of market, and so on. It may develop upon making the detailed plans that the first year's objectives cannot be met by confining activities to those originally planned due to factors previously unforeseen. In such circumstances, the profit plan must not be abandoned or discounted. Additional activities must be put into the annual budget or operations otherwise altered so as to permit the planned profits to be earned. If conditions change, it is the responsibility of managers to take appropriate corrective action.

Thus, by backing and filling, an annual budget is put together which ties in with the profit plan and which sets short-term (monthly) goals of revenues, profits, turnover of assets, and so on. The specific details as to how each department plans to achieve these goals will not be spelled out in the budget but nevertheless once the budget has been accepted, department heads must prepare their programs for securing them. Perhaps here we can visualize the inter-action of planning and control at various levels within the organization. The plans made at the highest level cover the longest period of time, and cover the broadest area in the least detail. At the lowest level, the plans cover the shortest time span and in the greatest detail. The longer the time period covered by the plans, the more likely they are to become affected by outside influences and therefore the more flexible they need to be. Planning should start at the top and, as we have discussed, be directed towards a consistent group of objectives. Plans for each level of authority downwards should be made in sequence so as to fit those of the authority immediately agove, just as a nest of boxes fit together.

* * * * *

So it can be seen that one purpose of the profit plan is to provide a means of controlling actual performance. We need a warning system that tells the right people at the right time where action is needed in order to keep our program on the rails. Proper control can only be exercised where good standards of performance are available; in fact, without such standards it would not have been possible to set realistic goals in the first place. What we need, therefore, is an integrated system of management reporting that ties together standards, plans, and actual results. The system of m a n a g e m e n t reporting might consist of the following:

1. Profit Plan: As already outlined, this is the long-term plan for growth built up by determining needs and goals, and establishing a realistic rate of progress at correct standards of performance from human, physical and financial resources.

2. Annual Budget: This breaks the first years of the profit plan into monthly segments and involves the detailed planning necessary to achieve the year's goals.

3. Monthly Financial Statements: These compare actual revenues and expenditures for the month and year to date with budget. The causes of variance from budget due to differences in volume and planned cost should be clearly indicated.

4. Labour and Material Cost Control: Prepared on a weekly or bi-weekly basis, these show where actual cost differs from planned cost. The planned cost is that used in preparing the budget and profit plan. Action taken on a small variance shown on this weekly report has a direct effect on achieving the total results perhaps five years hence.

5. Sales Performance Control: This ties together the total sales goals with the individual performance expected from each branch or salesman. It shows monthly where action must be taken if the sales objectives and selling costs in the budget and profit plan are to be secured.

There are, of course, other control reports which can be prepared. Management must exercise control over every activity and the number, form, and frequency of the reports depends on the amounts involved, the rapidity of changes, and the requirements of the individual. The purpose here is not to describe the processes of control but rather to make clear that there must be a very distinct link between long-term planning and short-term control of performance. The control reports such as those described above will indicate what is wrong, but action rests with individual managers. Sometimes an element of cost can get out of line quite beyond the influence of a manager. It is then the manager's responsibility to devise ways and means of recouping this loss in other ways — cutting other costs, increasing volume, substituting new activities — so that the profit goals are reached.

* * * * *

The fact that plans have been solemnly conceived and accepted is not in any way to be interpreted as freezing ingenuity or restricting flexibility. On the contrary, the more one's operations can be conducted according to an intelligent program, the more one will be free to consider the unusual.

This brings us to the question of revising the profit plan. This should normally be done annually, preparatory to drawing up the budget. All sections of the profit plan should come under review — objectives, plans, sales forecasts, new projects. At this time, the success in meeting the first year's goals will be evaluated and programs reshaped in light of experience gained. If actual performance is ahead of schedule this does not necessarily mean that timing of other segments of the plan should be advanced, nor objectives revised. Unusual conditions may have been experienced which will have the opposite effect next year. The main thing is to ensure that objectives and plans are right for the conditions as they are expected to be.

After updating objectives, plans for the remaining term of the old profit plan should be reviewed, sharpened, or revised. Plans should be extended to cover a new year or to a new "break point" in the company's activities. Projected financial statements should be prepared in the same way as previously. These should include the revenues and expenditures of new projects which detailed study has shown to be justified.

* * * * *

18 LONG-RANGE PLANNING AND CLOUDY HORIZONS

by Jack J. Friedman

Whatever other doubts he may have had, the average executive of the late 1950s was confident of one point: business was moving into the era of the Soaring Sixties when there would be growth markets aplenty and profits for everyone. But whatever happened to them? Dr. Herbert R. Brinberg, director of corporate commercial research at the American Can Co., feels that he knows at least part of the cause for the near disappearance of the Soaring Sixties. It was the same long-range planning that had first uncovered them for top managements on every side.

A surprising assertion? Not to Dr. Brinberg. "A few years ago," he points out, "everyone was trying to dope out the growth markets. As a result, everyone went into the same markets. The competition was intense, profits didn't turn out as expected — and that's one reason the economy has been under strain."

Certainly one need not search long for proof of Dr. Brinberg's assertion. Oil companies piled into petrochemicals in numbers that managed to sharply reduce the return on even that fabulous investment. The planemakers ran into heavy turbulence by over-producing jet transports. And so did the airlines, who are still waiting for customers to fill the vast numbers they bought.

All of which is not to say that all long-range planning has resulted in nothing but mishaps. Too many successful companies, too many newly developed markets, prove that long-range planning can be one of the most effective weapons in the corporate arsenal. Yet there are also the failures, where long-range planning led to what can only be called painful results. Somehow, it operated on a false assumption. Somewhere, it reached a fateful conclusion.

Reprinted from Dun's Review & Modern Industry, January, 1963, pages 42-43, 66, by permission of the publisher.

What Went Wrong?

That being so, thoughtful businessmen and not a few consultants these days are re-examining long-range planning, its concepts and its execution. For planning is too vital, too far-reaching in its consequences, to be left to the workings of mere chance. When it has gone wrong, they are asking, just what was the cause — and how can it be remedied?

From their findings come growing evidence that long-range planning is one corporate function that may well be more prone to error than perhaps any other. In view of its very nature — the task of trying to foretell the future — that is hardly surprising. What is surprising, however, is the lack of unanimity among corporations on long-range planning. Its basic aims sometimes are in doubt. Its execution is often based on misleading assumptions. And the question of just who should do the corporation's planning seems one that will bedevil top management for years to come.

Starting at the very beginning, it would appear that long-range planning often goes astray because management often tries to forecast the future with the approach of the past. For it will plan for the future by emphasizing that the corporation must adapt itself to change as it occurs, rather than anticipating or planning for it.

The need for a change in this approach is pointed up by no less an authority than Assistant Professor E. Kirby Warren of Columbia University, who spent a year studying the planning process of fifteen of the nation's largest companies. Says Warren: "With the growth of large corporations and the increased amount, speed and magnitude of change (economic, social, technological and competitive), adaptation alone has often proved inadequate to insure corporate survival and profitability."

Roughly a similar view is held by Michael J. Kami, director of long-range planning at International Business Machines and one of the most respected names in the field. Not only must the corporation prepare for change, Kami argues, it can expect those changes to come faster than ever.

Says Kami: "Major innovations use to occur in various fields every fifteen or twenty years. The intervals have now shortened to five or ten years — and may shrink even further in the period ahead. Since the allowable delay for decision making is becoming shorter, we must have at our disposal a background of information, facts and 'prethinking' with which to render rapid and informed decisions. Planning should provide a new and faster trigger mechanism for top management."

The fact that it sometimes does not may well be the fault of top management itself. For it appears that the question of just who should do the long-range planning has never been really resolved. Indeed, it may well be one of the most haphazard processes in all of business. Should it be the president or chairman? Should it be an operating man or a trained, dedicated planner? Should it be done by divisions close to the markets, or by central headquarters despite the danger of an ivy tower approach?

Kirby Warren is particularly emphatic in his assertion that long-range planning no longer can be carried out by the one or two top corporate officers as it has been in so many companies for so many years. The harassed chief executive can guess the reason for that. As Warren phrases it: "The sheer magnitude of the work when added to the numerous other responsibilities of these top officers makes this impossible."

But in trying to solve that problem, top management often commits a grievous error. As Warren describes it: "Typically; the president appoints a taskforce to study the feasibility of planning. The taskforce's report invariably urges a go-ahead. The president then appoints a planning committee and asks his key operating people to cooperate with it."

So far, so good. But almost immediately, complications appear. "The committee points out that it is too small and its budget too skimpy to be effective," says Warren. "Consequently, no one will expect much and a shoddy job won't be condemned." Warren's solution: a simple statement that top management does expect better, skimpy budget and small committee notwithstanding.

Yet it can be argued that top management, a perennial scapegoat if there ever was one, may be to blame for only some of the planning failures. For even the specialists appear to differ on many aspects of long-range planning.

Canco's Brinberg, for example, tends to the professional planner approach. "If the planner is not removed from the mainstream of business activity and assigned solely to plan," he argues, "you are not going to get good results. The man who has to worry about meeting next week's production quota is carrying a big emotional load. If pressed to do planning, he'll probably delegate the job — with disastrous results."

The Other Side

IBM's Kami, in contrast, favors operating managers, "the men who have the facts and can make the decisions." John O. Tomb, a director of McKinsey & Co., agrees. "Most planning and control systems," claims Tomb, "are not rooted in the realities of business. Executives are asked to put a number in a blank space on a form submitted to them by planning-staff personnel. They aren't even asked how the numbers are to be achieved."

Planning and control, Tomb goes on, should be integrated. Then if a sales manager has to produce a sales target, he will develop a marketing plan before setting his goal. Adds Tomb: "If poor distribution is holding back sales he'll plan a program to obtain better outlets before predicting a sales increase."

Some specialists insist that such a system would submit the sales executive to excessive pressure. It should be noted, however, that this has not been the experience of so eminently successful a company as General Electric. The nation's fourth largest company claims that long-range planning is intimately woven into the job of every manager.

Planning at GE starts at the operating department level, where the department general manager and his section managers draw up a rolling ten-year forecast of budgets and plans for their own product range. At the next level, division general managers map the future course of their divisions five and ten years in the future by balancing the plans of all their department managers.

To avoid one of the pitfalls of many companies, it should be noted that GE planning at the division level is a personal responsibility and may not be delegated. This planning concept threads its way to the very top of the corporate structure. At GE's executive offices in New York, the company's over-all objectives, policies and plans are hammered out by the chairman, president and fifteen other top executives.

Does it make sense to submit planning to GE's elaborate decentralization policy? Cramer W. LaPierre, one of the company's two executive vice presidents, thinks so. "About the worst that can happen under our system," LaPierre points out, "is the simultaneous occurrence of small mistakes in different divisions. The impact, company-wide, would be small. But a single mistake at the top could be a disaster."

The proof: "In 1949," LaPierre goes on, "one of our most highly respected scientists insisted that the ICBM was a fantasy. Suppose he had headed a centralized planning process? I shudder to think where we would be now."

The inevitable result of decentralized planning, it should be added, is some overlap in projects by divisions. GE views this as part of the price. As a check, though, GE controls planning through budgetary control, to avoid letting the divisions plan themselves into projects that, in total, would be too much for the company to bear.

At the other end of the spectrum — and this may be one of the few clear trends in the whole area of long-range planning — some corporations are trying to hit the happy medium between headquarters and the field. The way is to appoint a high-level executive with long operating experience to specialize in long-range planning.

For all its decentralization, GE recently placed LaPierre in just that position, with orders to think only about the over-all corporate future, from new business lines for the company to the role of technology in GE's future. Similarly, the American Can Co. named William F. May vice president and general manager of its new corporate planning and development department.

The selection of such a man, however, must be done with

extreme care. As McKinsey & Co.'s director E. Everett Smith points out, too many companies draft the "corporate achiever" to pilot their planning. "This simply doesn't work," says Smith. "The achiever is generally looking for short-term results. He's the man who made the big sale, swung the big deal or spun off a division painlessly. His personality seeks reward, applause and recognition. But no one applauds when a project takes fifteen years to bear fruit, even if it is a roaring success."

In contrast is the call to various departments to supply planners. Who appears? "Castoffs," snorts Herbert Brinberg. "Say the sales department has a man it wants to dump. Now it sees its chance. The result is a second-rate staff that guarantees planning will flop."

Aside from personnel, of course, the very nature of the long-range planning process itself can lead to error. In essence, and with all fancy verbiage stripped away, the job of the long-range planner is to foretell the future. True, he will use as many tools as possible to avoid error and the hit-or-miss approach. Nevertheless, he must make certain assumptions about the environment in which the company will function — the course of the economy, size of the market and so forth.

Very often, and perhaps quite understandably, that assumption can lead to trouble. A few years ago, by way of example, W.R. Grace & Co. realized that its basic shipping business was hardly a growth one. So Grace looked around for more fruitful endeavors. It could hardly be blamed for settling on chemicals; they were indeed a prime example of a growth industry. Yet no sooner had Grace built its massive chemical complexes than overcapacity settled around the entire industry. And only recently has Grace found the improved profits that it expected from the chemical industry.

One reason for miscalculations is that many companies confuse economic forecasting with long-range planning. The two are completely different. Economic forecasting is a basic tool in long-range planning, not the process. Says Columbia's Warren: "Too many companies mechanically extrapolate the figures on trends and call this planning." Adds GE's LaPierre: "Forecasts help to define the environment, but they don't dictate your decisions."

The Safe Ground

All of which is not to say that a company cannot make assumptions about the future. It must. Yet it would appear that it will be on safest ground if it adheres to assumptions that are close to its own business, to the field it knows best.

Once they have made their assumptions, American companies tend to spread their planning out over a five-year range. Here, though, the nature of the industry again must be considered a factor, for cycles vary greatly in length. Twenty years is roughly a single cycle for oil tanker procurement, but half the cycle of tree maturity in the paper industry.

Again, if a five-year program is followed, variations within the cycle must not be overlooked. Consider the program worked out by American Machine & Foundry Co. "We plan ahead in five-year cycles," notes President Rodney C. Gott. "But while the first year's planning is very detailed, the second year's is less so, though it is fairly accurate. We find that the third and fourth years are almost meaningless, and so we have tended to skip them. The fifth year, of course, is the objective.

Will long-range planning ever reach the point where that objective is fairly well assured? The last word must remain with Kirby Warren. "Only time," he comments, "will tell whether long-range planning is any good. In the meantime, there is no sure way of knowing. The only thing one has to evaluate over the short term is the way people plan. Did they take into account all the significant data? Did they give adequate weight to the right factors? Did they overemphasize the importance of competition, markets, foreign trade?"

They are questions more and more corporations are asking these days.

PART SIX:

CONTROL

19 CONTROL: A BRIEF EXCURSION ON
THE MEANING OF A WORD

by E. S. L. Goodwin

Everybody, or almost everybody, agrees that managing consists of, is divided into, has as its elements planning, organizing, directing, and controlling. There are those who will wish to add coordinating, following the lead of M. Henri Fayol, the French industrialist and management authority, who first (in 1916) analyzed management as a separate skill, universal to all human enterprise. There are some who will plug staffing (the assembling of managerial personnel) as a fifth member of the list, in answer to whom orthodox Fayolians will point out that staffing is obviously nothing but an aspect of organizing; and there are other departures — but these need not divert us now. For our present purpose we may regard planning, organizing, directing, and controlling as at least outlining the usually accepted analysis (basically Fayolian) of what a manager does when he manages.

There is general agreement that planning is making decisions about where you want to go and how you are going to try to get there; that organizing is erecting and tending the apparatus, material and social, that will carry you on the trip; that directing is steering the vehicle as the route unrolls — that is, telling your crew what to do along the way (coordinating can be fitted in here somewhere if anyone insists on it); and that controlling is . . . that controlling is what?

Excerpts, reprinted by permission from the January, 1960, issue of the Michigan Business Review, published by the Graduate School of Business Administration, The University of Michigan; pages 13-17, 28.

There is no general agreement on the meaning of control and, oddly, no clean-cut disagreement — merely fuzziness about the meaning, a condition of mild schizosemantia, most of whose victims seem happily unaware of their malady.

Control, most (but by no means all) agree, <u>starts with</u> observation and measuring — comparing what has just happened or is happening with what was supposed to have happened, or what had been planned to happen, or what used to happen. If we go only this far and no farther, we have the tidy and uncontroversial situation that control is a job made to order for staff — the job of checking-up, inspecting, keeping track; something which does not infringe on the line man's prerogative of directing and commanding; something which is, in fact, so inherently <u>non</u>-infringing[1] and at the same time so helpful to all concerned that it looms as a very large part of the raison d'etre of staff — maybe the largest part.

But there are management theorists who do not wish to leave it at that. They assert that control necessarily involves <u>doing something about</u> any deviations from plan that observation and measurement reveal.[2] And therefrom flows much confusion. Those who swallow this view whole tend to reject outright the idea of <u>any</u> "control" by staff — they are likely, typically and for example, to hold that cost <u>accounting</u> is a staff job, but that cost <u>control</u> is exclusively the job of the line. This view, it will be noted, in effect expels (unwittingly and contrary to actual desire, I suspect) the information-gathering element from the sphere of "control."

CONFUSED USAGE

A large group of the confused is composed of those who, in writing about management, use the word "control" in two different senses, without indicating their shifts in usage, and perhaps without being aware of them. The manifestations of this foible take two forms. The members of one subgroup besprinkle their paragraphs with occurrences of the word used, apparently unconsciously, in the commonly understood English sense (in which it is practically synonymous with "direction," or even with the all-inclusive "management" itself); and yet, in these very paragraphs, with no show of awareness of the anomaly

---

[1] Although some line executives may be inclined to suggest that having someone looking over one's shoulder is not without at least a faint odor of infringement.

[2] As an example, see Arnold F. Emch, "Control Means Action," <u>Harvard Business Review</u>, July-August, 1954.

which they are spawning, analyze managing into four (or more) elements of which one is controlling and another is directing. The second subgroup quote M. Fayol with apparent approval and with every evidence of eager affiliation; then, in their own expositions, with what must be misunderstanding rather than the perversity which it shouts, blithely give "control" meanings which are utterly incompatible with M. Fayol's. Some of the writing involved is reminiscent of passages from metaphysics or theology — it is doubtless extremely confusing to the new student of management theory.

RESOLVING THE CONFUSION

Can there be a clean-cut resolution of this? Yes, if we are willing to be logical and consistent. No one will deny that the information-getting element of control must be followed by action if control is to be of any use at all. So must thinking. So must planning. But this does not make action a part of thinking nor execution a part of planning. And, once we have agreed, in the interest of clarifying what managing is and entails, to analyze it into four component parts, why must we muddy our analysis by maintaining that one of these parts in some obscure way includes all of the other three? Yet this is what the control-means-action adherents, abetted by their less dogmatic but more careless fellow-errants, are in fact maintaining.

Let us suppose that a manager's information shows him that everything is going as he wishes, exactly according to orders and plans. What does he do? Nothing, of course (except possibly pinch himself to see if he is awake). So which of the things that he has done (if any) can be categorized as "controlling"? He has done nothing but gather and interpret information; so that, if he has controlled at all, it must have been in the act of gathering and interpreting information.

Or suppose that his information tells him that things are not going well, or as planned, or as hoped; and that he must take corrective action. What action does he take? There are just three categories of action that he can take, and these are (1) to modify his plan, (2) to revise his organization, and (3) to issue some new orders to his people. The first of these looks suspiciously like planning, the second is indistinguishable from organizing, the third is indisputably directing. What, then, of the various things that he has done or might do, remains to be labelled "controlling"? Clearly, nothing but the original gathering and interpreting of information.

Wait a minute! There is a fourth thing that he can have done, and that is to dig up more information or reinterpret and restudy some that he already has — in this sense one of the actions that results from control can be more controlling. But in any case the manager's controlling has been composed solely of the getting and treatment of information — nothing whatever more. What he does ultimately in the light of the information and aside from his treatment of it is always pursuant to some other aspect of managing, except in that special case where it loops back to more information-getting first.

What about the case where information and decision-making are made integral in one procedure, as in automatic line-item reorder at a specified inventory level — is this a case where control literally means and includes action? It is not. It is a case where a directing element has been tacked on to the end of a controlling element — two different things are still being done, despite the automaticity of their sequence.

How have we got ourselves enmeshed in thinking otherwise? Let us do a bit of etymological research.

ETYMOLOGY OF "CONTROL"

We start with the unabridged "Merriam-Webster," Second Edition, which tells us that the verb "to control" entered the language from the French "contrôler," and gives the following current meanings:

> 1. Originally to check by a duplicate register (contre rôle in the French; counter roll in English) or account; now, to check or regulate (expenditures, payments, etc.)
> 2. To check, test, or verify by counter or parallel evidence or experiments; to verify by comparison or research; as to control a statement or experiment.
> 3. To exercise restraining or directing influence over; to dominate; regulate; hence, to hold from action, to curb; to subject.
> Synonyms — restrain, rule, govern, guide, direct, check, subdue.

Meaning number one (except for that contaminating "regulate") comes very close to the management sense of the word. Meaning number two is even closer, although it seems to be slanted toward the limited application in scientific experimentation. Meaning number three, which makes "control" and "direct" synonyms (and note that the entire list of synonyms, with the possible exception of "check," is associated with this third meaning), is quite incompatible with an analysis in which "control" and "direct" both appear as presumably different parts of one whole.

And yet meaning number three is the dominant English meaning! It is the meaning intended by engineers when they use the word. It is the sense usual in aeronautics. It is what we have in mind when we speak of a baseball pitcher's performance or a parent's influence over his offspring. The military term "fire-control" means more than merely the spotting and reporting of fall of shot; it really means "fire-direction." If asked which of the two, the steering wheel or the speedometer, is a control mechanism in our car, most of us will unhesitatingly pick the wheel. Yet, in the management sense, the only correct answer is the speedometer.

Let us continue digging. The Oxford English Dictionary tells us that the word came over from the French in 1475 with the sole meaning "to check or verify." The restrain-prevent-regulate-dominate-direct senses (the "action" senses) appeared later, apparently as a spontaneous addition, unilaterally English (the Oxford dates the first occurrence in these senses at 1495). "Well, what difference does that make?" you may protest; "Doesn't usage properly change the meanings of words? Language is not a frozen thing. Dictionaries don't govern language — language governs dictionaries. Control means to English-speaking people what it has come to mean to them, regardless of what the French originally meant by it or now mean by it. We thank them for the word, of course; but they can't dictate what we shall do with it now that we have it."

All right. Granted. But "control" in the management sense did not enter English from the French "contrôler" in 1475; it entered English from the French "contrôler" in 1929. It made that second trip across the Strait of Dover because, in that year, a Mr. J. A. Coubrough, an Englishman, mistranslated "contrôler" as "control," and the result was printed by the International Institute for the Scientific Organization of Work at Geneva in the first published English version of M. Henri Fayol's Administration Industrielle et Générale which, originally presented in French in 1916 by the Society of the Mineral Industry of France, had introduced the prévoir-organiser-commander-coordoner-contrôler[3] list into management theory.

"CONTROL" A MISTRANSLATION

I say "mistranslated" because the word used by Mr. Coubrough to render "contrôler" had come, since 1475, to mean something altogether different from "contrôler." What M. Fayol meant by "contrôler" may be found in the unabridged Pierre Larousse where (take my brief word for it; the Larousse devotes some 250 to the subject) the dominant meaning is checking, comparing,

---

[3]Meaning (forecast and) plan-organize-direct (or command)-coordinate-?????

verifying; and the idea of directing, restraining, using overriding power <u>does not appear at all.</u>[4]

Those who have ridden in the Paris Metro may recall a sign posted in the cars which says:

> Save your ticket.
> It might be checked (contrôlé) enroute.

FAYOL'S ORIGINAL TEXT

That M. Fayol meant his "contrôler" in this sense is perhaps adequately attested by the fact that he was a Frenchman writing in French. But we can further clinch the matter by quoting several of his own passages from the original text of <u>Administration Industrielle et Générale</u>[5] (I translate, using "c ——— " for every occurrence of "contrôler" or its inflections or the corresponding noun or adjective. The reader may like to read "checking" or "check-up" into these places. All emphases are supplied.):

"In an enterprise, c ——— consists of verifying whether[6]

---

[4] By "unabridged Pierre Larousse" I am referring to the monumental <u>Grand Dictionnaire Universel du XIX Siècle</u>, published in France between 1865 and 1876, with Supplements in 1878 and 1888. A second great Larousse, the <u>Nouveau Larousse Illustré</u>, came out between 1898 and 1904, with a Supplement in 1907. Under "contrôler" it adds nothing significant to the material in the earlier version. The name Larousse means much more to the French, in its implications of authority, than the name Webster means to Americans; and, since M. Fayol was born in 1841 and died in 1925, I think that we can accept these two Larousses as authoritative guides to his mother tongue as he knew and used it.

A third great Larousse, the <u>Larousse du XX Siècle</u>, publication of which began in 1928, gives the same meanings for "contrôler" as do the two earlier ones, but with the addition, at the end, of the following (for our purpose) extremely significant and illuminating "Remark" or note (I translate):

> There is sometimes given to this verb the sense of "be master of," "govern," "direct": thus — "The territory controlled by the Marshal Chang Tso Lin." This is an anglicism.

[5] Since 1925, published by S. R. L. Dunod, Publishers, Paris.
[6] The French here is ". . . consiste à vérifier si tout se passe. . . ." Mr. Coubrough's 1929 translation renders this

everything happens according to the program adopted, the orders given, and the principles established. It has as its aim <u>to point out</u> faults and errors <u>so that they can be</u> rectified and their recurrence prevented."[7]

"Each department exercises surveillance over its own people, and top authority keeps its eye on everything. But when certain c —— operations become too numerous or too complex or too extended to be done by the regular supervisors of the various (line) departments, recourse must be had to special functionaries called controllers or inspectors."[8]

"For c —— to be effective it must be done sufficiently promptly, and it must be <u>followed up</u> by sanctions. It is obvious that, if the results of a c —— procedure, even a very good one, arrive too late to be of use, the c —— procedure will have been futile. It is no less clear that c —— is useless if the practical conclusions which flow from it are obstinately ignored."

"Well done, c —— is a valuable auxiliary of top management. It can give it certain necessary information which the hierarchic chain is sometimes incapable of furnishing....Good c —— insures against those troublesome surprises which might degenerate into catastrophes."

Perhaps an even better statement by M. Fayol of what he meant by "contrôler" is to be found in an address of his, entitled "The Administrative Theory in the State," before the Second International Congress of Administrative Science at Brussels,

---

".... consists of seeing that everything is being carried out. . . . ." The English idiom "to see that" so-and-so happens carries the clear implication to cause it to come out that so-and-so shall happen; in other words, to make it happen. The French phrase "verifier si" does not say this. Another black mark for Mr. Coubrough! A later translator, Constance Storrs, who is responsible for the Pitmans' version of the same text issued in 1949, avoids this pitfall by using "verifying whether," and I follow her lead in my own rendering.

[7] Although Mrs. Storrs avoids the "see that" trap (see last footnote), she gets drawn into the anglicization cited by the Larousse in her treatment of the next sentence. The French is: "Il a pour but de signaler les fautes et les erreurs <u>afin qu'on puisse</u> les reparer et en eviter le retour." Mrs. Storrs renders this: "It has for object to point out weaknesses and errors in order to rectify them and prevent recurrence" — a version which will be seen to be either bad translation or bad English, or possibly a little of both.

[8] In interesting contrast with this passage is a section in Mr. Emch's article, previously cited, whose sub-title and theme is "Controllers don't control."

September 13, 1923 — just two years before his death (I retain the convention of recording the controversial word as "c —— ").[9]

"To prepare the operations is to <u>plan</u> and <u>organize</u>; to see that[10] they are carried out is to <u>command</u> and <u>coordinate</u>; to watch the results is to c —— ."

"C —— is the examination of results. . . . C —— compares, discusses, and criticises; it tends to stimulate planning, to simplify and strengthen organization, to increase the efficiency of command and to facilitate coordination."

The duplicate transformations of "controler" into English, 450 years apart, remind me of a gimmick in some science-fiction plots in which the hero, time-traveling into the future, encounters his older and of course altered self. The confusion to all concerned is quite similar in both situations.[11]

WHOSE FAULT?

M. Fayol might have saved us all this by writing in English; but we can hardly take him to task for not having done so. Mr. Coubrough might have served us better by translating "controler" as "measure," or "compare," or "check-up," or "verify," or "inspect" . . . his little sin in not having done so seems to have misguided a large segment of a generation of English-speaking management theorists.[12] Finally, I suggest that we might relieve Mr. Coubrough of <u>some</u> of the blame and shift it to the shoulders of the misguided segment itself, on the ground that they could have avoided being misguided if they had given somewhat more attention to testing their own internal consistency — that is to say, <u>controlling</u> it.[13]

---

[9] Translation by Sarah Greer, in Luther Gulick and Lyndall Urwick (eds.), <u>Papers on the Science of Administration</u> (New York: Institute of Public Administration, Columbia University, 1937).

[10] Note "see that" here in its proper role. Contrast with subject matter of footnote 6.

[11] Professor Albert H. Marckwardt of the English Department at the University of Michigan assures me that this disturbing event is far more common in philology than it is (as far as we know) in tourism.

[12] And a scattering of Controllers (which is, I suggest, what was bothering Mr. Emch, previously cited).

[13] My quarrel is not with those who use the word simply in the anglicized sense without pretending to combine this usage with a Fayolian or quasi-Fayolian treatment — it is rather with those who use the Fayolian analysis without understanding Fayol. In fairness to Mr. Emch, previously cited, I should state that

The cure? As the veterinary doctor said when called into the case of the ailing but still ebullient gorilla, the prescription is easy; it's the administration of it that poses problems.

The prescription in the case of "control" is, of course, to drop the word from membership in the list of the elements of managing and substitute something else. Moorehead Wright of General Electric likes "measurement." Luther Gulick uses "reporting" (presumably implying and including the reciprocal — being reported to). Another possibility is "comparison." Still another would be the obvious, and simple, "supervision," except that this word has come to apply mainly to the lower levels of managership. There is one word which is perfect for the purpose, and this is "surveillance." The fact that its companion verb, "to surveil," is not yet in Webster need not be a decisive deterrent.

But the difficulty is to get this prescription into the patient. Once a confusion has become embedded in a language, and hence in a culture, there is sometimes only one thing that one can do about it — and that is to wait a couple of centuries.

---

he does not mention Fayol, shows no evidence of familiarity with Fayol's analysis, and makes no comparable one of his own.

20 CONTROL AND EVALUATION

by Albert H. Rubenstein and Chadwick J. Haberstroh

To many authors, the subject of "Control and Evaluation" is as broad as the question of "how to organize." One might surmise two reasons for this: the subjectivity of most writing on management and the fact that control or evaluation presupposes a great deal about organization. By subjectivity is meant the absence of the qualities of cumulativeness of contributions, systematic formulation, and communicability that were discussed [earlier], as well as the custom of writing from the viewpoint of a practicing manager. Given these considerations, an author is driven to express much of his basic philosophy of administration before addressing himself to the question of control. Furthermore, viewed from the situation of the practicing manager, the question of control becomes, "How do I get my subordinates to do what I want them to?" which is, for the manager, equivalent to the question, "How do I organize?"

Inasmuch as we have not proposed this book as a handy guide to the practicing manager and have declared our intention to concentrate on that which is systematic, cumulative, and communicable, the place to start is with the presuppositions of control and evaluation. The first, of course, is a going organization larger and more complex than can be compassed by a face-to-face group. It is also supposed that the organization is rationally structured and goal-directed (i.e., bureaucratic). The question of control may then be phrased," How do organizations act so as to co-ordinate human and other resources in support of goals?"

Excerpt, reprinted from Some Theories of Organization, edited by Albert H. Rubenstein and Chadwick J. Haberstroh (Homewood, Ill.: Richard D. Irwin, Inc., 1960), pages 323-330, by permission of the publisher. Unless otherwise indicated, titles enclosed in quotes in the present selection refer to other articles appearing in Some Theories of Organization.

The answer to this question must necessarily be partly general and partly specific. Each organization has differences from all the others in the content of its goals, in the specific resources with which it has to deal, and in the technology available to it. But organizations have similarities too: they are goal-directed; they differentiate executive roles from other member roles; and they all are constrained by the "human nature" of their members.

GOALS

The consideration of values is basic to any discussion of control — and it is relevant in more ways than may appear on the surface. The first and most important set of values is what Selznick calls "the evolving character of the organization as a whole." This defines the goals or objectives. Goals, of course, are specific; but, being determined, they provide the criteria by which the effectiveness of the organization is judged. It would be unreasonably formalistic, however, to hold that these are the only relevant values. A second way in which values are relevant stems from the commitment of the organization to its members. The human beings involved are not passive but react in terms of their own values to the controls imposed upon them. This thesis has been amply developed in [earlier sections.] Third, and less obviously, enter the values of any nonmembers of the organization who have interest and power. All three of these impose imperatives on organizational functioning. It is through the executive apparatus that these imperatives are realized.

THE EXECUTIVE ROLE

In his classic work, The Functions of the Executive, Chester I. Barnard outlined the vital components of the executive role as: (1) the maintenance of communications within the organization, (2) the elaboration of purpose, and (3) the eliciting of member contributions. These functions, systematically arranged, provide the beginnings of organizational control.

The executives' communication functions include the formal aspect of establishing the system of positions and the informal one of insuring the adequacy of communication by departing from official channels when necessary. In most organizations, there are also routine formal channels of communication that transcend the "line of command." These include media, such as the company house organ, that are disseminated indiscriminately and reports, such as periodic accounting and statistical bulletins, that are regularly transmitted to designated executives without recourse to "channels" on each occasion. Both of these types are important to the control function. Granick[1] points out how the Soviets use broadcast communication to secure changes in emphasis in industrial programs; this method seems especially appropriate for communicating information on goals. The role of routine reports of performance is developed in several of the articles reproduced below. Although communication is necessary to control, it does not by itself normally establish executive responsibility.

Elaboration of purpose means more than formulating over-all goals. It includes the determination of subgoals and methods down to the assignment of specific tasks to specific individuals. The larger aspects of this function are departmentalization (the grouping of positions and tasks) and the related process of commitment of resources to relatively more specific forms, such as land, buildings, machinery, hiring and training of personnel, etc.

In an [earlier] section we examined many of the factors conditioning the ability of the executive organization to elicit member contributions. This subject is generally discussed in two parts: the decision to participate in the organization and the influencing or organization members after they have achieved that status. Although the act of joining evokes a significant increase in the member's regard for the legitimacy of organizational authority, co-operation is held by the same methods it is won: by members sharing the organization's goals, by the payment of incentives (including nonmonetary), by members' acceptance of the legitimacy of their role vis-á-vis the organization, and by sanctions.

Faced with these characteristics of organizations, we may begin to inquire how it is that they can achieve the degree of technical superiority alleged for them by Weber and so readily observed in the course of our daily lives. What properties of the organization overcome the very real limitations we have studied and permit the great achievements of which organizations are capable? The technical advantages of specialization and definite allocation of jurisdiction according to formal rules, as discussed by Weber, help to explain the organization's power over its external environment. We must also explain the ability of the organization to maintain control over itself.

The application of cybernetic models to this question is the subject of the articles by Haberstroh, Dean, and Rubenstein. They suggest that the kind of rationality necessary for control takes a somewhat different form from that envisioned by Weber. In particular, there is needed a feedback of information on the results of the organization's efforts, an appropriate measure of the effectiveness of organizational action. Coincidental with this is the need for accurate and timely communication of the results of

------

[1] David Granick, Management of the Industrial Firm in the USSR, Chapter 4 (New York, 1954).

performance measurement to the appropriate part of the organization. Beyond this, there still remain the problems of correcting performance, to be discussed under the headings of <u>executive responsibility</u> and <u>power</u>.

The <u>servomechanism</u> model is an attractive and appropriate analogy in the discussion of organizational control. Although frequent use is made of it in the literature, there have been few attempts to build genuine, mathematical models such as those commonly used in engineering control systems. The reasons for this can be appreciated from a study of the case reported by Haberstroh. Although this study attempted to model only the safety function in the plant, the control chart is fairly complex and, if modeled fully, would require a nonlinear operator that is beyond the power of present analytic methods. If the entire organizational control system were modeled (or even the entire safety function including departmental loops), sheer complexity would probably prohibit an analytic solution. Moreover, testing of such a model is hampered by the paucity of data. Only one measurement of annual performance can be taken each year. It is these features that attract some investigators to techniques of <u>simulating</u> organizational performance.

Evaluation procedures are usually thought of as ascertaining the effectiveness of particular executives, operating units, projects, methods, apparatus, or organizational forms. Since these procedures usually begin with an audit of <u>past</u> performance, they may be thought of as distinct from <u>control</u> functions, whose purpose is to regulate <u>current</u> performance. Actually, if evaluation procedures have any impact, it is as the long-run counterpart of control. Control at the highest levels largely consists of changes in executive personnel or formal organization, based on the results of formal or informal evaluation procedures. This principle appears recurrently in the articles in this section as well as elsewhere in the literature.[2] In "A Research Plan for the Study of Organizational Effectiveness," Andrew L. Comrey presents a general design for a series of studies which was later carried out in several different kinds of organizations.[3] If this research had been planned and executed by a practicing manager or his staff in his own organization, it would clearly qualify as an evaluation procedure since it attempts to relate various design characteristics to over-all organization effectiveness.

---

[2] C. I. Barnard, <u>Functions of the Executive</u> (Harvard, 1938), page 223.

[3] The final report of this study was Andrew L. Comrey, John M. Pfiffner, and Wallace S. High, <u>Factors Influencing Organizational Effectiveness</u> (Los Angeles: University of Southern California, 1954). Three partial reports of this study also appeared in <u>Personnel Psychology</u> for 1953, 1954, and 1955.

Implicit in the theory of control or evaluation procedures are standards of performance. In each of the cases which are examined in the readings to follow, the existence of some standard is pointed out or recommended. Standards are usually the creation of the participants, although it is possible to find cases (e.g., the subordinate organizations discussed in the readings) where the standards are given by the environment (superior organizations). The more interesting case and the one of most importance to the businessman is the standard that has to be self-generated. The standards may be derived as indicated below from some model in use by the organization. They may also be set intuitively, or on the basis of historical experience, or by a consideration of the experience of other similar organizations.

In management literature, in economic theory, and in operations research the standards are usually conceived of as optima of some sort. The most common example is the maximization of profits. There is a relation between the concept of standards as used in our theory of organizational control and the concept of optimum performance as just stated. Standards may be intended as optima, but they are rarely demonstrable as such. In the context of organizational behavior the existence of optima can be affirmed within the framework of some model of the organization's functioning that admits of analytic methods (like the infinitesimal calculus) for defining the optima. An optimum value is then a property of a model used by or recommended to an organization. A model in use is a design characteristic of the organization, a part of the formal organization usually, and possibly itself subject to an evaluation procedure. Frequently, the optima of a model are clearly not identical with the attainment of the over-all goals of the organization, but the model is used as the best available alternative. In such instances, the act of constraining organizational behavior in ways suggested by the optimality criteria of the model is referred to as suboptimization.

A measurement of performance can disclose whether performance is up to standard, but not whether it is optimal. In each of the articles in this section, one or more measures of performance are reported and analyzed.[4] The main difficulties with systems of performance measurement lie in determining standards and measures that really reflect the goals of the organization. If this is not the case, the organization is more likely to achieve what is being measured than to realize its actual goals. In the language of the preceding discussion of models, suboptima are

---

[4] An excellent annotated bibliography of material on this subject, including much material on control in general, is P. Wasserman, Measurement and Evaluation of Organizational Performance (Ithaca, N. Y.: Graduate School of Business and Public Administration, Cornell University, 1959).

likely to displace original goals. This is essentially the main thesis of the article by Ridgeway, "Dysfunctional Consequences of Performance Measurement."

The existence of a good measurement of performance is not useful unless the information is present at the point where it can be used. This implies that information on achievement of the organization's most general goals is reported to the highest executives and, correspondingly, information on subgoals, to the subordinate officials in the appropriate positions. If we judge by cybernetic models, these communication links are crucial to organizational control. This may account for some of the trends in organizational development: specifically, the development of elaborate systems of quantitative reports and the growth of extensive staff organizations paralleling the usual line of command. Both of these developments provide alternative chains of communication to the normal hierarchical flow of reports. The establishment of multiple channels of communication is probably a calculated step; it is often easier to improve one's performance by manipulating reports than by actually correcting deficiencies. Dalton, for example, reports case material illustrating top management's use of staff services for control purposes and also illustrating a rich variety of ways in which reports were falsified to show better than actual performance.[5] Some of the examples cited by Ridgeway (e.g., sacrificing maintenance for production records) also illustrate ways of manipulating reports.

This brings us to the question of what is actually done in organizations to assure adequate performance, the matter of executive responsibility. According to Barnard,[6] responsibility is the capacity and determination of an individual to work within his own moral codes relevant to the situation in which he finds himself. By interpretation, executive responsibility thus refers to the executive's capacity to anticipate and to direct his actions toward their consequences for the imperatives of the situation. Elliott Jaques, in the context of working out performance standards for a large engineering company, defined a measure of responsibility as the time span between the executive's initiation of action and the feedback of the results of his actions.[7] Since the relevance of feedback is determined by the imperatives of the situation, there is more than a hint of similarity between the two definitions. The responsible executive is the one who can manage his affairs so that the imperatives of the situation are met, the test of whether or not they are met being implicit in the feedbacks received. This means that the executive is bound not only by his own values

---

[5] Melville Dalton, Men Who Manage, Chapter 4 (New York: John Wiley, 1959).

[6] Chester Barnard, Functions of the Executive, Chapter 17.

[7] E. Jaques, Measurement of Responsibility (Harvard, 1956).

and the goals of the organization, but also by the values of other members whose co-operation is needed and of outsiders, if their values can be brought to bear on the immediate concerns of the executive. Government regulatory agencies and customer boycotts are relevant examples of the latter.

If the network of feedbacks is appropriately arranged, then the maintenance of responsibility will be sufficient for achievement of the organization's goals. But what of the executive who fails to be responsible? The usual answer is, of course, that this forces into action another executive whose responsibility is thus jeopardized. The supervisory system thus assures that the failure of one executive will not prejudice the goals. Nevertheless, control systems are subject to certain malfunctions and these are also illustrated in the literature. The manipulation of reports of performance has already been discussed. Another way of maintaining overt responsibility is by the collusion of a superior and subordinate to keep the superior formally ignorant of malfunctions. An example of this is the inspection procedure described [elsewhere] by Dalton in "Managing the Manager." . . . Hemphill and Sechrest, in "A Comparison of Three Criteria of Air Crew Effectiveness in Combat over Korea," illustrate still another type of malfunction. Here is an evaluation procedure used by the Air Force, involving an apparently objective criterion, and shown by the researchers to be itself irrelevant to performance. Other examples are cited by Ridgeway.

There is a second theme implicit in Dalton's case analysis in "Managing the Managers": whether apparently evasive action by subordinates is to be judged by "the book" or whether it is to be judged by the over-all goals of the organization. This appears in his contrasting the "strong" executives who get things done with the "weak" executives who place excessive reliance on compliance with formal requirements. Executive malfeasance is thus a possible cure for misdirected formalism and a source of adaptive flexibility in times of crisis.

The entire problem of control logically presupposes the existence of executive power. Since control is by and large achieved, one may infer that executives do indeed hold power. Nevertheless, the qualifications and limitations on the holding and exercise of power have important consequences for organizational functioning. As we may infer from Section Two, the possibility of struggles for power is as great within organizations as in social, economic, and political systems. Empire building in subordinate departments may greatly reduce the power of higher executives to establish and enforce goals for those departments. This has become a commonplace in governmental administration, and it is often correct now to regard the bureau, and not the President, as the seat of executive authority in certain spheres. The existence of power centers outside the executive hierarchy, especially unions and government regulatory agencies, also imposes restraints on the freedom of executive action. The institutions developed by organizations to assure stability can also impose limitations on executive power. For example, the widespread custom of (officially or unofficially) guaranteeing job security to executives restricts the sanctions which may be used against them and also limits the organization's freedom to "put the right man in the right job." The legitimacy of authority and the indirect sanctions which an organization may hold over an executive's promotion chances, perquisites, freedom of action, etc. still represent considerable power.

*   *   *   *   *

21 FINANCIAL REPORTING
. . . For Control or Creation

by John Coughlan

Perhaps the most obvious and important requirement of a good system of financial reporting is that it should relate results to the people who achieve the results. It should relate performance to responsibility.

Locate the Decision Centers

Let us consider the problems of the large decentralized corporation. If the divisional breakdown is on a geographic basis, then the important breakdown of overall corporate results is on a geographic basis, for the decisions that spell more or less profit are made by the managers of these geographical divisions. If the corporation is divisionalized on a product basis, then breakdowns must be given on a product basis. As obvious as this point may seem, yet in the large corporation with its numerous divisions, its multiplicity of products, its staff and service departments, reports are often segmented in such a way that some segments present the results of not one person, one team or one unit of the organization but rather the composite results of unrelated teams and efforts, while other segments present results unique to one group or organizational entity but are only a part of the results of that group of entity. Just as cost accountants attempt to accumulate costs by "cost centers" so the financial reports should report results by "decision centers."

Excerpts, reprinted from Advanced Management — Office Executive, November, 1960, pages 20-24, by permission of the publisher.

Don't Hold Executives Responsible for Costs
Incurred by Others

Failure to report by decision centers is not as common as the error of allocating to divisions and plants costs that were incurred by executives in other organizational units. The commonest example of this zeal for allocations occurs in connection with central administrative and overhead expenses. In the top half of Exhibit I, corporate administrative expenses and advertising expenses have been allocated to the operating divisions, leading to the charge by Division I personnel that they are "paying the rent" since they show a pre-tax profit of $1,166,667 in contrast to a Division II pre-tax loss of $166,667. In the bottom half of Exhibit I, none of the corporate administrative expense has been allocated, and neither has that part of advertising expenses designed to create a "favorable corporate image." The divisions are only held responsible for their own selling and administrative expenses and for the advertising expenses directly related to their own products. It is apparent that both divisions made some contribution toward the corporate overhead and advertising expenses. For the manager or president of the divisions, this is a better presentation and one which assures them that the costs related to their own efforts will not be swamped in the allocated costs incurred by other organizational units. Under the presentation appearing in the top half, the president of Division II had little reason to put on a concentrated drive to reduce selling and administrative expenses since the expenses for which he was responsible and over which he had authority constituted only a small part of the total administrative, selling and advertising expenses charged to his operations. Under the preferable presentation in the bottom half of the Exhibit, the division is charged with no expenses that the division president has not approved.

Where corporate-level expenses can be related fairly directly to the mission of the divisions, some case can be made for allocations. Suppose that most of the time of the corporate officers is spent making decisions relating to production and sales problems and in supervising the efforts of the division managers. But even here where the organization is still highly centralized, there are dangers in attempting to allocate corporate-level expenses. In the top half of Exhibit I, these corporate-level expenses were split on the basis of sales. More precise methods are available for certain departments such as purchasing and billing, but allocations of such overhead items as the president's salary and the cost of the treasurer's department are bound to be very arbitrary. An even worse fault of these allocations, however, is the fact that, whether or not central administrative expenses can be related to the operating divisions, the division managers rarely request these corporate-level services and are seldom in a position to turn them down or limit them. Holding the division manager responsible for expenses incurred by others and over

EXHIBIT I.   Operating Statement.

NOT This

	Division I	Division II	Corporate
Sales	20,000,000	40,000,000	60,000,000
Less: Cost of Sales	14,000,000	32,000,000	46,000,000
Manufacturing Profit	6,000,000	8,000,000	14,000,000
Division Selling and Administrative Expense	1,000,000	1,000,000	2,000,000
Corporate Administrative Expense	3,000,000	6,000,000	9,000,000
Advertising Expense	833,333	1,166,667	2,000,000
Total Expenses	4,833,333	8,166,667	13,000,000
Pre-Tax Profit	1,166,667	(166,667)	1,000,000

BUT This

	Division I	Division II	Corporate
Sales	20,000,000	40,000,000	60,000,000
Less: Cost of Sales	14,000,000	32,000,000	46,000,000
Manufacturing Profit	6,000,000	8,000,000	14,000,000
Division Selling and Administrative Expense	1,000,000	1,000,000	2,000,000
Product Advertising	500,000	500,000	1,000,000
Total Divisional Expense	1,500,000	1,500,000	3,000,000
Division Contribution to Overhead and Profit	4,500,000	6,500,000	11,000,000
Corporate Advertising			1,000,000
Corporate Administrative Expense			9,000,000
Corporate Level Expense			10,000,000
Pre-Tax Profit			1,000,000

Moral: Don't allocate expenses to units that don't control the expenses.

which he exercises little influence can only encourage the attitude that the "figures don't really tell the story." It is better to let Division I argue, as it might in connection with the statement in the bottom half of Exhibit I, that its operations are more important to the company because little of the corporate overhead is related to its activities than to have the accounting department enter the controversy by assigning a part of these corporate expenses to the divisions which had nothing to say when they were incurred. The financial reporting department should leave the expenses (and the revenues) where it finds them.

MAKE MEANINGFUL COMPARISONS

Relate Inputs to Outputs

It is important that the reporting system make meaningful comparisons between inputs and outputs, between costs and revenues, between effort and achievement. For the corporation as a whole, probably the most meaningful measure of performance is return on investment, the relationship between income and investment.[1] For the sales department, important comparisons include the ratio of selling expenses and sales commissions to such measures of success as total sales and gross profit. (While the ratio of selling expenses to sales is a significant indicator of the success of the sales department, it does not indicate whether it is selling the most profitable lines; therefore, a measure that takes into account the profitability of the product mix such as the ratio of selling expenses to gross profit is sometimes even more significant.) For staff departments, comparing costs to performance is often more difficult and sometimes requires adoption of a non-financial measure of performance. Thus the cost of the purchasing department may be compared to the number of purchase orders issued to find the average cost per order. Even here, financial measures of performance, measures in which both the input and the output are in monetary form, are usually possible and preferable. For example, the cost of the purchasing department may be compared with the cost of items purchased. Always present is the danger of relating costs to activities rather than costs to results. Both costs and activities relate to inputs; it is much more important to compare such inputs with the result or product of these inputs. The ratio of the cost of the purchasing department to the number of hours worked in the purchasing de-

---

[1] See Othel D. Westfall, "Use of Rate of Return on Investment," Advanced Management, January, 1958, pages 19-23; and James H. Rossell and Reuben E. Slesinger, "Rate of Return on Capital Employed," Advanced Management, September, 1959, pages 14-15, 23.

partment, for example, would not necessarily indicate that the department was becoming more efficient; the quantity of output achieved in that hour of work might also have declined. It is more important to assess results rather than effort. What was the cost per dollar of purchases, how much lower was the cost of items purchased than the list price of such items, and what trade discounts were obtained?

For some staff departments — the legal department, the public relations staff — the output is so difficult to measure or express in financial form that the use of a ratio of output to input is often not attempted. Even here, however, diligent research will disclose some meaningful measure of performance and efficiency. Government, particularly the Federal Government, is devising various measures of performance and ratios for the measure of efficiency for departments and agencies where the output is extremely intangible and difficult to identify. The problem which the corporation faces in measuring performance, particularly since performance is all directed to maximizing return on investment, should be less difficult to solve. For a public relations department, for example, measures of performance such as number of favorable mentions per dollar of cost or number of lines of newspaper devoted to corporate activities per dollar of "pr" cost, while they leave much to be desired, are better than no measure of performance.

Make Comparisons with Other Organizations, Current Budgets and Prior Periods

A ratio of output to input by itself means little. It is more important to know whether the ratio is better or worse than it was in prior periods, whether it differs favorably or unfavorably from the budget, and whether it compares favorably or unfavorably with that of other divisions and competitors.

For the overall corporate performance, a comparison is commonly made between the corporation and other corporations, particularly close competitors. To the extent that the overall goals of different corporations are comparable — particularly to the extent that corporations are in business to earn a favorable return on capital — a comparison of the rate of return earned is valid whether the comparison is with close competitors or with unrelated enterprises. If the purpose is not just to compare overall performance but also to identify some of the reasons for the differences in overall performance, it is essential that the comparisons be made with close competitors. Quite commonly, return on investment is broken into, or analyzed in terms of two other factors: the profit margin on sales and the turnover of capital.

Comparisons between actual data and budgeted data, while extremely common in many reporting systems, are only useful where the budget system has two important characteristics. First, the division or department whose results are being compared with the budgeted figures must have had a loud voice in the preparation of the budget figures. Otherwise, the executives whose operations are being appraised will shrug off unfavorable comparisons with budget by asserting that the budget officer wasn't sufficiently familiar with their operations. A second requisite of the budget system is that its adoption should be the occasion of considerable discussion and comment. Only if it receives spotlight attention when it is adopted will it reflect goals consistent with the potentials of the organizational units. If the adoption of a budget is largely a matter of filling in forms that are then filed away without comment or controversy, there is always the danger that budgets will not reflect attainable goals but will be set with a view toward providing a favorable comparison with actual figures at a later date.

Comparisons between current year's performance and prior year's performance are almost always valid and useful. Unlike comparisons with competitors, there is no question about the comparability of the organizations and little difficulty arises from diversity of accounting practices. Unlike budget comparisons, nobody can assert that prior figures represent unattainable objectives nor can they be set too low to provide a favorable comparison.

Tell Enough but Not Too Much

Financial reports should disclose all relationships that are important to the decisions made by management, but this requirement does not mean they should be honeycombed with intricate details. To illustrate an area of reporting where important relationships are often omitted, consider the typical disclosure of purchases discounts earned. To illustrate the other sin, consider next the typical type of comparison between actual and budgeted figures prepared for staff departments.

The Iceberg Report

Here's the manner in which purchases discounts are handled in many, perhaps most, income statements:

	1959	1958
Operating Income	253,000	312,000
Add: Purchases Discounts Earned	14,000	10,000
Net Income Before Tax	267,000	322,000

Statements such as this may well be characterized as iceberg reports. The purchases discounts figure is only part, and not necessarily the most important part, of the iceberg. It might appear from this statement that the amount of purchases discounts earned has increased significantly from the prior year, and that the efficiency of those responsible for paying bills within the discount period had increased significantly.

Perhaps the full picture is as follows:

	1959	1958
Purchases Discounts Earned	14,000	10,000
Purchases Discounts Lost	23,000	15,000
Purchases Discounts Available	37,000	25,000
Percent of Purchases Discounts Taken	38%	40%

From this schedule, it is apparent that the purchases discounts lost are indeed the dangerous, submerged portion of the iceberg. The purchases discounts taken are only a portion of the discounts available, and furthermore the portion has declined from 40 per cent to 38 per cent. The only reason those responsible for paying the bills of the company appeared to have done better in 1959 than in 1958 was that the discounts available from its suppliers had increased considerably. (Perhaps tightness in credit conditions had led to the offer of substantially better discount terms in an industry from which the above enterprise obtained the majority of its materials and supplies.) The income statement of this company is presenting an incomplete and misleading picture.

This misleading picture can be corrected by supplementing the income statement by the above schedule of discounts earned, lost and available, or the full disclosure can be built right into the income statement by a presentation such as the following:

		1959		1958
Operating Income		253,000		312,000
Add: Purchases Discounts				
Available	37,000		25,000	
Less: Purchases Discounts				
Lost	23,000		15,000	
Purchases Discounts				
Taken		14,000		10,000
Net Income Before Tax		267,000		322,000

Whatever the presentation, it is important that the figure for discounts taken be supplemented by either discounts lost or discounts available.[2]

---

[2] <u>Accounting Reports for Management</u>, Chapter 1 (Englewood Cliffs, N. J.: Prentice-Hall, 1957).

As long as the amortization of past costs and the careful matching of past costs with future receipts remains the principal activity of the accounting department of the modern corporation, so long will financial reports be cluttered with misleading and meaningless figures.[3]

*   *   *   *   *

CONCLUSION

Financial reporting should be a creative activity. It is intended not to implement some narrow and negative concept of "control," but to encourage positive accomplishment and to facilitate the search for new solutions to old problems. Such an objective requires creative talent, not only on the part of those who use the reports, but also on the part of those who prepare the reports. Reports that are hackneyed and stereotyped are soon filed and forgotten. Financial reports that are quick to recognize changing needs, reports that present the old figures from new points of view, reports that are not afraid to depart from fixed formats and are willing to scrap, on occasion, long-standing habits of presentation, such reports remain the subject of continuing analysis and aggressive action. Until recently, American homes were rectangular in shape, divided into numerous rectangular rooms by walls, and with floors having only one level. In recent years, homes have been built in spherical shapes, with little or no division into rooms, and with floors of various levels. These modern homes have provided beauty and comfort unknown to the home owners of former years. Similar experimentation is almost unknown in financial reporting. Couldn't financial reporting serve new needs and provide new insights into American business if it experimented with the monetary unit, if it sometimes scrapped old formats, and if it sometimes scrapped the traditional financial statements in favor of statements designed to meet new needs?

---

[3] I recently proposed a new approach to accounting that would not involve this detailed matching of costs and revenues. See, "Industrial Accounting," Accounting Review, July, 1959, pages 415-428. It involves no depreciation accounting and no inventory pricing.

22 THE CRISIS IN CORPORATE CONTROLS

by Scott Nicholson

"Knowledge," wrote Francis Bacon, "is power." As American business continues to decentralize, executives at the highest levels of industry are coming more and more to realize the truth of Bacon's statement. The more decentralized a company grows, the more difficulty the president generally has in finding out what is going on. Yet without this knowledge he can hardly hope to exercise his power in the most effective way.

Adding to the difficulty, the problem cannot be solved simply by doing away with decentralization. As most executives agree, the $300-million or more (annual sales) company of today, with its global sprawl and its far-flung divisions, can operate effectively only through a decentralized structure.

The resulting dilemma is described by Frederick Stahl, president of Standard Research Consultants. "To say that the president of a giant corporation wants more control," says Stahl, "does not mean that he wants to reverse the progress achieved over the past ten years through delegation and divisional autonomy. What he wants is the knowledge that he's on top of the job, not blindly rubber-stamping programs that come to him for approval."

But can this crisis in control — as it has quite literally become in many companies — be resolved? Finding the answer has become one of the most compelling of company projects these days. On every side corporations are attempting to set up what might be called a centralized-decentralized system of control built around a kind of two-way channel: fast, thorough reporting of facts to the president, and an effective system for carrying his orders back to divisions.

To do that, corporations are strengthening their central corporate staffs, sharpening their committee procedures and trying

Reprinted from Duns Review & Modern Industry, July, 1963, pages 38-39, 61-62, by permission of the publisher.

to improve the quality of their field reports. And they also are taking a new, hard look at those areas where information tends to be the most obscure, such as in the forward-planning phases of R&D, engineering and market forecasting.

From this reassessment already has come one notable reversal in the management power structure of recent years. Where the man in the field was operating with virtual (sometimes real) autonomy, this new era in organization is seeing the rise of the specialist back at corporate headquarters. The staff man is receiving far more authority than he had, and his numbers are being increased both by the creation of new staff assignments and by the return to headquarters of many activities formerly handled in the field.

The staff now is taking back, in fact, the reins of power that it had been losing to the division. Secretary Keith F. Kennedy of Reigel Paper Co. believes that this is the one strongly developing trend in management today. The corporate specialist is beginning to share command with the division manager, whose service group corresponds to the specialty of the headquarters man.

This changing of the corporate guard already has taken place in scores of companies. At General Tire & Rubber and Cluett-Peabody, by way of example, certain staff specialists now hold the power of line authority over their counterparts in the divisions. Similarly, Johns-Manville's marketing director now has the authority to command information from the divisional sales office — a far-reaching and radical change, as any marketing man will attest.

Still other companies are making similar moves on the organizational chessboard. Alco Products, for example, has recentered the functions of product planning and market forecasting, taking those jobs away from the field and turning them over to its corporate staff. Reigel Paper, going a step further, has eliminated some staffs in its divisions entirely, with their work now being handled by people at headquarters. And the Interchemical Corp. has formed a capital additions committee to approve all expenditures over even so small a minimum as $1,000.

Given that mushrooming of power at headquarters, it is not at all surprising that some entirely new functions are cropping up at the staff level. Significantly, many of them revolve around the flow of information. One proliferating breed, for example, is the technical information officer, whose job is to keep abreast of the details and status of engineering projects and keep the entire management team advised of them in language that business executives (as opposed to engineers) can understand. Other new staff roles include information retrieval specialists and advisors on product engineering coordination and automation.

Not all of these drives to keep management abreast of its scattered divisions, it should be noted, are effective. Some, in fact, actually hurt. In the instruments industry, for example, there is a widely disseminated joke about the company that delivers a monthly operating report to 32 of its key executives each month. Seemingly a worthwhile project, the report contains 12,000 separate figures — far more than any one executive can assimilate.

Sash A. Spencer of McKinsey & Co. of New York refers to such reports as "encyclopedic reporting" and notes that they are designed to cover up the lack of a true informational system. "Many divisions," Spencer goes on, "deliver tomes about their operations. Such masses of detail convert the president into a high-priced clerk, forced to sift through volumes of paper to find the bits of information that are important to him. On the other hand he may not bother, and this costs even more."

In some cases, of course, the president has merely become a victim of progress. As Martin Schwab, vice president of United Merchants & Manufacturers, succinctly explains: "Machines provide more information than people can assimilate."

The trick, of course, is to get just the right information to the president in quantities that he can digest. This is not always done. As Chairman Burl S. Watson of Cities Service once confessed, his reading during the course of the business year amounts to 1.5 million words, the equivalent of reading the Bible twice.

To cut down on this "bible reading," virtually all companies are permitting the division manager to report by exception; that is, to report only those matters that are at variance with routine. While this cuts down on headquarters reading, the practice does have a built-in danger. Most managers prefer to report only favorable exceptions, omitting the looming troubles which they know will require explanations — and which they hope eventually to lick.

Division operating balances, to be sure, do not fall under the "exception" rule. They are invariably complete and factual. And few company presidents have any trouble obtaining a clear picture of divisional sales, earnings, inventories, new orders and expenses along with comparisions of the year before and amounts budgeted.

Even here, though, management is trying to cut down on the size. At Daystrom (where, as one evidence of the shift in corporate power, Controller Russell E. Norem can remove divisional finance officers), reports have been drawn up so that they emphasize return on investment. Daystrom has drawn up the formula for that figure in a way that allows President John B. Montgomery to peer closely at all the elements that make up the final profit.

Thus Daystrom's formula for return on investment is computed by using earnings as a percent of sales multiplied by turnover. By using this formula, the company isolates the separate effects of earnings, sales and turnover. Thus earnings as a percent of sales reflects the division manager's success (or lack of it) in keeping a satisfactory lid on costs. And turnover measures his success in parlaying the capital entrusted to him into sales volume.

While such formulas undoubtedly cut down on chief executive reading, Norem himself puts his finger on their weakness. In so doing, he also points up the second big informational need of top management. "The controller's facts," Norem observes, "are historical; they leave the president in the stern of the boat saying, 'Hey, look at the rocks we just missed.'" In other words, the data which a controller normally gathers is not of much use in the forward-planning areas of market forecasting, research and engineering.

United Merchants and Manufacturers' Schwab puts the problem in slightly finer perspective. "Operating balances are fine as far as they go," he observes, "but they fail to spot weaknesses in the division's planning efforts, where the key decisions are being made."

Gradually, industry is working out this problem in a way already mentioned: by bringing more power back to headquarters. At the Ruberoid Co., for example, divisional sales forecasts are sent to the corporate marketing vice president, who studies them, compares them to the general economic forecasts assembled by the corporate office and keeps Ruberoid's President Ernest J. O'Leary thoroughly abreast of them. Similarly, Ruberoid's Vice President of Operations William J. Van Akin has all the facts on manufacturing plans, plant expansion, inventories, materials and new equipment. In both cases, of course, central management can then take a hand in forward planning.

Still other companies are copying a plan worked out by Interchemical for keeping abreast of corporate developments in the all-important area of R&D. First, Interchemical requires project leaders to submit monthly and quarterly R&D progress reports that describe in detail the objectives, schedules and accomplishments of each project. Divisional laboratory managers are required to forward a copy of their own reports to the vice president of engineering on the corporate staff, who then analyzes their contents for the information needed in forward planning.

Pressures and Pipelines

At the same time, top management also has been working to get the facts earlier, both to avoid trouble and to have more time for the decisions that inevitably follow the figures. One way is through frequent management committee meetings; these create deadline pressures, and the pressures keep the pipelines flowing. At the newly resurgent Chrysler Corp., for example, half a dozen specialists are usually found working around the calendar to organize data for the weekly meetings held by President Lynn A. Townsend.

Another type of meeting, it should be noted, also plays a part in advance planning on R&D. This is the "research review." In this meeting the leaders of all R&D projects in the divisions report to the president and to one another on the status of their technical programs.

Are the reviews useful in that all-important area of forward planning? "Very much so," answers C. Stewart Hoagland of Interchemical. "The only comparable way to form a clear picture of what's going on in the lab is by an actual visit, which we also do quite frequently."

But of all the information vehicles available to management, the one receiving the sharpest scrutiny is also the most widely used: the plain, humble written report. Phillips Petroleum, General Foods and Republic Steel are only three of dozens of large corporations that are setting up special corporate offices to raise the quality of written reports. Usually their efforts at improvement center around three goals: making the reports readable, processing them faster and pruning them for brevity.

Here, again, company presidents are turning to specialists by employing technical editors for the editing skills needed at the corporate staff level. Men with ten years or more of experience in editing technical manuals are being assigned to the president's staff with the job of clarifying the mass of reports that flow to the president's desk.

In one respect, interposing an editor between the president and his divisional people is an impediment. First, a technical editor, with a necessarily limited viewpoint, may miss the significance of an important point in the report. "It creates," adds the controller of one electronics company, "a time delay. It seems to me that a faster way must be worked out to get reports to the home office within the day."

Custom-tailored Data?

One logical question: If such ways are possible, why is it that many presidents still have trouble finding out what is going on? Surprisingly, part of the answer seems to be a point largely overlooked by the men who are the most affected. It is a simple one: to do a truly effective job, data must be tailored to the individual preferences of the man who receives it.

A logical answer, yet few companies think of it. "When a new man moves into the president's spot," observes McKinsey's Sash Spencer, "companies will paint the office and change the sign on the door, the organization chart and the telephone directory. But they almost never re-examine the information with which the president is supposed to run his operation, and most of the time the new president will uncomplainingly accept the existing information as it is."

Yet even a casual glance at the top management ranks will show that just as executives operate in different fashions, they also differ in their informational needs. Yale & Towne's President Gordon Patterson, for example, stresses clear writing in the reports he receives. Celanese Corporation's Harold Blancke, in contrast, works with columns of figures rather than prose reports. And Executive Vice President Carl Holschuh of Sperry Rand sidesteps both; he finds that all the statistical information he needs each month can be obtained from twelve simplified charts.

But as companies continue to decentralize and information grows correspondingly harder to obtain, it is likely that management will begin to discover that it must look at itself as well as its information channels. For only in that way will it obtain Bacon's knowledge that leads to power.

PART SEVEN:

STAFFING

23   DO YOU WANT A WEAK SUBORDINATE?

by Lewis B. Ward

If you had to choose between two men, one courageous but not very ambitious, the other ambitious but somewhat lacking in courage, which would you rather have as a subordinate?

Again, which man would you find less desirable — a subordinate who was apathetic or one who was intolerant?

We posed 56 questions like these as part of a lengthy questionnaire on finding and developing management talent, which was completed by over 4,000 H[arvard] B[usiness] R[eview] readers — 39.9% of the cross-section polled. This high rate of return, along with the many thoughtful comments written by these administrators in anonymous replies to questions about their company practices, reflects the widespread interest in management development on the part of today's managers and executives.

*   *   *   *   *

Because the business leaders of tomorrow are being selected and trained by today's executives, we believed that it would be of interest to examine executives' views about the qualities they seek in their subordinates. Are the qualities sought by those near the top of the management ladder the same as those desired by men at lower executive levels? And are the desirable and unde-

Excerpts, reprinted from Harvard Business Review, September-October, 1961, pages 6-8, 10, 12, 14, 16, 18-20, 22, 179-182, 184, 186, 188-189, by permission of the publisher.

sirable qualities in subordinates thought to be the same by executives in various functional areas? The replies received in our survey provide some interesting evidence bearing on these and other issues relevant to this important area of management activity. Here are some of the high lights:

1. Lumping all executives together, we find a strong consensus as to what personal qualities and traits they consider to be desirable or undesirable in their subordinates.

2. Within this general agreement, individual executives differ from the majority of their colleagues in favoring this or that quality, and show tremendous variety as to which particular quality they differ on. The same holds true for the undesirable traits.

3. Analysis in depth of executives' preferences between pairs of traits or qualities reveals two general patterns. One pattern is characteristic of executives who are more likely than others to accept qualities such as "dull," "apathetic," and "retiring" in preference to "argumentative," "intolerant," and "egotistical." The second pattern is characteristic of executives who more often favor "accurate," "careful," "precise" subordinates in preference to those who are "courageous," "tolerant," and "capable."

4. Commonly held stereotypes — consisting of groups of qualities thought important in the different functional areas — show up in the answers of respondents. That is, marketing men tend to select the same group of favorable qualities and reject similar unfavorable attitudes. The same tendency holds for executives in finance, personnel, production, and so on.

5. Members of top management differ from executives at other levels mainly in their avoidance of the subordinate who falls in the trouble-maker pattern and their willingness to accept in his place a "dull," "apathetic," and "retiring" subordinate. With this exception, there seems to be little or no difference between the personal qualities desired in subordinates by members of top management and the qualities desired by executives at lower levels of responsibility.

6. Respondents agree that in deciding which college graduate to hire the most important information is class standing and field of study. Among executives in different functional areas only those in the engineering and R & D group are interested in the particular college or university attended.

7. Respondents also agree with recommendations of recent major reports on business education that 4 years of liberal arts plus 2 years of business administration training is the best preparation for a career in management. Not unnaturally, engineering and R & D executives are in favor also of 4 years of engineering plus 2 years of business administration training.

8. In advising young men on how to develop their management talents, executives in top management view harder work on the job as more important than do other respondents.

One often hears it said that business is recruiting and developing good organization men who fit in well and cause no trouble. If this is so, where will business in the future find the agressive innovator, the leader who carries his company to new heights of success? Are the qualities sought in those entering the lower ranks of management ones which will make men unfit for the top jobs?

To throw some light on this question we compared the answers given on our questionnaire by presidents and company officers with the answers given by the other executives in our sample.

Our data show no differences at all between the top-management group and other HBR respondents for most of the adjective pairs in our questionnaires. Interestingly enough, the only difference we find is small. . . . Top executives show even greater preference than do other respondents for the bashful, retiring, or apathetic subordinate as opposed to intolerant, argumentative, or rebellious individuals. . . .

One possible way of accounting for this difference was suggested by Mr. Donald Reynolds, President, Donrey Media Group:

> "Possibly a top executive doesn't really get close to his subordinate line executives. His dealings with them often are filtered through a screen of personal assistants who, more or less, carry the message. Perhaps it is these staff assistants — who are 'bashful,' 'retiring,' and 'apathetic' — that the top executives are describing as ideal subordinates. The main reason I think so is that I believe that otherwise the normal ego of the type of man who becomes a top executive would necessarily cause him to identify the subordinate he wants as a man who has most of his own qualities — or qualities, at least, that he thinks he has. And, quite frankly, most of the company presidents I know are certainly not Caspar Milquetoasts!"

A similar reluctance to accept the findings of our study was expressed by Mr. Richard E. Krafve, President, Raytheon Company. As he stated:

> "The three things I look for in a man, and in a subordinate of mine, are integrity, courage, and capability. By integrity, I mean his knowledge of what is right; and by courage, I mean his willingness to do what he knows is right. By capability, I mean his intelligence and

experience. But integrity and courage are the most important. I want a man with the 'guts' to stand up for his convictions, even when it might be impolitic to do so at the moment.

"I find it difficult to believe that some company presidents and top executives would want weak subordinates. I think you'll find that strong companies have strong executives. When you don't have strong executives, your company tends to deteriorate. Momentum will carry a company quite far, but it diminishes and disappears after a while."

* * * * *

FUNCTIONS AND PERSONALITY

There is probably no place where thinking of people in terms of personal traits or qualities is more common than in connection with jobs in different business functions. When we think of a salesman, most of us envisage someone who is energetic, personable, and popular, while the accountant brings a very different set of traits to mind. Do HBR executives think about their subordinates in similar terms? We compared the choices among adjective pairs for executives in our sample who held jobs in different functional areas. The differences we found certainly confirm the popular view of what it takes to succeed in the different functional areas.

Thus, the qualities which are more often chosen as desirable by executives in marketing [differ from those chosen by] executives in other areas. There are a few surprises in this list. Perhaps the most interesting preferences are those of an "energetic," "enterprising" subordinate over a "responsible" and "intelligent" one. Both of these choices highlight the importance of sheer energy in many sales activities.

* * * * *

As for the HBR executives working in finance, they show quite a different set of preferences as to qualities desired in subordinates. . . . The contrast between the choices of finance executives and marketing executives could hardly be more striking. Again, however, the choices closely fit the stereotype many people harbor about what a financial manager should be like.

For some reason executives in the accounting area had fewer choices which distinguished them from executives in other areas. . . . At the same time, one preference stands out here: that for "independent" over "attractive." This would seem to reflect the auditing function and the nature of public accounting activities. Otherwise accounting executives have preferences quite similar to those of finance executives.

Still another set of choices characterize the HBR executive sample in production. The qualities chosen more often than in the case of other executives reflect the dual aspects of production: (1) production control and (2) getting the job done through people. Thus, we have a greater preference for subordinates who are "precise" as well as for subordinates who are "popular" and "courageous." . . .

Executives in the HBR sample working in the labor relations and personnel area showed some of the same preferences as those working in production. In addition, however, they showed special preferences for such human-relations qualities as "tolerant," "pleasant," and "kind." We do not find great concern over qualities such as "precise" and "systematic" in this group. . . .

Next, it is not at all surprising to find engineering and R & D executives favoring such qualities as "intelligent" and "sharp-witted" more than do most other types of executives. Likewise, "foresighted" and "independent" fit our ideas of the work of R & D men. . . .

The final functional area of interest is that of general management. It is rather reassuring to find there are no choices that characterize this group as markedly different from other executives as a whole. The fact is, executives in general management have usually (but not always) come up through one of the more specialized functions, and therefore have such a conglomeration of different backgrounds that they show no shared preferences for any particular qualities. Furthermore, many of them have executives in more than one functional area reporting to them; hence, in reacting to the adjective choices they may have been trying to find a common denominator and had fewer strong preferences.

*   *   *   *   *

ADVICE TO YOUNG MANAGERS

*   *   *   *   *

Apparently HBR respondents in general agree that "his class standing" and "his degree and major field of study" are the most important details to be considered in hiring a college graduate. Least important by a considerable margin is "the college or university he attended." If these executives actually act in accordance with the way they answer this question on the survey, the result should be encouraging to the smaller, less well-known colleges and universities. At the same time, it should lessen the "pressure" on admissions at the better-known institutions, reflecting the widely held view that graduation from one of these schools is of great assistance in starting a business career.

When it comes to educational background the only differences that top executives show between their views and those at other levels are (1) a slightly less negative attitude toward a high school education as preparation for management; (2) a somewhat less negative attitude toward 5 years of liberal arts; and (3) an even greater preference for a combination of 4 years of liberal arts and 2 years of business (a majority of all groups voted for this combination as "excellent preparation." In other words, presidents and company officers had a wider range of attitude than other groups about educational preparation for a career in business management.

*   *   *   *   *

IMPLICATIONS

Our broadly ranging survey of the qualities executives want in their subordinates supports some commonly held notions about executive traits, and casts doubt on others. The pervasive effect of what social scientists call social desirability is clearly present in the thinking of our sample of executives, for example. To some degree widely recognized stereotypes exist in terms of the differing qualities desired in subordinates in the major functional areas of business. Does this tend to freeze the differences between functions?

To the extent that it may be important for a man to fit the expectation pattern of his superiors in a functional area, it may well be that some matching of the personal qualities of the man — as seen by others — with the qualities typically desired in a functional area would lead to more satisfactory or at least more pleasant job placement. On the other hand, the continuing vitality of the company may require executives to deliberately run counter to their own natural inclinations in selecting subordinates. This is a question to ponder.

The old saying that "the proof of the pudding is in the eating" is pertinent here, however. The issue is not whether executives agree in desiring these qualities in their subordinates, but rather what qualities lead to long-run successful performance in the area. Presumably executives responded to our questions in part, at least, on the basis of their experiences with many different kinds of subordinates. Yet there are too many gaps in our knowledge for us to use data of the sort reported here as a major basis for executive selection. No survey of opinions is likely to answer the question as to what personal qualities lead to success in the field of marketing, for example. Only systematic observation of the fate of many aspiring managers of differing personal qualities can really answer that kind of question.

The fact that substantial numbers of executives report such traits as "retiring," "dull," and "apathetic" to be less undesirable than "irritable," "argumentative," and so on, raises again the question of the importance of conformity in the life of an organization. Is the generally intense dislike for the trouble maker a sign of danger? The results of our survey merely raise this question — they do not answer it.

The comment of Frederick R. Kappel, President of the American Telephone and Telegraph Company, in talking to this year's graduating class at Rensselaer Polytechnic Institute about the kind of manager a vital business enterprise needs, is pertinent here:

> "Judgment, imagination, sensitivity to the life around one, clear perceptions of just what problems are and how to attack them — these are the major factors that will distinguish professional achievement. These, and courage also, because after all the available facts are assembled and all the data evaluated, they will still not add up to the answer. It is the manager himself who must decide, and in so doing risk his reputation and career."

But this is not the attitude that executives revealed to us. They may _want_ to feel this way, but _do_ they? _Should_ they?

An interesting note to end on comes from the comments of Charles N. Brennecke, Director — Management Selection and Training Procedures, John Hancock Mutual Life Insurance Company:

> "What sort of a man are we looking for as a manager? Well, this is hard to put into words. At present I think we rely a lot on the test of experience. We look for a man who has survived his share of tough knocks, has had a variety of experiences. Counterbalancing this, we look for an ability to break away from old routines, to welcome new experiences.
>
> "Some day, when we find out more about how management works, maybe we will change our sights. Who knows, we might even decide we should look for someone more docile, more oriented toward his boss. But I hope not."

24 THE EFFECT OF MEASUREMENTS ON MANAGEMENT PRACTICES

by Rensis Likert

Two generalizations emerge from the results which have been examined . . . :

1. The supervisors and managers in American industry and government who are achieving the highest productivity, lowest costs, least turnover and absence, and the highest levels of employee motivation and satisfaction display, on the average, a different pattern of leadership from those managers who are achieving less impressive results. The principles and practices of these high-producing managers are deviating in important ways from those called for by present-day management theories.

2. The high-producing managers, whose deviations from existing theory and practices are creating improved procedures, have not yet integrated their deviant principles into a theory of management. Individually, they are often clearly aware of how a particular practice of theirs differs from generally accepted methods, but the magnitude, importance, and systematic nature of the differences when the total pattern is examined do not appear to be recognized.

[These generalizations raise] a perplexing question. The data reported present a consistent pattern and lead to the same general conclusions. If this pattern is so consistent, why is it that the majority of supervisors, managers, and top company officers have not arrived at these same conclusions based on their own experience?

The answer lies in the inadequacy of the measurement processes used by most companies. These processes leave large gaps in the amount and kind of information available to company

---

executives. Virtually all companies regularly secure measurements dealing with end results, such as production, sales, profits, and percentages of net earnings to sales. The accounting procedures reflect fairly well the level of inventories, the investment in plant and equipment, and the condition of plant and equipment. Most companies have a fair amount of information about the market and their share of it. Some companies have continuous information as to customer reactions to their products and to competing products.

Much less attention is given, however, to another class of variables which significantly influence the end results. These variables, seriously neglected in present measurement, reflect the current condition of the internal state of the organization: its loyalty, skills, motivations, and capacity for effective interaction, communication, and decision making. For easy reference these variables will be called intervening variables. In a few companies, experimental programs are now under way to develop measurements of these intervening variables so that the quality and performance capacity of its human organization will be revealed.

The present practice of watching closely only the level of performance of the end-result variables such as production, sales, costs, and earnings is leading to faulty conclusions as to what kinds of management and leadership yield the best results. What often confuses the situation is that pressure-oriented, threatening supervision can achieve impressive short-run results, particularly when coupled with high technical competence. There is clear-cut evidence that for a period of at least one year, supervision which increases the direct pressure for productivity can achieve, typically, significant increases in production if the operations are highly functionalized and if standard operating procedures have been established. Such increases, however, are obtained at a substantial and serious cost to the organization. (Direct pressure for increased performance does not seem to yield even short-run improvement in jobs, such as conducting research, which have not been or cannot be highly functionalized and standardized.)

* * * * *

MANAGERS' INTERPRETATION OF MEASUREMENTS

Let us look at the situation which virtually all supervisors and managers face today. The only measurement provided them are measurements of such end-result variables as productivity and costs. With only this information available and knowing that they are being appraised in terms of it, what conclusions are managers likely to draw as to the kind of leadership they should use to achieve the level of performance expected by higher management? In considering the answer to this question, it is important to keep in mind that these managers usually experience rewards and promotions for achieving high production and low costs over the short run rather than the long run. Moreover, since many managers are transferred after about two years, their attention is focused primarily on short-run results. Given these conditions, the answer is clear. If we look only at the productivity and cost data in the clerical experiment, the hierarchically controlled pattern of leadership is superior, at least for a period of one year.

The great majority of managers in charge of low-producing units and a substantial proportion of managers who achieve moderately good results have reached this conclusion and have adopted an authoritarian style of leadership.

In using this method of leadership, managers may be worried from time to time by seeing the absence and turnover in their units become greater than they wish. And they may be concerned by the high scrap loss in their departments and the excessive attention to inspection and quality control required for their units. They may also be disturbed by the resentment and hostility displayed by subordinates, and they may be perplexed by the higher rates of grievances, slowdowns, and similar disturbances in their units. All such developments as these may lead them to ease up from time to time on the tight controls and the threatening pressure for production. They may attribute the difficulties and hostility which they encounter to perverse human nature or the unreasonable hostility of labor leaders. But they would have little objective evidence to persuade them that their present leadership practices are inefficient and inadequate. This would be especially true in situations where their own bosses shared their views as to what leadership principles achieve the best results.

* * * * *

For this reason, if managers are to make the best use of their experience, they need measurements which will paint for them a full and accurate picture of their experience. This will not happen until the measurements which companies obtain routinely are far more extensive and complete than is now the case.

An organization's need for accurate measurements increases as it increases in size, as its investment in plant and equipment increases, and as it uses more effective but more complex forms of social organization. Crude impressions become less accurate and more out of touch with reality as size increases. Moreover, the cost of inadequate and erroneous decisions becomes greater as the organization becomes larger and the investment greater.

The clerical experiment and the subsequent discussion of the relationships between the different kinds of variables help to clarify an important research finding. The different variables such as the intervening and end-result variables need not necessarily change in the same direction (e.g., favorable) at the same time. For example, in the participative program of the clerical experiment, attitudes became more favorable while productivity was increasing. In the hierarchically controlled program, however, the opposite pattern occurred: attitudes became less favorable while productivity was increasing.

These results help to illustrate the point that widely different trends can occur among the intervening and end-result variables, depending upon the character of the causal variables. Hierarchically controlled patterns of supervision yield different trends and relationships than do participative patterns.

A second aspect of this general finding is that, at any one point in time, each of the different variables may or may not display corresponding degrees of favorableness. Thus, production may be reasonably high for a time even though relatively unfavorable attitudes exist; or at a given point in time, high productivity can be accompanied by favorable attitudes toward job-related matters; or, at certain times, there may be no relationship at all between level of productivity and the degree of favorableness of employee attitudes. To assume, as is often done, that there is or should be a simple correspondence in the relationships between the intervening and end-result variables is unwarranted. The interrelationships are much more complex than this assumption implies.

LIQUIDATING THE INVESTMENT IN THE HUMAN ORGANIZATION

Let us examine some additional reasons for measuring, periodically, all the significant variables. As was demonstrated in the hierarchically controlled program of the experiment with clerical workers, putting pressure to increase production on a well-established organization engaged in work for which performance standards can be set can yield substantial and immediate increases in productivity. This increase is obtained, however, at a cost to the human assets of the organization. In the company we studied, for example, the cost was clear: hostilities increased, there was greater reliance upon authority, loyalties declined, motivation to produce decreased while motivation to restrict production increased, and turnover increased. In other words, the quality of the human organization deteriorated as a functioning social system devoted to achieving the institution's objectives.

It costs money to hire competent personnel, to train them, and to build them into a smoothly and efficiently functioning organization. Virtually all companies today ignore these costs in their accounting and in their decisions as to the relative efficiency of different systems of management. This was true of the company in which the clerical experiment was conducted. If that company had had accounting procedures showing the investment in the human organization, it would have seen that in the two divisions in the hierarchically controlled program the value of the human organization to the company was significantly less at the end of the experimental year than at the beginning. In other words, it would have been evident that some of the increased productivity was gained actually by liquidating part of the company's investment in the human organization. The increase in productivity should have been charged with this cost.

On the other hand, had the company's accounting records reflected the value of the company's investment in the human organization in the two divisions in the participative program, the management of the company would have seen a different picture. The research data revealed that the value of this investment increased during the year. The management of the two divisions had been of such a character as to advance the productive capacity of the organization as a functioning social system: loyalties had increased, hostilities had decreased, communication was improved, decisions were better since they were based on more accurate and adequate information, and production goals and motivations to produce were increasing. Measurements of these intervening variables showed a significant improvement in these two divisions.

Unfortunately, the accounting operation of this company did not have data on the human costs and investments to make proper charges and credits to the divisions involved. If the changes in productivity levels and costs had been appropriately charged with the liquidation of human assets, on the one hand, and credited with the increased human assets on the other, the financial results achieved by the two experimental programs even during the first year would have been appreciably different.

FINANCIAL REWARDS FOR LIQUIDATING INVESTMENTS

Companies are very careful not to let managers of decentralized plants show spurious profits and earnings by juggling inventory or by failing to maintain plant and equipment. Their accounting procedures measure and report regularly on inventory and on the condition of plant and equipment. "Earnings" achieved by liquidating the assets represented in the human organization are just as spurious as those achieved by liquidating the investment in the plant. Yet under present management practices, companies are encouraging their managers, by the facts used in deciding about promotions and by the formulas used to compensate them, to press unduly for immediate production, cost reduction, and similar goals, and thereby to profit personally by reducing the value of the company's investment in the human organization. Other contributing factors are job evaluations focused on the immediate contribution to earnings and profits and measurement of only the end results, which permit the liquidation to occur without the company fully realizing it.

Let us look, for example, at a series of events which often take place in a department or plant engaged in an operation where performance standards and production schedules can be set. A man is put in charge of such a plant or department knowing that he will be favorably judged and rewarded if his department achieves a high level of production. He puts a good deal of pressure on his subordinates and pushes production up. Measurement of the end-result variable indicates that he is a "fine manager." In a year or two his reputation earns him a promotion to another department, where he repeats the performance. In the meantime, hostilities have been developing in his subordinates and those below them in the organization. Just about the time that he moves on, the results of his unreasonable pressure begin to show up in decreased loyalty in the organization, lack of motivation to do a job, turnover, slowdowns, and scrap loss. The new manager reaps the fruits of the promoted manager's behavior and gains the reputation of being a "poor manager," for almost as soon as he takes over, things begin to fall apart. Sometimes the department is so relieved at getting rid of the pressure-oriented manager that they are willing to give the new manager the benefit of the doubt. Even then, however, there is usually deep-seated distrust and hostility, which handicaps him and requires years or organization rebuilding to overcome.

A solution to this undesirable sequence of events is the introduction of adequate periodic measurements of the intervening variables to reveal the current character and quality of the human organization. Estimates or impressions as to the state of these variables usually prove to be seriously inaccurate. For example, the estimates of superiors as to the expectation, perceptions, attitudes, and motivations of their subordinates usually display appreciable erros. Not only is judgment alone inaccurate, but it tends to be most inaccurate in those situations which are unsatisfactory or deteriorating.

25 THEORIES OF BUREAUCRACY

by James G. March and Herbert A. Simon

* * * * *

THE SELZNICK MODEL[1]

Where Merton emphasizes rules as a response to the demand for control, Selznick . . . emphasizes the delegation of authority. Like Merton, however, Selznick wishes to show how the use of a control technique (i.e., delegation) brings about a series of unanticipated consequences. Also, like Merton, Selznick shows how these consequences stem from the problems of maintaining highly interrelated systems of interpersonal relations.

Selznick's model starts with the demand for control made by the top hierarchy. As a result of this demand, an <u>increased delegation of authority</u> (1.14)[2] is instituted [1.14:1.1].

Delegation, however, has several immediate consequences. As intended, it increases the <u>amount of training in specialized competences</u> (1.15) [1.15:1.14]. Restriction of attention to a relatively small number of problems increases experience within these limited areas and improves the employee's ability to deal with these problems. Operating through this mechanism, delegation tends to decrease the <u>difference between organizational goals and achievement</u> (1.16) [1.16:1.15], and thus to stimulate more

---

[1]The following is a discussion of the Selznick and Gouldner models of bureaucracy; it makes up the larger part of a section entitled "Theories of Bureaucarcy," which begins with a discussion of Max Weber's ideas, followed by one of R.K. Merton's. — Ed.

[2]The numbers in parentheses and brackets refer to numbered blocks in the chart diagrams. — Ed.

Excerpts, reprinted from <u>Organizations</u> (New York: John Wiley & Sons, Inc., 1958), pages 40-47, by permission of the Publisher.

delegation [1.14:1.16]. At the same time, however, delegation results in departmentalization and an increase in the <u>bifurcation of interests</u> (1.17) among the subunits in the organization [1.17:1.14]. The maintenance needs of the subunits dictate a commitment to the subunit goals over and above their contribution to the total organizational program. Many individual needs depend on the

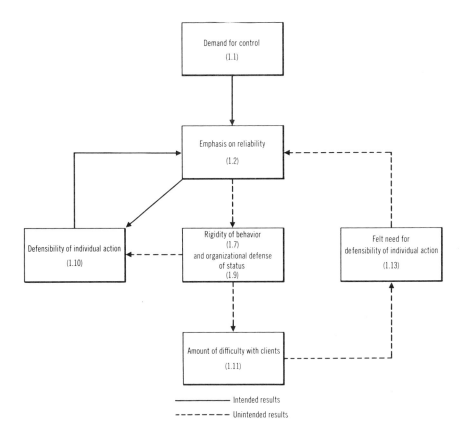

FIG. 1.2   The Simplified Merton Model.

continued success and even expansion of the subunit. As in the previous example, the activities originally evaluated in terms of the organization goals are seen to have additional important ramifications for the subunits.

Bifurcation of interests is also stimulated by the specialized training that delegation (intendedly) produces. Training results in increased competence and, therefore, in increased <u>costs of changing personnel</u> (1.18) [1.18:1.15] and this results, in turn, in further differentiation of subunit goals [1.17:1.18].

The bifurcation within the organization leads to increased conflict among organizational subunits (1.19) [1.19:1.17]. As a consequence, the content of decisions (1.20) made within the organization depends increasingly upon considerations of internal strategy, particularly if there is little internalization of organizational goals by participants (1.21) [1.20:1.19, 1.21]. As a result there is an increase in the difference between organizational goals and achievement [1.16:1.20] and this results in an increase in delegation [1.14:1.16]. (The general subject of intraorganizational conflict is discussed elsewhere.)

This effect on daily decisions is accentuated by two other mechanisms in Selznick's system. The struggle for internal control not only affects directly the content of decisions, but also causes greater elaboration of subunit ideologies (1.22) [1.22:1.19]. Each subunit seeks success by fitting its policy into the official doctrine of the large organization to legitimize its demands. Such a tactic increases the internalization of subgoals by participants (1.23) within subunits [1.23:1.22].

At the same time, the internalization of subgoals is reinforced by a feedback from the daily decisions it influences. The necessity for making daily decisions creates a system of precedents. Decisions depend primarily on the operational criteria provided by the organization, and, among these criteria, subunit goals are of considerable importance [1.20:1.23]. Precedents tend to become habitual responses to the situations for which they are defined as relevant and thus to reinforce the internalization of subunit goals [1.23:1.20]. Obviously, internalization of subgoals is partially dependent on the operationality of organizational goals (1.24). By operationality of goals, we mean the extent to which it is possible to observe and test how well goals are being achieved. Variations in the operationality of organizational goals affect the content of daily decisions [1.20:1.24] and thus the extent of subunit goal internalization.

From this it is clear that delegation has both functional and dysfunctional consequences for the achievement of organizational goals. It contributes both to their realization and to their deflection. Surprisingly, the theory postulates that both increases and decreases in goal achievement cause an increase in delegation. Why does not normal learning occur here? The answer seems to be that when goals are not achieved, delegation is — within the framework of the "machine" model — the correct response, and the model does not consider alternatives to simple delegation. On the other hand, the model offers explicitly at least two "dampers" that limit the operation of the dysfunctional mechanisms. As is indicated in Figure 1.3, where the skeleton of the Selznick model is outlined, there are two (not entirely independent) variables treated as independent but potentially amenable to organizational control, each of which restrains the runaway features of daily decision-making. By suitable changes in the extent to which organizational goals are operational or in the internalization of organizational goals by participants, some of the dysfunctional effects of delegation can be reduced. (To be sure, this ignores

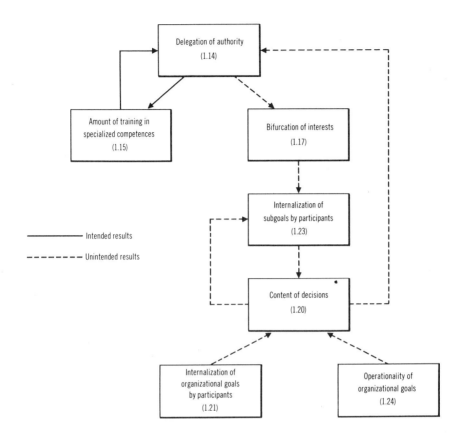

FIG. 1.3.   The Simplified Selznick Model.

the possible effect of such procedures on the maintenance problems of the subunits and the consequent results for the larger organizations, but these are problems we are not prepared to attack at the moment.)

THE GOULDNER MODEL

In terms of number of variables and relations, Gouldner's model . . . is the simplest of the three presented here; but it exhibits the major features of the two previous systems. Like Merton, Gouldner is concerned with the consequences of bureaucratic rules for the maintenance of organization structure. Like both

Merton and Selznick, he attempts to show how a control technique designed to maintain the equilibrium of a subsystem disturbs the equilibrium of a larger system, with a subsequent feedback on the subsystem.

In Gouldner's system, the use of general and impersonal rules (1.25) regulating work procedures is part of the response to the demand for control from the top hierarchy [1.25:1.1]. One consequence of such rules is to decrease the visibility of power relations (1.26) with the group [1.26:1.25]. The visibility of authority differences within the work group interacts with the extent to which equality norms are held (1.27) to affect the legitimacy of the supervisory role (1.28) [1.28:1.26, 1.27]. This, in turn, affects the level of interpersonal tension (1.29) in the work group [1.29:1.28]. In the American culture of egalitarian norms, decreases in power visibility increase the legitimacy of the supervisory position and therefore decrease tension within the group.

Gouldner argues that these anticipated consequences of rule-making do occur, that the survival of the work group as an operating unit is substantially furthered by the creation of general rules, and that consequently the use of such rules is reinforced [1.25:1.29].

At the same time, however, work rules provide cues for organizational members beyond those intended by the authority figures in the organization. Specifically, by defining unacceptable behavior, they increase knowledge about minimum acceptable behavior (1.30) [1.30:1.25]. In conjunction with a low level of internalization of organizational goals, specifying a minimum level of permissible behavior increases the disparity between organization goals and achievement by depressing behavior to the minimum level [1.16:1.21, 1.30].

Performance at the minimum level is perceived by hierarchical superiors as a failure. In short, the internal stabilizing effects of the rules are matched by the unbalance they produce in the larger organization. The response to the unbalance is an increase in the closeness of supervision (1.31) over the work group [1.31:1.16]. This response is based on the "machine" model of human behavior: low performance indicates a need for more detailed inspection and control over the operation of the "machine."

In turn, however, close supervision increases the visibility of power relations within the organization [1.26:1.31], raises the tension level in the work group, and thereby upsets the equilibrium originally based on the institution of rules. The broad outline of the model is shown in Figure 1.4.

Gouldner's model leaves some puzzles unexplained. In particular, why is increased supervision the supervisory response to low performance? It seems reasonable that the tendency to make such a response is affected both by role perceptions and by a third equilibrating process in the system — the individual needs of the supervisors. Thus, the intensity of supervision is a function

of the <u>authoritarianism</u> of supervisors (1.32) and a function of the
<u>punitivity of supervisory role perception</u> (1.33) [1.31:1.32, 1.33].

As in the Selznick model, the existence of "dampers" on the
system poses the question of their treatment as external varia-

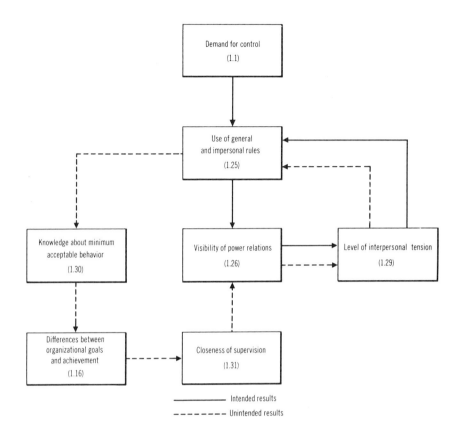

FIG. 1.4.   The Simplified Gouldner Model.

bles. Appropriate manipulation of equality norms, perceived
commonality of interest, and the needs of supervisors will restrict the operation of the dysfunctional features of the system.
The failure of top management to use such techniques of control
suggests that the system may be incompletely defined.

PROBLEMS OF VERIFICATION

We have sketched three major "models" of bureaucratic behavior. To what extent are the hypotheses empirically verified?
Both Selznick and Gouldner base their propositions on extended

observations of single organizations in the field. The data on which Merton relies are somewhat less specific but appear to be distilled from a set of generally accepted characterizations of organizational behavior.

Such evidence raises two major problems. First, what is the role of field research in verifying hypotheses about organizational behavior? The field situation fails to meet many of the major assumptions underlying standard techniques of statistical inference. The second problem is distinctly related to the first. What is the standing of the single case as evidence? For example, one of the knottier complications in this area is deciding what the sample size really is.

At least some of the propositions advanced by these three writers will be re-examined below in different contexts. Some hypotheses relating the closeness of supervision to employee satisfaction are considered later in the present chapter, and some hypotheses concerning organizational conflict can be found elsewhere. As we will suggest in those passages, there is evidence for some of the propositions over and above the single field studies discussed here. The evidence is scarcely conclusive and far from complete, but on the whole tends to be consistent with the general models used by Merton, Selznick, and Gouldner. What little we can say beyond that is indicated below.

IMPLICATIONS OF THE BUREAUCRACY MODELS

Other quite comparable models could be added to those examined here. Bendix . . . has discussed limits on technical rationality within an organization and pointed out the intriguing complications involved in the use of spy systems as systems of control. Dubin . . . has presented a model quite similar to that of Merton. Blau . . . has examined the changes in operating procedures that occur at a relatively low level in the hierarchy under the pressure of work group needs.

In the sample of three cases from the "bureaucracy" literature we have presented (as well as in the others mentioned), complications arise in each of the three ways predicted from the influence model outlined previously. The elaboration of evoking connections, the presence of unintended cues, and organizationally dysfunctional learning appear to account for most of the unanticipated consequences with which these theories deal.

Many of the central problems for the analysis of human behavior in large-scale organizations stem from the operation of subsystems within the total organizational structure. The sociological studies of the work group analyzed here have focussed on the ways in which the needs of individuals, the primary work group, and the large organization interact to affect each other. We now turn to the study of morale and productivity, where we also find that the study of the psychology of work has focussed on the same interactions, with perhaps a greater emphasis on the relations between the needs of individual personalities and the needs of the organization.

26 DELEGATE BY THE RESULTS YOU EXPECT

by Edward C. Schleh

When we say delegate by results expected we mean: State what you <u>want done</u>, rather than what people <u>should do.</u> But this must be carried all the way down through the whole company. An executive wants to make sure that people under him are delegating responsibilities in this way at every level.

If this is not done, people will be carrying on a lot of activities; but they won't be getting as much done as they could. In addition, what they do get done may not be aiming at the company goals.

When an executive sets over-all goals for the people directly under him, in a broad sense he is delegating by the results he expects. This thinking should be carried further, however.

<u>First</u> of all, the broader goals should be broken down into the sub-results that you expect from the people directly under you.

<u>Secondly</u>, these sub-results should be broken down, in turn, for the people under them. Every man should know what is expected of him in order to do a real job. And he should know beforehand.

If you want to get the best results from people, (1) state <u>what</u> you expect, (2) <u>when</u> you expect it, and (3) from <u>whom</u> you expect it.

In order to do this, use this rule on supervision:

> It is the supervisor's responsibility to make sure that his people know what is expected of them. In no way can a supervisor dodge this responsibility.

Edward C. Schleh, <u>Successful Executive Action.</u> © 1955. Reprinted by permission of Prentice-Hall, Inc., Englewood Cliffs, N. J.

If you make sure that this rule is followed, you will have taken a major step in welding an organization that works toward a common goal. This helps develop leaders all the way down the line. You can see that it makes the supervisor take the lead. It doesn't let him "pass the buck" down if someone under him hasn't understood what was expected of him.

Delegating by results gives a basis for a "live" compensation plan — a compensation plan based on the results that you expect from a man. In other words, delegate by results and let people know what the results are that you expect. Then carry through and pay them according to whether or not they accomplish these results.

You can tie in a realistic employee-appraisal plan, rating the employee on whether he accomplishes the results that you expect from his job. If this appraisal plan is carried all the way down the line, you know that people are working in the right direction. There is an accountability at every level for working toward the goals that you set.

In the first place, remember that delegations come from an executive down to the people under him. These delegations are parcelled out by them, in turn, to their people, and so on down the line. . . .

In other words, the top man has the full responsibility for all accomplishment. He, in turn, divides this responsibility into parts. He delegates these parts to the people under him. They, in turn, divide these parts further and delegate. All delegations must be part of the responsibility of the man at the top. . . .

However, if you want to get the most value from a man, you have to interpret these results expected from the point of view (and I emphasize from the point of view) of the man on the job. The results expected should be shown to lead to the results of the man above.

In other words, at the very lowest level in the company, all the results expected of a man or a woman should lead to the results expected of the job above. This progression should hold on up the line to the very top of the organizational echelon. Anything that does not lead to the results expected of a man's boss should be cut out. . . .

It is usually helpful if the results are written down. . . . It is hard to get an agreement verbally between two people that seems to hold the same meaning permanently. People forget. . . .

These descriptions of the results expected should point up horizons. They should point up over-all limits but provide as broad a latitude as possible in getting results. Allow a man to strive to the very limit of his capacity to do the best job he can for the company.

On the other hand, you must guard against overlap with other people's responsibilities. Strangely enough, overlapping doesn't always cause the trouble you might expect with the people reporting directly to the executive. In actual practice, it is often cleared up through normal face-to-face contacts. The trouble occurs between people two or three levels down because they aren't sure if or where overlapping of responsibility is taking place.

Descriptions of the results expected should state the key relationships between people. There are always places where a man is doubtful as to how far he should work with someone else. If this point isn't made clear, he often makes wrong guesses that retard his work.

The executive who makes sure that results are well defined up and down the line finds it easier to get things done. People seem to assume responsibilities better. If you don't write them out, you will still want to insist that every supervisor and executive review with each man under him the results he expects.

The executive has much to gain from making certain that the results expected of every job are well understood up and down the organization. This procedure sets up the foundation for over-all administration. It gives him a means for carrying out any of the work or any of the programs that he feels he needs.

If you don't define the results that you expect of every job, you find very often that people do a lot of work but "things do not get done." In other words, people are working at "activities" instead of working toward accomplishment. It is often easy for a man to be working steadily, doing a great deal of work, and yet accomplishing little for the company. He is spinning his wheels with a great flurry of activity but producing little of value to the company.

I am reminded of a research engineer in a food processing plant. He had worked for three years on various projects and seemed to be working all the time. He seemed to be working on very important projects, too. Yet, in the three years, no worthwhile project was finished and turned over to the sales department to improve the product line.

Right alongside of him, another research engineer was working on essentially the same kinds of projects. In spite of the fact that his boss had not set goals, this man had set them for himself. He had decided that he had to turn out products for the sales department. In the same three years he contributed five major items to the line.

When the research head reviewed these two people, he recognized the error. He sat down with the first research engineer and explained very carefully what was expected of him. In fact, he held back a raise because no real accomplishment had been made. In the next year this research engineer brought to a head three of the items on which he was working and turned them over to the sales department.

You fix accountability — an essential of good administration — when you set up results expected. You prevent people from "passing the buck." People take personal responsibility for results or lack of them. This personal responsibility is the very crux of administration. Anyone who takes authority must, by implication, always assume accountability. He must "take it on the chin" if things go wrong.

By fixing a responsibility you tend to develop in your staff people broader thinking concerning their accountability. For example, a training director in a chemical plant had carried on quite a few programs. He felt that he was accomplishing big things for the company because he had all these programs going.

His boss sat down with him and told him, "Unless your training results in improved efficiency, better production, or more results from the line people, you're doing little."

He then reviewed his whole program in this light. He actually cut out two-thirds of it, revised the other third, set up records on it, and was able to make a much greater contribution to the company at a lower cost.

Every job, no matter what it is, needs some kind of standard. But you can't set up standards for a job until you know what results you expect from it. Deciding the results you expect from a job leads you to standards of performance for it.

It is hard to make a realistic appraisal of a man until you have set some kind of standard. It gives the man incentive toward accomplishment when there is a standard of performance and he knows what it is. . . .

A standard does not necessarily have to be a strict objective record in so many units per hour. Simply ask yourself, "What accomplishment do we expect from this job? What do we expect it to do for us?" This appraisal should automatically lead to some kind of over-all standard. To keep these standards alive, it is a good idea to consider changing them each year in line with any changes in company or job objectives. Some examples of pinpointing standards of performance are shown in Figure 1.

Sometimes people on staff jobs say that you can't set up standards for their jobs. . . . In a sense, aren't they saying, "We are not expected to accomplish anything for the company"? There shouldn't be any job in the company that is not expected to add, in its way, to the over-all welfare of the company. In actual practice it is surprising how often you can set a standard (even though it is rough) for staff jobs.

Ask "Why did we set up this job? What is it supposed to do for us?"

Sometimes, when you do this, you find that many staff jobs just have no place in the organization. They shouldn't have been there to start with.

The right arm of any executive is often a good control system. Let's look at it as a control of men, rather than a group of control records sent up to top management for review. What do we mean by control of men? Simply this: The control should be

FIG. 1. Set Definite Standards of Performance.

Don't Say:	Say Instead:
Decrease costs.	Cut X line costs 5 per cent in six months.
Improve sales effort.	Get 25 per cent of sales potential.
Improve sales effectiveness.	Increase average sales profit by 15 per cent in one year.
Get more efficient production.	Increase output per man-hour by 10 per cent.
Get less waste.	Cut waste to 4 per cent average.
Improve inspection.	Cut rejects to .1 per cent.
Develop cost records.	Eliminate cost deviations over 5 per cent.
Improve employee selection.	Keep duds below 15 per cent.
Train new employees properly.	Cut training time to one-half.
Keep new products coming through.	Have X product on the market by (date).

used to encourage men up and down the line to do their best and do it in the right direction. The control should show whether or not the men are getting the results expected of their jobs.

You can see that first you have to decide what results the men are accountable for.

The control should show whether or not there are deviations from what is expected. If these are reviewed with the man, he knows whether or not he has accomplished the result expected of him. But if there isn't a clear understanding of the results expected in the first place, this is hard to do.

*   *   *   *   *

Some firms have felt that they would rather not define the results expected. Instead, let "the cream come to the top." In some cases it may be true that the cream comes to the top. You might get a great deal of sour milk along with this cream, however.

It's surprising how often this cream is merely a good politician or a good talker. The "rising cream" philosophy often forces everybody to be a terrific salesman of himself, a braggart. This can go through the whole company. Perhaps that works well in certain kinds of companies. In a firm that must blend good production methods, down-to-earth planning, live statistical work, farsighted research, and so on, it may actually disrupt the work of the whole company.

I know of a hard goods firm that had followed the "rising cream" philosophy. In the course of about ten years the indirect office staff almost doubled compared to sales volume. Since sales increased in this period, you would expect the office staff to have increased, but it should not have increased more than sales did. There should have been increased efficiency with greater volume.

*   *   *   *   *

27 HOW TO STAY ON TOP OF THE JOB

by James C. Harrison, Jr.

Think of four executives you know. How many of them delegate responsibility to a subordinate the same way you do? One?
Two? More than likely, <u>none</u> of them does.

Styles of delegation can range all the way from the executive
who turns over an assignment carte blanche, to the executive who
treats his subordinate as an "assistant to," giving him a minimum of authority and responsibility. To be sure, most executives
are familiar with and probably share the common business tenet
that "the delegation of responsibility for performance should
never be conferred without the delegation of authority for directing the performance." But what about the act of delegation itself?
Specifically:

1. How much responsibility can an executive delegate to a
    subordinate?
2. When delegation proves unfruitful, can an executive excuse
    himself by placing the blame on the delegated-to subordinate?
3. Does the delegating executive have equal responsibility for
    the failure?
4. If so, how can an executive use delegation to reduce the de-
    mands on his time, develop his subordinates, and still keep
    on top of every job?
5. In sum, what do executives really mean by the word <u>delegation</u>?

The plain fact is that some executives are able to use delegation successfully and others are not. And the differences in practice that go to make up delegation undoubtedly relate to the

Excerpts, reprinted from <u>Harvard Business Review</u>, Novem-
ber-December, 1961, pages 100-108, by permission of the
publisher.

indication that there is a good deal of confusion among executives as to exactly what delegation is.[1]

[AN EXAMPLE]

I happened to be present when a company president called a hurried conference with his staff following a meeting of the firm's board of directors. The board had been very critical of a recent decline in sales and profits, and had strongly intimated to the president that the fault lay not in the capabilities of the staff but in a lack of energetic application of their talents. The president concluded his post-mortem with this admonishment:

> "I don't intend to subject myself to such humiliation again. You men are paid to do your jobs; it's not up to me to do them for you. I don't know how you spend your time, and I don't intend to try to find out. You know your responsibilities, and these figures bear out that you haven't discharged them properly. All I can say, men, is that if the next report doesn't show a marked improvement, I can't guarantee that all of us in this room will be together when another conference of this nature takes place."

* * * * *

[Notice that] the humiliated company president's interpretation does not include follow-up: "I don't know how you spend your time. I don't intend to try to find out." This is delegation in the extreme: interim relinquishment of participation. He interprets the word delegation to allow him to shed not only the burden of responsibility, by his manner of delegation, but also the mantle of leadership. He makes no attempt to stay on top of the job; he wants only to get out from under it.

Yet the company president undoubtedly does not believe that he is shirking his duties. . . .

* * * * *

---

1 To illustrate his point, the author gives two opposite examples of delegation: one where the head executive, while delegating specific powers and responsibilities to subordinates, strives personally to "keep on top of," or maintain steady surveillance over the employment of those powers; and the other where he allows their employment to occur independent of any central control. The passages reprinted here include chiefly those dealing with the second kind of delegation. — Ed.

Webster's New International Dictionary defines delegation as the "act of delegating, or investing with authority to act for another." But what is meant by "investing with authority"? Here is the root of the problem.

The key semantic, and consequently behavioral, difficulty arises in defining what degree of authority and what type of behavior are to be invested. For the amount of power or the kind of power to be given is not an inherent or specified part of the written definition. Rather, the degree of authority is dependent on the extent to which a person is allowed to substitute one behavior for another. And this is usually — in daily business practice — a matter of subjective interpretation and operating behavior on the part of the delegator.

*   *   *   *   *

SCOPE OF OBLIGATION

The decisive answer . . . to the confusion over the meaning of delegation, is one word: accountability. An executive can delegate responsibility, that is, obligation. He can hold another person accountable to him as the delegator of responsibility to do a certain job. But this act by no means diminishes the measure of his own accountability to his own superiors. He can no more divorce himself from this liability than he can excuse himself from blame in the event of his subordinate's failure, or take full credit for the success. The executive himself, not his subordinate, possesses the full obligation.

Thus, in every single act of delegating there are two sets of correlative and equal responsibilities: (1) the obligations which the delegate has to his principal, and (2) the obligations for which the principal is accountable to those whom he represents.

The obligation in the principal's case is not solely that of setting action in motion, such as by assigning the work to his subordinate. Far from it. His responsibility is for final results, irrespective of the style or type of delegation he uses. The same holds true for his subordinate if the latter in turn delegates the job to his own assistant.

A president, for example, is a delegate of his board of directors assigned to the task of increasing sales and profits. He, in turn, since this assignment is no one-man job, delegates specific aspects of this responsibility to members of his staff. Because of this delegation, they are obligated to him to produce the desired results. However — and this is the emphatic point — he cannot delegate to them his accountability to the board; this is his and his alone.

Nor can his assistants delegate to their assistants their accountability to the president. The proper discharge of their responsibilities will pay off the obligation he imposed on them, but a failure on their part will not make the president blameless for the outcome as far as the board is concerned. His assignment may have been more than a one-man job, but his accountability for its successful completion is a one-man burden. Only the labors can be shared.

Keeping on Top

If one must delegate and yet retain full accountability for the results, then some sort of supervision is necessary. How can a busy executive keep on top of every job he must turn over to others? The ease that an executive will have in doing this job depends on the style of delegation he selects.

Many executives, such as the company president cited earlier, behave as if keeping on top means only that they should watch what is going on, as spectators. But in this guise a man is actually not an executive; he is not, as is demanded in his title, working through others. Rather, he has simply turned a job over to others. And he has all the confining characteristics of a helpless onlooker. He can really be an executive only when he works through others; only when they are extensions of himself; only when he is well enough informed of their efforts to protect his own accountability, to be certain of the outcome.

*   *   *   *   *

Keeping a Hand In

But to delegate and at the same time remember one's own full accountability requires self-discipline. Let me give you a very personal example. At one time I headed an advertising agency. One day there came to our door an account which was very foreign to my experience: publicizing a series of evangelistic meetings conducted by Billy Graham. On the advice of his friends, he was making his first public appearance outside his adopted home of Charlotte, North Carolina. The account was placed with our agency by a committee of local citizens whose sole responsibility to Graham consisted of engaging advertising services, setting the dates of meetings, and stipulating the amount of money to be expended on the campaign.

I knew that the head of our art department was a running mate of the members of the sponsoring committee and, realizing my own inexperience with this type of account, "delegated" the task to the artist. I dismissed the matter from my mind until Graham's business manager (whose name I have since forgotten) came into the agency prior to the first evangelistic meeting. I sent for the artist, and he showed up with layouts far more suitable as illustrations for religious works than as a mass appeal to the audience that Graham hoped to reach. Well, shamefacedly, I banished the artist along with his works to their northern-lighted quarters, and begged for another day of grace. The business manager granted it, but with some memorable parting words:

> "Mr. Harrison, may I give you a little advice? A good executive has to delegate, just as you have done in this case. And the power to delegate enables a man to multiply his abilities many times. But, in order to do this, he must learn one basic rule: to keep his hand in whatever he delegates."

Most executives do want to multiply their abilities by spreading the actual work to be done among subordinates. But to do this successfully requires that an executive remember that accountability cannot be delegated. In sum, an executive must select delegating behavior that will concurrently allow him to:

1. Spread the physical work among his aides.
2. See to it that the job is done correctly.
3. Have enough time to take corrective action should something go wrong.
4. Develop his subordinate's talents and abilities.

It is combining these four elements into practice that most executives find difficult. Yet only by selecting a style of delegation that includes these four elements can an executive keep his hand in sufficiently to protect his accountability.

AUDITING PROGRESS

But just how can an executive keep his hand in every job, considering the multiplicity of demands on his time and energies? Obviously, such limitations prevent a complete sharing of the assignment. However, time is not so short (and, in fact, cannot be) that it prevents an active participation in every delegated job.

Such participation is possible, not by supervising every detail of the job, but by periodic audits of what is going on. . . .

However, auditing, like delegation, can denote many different kinds of specific activities. So rather than fall into semantic traps, let us define auditing by looking at some methods that successful executives use to audit progress. From time to time I have observed various styles of delegation which businessmen use to protect their accountability. Each of these methods has as a goal the four elements outlined above, and stresses active executive participation in the delegated activity, giving ample opportunity for correction before it is too late.

Now I confess that in only rare instances did I find uncompromising adherence to any single one of these methods for auditing delegation. Rather, the choice of a particular device depended on the nature of the responsibility delegated. The same executive should use several of them concurrently, each for different individual assignments. Conditions, not the executives, determined the selection of a specific plan of delegation. But more about this later. First, here are the methods of delegation.

1. Previewing Direction. In this method, an executive gives his subordinate the problem and asks him to submit in writing at a specified time a synopsis of his plan of action. By this process the executive receives at the very start his subordinate's interpretation of the problem, a definite and concrete line of attack, and a detailed plan of procedure that can be corrected or adjusted.

2. Questioning on Progress. This is the most informal, the most revealing, and the most time-consuming style of delegation emphasizing executive participation. It requires that an executive send for or go to his subordinate at or during the most propitious stages of development for the project in question. This method requires deft timing and a clear attitude of friendly interest. The executive cannot risk the appearance of "checking up," lest he destroy his subordinate's self-confidence. This method is inconvenient because it requires an executive to stop work at the most inopportune moments, takes time to carry out, and interrupts the subordinate. Yet the executive does maintain a maximum grasp of what is going on.

3. Demanding Reports. This method requires that the subordinate submit periodic progress reports, with or without specific deadlines. It can be the most pleasant of all audits, since it saves the time of all concerned. Yet it can also be the least satisfying method because its effectiveness depends on the ability of the subordinate to express himself in writing, the inclusion in the report of all facts necessary for judgment of progress (usually making the report unwieldy), and mutually understood measurements of development and progress which allow the accountable executive to be aware of deviations from an apparent pathway to the desired goal. In sum, this method relies heavily on the subordinate's talents and the executive's clarity in putting across his ideas originally. It may be doubly difficult to use if the project is complex.

4. Scheduling Conferences. By scheduling oral reports or conferences for definite dates in the future, this style of delegation attempts to alleviate the complications of Method 3, while at the same time gaining the merits of the informal questioning used in Method 2. It is most useful when the project to be audited is one which has a series of events that can be planned and timed in advance. Success is contingent on a carefully planned chronology of developments, an assumption that the forecasts or scheduled events will actually materialize at the times anticipated, and a presumption that the original plan of attack decided on is the only feasible approach. The drawbacks consist of the pressure imposed by time, a blind conformance to a prearranged method

of attack, and a prohibition of creative experimentation by the calendar-bound subordinate.

5. Setting Deadlines. This method of delegation sets a time limit for completing delegated assignments. It is fairer than scheduling conferences in advance, since it abolishes all of the drawbacks except for the pressure imposed by time. But it also entails a maximization of certain potential liabilities.

These include loss of all time and materials consumed in the event of an impractical or unworkable solution, denial of all possible interim help and advice the delegator could have given his subordinate, and setback in the morale of the work force if failure should result.

Against these must be weighed freedom of thought and action extended to the delegated-to person, development of the subordinates' talents through the thrust of full and unrestrained authority, and minimizing interruptions of the work of the delegating executive.

Obviously, the only difference between this method and that employed by the company president in our vignette is the length of time during which there is, for all intents and purposes, complete abandonment of executive control. Naturally, the shorter the period, the better. This style of delegation is warranted only when the subordinate has proved his ability to perform successfully, his mode of performance is identical to that of the delegating executive, or the task is so perfunctory that the path to its completion is unmistakable.

6. Checking Results. This method, unlike No. 2, can be used only when the particular project has tangible results while in progress. It is the most accurate, the most convenient for all concerned, and the least trouble to the subordinate.

The real test in using this method is in the self-discipline of the delegating executive, since he must schedule and prod himself to witness the progress (or lack of it) firsthand. This style requires available time to travel to and make an inspection of the progress, a knack of showing interest in the progress instead of reflecting suspicion on the abilities of the delegate (as in Method 2), and an ability and temperament to make constructive suggestions, as well as to leave behind an aura of encouragement.

7. Measuring by Crosscurrents. Few problems are separate entities. The solution of one problem is usually reflected in other phases of an enterprise. For example, relieving a bottleneck in filling orders will automatically minimize the number and vociferousness of the complaints from the shipping department. In fact, the great majority of business problems are made known, not by their noticeable presence, but by their hindrance to other activities.

These crosscurrents of work flow provide measuring devices and warning signals, if an executive is attuned to them. This style of watchful delegation is effective where there is no damaging delay due to time lags in the crosscurrent warning signals, and where there is a dependable and direct relationship between the warning sign and its designated cause, and isolation and control of all other factors that filter into the crosscurrent.

8. Delegating by Interdependence. This method can be used when the start of one activity begins with the culmination of another, or when the solution of a problem in one department becomes a problem in another, much like a relay race. Though devoid of intermediate participation by the top executive and consequently subject to inherent dangers, this style of delegation redeems itself on the strength of the adage: "Two heads are better than one." In effect, the report of progress is automatically given by the start of the next phase in the sequence. The delegated subordinates check on each other, for any one's performance is dependent on the others.

Such chains are quite often the case in business, as when the production, sales, and advertising departments are charged with increasing the volume of goods sold. Production must come forth with a product which sales thinks it can merchandise successfully; sales must invent a strategy in its area of marketing which will lend the greatest support to advertising; and advertising must originate a campaign designed to promote the salability of the product and to accelerate the effectiveness of the sales strategy. The responsibility and compliance of one group are, under such an alignment, mutually dependent on and therefore limited by the efforts of the others. The top executive has a built-in audit of progress.

Naturally, delegating by interdependence relies for favorable outcome on a marked degree of departmental interdependency for final results, separate and distinct functional responsibilities for each department involved, and sharp lines of demarcation whose boundaries, while contiguously dependent, are mandatorily independent in that they circumscribe departments whose progress can be measured by their own results and not by the shortcomings of others.

9. Delegating by Correlation. In contrast to the preceding method, this one depends on parallel activities: two or more departments predicate their plans on the fact that all the others will complete their roles successfully and simultaneously. The chief advantage over delegation by interdependence is a reliance on concurrent employment of efforts, so that all related (but departmentalized) goals will materialize at the same time. By the same token, the main disadvantage is that such a parallel relationship of results will end up in failure for all if there is a failure for one. This type of delegating arrangement can be employed whenever a successful conclusion can be pinpointed in time. For example:

A bakery might be faced, in its wrapping area, with the problem of adapting machines to the use of a new wrapping film. A deadline of three weeks is given. During this same interval, the sales department is to formulate merchandising plans to introduce the bread in its "new dress." The same length of time is granted to the advertising department to prepare, and have ready to go, a specific promotion and media plan. Thus, on a stated date, all three responsibilities must be fulfilled: the bread must appear in its new wrapper, the merchandising must begin, and the advertising must appear.

Obviously, delegating by correlation needs to take into account assurance of satisfactory results, assumption of scheduled performance, and willingness of the top executive to accept accountability in the event of failure in any or all departments.

Combining Methods

As must be clear to the reader by now, all these styles of delegation can be easily combined. For example:

1. Delegating by correlation can be supplemented by scheduling conferences in order to obtain reports.
2. Delegating by interdependence can also include demanding reports of the subordinates.
3. Measuring crosscurrents may be made more accurate by checking of results.
4. The method of previewing direction offers an effective start to setting deadlines.
5. The system of demanding reports may be improved by questioning on progress as well.

In many instances more than two of the methods may be combined. One successful method for delegating and still keeping a hand in might combine previewing directions, scheduling conferences, checking results, and also delegating by interdependence.

* * * * *

Necessity for Compromise

Three tentative evaluations [have to be made] by an executive selecting a style of delegation: the specific terms of the information needed; the crucial measuring points; and the optimum method of auditing. Yet these three elements are not always harmonious, nor can the executive always be certain that he will have the time or money to carry them through effectively. The final selection of a method of auditing, then, is a matter of compromise, a matter of weighing the following five considerations and resolving them to a solution:

1. How important is this job? What are the costs of imperfect final results?
2. How much time and money will it take to make the optimum measurements and audit?
3. Do I have this much time? Must I make the time available?
4. Can I interrupt this project to make an evaluation? For how long? How important is the deadline for completion?
5. How much faith do I have in the man carrying out this project?

Such conflicts demand adherence to the principle of "first things first." For example, if the job is so important that the executive cannot risk failure, then, of course, control is his primary objective. In such a situation, a relatively time-consuming method giving good control may, in the end, be a small price for seeing to it that the job is completed successfully — may be cheap in light of the costs of failure. Even drawing time and effort away from other projects may be less costly in the long run.

* * * * *

CONCLUSION

An executive can never delegate accountability. Though he vest his assistant with full responsibility and complete authority, the executive, nevertheless, cannot escape final full accountability for the results. His only recourse for seeing to it that things go right is through executive participation — maintaining enough contact with every job so that he is "on top of it" by "keeping his hand in."

This article suggests a number of styles of delegation which accomplish this goal. Their purpose is to advise the executive of the status of an assignment in time to take corrective steps before failure either renders success hopeless or becomes unnecessarily costly.

However, the selection of one style or a combination of them is not a matter of arbitrary choice. Rather, it is dictated, first, by the type of job to be delegated and, secondly, by the amount of time an executive can invest in protecting his accountability. The weighing of these two factors, resolved one against the other, determines the optimum style of delegation to be selected.

28 THE INTERRELATIONSHIPS BETWEEN RESPONSIBILITY, AUTHORITY AND ACCOUNTABILITY

Earlier   in this Book, it was stated that assigning responsibility, transferring authority, and expecting commensurate accountability are not separate concepts but rather are all intra-related parts of the same basic organizational and managerial process — the process of delegation.

They should, therefore, be considered to be bounded by the same limits in time and scope and evaluated in the same units of measurement, simultaneous, co-terminous, and commensurate. The manager assigns responsibility and transfers all authority necessary to the discharge of the duty as defined. When a man accepts the responsibility, he thereby assumes personally the obligation for carrying out the duty assigned to him and the accountability for so doing. These are relationships between two individuals. A responsibility cannot be shared by a group of individuals. An individual has a responsibility, or he does not. Also it has been stated that a person should have only one boss, that a man should know to whom he reports and, if he is a manager, he should likewise know who reports to him.

Thus, ideally, every employee in the Company is assigned to a position or job in one — and only one — organizational line of responsibility. This organizational arrangement defines his line relationships in the common usage of the term. There is a "line" connection from each individual contributor to his immediate manager and through intermediate managers to the President of the Company. Therefore, the employee in each position or job has a personal, unique, and distinct place in the total Company Organization Structure. In this manner, organizational arrangements are made, and relationships are established for planning

Reprinted from Professional Management in General Electric, Book II: General Electric's Organization (General Electric Company, 1955), pages 186-189, by permission of the publisher.

and for doing all the work, and every type of work, that needs to be done by all the employees of the enterprise.

Ideally again, each employee should know what work he should do, when it should be done, and what are its teamwork, or relationship, requirements just as much as its internal work, or functional, responsibilities. Furthermore, his "citizenship" in the working community of the enterprise includes understanding and voluntary acceptance of whatever duties go with doing the work which has been assigned to him for performance.

These considerations lead to the statement that responsibility, authority, and accountability are three parts of the same package.

A particular piece of work is assigned to an individual for performance. His position, as designed and defined in the Organization Structure, provides for him the necessary authority for doing the work. By accepting the position and the assigned work, he assumes the obligation and the accountability for doing the work as assigned, as long as he retains such position and relationships.

Therefore, it is stated that "responsibility, authority, and accountability are simultaneous, co-terminous, and commensurate." Furthermore, the definition of work to be done and of the relationships between particular pieces of work and all other parts of the total work being done by employees of the enterprise cannot be complete until the responsibility, authority, and accountability pertaining to each piece is thus adequately stated and understood.

The Organization Structure — with its designed Position Guides and its Function Guides, or charts, for components — is the general and integrating expression of these relationships.

The Organization Chart is an attempt to picture — as best this can be done, statistically and on a flat plane — the basic elements and relationships of such organization pattern and structure.

As such, the Organization Chart is useful and constructive. It does not "put men in little prisons or boxes with walls or lines around them." On the contrary, by helping each man to visualize both his work and his teamwork responsibilities more clearly — and to see them more fairly as a part of the whole which embraces them — it is a device for letting a man go about his work with greater freedom, with greater confidence that both he and his associates will be together in common purpose on plays requiring team as well as individual integration; and yet always remembering, as Dr. Harry Hopf[1] warned, it is a "curious illusion that it is possible to convey a full appreciation of sound organization through the medium of a two-dimensional chart."

---

[1]Harry A. Hopf, Adapting the Industrial Organization to Changing Conditions, Address delivered at Rutgers University, 1946.

Yet, when the structure is clearly defined, simple, and straight-forward, the understanding of jobs and relationships will be correspondingly easy; duplication of effort and waste will be minimized; and over-all efficiency in work and teamwork will be enhanced. Because the working setup is smooth, because each sees both his own position and its place on the team, morale will be high.

On the other hand, complicated, complex, entangled, poorly defined organization structures lead to overlapping and confused work assignments, work omissions, misunderstandings, frustrations, bad personal relationships, and over-all inefficiency. Under these conditions, morale and worker output are only too likely to be low despite any inspiration which even an understanding and gifted Manager can bring to bear.

In designing an Organization Structure — either for a business or for a functional component — therefore, it is essential to remember that responsibility, authority, and accountability need to be thought of fundamentally as inseparable parts of one concept. Like a shamrock, they are three distinct leaves always found and thought of together.

And it is also to be kept clearly in mind that any action or device that weakens one part or tends to separate one part from the other two, as far as one individual's work is concerned, will automatically weaken total performance.

One person cannot have the responsibility and another the authority, or another the accountability for the identical piece of work, but all have a joint teamwork responsibility to see that their assigned separate pieces of work — as they are diligently and timely performed — do fit smoothly together, so that over-all organization performance and timing may be as successful as that of the individual pieces. The important point is that this is an individual responsibility for each man on the team, not merely that of the manager, even though the latter's personal accountability does embrace it also.

29 LEGAL AND OPERATING AUTHORITY

* * * * *

LEGAL AUTHORITY THAT EXCEEDS ADMINISTRATIVE OR OPERATING AUTHORITY

We court confusion when we assume that legal authority is always equal to administrative or operating authority. Legal authority is principally a matter of the relationship of outsiders to an enterprise; what we have been discussing is the supervisor-subordinate relationship of people within the enterprise. A company always has a number of people who can represent it to the outside world, that is, to customers, suppliers, prospective employees, bankers, and government officials. These agents can make contracts and otherwise act as legal representatives of the company.

A firm may give a salesman, explicitly or by implication, legal authority to sell to any customer who places an order. His operating authority, however, may be much more restricted, confining him to certain types of customer, and requiring him to secure internal approval from, say, the credit department, before he takes a specific order. Similarly, a company may legally authorize a purchasing agent to buy large quantities of raw material, although operationally he must stay within budget limits and purchase only the kinds of material that other departments requisition. The legal authority of a treasurer to write checks on a company's bank account normally far exceeds his actual rights to spend the company's money. We could give other illustrations of our point that, for practical purposes, an enterprise

William H. Newman and Charles E. Summer, Jr., The Process of Management: Concepts, Behavior and Practice. © 1961. Reprinted by permission of Prentice-Hall, Inc., Englewood Cliffs, N. J.

must often transfer to a member of its staff legal authority far in excess of the permission it grants him to exercise that authority.

Legal authority need cause us no trouble if we recognize that it is different from the administrative rights we have been talking about. In a business enterprise, at least, we can establish a sound management organization and then let lawyers provide for legal authority wherever we need it.

FAILURE TO MAKE LIMITS OF AUTHORITY CLEAR

Effective delegation requires, among other things, that we make clear the limits of authority to each subordinate. A worker, his boss, and any other people who may be affected, should have a mutual understanding of (1) the worker's rights — to act, to request others to act, to discipline — and (2) any restrictions on how or when action may be taken. Such mutual understanding is not always easy to achieve.

Written job descriptions, policies, and procedures should give some indication of the authority of each member of an organization. Many companies, however, have not felt it worthwhile to prepare such documents; in other companies whatever documents exist give an incomplete picture. In the normal course of business, variations in operating conditions arise that call for shades of meaning to the authorizations that have been granted. Moreover, as men work together over extended periods of time, their relationships will change. An administrator will grant more freedom to an experienced man, particularly as the man demonstrates sound judgment, than he would to the same man when he is first employed. It is obviously impractical to attempt to spell out explicitly and formally all the details and subtle qualifications of each supervisor-subordinate relationship.

In practice, the full meaning of a delegation depends largely on tradition and habit. For example, a foreman may customarily requisition expensive raw materials and supplies according to his own judgment whereas to purchase new equipment, even though a much smaller sum is involved, he must "always clear with Mr. Jones, the treasurer." A subordinate learns how far he is expected to go — partly through training on the job, partly through occasional consultations with his boss, and partly through trial and error. Many of the limits of authority are only implied, and each subordinate must learn to sense them.

A subordinate gets into trouble when the limits of authority are so vague that he either goes far beyond his appropriate sphere of action or fails to exercise the initiative he should. The superintendent of a textile mill, for instance, knew he could lay off a few men when they were not needed, but found himself in a row with the unions and with other mill superintendents in the same company when he cut his entire plant back to a four-day week. To avoid such problems, a wise manager — from president to first-line supervisor — is continually aware of the need to clarify and interpret delegations to each of his subordinates. In dealing with day-to-day problems and in reviewing past performance, he must consciously consider how his subordinates will interpret his attitudes as well as his actions. To cite a simple case, a sales manager puts meaning into the degree of a salesman's authority to phone out-of-town customers by endorsing, or by frowning on, frequent and lengthy long-distance calls. By labeling a particular action — perhaps warranted in an emergency — as an exception to the normal standard of behavior, or by calling attention to failures to make aggressive use of authority, a manager can put substance into broadly stated job descriptions.

Occasionally, people will argue that management should leave the boundaries of authority fuzzy in order to encourage cooperation. This contention is based on a false premise. Clear-cut duties and authorities do not imply that each man should work in his own isolated corner. Instead, in most delegations, managers make it very clear that a subordinate should consult with others and keep them informed as he proceeds with his own duties. Furthermore, a few assignments are specifically joint undertakings. Some companies emphasize their concern with cooperation by saying that a man is accountable for both work and teamwork, and they are dissatisfied with a man's performance unless he measures up well on both counts. Cooperation is simply a part of a job and should be as clear as other duties.

INCONSISTENT BEHAVIOR OF MANAGERS

A delegation of duties and authorities can work no better than a manager allows. His plans and controls should be consistent with the assignments he gives to his subordinates. The merchandising manager of a department store, for example, told all his buyers that they would be responsible for preparing spring programs for their respective divisions. Several buyers exerted a great deal of effort to compile detailed tables of what to buy and when to have goods delivered, only to have the merchandising manager make substantial changes because he "didn't think that stuff would sell." Here, after the merchandising manager had clearly delegated a planning task, he went ahead with his own spring program regardless of the disappointment and frustration of his buyers.

Control actions are especially apt to be inconsistent with previous assignments. One of the large hotel chains in this country, for instance, is presumably operated on a profit-decentralization basis. Nevertheless, the president requires detailed expense figures and ratios each month, and he is likely to call to task any of his hotel managers for insignificant expenses that he thinks are out of line. Some of the managers are able to keep this needling from interfering with their main tasks, but others spend an unwarranted amount of time preparing for a possible call from "the old man."

Another company, which was decentralizing its operations, had spent a lot of effort convincing its district managers that they were in the best position to determine how much additional equipment they needed to develop their respective territories profitably. The company did not modify control procedures, however, to conform to the new delegation of authority, and a central engineering staff continued to approve or disapprove all new equipment that cost more than ten thousand dollars. Theoretically, the central staff was to be available to advise the district managers at the time they formulated their plans; in fact, the staff exercised a control that was inconsistent with the new set-up.

OBSTACLES TO ACTUAL DELEGATION

Still another practical difficulty in delegating occurs when, although both boss and subordinate agree on the desirability of transferring certain duties and authority, for some reason the transfer does not actually take place. To understand the reasons behind such mere lip-service to the desirability of delegating we must examine the attitudes and behavior of both a boss and a subordinate.

Possible Reasons Why a Boss May Fail to Delegate

Many a manager wishes to transfer his heavy load to his subordinates and yet fails to let loose of the work he is doing. What causes this paradox?

1. Some executives get trapped in the "I can do it better myself" fallacy. Even if an executive can do a job better than anyone else (which is not true quite so often as he thinks it is), he must nevertheless reconcile himself to turning the job over to someone else whose performance will be "good enough." The choice the executive must make is not between the quality of his work and that of his assistant; rather, he should weigh the advantages of higher-level performance if he does the work himself against the benefit to the total operation if he devotes his attention to the planning and supervision that only he can undertake.

2. An executive's lack of ability to direct is another barrier to successful delegation. One of the authors remembers well one of his first bosses, a very friendly individual who had keen business judgment, but who simply could not tell a man working for him what to do more than a few hours ahead. Life for the subordinates was a bit precarious because their success depended on guessing how the boss's mind would work before the boss himself had formulated his ideas. Here was a man who wanted desperately

to delegate. But he could do so only in repetitive situations, because he was unable to identify and communicate the essential features of his long-range plans.

3. A third possible block to effective delegation is <u>lack of confidence in subordinates.</u> When we recognize this cause for withholding authority, the remedy is clear: Either we should start a training program immediately, or, if this is impractical, we should find a new subordinate. Often, however, the situation is by no means so clear-cut. An executive may not be fully aware of his lack of confidence; his reaction is subjective and he simply feels uneasy about how someone else will do the work. When this is so, the executive is likely to pay lip-service to the principle of delegation, but be reluctant in an actual working relationship to let go of authority or duties.

4. A related obstacle to delegation is an <u>absence of sensitive controls that warn of impending difficulties.</u> Since a good executive is sensitive to his continuing obligation even though work is delegated, he obviously needs some "feed-back" about what is going on. He wants to be sure he will know of serious trouble in advance so he can help overcome it. If the control set-up fails to keep him informed as he feels he should be — at least on major matters — he will probably be cautious about delegating.

5. Finally, a manager may be handicapped by <u>a temperamental aversion to taking a chance.</u> Any manager who delegates must take a calculated risk. Even with clear instructions, dependable subordinates, and selective control, the possibility remains that something will go wrong. Unless the executive adjusts emotionally, as well as intellectually, to this element of risk, he is likely to be reluctant to delegate anything to anyone.

Possible Obstacles to a Subordinate's Accepting Delegation

Even when a boss is ready and able to turn over authority, a subordinate may shrink from accepting it.

1. Often a subordinate finds it <u>easier to ask the boss</u> than to decide for himself how to deal with a problem. Making a wise decision is usually hard mental work. If a man finds that he can take any troublesome problem — with at best only tentative suggestions — to his boss for an answer, it is natural for him to do so. In addition to being easier, this course has the advantage that if the boss does make the decision, the employee is less liable to suffer severe criticism for consequences later.

An executive can break a subordinate's habit of bringing all tough problems to him by insisting that the subordinate either take action or at least recommend a fully thought-through solution on which he is prepared to stake his reputation. The boss will probably want to continue to give advice in his role as coach. He must, however, be constantly on his guard lest his advice undercut the initiative and sense of obligation he is striving to build.

2. A second factor that may deter a man from embracing greater duties is fear of criticism for mistakes. He will usually welcome constructive review, but will resent negative and unreasonable criticism. A subordinate will naturally be inclined to be cautious and play it safe if he has learned from experience that when he takes on more duties, he risks an embarrassing and unwarranted bawling-out. His feeling is, "Why should I stick my neck out for this guy?"

3. Most men hesitate to accept a new assignment when they believe they lack the necessary information and resources to do a good job. A person accustomed to a restraining web of budgetary and personal limitations may accept new duties, knowing full well that he will have to battle at each step. In general, however, because of frustrations of trying to work handicapped by inadequate information and resources, a man will reject assignments with such a drawback.

4. Lack of self-confidence stands in the way of some men in accepting a delegation. Ordering a man to be self-confident will have little effect. In many cases, however, he can develop self-confidence if, by carefully providing experience with increasingly difficult problems, we help him to sense his own potentialities.

5. Positive incentives may be inadequate. Accepting additional duties usually involves mental effort and emotional pressure. If we expect a man to take on an additional load enthusiastically, we should offer positive inducements. The inducements may be pay increases, improved opportunity for promotion, a fancy title, acknowledged status in the organization, personal recognition and approval by the boss, and other rewards, both tangible and intangible. We shall explore the whole matter of incentives in a later chapter of this book. The important point here is that a subordinate is more likely to accept new duties when they are sweetened by an incentive that is important to him.

* * * * *

PART NINE:

DECENTRALIZATION

30 DECENTRALIZATION REAPPRAISED

by Lounsbury S. Fish

Many people talk a good game of decentralization; fewer understand its full implications. It takes a lot of doing to fit the concept of decentralization to the particular needs of a large business and make it work!

TENDENCIES TOWARD CENTRALIZATION

Many human factors and frailties conspire toward the over-centralization of management:

1. Higher management is concerned with the satisfactory progress of the business. It naturally feels that if it makes all the decisions and watches all the details of the business itself, the situation will be well in hand.

2. There is widespread reluctance among executives and supervisors (and fathers and mothers) to delegate a sufficient measure of responsibility and authority to their subordinates.

3. Executives advanced to higher positions tend to hang on to the responsibilities they exercised at lower levels; their successors, they feel, lack their own breadth of judgment — "nice boys but young yet!"

4. It often seems easier and quicker for the executive to handle particular matters himself than to find and train others to handle them satisfactorily for him. Unfortunately, in so doing the executive limits his capacity to one manpower.

5. Every time a subordinate makes an embarrassing mistake or error in judgment, there is a tendency to curtail delegated authority and exercise closer control from a higher level.

The result of these human tendencies, on a corporate scale, is that too much of the management burden frequently rests upon

---

Reprinted from Management Record, April, 1960, pages 14-17, by permission of the National Industrial Conference Board.

the chief executive, the top group, the central office; too little responsibility and authority are given to those in immediate charge of operations who could be most effective in ministering to the needs of the business on the firing line.

Countering and overcoming these natural, gravitational pulls toward centralization cannot be accomplished by decree. It requires changed concepts of organization at the head office and in the field; it necessitates important changes in the system of controls; it calls for a conscious change in attitudes of mind, both topside and at the outposts.

LIMITING FACTORS IN DECENTRALIZATION

Regardless of the desire and determination to decentralize, there are certain fundamental factors that limit the extent to which decentralization can be successfully applied in any given organization.

For instance, it is necessary to bring management decisions to a level that has appropriate jurisdiction and adequate knowledge of related requirements of, and consequences to, the business. "A man's judgment is no better than his information, his decisions no better than his knowledge."

So you can safely decentralize management authority only to the extent that you are organized at the receiving end to assure balance, coordinated management decisions — taking all consequential business factors into account. For example, resident managements may know most about conditions, needs, and fields of opportunity within their own areas; but they are less well informed about the relative needs and opportunities of the business in other areas.

Therefore, the degree to which knowledge and experience of the best industry practice can be made available to divisional managements to guide their decisions has a bearing upon the practical extent of decentralization.

Decisions which must take into account the relative needs, risks, and opportunities of the business in different areas can only be made at "the hub of the wheel." These include the following decisions affecting the disposition of limited resources among the different areas of need and opportunity:

1. Investment of limited capital funds among competing needs.
2. Determination of which areas offer greatest possibility for growth.
3. Assignment of executive personnel among different operations, considering the relative needs of the business and the training value of the experience in the rounded development of men for senior executive posts.
4. In our oil business, determination of which areas offer the best possibilities of finding oil.

It is essential that the management organization, both at the head office and in the field, be geared to the special requirements of management on a decentralized basis. Among the factors which must be taken into consideration in this connection are the following.

First, the extent to which the business as a whole lends itself to subdivision into principal operating components has an important bearing upon the feasibility of decentralizing management decision and action. To facilitate decentralization, the business as a whole should be broken down into operating components that can be made relatively self-sufficient. Each component should, as far as possible, be —

1. Big enough to justify a potent management team.
2. Small enough for that team to "get its arms around" and do a first-class job.
3. Complete and separable — a logical, definable, management "package," embracing or having adequate control over elements, facilities, services, and related operations vital to the achievement of its primary objectives.
4. Measurable as to results achieved, as an essential basis for management accountability.

Where the nature of the business permits, subdivision into semiautonomous smaller businesses — such as product divisions or geographical divisions, which can be held accountable on a profit-and-loss basis — has the following great advantages in facilitating decentralization.

1. Each component business has within itself the means of coordinating and controlling many or most of its own business problems without burdening the high command.
2. Components which thus qualify as complete sub-businesses can safely be given wide latitude in making their own management decisions — "in running their own businesses." As a result the primary centers of profit responsibility are multiplied.

Many of the large manufacturing industries have created relatively autonomous product divisions. The oil industry, on the other hand, finds it very difficult to subdivide on a product basis, as all the products usually come from the same barrel of crude in a common plant. In many cases, however, a satisfactory breakdown has been achieved on the basis of geographical divisions.

Another consideration in organizing for management decentralization is the provision for effective staff services. In order to make sound decisions, decentralized managements must have ready access to highly competent staff advice and services.

Certain types of staff services should be established "at the elbow" of the operating executives who require them as an inherent part of the day-to-day management process.

Other types of services, such as engineering and mechanized accounting and data processing, can often be supplied satisfactorily from central offices, where greater volume, more experienced personnel, better equipment, and higher-powered technical supervision can result in improved service at reduced cost. In this connection, it is important to recognize that the heart and core of management decentralization is the decentralization of management initiative, decision, and action. So long as the decentralized management is able to get the staff advice and service it needs as a basis for sound decision — promptly, competently, and conveniently — this service can come from, or be based at, central offices without impairing the concept of "decentralization."

Finally, the business must be so organized that top management can effectively oversee the decentralized units without making all the detailed decisions. In carrying out this surveillance, many managements appreciate that even well-designed operating reports can, at best, convey only a part of the picture and, hence, place increasing reliance upon systematic visits by top executives to divisional headquarters.

The substantial amount of time required to do full justice to this important, top-management obligation should be taken into account in the plan of organization. In the smaller or more compact businesses, it is possible for the president and his functional officers to maintain sufficiently close personal contact with subordinate managements to fully satisfy this requirement.

In the case of very large enterprises, operating through many divisions and over a wide area, this becomes increasingly difficult. In such cases, there is a growing tendency to expand the president's office through the creation of group executives or regional executives, usually at the vice-presidential level, to assist the president in furnishing effective over-all guidance, leadership, and coordination to the respective operating managements.

CHANGES IN CONTROLS

With the organization requirements satisfied, we turn next to the question of controls. The successful decentralization of management depends upon the development of a system of controls that will permit the extension of the widest practical authority to local managements in the current conduct of the business. In designing such a system, the following are important requirements:

A. As previously mentioned, the company's over-all objectives, long-range plans, guiding policies, and allocation of limited resources among competing needs and opportunities must, of course, be determined at the head office, where all the pertinent information is available. Based upon this over-all planning, "policy guidance" must be furnished to field managements as to the directions and dimensions toward which they should work.

B. Within this framework, each field management must establish its objectives, plot its course, estimate its requirements, and forecast its results.

C. Head office and field managements then must agree on whether the projected course is a satisfactory basis of performance and accountability for the period ahead. This can best be accomplished through the medium of a carefully prepared "annual operating program" or operating budget.

D. There needs to be an effective system for comparing actual results with agreed-upon significance rather than volume (the really important figures, not all the figures; one does not have to resort to "paralysis by analysis").

E. Finally — on the principle that a good look, on the ground, is better than a ton of paper at head office — there must be thorough visits, at appropriate intervals, by the responsible head-office executives to each of the principal operations:

1. To provide policy guidance and counsel.
2. To secure first-hand knowledge of local needs and problems.
3. To appraise past performance and results.
4. To appraise forward programs, projects, and budgets.
5. To appraise management strengths, development needs, and potential.
6. To correct unsatisfactory conditions.
7. To make many decisions or recommendations on those matters worthy of general management attention that can best be resolved in the field, where relevant facts are readily available, and the views of local management can be taken into proper account.
8. To secure first-hand knowledge of situations requiring final decisions at the head office, and thus be in the best position to be convincing in securing necessary support at that level.

These relatively simple measures, well designed and well administered, can provide the means for effective over-all management guidance, coordination, and control and, at the same time, provide wide latitude for management initiative and action on a decentralized basis.

CHANGES IN ATTITUDE

Finally, we come to decentralization as a way of life. It has been truly said that "decentralization is 95% an attitude of mind." Certainly, successful decentralization requires a conscious point of view. From the head-office end, this point of view might be characterized as follows:

1. Members of head-office management should constantly remind themselves that the operating components are the heart and core of the business. These operating components should be recognized and respected as the "money-making elements" of the business.

2. Head-office personnel must remember that a large part of the purpose and justification for the "overhead" or head-office organization is to help the respective operating managements do the best possible job in maximizing company profits.

3. It should be kept in mind that decentralization works only if real authority is delegated, and won't work if details have to be reported — or, worse yet, "cleared" — before action can be taken.

4. It should be appreciated that occasional mistakes by subordinate executives that contribute to their knowledge and development are usually cheaper than the ponderous processes of centralized management.

5. Senior executives have to remember that junior has grown up — he is a big boy now — he wears long pants — he is usually able to carry the load if papa will relax and give him a chance.

In the same way, successful decentralization requires a complementary point of view at the receiving end.

In the first place, decentralization has to be earned. Accepting the heavy obligations of decentralized management is a solemn undertaking. It is one thing to refer possible courses of action to higher management to ponder, weigh, and decide upon; it is quite another to have to "sweat out" the decision yourself.

The decentralized manager needs to have the same motivation and concern, in every move, that he would have if it were his own business and his own money at stake. Knowing what he does about the opportunities and risks of the business, would he put his own money into this new service station, these new trucks, this new terminal; which segments of the market would he train his heaviest guns upon; would he follow this or that course or policy? It is a mightly lonesome position to be in, but good men thrive on it. It is the spirit of decentralization.

ADVANTAGES OF DECENTRALIZATION

Fitting these building blocks of decentralization together and adapting them to the needs of the business is quite a job. But a summary of the more important advantages and objectives of decentralization shows that the effort is worthwhile.

1. Decentralization distributes the management load. As an enterprise increases in size and complexity, it becomes more difficult, and finally impossible, to effectively handle it from some remote headquarters. It becomes increasingly necessary

to develop management initiative, responsibility, and authority at logical centers, closer to the scene of action, throughout the company.

2. Decentralization multiplies management effectiveness and firepower. Instead of a single center of management, decentralization stimulates and multiplies management initiative, resourcefulness, and the sense of profit-making responsibility throughout the organization.

3. Decentralization capitalizes on the natural decision-making advantages possessed by management-on-the-spot.

4. Decentralization strengthens, simplifies, and speeds the management process. It minimizes the amount of detail which must be referred to headquarters; it eliminates unnecessary red tape, multiple handling, and overloading of central offices and staff costs.

5. Decentralization develops strong, self-reliant managers. It multiplies the opportunity for development of well-founded executives and businessmen. It tends to produce leaders rather than leaners.

6. Finally, decentralization gives added challenge, stimulus, zest, importance, and value to "management-on-the-firing-line." There is nothing more challenging and interesting than being on your own, with full responsibility and accountability for results. Because of the heavier responsibilities entailed, decentralization substantially enhances the importance of management positions.

In recognition of these fundamental needs and advantages, it is easy to understand why there has been a marked trend toward decentralization of management among progressive companies with large-scale operations in many parts of the world.

31 CENTRALIZATION AND DECENTRALIZATION

by George A. Smith, Jr.

At present, to make the words "centralization," or "decentralization," or "delegation" really useful, one must amplify them. Better to use more words and convey a definite idea than to try to make a single, but ambiguous, word describe a complicated relationship.

One can probably be understood if one says, "Our company is geographically decentralized, or physically decentralized." That seems to mean it conducts operations at several locations. Even so, the listener will not know at how many locations, or whether they are widely scattered or closely concentrated. Better understanding would result if one said, for example, "Our company has ten plants located in eight cities or states."

Certainly there is no brief and yet adequate way to indicate how, in a particular company, various action-taking or decision-making powers are allocated among the several levels in the management hierarchy. This cannot be done by simply categorizing the company as "decentralized" or as "highly decentralized." Nor can it be done by stating that "power is delegated downward as far as possible." Such a statement merely shifts attention to the question, "How far down is it believed possible to delegate what powers?" A meaningful answer to this question needs to be a fairly long answer.

Instead of merely saying that "power" has been "delegated" or "decentralized," it is somewhat more specific to indicate the areas into which the delegated authority extends. For example, one might say, "Production is decentralized, but marketing is centralized." But even this is not enough. Production is not just one thing; neither is marketing. Each main area or business

Reprinted from Managing Geographically Decentralized Companies (Boston: Division of Research, Harvard Business School, 1958), pages 15-22, by permission of the publisher.

function comprises a variety of activities. Marketing, for example, includes selecting the line of goods to be offered, pricing, selling, advertising, supervising salesmen, and many other things. Power or authority over different activities within this broad area might well rest with different echelons. For example:

> In a large manufacturing company, the author was told by the general sales manager, "Marketing in our company is decentralized." It did prove to be true that all selling was done by people in the regional divisions; no one at headquarters actually made any sales. But the headquarters organization made up the line, set prices, approved the hiring of salesmen, conducted sales training programs, set salary limits, moved salesmen from one region to another, and handled the company's advertising. Moreover, people at headquarters kept track of sales by salesmen, by customers, and by products, and continually gave advice to regional sales managers. When the author talked to some of the regional officers, they gave a different view from the one expressed at headquarters. They described the company's marketing department as being "highly centralized" — "much too highly centralized," they seemed to imply.
>
> In the same company, the vice president in charge of purchasing told the author he had recently completed a program to decentralize purchasing, and the "purchasing is now 100% decentralized." The facts proved to be these: The headquarters purchasing department contracted for virtually all the basic raw materials used by the factories. (This outlay amounted to something like 60% of the company's sales dollar.) Moreover, headquarters was responsible for quality control of all raw materials. This arrangement had existed for many years, and in view of the need for uniform high quality of output in this company's industry, it appeared to be a wise one.

What then had the purchasing vice president meant when he spoke of his "decentralization program"? It involved only a change in the method of ordering shipments from suppliers. Formerly orders for raw meterials had been sent by the divisions to the company's own head office, which then sent shipment orders to the vendors. After "decentralization," the divisions could order shipments as needed directly from the suppliers, who shipped the materials under the terms of the company-wide contracts. There were no other changes.

And what of the vice president's statement that purchasing was now "100% decentralized"? He was not trying to deceive. What he meant was that his particular program of delegating a small amount of additional authority to the divisions was now in effect. A more accurate statement would have been, "The amount of authority in the purchasing area, which we at headquarters now think is the correct amount to give the divisions, has been delegated, and they are exercising it." He might also have added, "And this amount of delegated authority is not, in fact, very much." By no stretch of the imagination would an outside observer say that "purchasing was 100% decentralized."

DECENTRALIZATION AND DELEGATION

It should be clear that geographical decentralization of physical properties is not necessarily accompanied by a general downward delegation of management powers. These are two separate concepts, and the distinction should be observed. "Delegation" appears to be a better word than "decentralization" in most instances when reference is made to a distribution of authorities, powers, and responsibilities within the management hierarchy of a company.

It should also be clear that the degree of local autonomy in a multiple-unit company may be much or little, whether the company is managed by geographical regions, by product divisions, or by functions. These three types of management patterns will be described and illustrated in the next chapter. They are mentioned here merely to point out that the decision to use any one of these patterns does not settle the question of how much of what authority to delegate to whom. The settling of this latter question involves a separate set of decisions.

How much power to delegate down the line has long been one of the most debated issues in business and business literature. Many executives pay at least lip service to the ideal of a "democratic" organization; fewer are willing to foot the bill that they fear may be involved if they give subordinates more authority. Here, parenthetically, the author would like to enter a plea for more boldness in this respect. The costs of delegation might well be regarded as a long-term investment — in management training, in improved morale, in increased energy and initiative among all ranks that should pay off in an abundance of new yet critically scrutinized ideas. It is not always possible or wise, from a purely business or economic point of view, to delegate; wherever, then, it does seem possible, management should have the courage to try it.

In speaking of organizational arrangements, it is important to realize that each company must devise its own — there is no such thing as a common pattern; indeed, there are as many different administrative arrangements as there are companies. In this study, no two companies were found to be operating with the same arrangements, even if they were in the same industry. Some were similar, but never identical. This is appropriate, for no two companies have exactly the same circumstances. Each has its own problems, its own opportunities, its own environment, its own history, its own strengths and weaknesses, and, above all, its own people. What is a suitable and effective working arrangement for one group need not necessarily be good for another. Indeed, it probably would not be.

Still another matter to bear in mind is the fact that the "proper" set of arrangements for any one company will change from time to time. There is and should be a flow of authority back and forth between the headquarters and the divisions. It is a mistake to assume that a "best possible" alignment of powers and responsibilities can be devised, put into effect, and then forgotten. In making a plan, there is of necessity a great deal of trial and error. In putting a plan into effect, there is much that has to be adapted to human eccentricities or to temporary conditions. Once the plan is working, it may soon have to be changed, for someone will leave or die, and be replaced by a man with differing abilities. Or changing competition and business conditions may signal the need for some sort of answering administrative change.

EXPLAINING CHANGE

Because this flow back and forth is a real, an unavoidable, and a continuing thing, a management should probably not think or talk of a "decentralization program." This phrase has three misleading implications:

1. That it will start at a definite time and be completed at a definite time.
2. That all the intended changes in authority are downward delegations.
3. That this program is somehow separate and separable from the regular routine job of running the company.

It is probably wiser — that is, less disruptive and more educational — for the members of a business organization, if the manager would think and talk along these lines: "Let us look, perhaps more intently than usual for a while, at the way we have allocated authorities and powers between the headquarters organization on the one hand and the local divisions on the other hand. Let us see if we are having decisions made and actions taken at the levels where they can best be made. Let us ask the divisions what things they would like to decide which they now can't decide. What do they have to decide which they wish the headquarters would decide for them? Let us ask similar questions of the headquarters people."

He might say, also, if he believes it, "I hope we will end up with more power delegated to the divisions; but there may be some areas wherein some authority ought to be brought back to headquarters."

A statement like this, as against a "let's decentralize" statement, would have the following virtues:

1. It avoids the use of ambiguous terms.

2. It avoids the implication of a "once and for all" program. It suggests a continuing scrutiny of all arrangements, and even leaves the door open for major future changes in management philosophy. The emphasis is on "what seems to be a good arrangement for us at this time."

3. It implies that there may be some give and some take on the part of the local officers as well as on the part of headquarters. It also suggests that people from both levels will have a share in working out the new arrangements. It stresses the underlying concept that central office and local branch form a cooperative partnership which gets things done together on a mutually acceptable basis. It plays down the idea of a competitive struggle for power with resulting domination of one group by the other.

SEMANTICS AND MORALE

Obviously, members of an organization will be confused if plans are described to them in vague or ambiguous terms. But confusion alone is not the only penalty that management must pay for relying too heavily on imprecise terms. There is also an important damage to morale whenever people feel they were promised something in words that then does not accrue to them in practice. For example:

> A few years ago the president of a large multi-unit firm decided to change the management pattern of his company. The change he had in mind involved dividing the company into regional divisions and creating a new level of managers, each of whom would be supported by a staff of functional department heads. The men at headquarters, who formerly had actively administered the company under a system of functional divisions, were to become "elder states-

men," "general advisers," "policy formulators."
This plan was referred to by the president as
a "decentralization program."

In the president's mind, it was clear that
before much authority could in fact be delegated
downward, the regional organizations would have
to be created and trained. This would take time.
And it would take time for the men at headquarters to adjust themselves to the new organizational circumstances.

As it worked out, officers of the company at and below the new
regional level had their eyes on the word decentralization and
the connotation it had for them was downward delegation of power.
Most of these officers were eager to have more authority — and
to have it quickly. When the change they expected did not soon
materialize, they became impatient; some felt they had been
deceived. The president had to work hard and long at the job of
clarifying his views and his objectives, at educating his officers
at all levels — educating them both intellectually and emotionally.

The president would have had to do much of this work no matter
what words he used, for his plan involved a major change in the
working habits and relationships of many people. Nevertheless,
it seems likely that the transition could have been made somewhat less painful if the prospect had been described in different
words. The president could have called his plan "regionaliza-
tion," to be followed, "as fast as possible, by a realignment of
powers and responsibilities between the headquarters people, who
would now have a new kind of mission, and the regional officers,
whose positions hitherto did not exist."

32 CENTRALIZATION VS. DECENTRALIZATION

by Auren Uris

The executive looking for certainty won't find it on the centralization/decentralization seesaw. Despite all the years of discussion and implementation of these two conflicting concepts, no clear-cut claim to "rightness" can be made by either side.

For a long time managers have been trying to mix a palatable combination of the two ideas, but we're still pretty much in the trial-and-error stage. As long as the talk remains in the abstract, executives agree that both types of organization have good and bad points. But disagreement erupts, sometimes violently, when practical decisions must be made concerning the precise form a real organization should take.

An interesting exercise is to take an organizational problem and develop hypothetical solutions by devising centralized or decentralized versions of the operation. You then realize how arbitrary many of our organizational decisions are.

The fact is that a flexible company structure can make use of both centralization and decentralization. At General Motors, for example, operating divisions are decentralized both geographically and by products, while financial and legal functions are centralized. At Koppers, a company with strong leanings toward decentralization, the purchasing of most products is done out of a central office. It's interesting to note that personnel is one function that frequently is centralized.

Of course, real pressures shape real organizational decisions, even when the specific choice is made arbitrarily. This becomes increasingly clear as centralization/decentralization argument is probed in detail.

"When I later talked with Mr. Khrushchev, he told me frankly that the old system of centralized management was 'impossible.' You can't run the industry of such a big country from one center, he said emphatically, and added that the effort to do it had only caused paralysis, duplication, and waste while able men in the outlying areas sat around waiting for directives from above." So wrote Adlai E. Stevenson in describing an interview he had with the Soviet Premier during his visit to Russia in 1958.

The realities of management, it seems, can even pierce the Iron Curtain. Certainly, Khrushchev's complaint about the inefficiency of centralized control is an old story to Western businessmen. "Paralysis, duplication, and waste" are symptomatic of overcentralized control everywhere. Before we hand over the prize to decentralization, however, there is further evidence that must be considered.

The literature of management abounds with case studies of organizations that have changed from a centralized to a decentralized form of organization. Reading this material, you get the impression that all organizations flee from a centralized structure as from the plague. And, certainly, there has in recent years been a strong trend toward decentralization. One reason is that, in our present stage of development, many companies have expanded their operations to the point where decentralization seems to be a logical solution to their problems. But actually there's no reason why the process may not be reversed. It may be just as sound a solution to operating difficulties to centralize an activity that has been decentralized.

A CASE OF CENTRALIZATION

The following case history, which describes a changeover from a decentralized to a centralized form of control, illuminates some of the factors that must be considered in making such an organizational change.

> A small chain of restaurants in the Midwest had been built up over a five-year period after a highly successful one-location operation. The additional branches were placed under the authority of individual managers, each of whom had been personally trained by the head of the firm, who was himself the successful manager of the parent restaurant.
>
> By and large, the managers were given complete antonomy. As a result, their individuality gradually created noticeable differences

among the restaurants. In one case, a unit located in a better neighborhood began to cater to the more sophisticated eating tastes of its patrons. Naturally, with the choicer menu came a price rise. In another location, because of strong pressure from a nearby competitor, the manager steered a course that resulted in a lowering of price and ultimately of quality.

The company president found difficulties piling up. First, costs were getting out of line. Decentralized purchasing resulted in a widely varying cost of food and supplies. Second, because of the variation in the quality of food and service from one restaurant to another, unified advertising became a problem. Third, and most important, the customer appeal of a chain restaurant operation was lost because of the dissimilarities among the various chain units. The single-organization image that would assure the public of a uniform standard of food and service had been destroyed.

At this point the president decided to centralize. The managers of the individual units were brought together in a top-level conference at which plans were developed for the standardization of policies and procedures in all the locations. Planning was done in detail, with the original restaurant's methods of operation adopted as a model. Everything from the way a table should be set to how the waitresses should wear their hair was spelled out in a procedures handbook. Purchasing of all supplies was centralized. A delivery truck was bought, so that foodstuffs could be centrally purchased and distributed to the branches. Price levels were standardized among all the units. Now a customer would know the cost of a meal when he entered any branch of the chain.

Note that, in making the change, the president chose a course that was not clearly "better" by any and all standards. He realized that the efforts of the individual managers to build up their own restaurants through price and quality modifications had not been ill-advised. On the contrary, he recognized that these efforts represented intelligent attempts to build patronage. As he pointed out to the managers, however, these efforts ran counter to a policy of uniformity that promised to pay for the whole company in the long run.

One of the factors that led to the decision to centralize was a plan to add more units. Without a uniform institutional face on which to capitalize, the investment could hardly be justified.

The company president counted on a period of loss taking. A certain number of old customers who had been attracted by the modified menus and types of service were bound to drop away. But it was expected that eventually the volume of business would build up after the period of readjustment.

It's worth noting that neither before nor after the changeover was the company completely decentralized or centralized. This fact brings us to an oversight that occasionally serves to add to the heat of the controversy over centralization versus de-centralization, or "C/D," as we shall call it.

* * * * *

BALANCING THE ADVANTAGES AND DISADVANTAGES

It's not difficult to list the advantages and disadvantages of centralized and decentralized organization in a way that would generally be approved by both sides in the controversy. They are presented in Table 1. With the advantages and disadvantages clearly defined, it's not at all surprising that managers eventually channel their energies toward the development of a structure that avoids the inherent limitations of each approach.

The top executive group of a large, two-plant food-processing company decided that there were potential economies to be gained by centralizing their production planning. To minimize the obvious communication problems that would result, they mapped out an information exchange formula involving everything from direct-phone hookups to daily written reports.

Another typical attempt to avoid inherent weaknesses is that of a decentralized organization seeking to give the head of its sub-units a "centralized view." A drilling and test-boring company with headquarters in North Dakota had widely scattered field operations. According to one of the top operating executives:

> "Our work groups are small and work in a dozen different states. Our group leaders have very little direct supervision from the home office. Despite these difficulties, we have been able to give our group heads the 'long view' of their operations. We have done this principally by acquainting them with the cost of operations."

Don't confuse this cost solution with the idea of "talking costs" to employees for motivational purposes. Here the purpose was to get decentralized managers to view their operations in

TABLE 1.

Centralized Organization

Advantages	Disadvantages
1. Uniformity of standards and activities among organizational units.	1. Stretching communication lines to the breaking point.
2. Utilizing the talents of outstanding executives by the entire organization.	2. Excessive demands on executives' time.
3. Uniformity of decisions.	3. Undesirably "personalizing" management policy by concentrating authority in a few hands.
4. Consistency of operating.	
5. Cost savings due to elimination of overlapping or duplicated activities.	4. Forcing top executives to develop a breadth of interest that is beyond their capacity.

Decentralized Organization

1. More manageable scope of operations.	1. Lack of uniformity in policy and procedures.
2. Development of more executives capable of decisive action in setting and administering policy.	2. Difficulty in finding executives able and willing to assume primary responsibility.
3. Shortening lines of authority and communication, thus increasing efficiency.	3. Acceptance of second rate executives in top jobs, simply because they are available and in line.
4. Vesting decision-making responsibility in the individuals closest to situations.	4. Poor coordination between decentralized units.
5. Creation of more chains of promotions.	5. Inter-unit rivalry interfering with operations.

Research Institute of America

the same light as the home office. The group leaders were being given the same yardstick used by headquarters executives to measure success and failure. In short, when they were talking money, both home and field executives were talking the same language.

CENTRALIZED PLANNING, DECENTRALIZED DOING

In Human Relations in Industry, Burleigh B. Gardner and David G. Moore say that a primary objective of organizational planning "is that of building large organizations and of retaining, at the same time, the quality and strength of small, well-integrated work groups."

Attainment of this objective, says Raymond Villers in the Harvard Business Review, may be blocked by two obstacles:

> "1. The difficulty of decentralizing down to a sufficiently small unit. (The decentralized unit of a large corporation is generally of substantial size, often including many plants and several thousand employees. There is little or no decentralization within such a unit.)
>
> "2. The difficulty of controlling the decentralized unit. (Simplified controls, such as those based essentially on the well-known criterion of 'return on investment,' often prove to be deceptive and can be applied successfully only to decentralized units of substantial size.)"

To overcome these difficulties, Villers and some other management authorities favor an organizational setup with centralized planning and control and decentralized authority and responsibility. Essentially, this approach offers a division of the "planning" and "doing" functions. To be sure, the heads of the decentralized units have "authority and responsibility." But, by and large, they are forced to play the home office's game.

Villers himself points out the limitations and dangers of the technique: "A department or an individual is entrusted with a given assignment and left alone in accordance with the principle of decentralization of authority and responsibility. That is fine if he succeeds, but what happens if he fails?"

He concludes: "A policy of decentralization of authority, based on the concept that individuals may be entrusted with the full responsibility for certain assignments, is acceptable only if the risk entailed by failure is not of excessive magnitude."

ACCOUNTABILITY AND C/D

Once the element of failure is introduced, much of the elusive C/D discussion solidifies. We see more clearly not only that "what works, works," but that "what works is right" — in other words, that the only real test is success or failure. The heart of the centralization-decentralization problem lies in the concept of accountability for success or failure.

There is no instance on record of a company president handing over a substantial part of his organization to an executive with the simple invitation, "Run it or ruin it." For that matter, neither does the chief executive of a centralized operation have such latitude; he too is usually accountable to a higher authority.

Even the top man of a corporation may have his head handed to the stockholders on a platter because of failure.

Yet different standards must be applied in judging the success of a centralized executive on the one hand and a decentralized executive on the other. The distinction seems to lie chiefly in two factors: magnitude of risk and time limit. The top executive of a centralized organization generally plays for larger stakes and is given a longer period of time to prove the value of his efforts.

In other words, from the larger perspective, decentralization may be looked at as a means of (1) decreasing the size of an investment risk and (2) shortening the length of time of the trial on which a judgment of success or failure is made.

33 THE DECENTRALIZED ORGANIZATION OF A DIVERSIFIED MANUFACTURER AND RETAILER—GENESCO

by W. Maxey Jarman and B. H. Willingham

Genesco is a diversified manufacturer and retailer of footwear and apparel. Inasmuch as size and composition of a company have a great deal to do with the organization plan, certain facts should be stated. The Company has about sixty manufacturing plants and about eight hundred retail stores, with about twenty-five thousand employees. The original company started as a men's shoe manufacturer thirty-five years ago and from a volume of one million dollars in its first year has grown, both internally and through acquisition, to an annual sales volume of 325 million dollars and has enlarged into various other fields, all related in some way with footwear and apparel.

The organization structure consists basically of sixty-six operating companies, loosely grouped together for administrative purposes in ten different groups. There is a central executive committee consisting of nine executives who coordinate the activities of the business. There are also several central functional staff departments which work with the various operating companies.

The operating companies are set up in various ways: on a product basis — for example, Johnston and Murphy, a men's high-quality shoe company; on a geographic basis — e.g., the Innes Shoe Company, a family chain to service the Greater Los Angeles area; on a type of market basis — e.g., children's lingerie; or on a type of function basis, such as box manufacturing for internal use. There are some operating companies that are primarily manufacturing businesses, others that are primarily sales

Exerpts, reprinted from Organization Theory in Industrial Practice, edited by Mason Haire (New York: John Wiley & Sons, 1962), pages 57-67, by permission of the Foundation for Research on Human Behavior.

TABLE 1. Names That Mean Genesco

Important Brands Sold Through Independent Retailers

Men's Footwear

    Johnston and Murphy
    Jarman
    Fortune
    Douglas

Women's Footwear

    Delman
    I. Miller
    Christian Dior
    Mademoiselle
    Mannequin
    Valentine
    Cover Girl
    Fortunet

Juvenile Footwear

    Number 26
    Acrobat
    Storybook

Men's Clothing

    Griffon
    Fenn Feinstein

Women's Intimate Apparel

    Formfit
    Rogers

Important Owned Retail Stores

Men's Footwear

    Flagg Bros.
    John Hardy

Women's Footwear

    Berland
    Holiday
    Wise

Family Footwear

    Innes
    Sommer and Kaufmann
    Bell Bros.

Women's Specialty Stores

    Bonwit Teller
    Henri Bendel

Men's Clothing Stores

    Whitehouse and Hardy
    Frank Bros.
    Roger Kent

Jewelry and Gifts

    Tiffany and Co.

agencies, and still others that are retail stores such as Bonwit Teller or Flagg Bros.

Some of the operating companies deal only in footwear, others in men's clothing, others in women's garments. Some of them, in the retail field particularly, will buy a great deal of merchandise from other manufacturers outside the Company. In other operating companies, some of the retail operations will buy primarily from within the Company. The operating companies are decentralized in authority and, with certain exceptions, are autonomous in their operation. . . .

THE PURPOSE OF DECENTRALIZATION AT GENESCO

1. Decentralization brings decision-making nearer to the point of action; e.g., the head of each retail operating company makes his own decision as to new store locations. He picks the location, he decides on how much rent he can pay, and he plans the economic operation of the new store.

2. Decentralization permits the people closest to the problem to decide the proper course of action; e.g., each manufacturing company makes its own decision within the limit of its capital budget in its need for new facilities. In 1955, after acquiring an established women's shoe business, the Company decided that a new plant was needed. The head of the operating company could not believe it when he was told to select the land, employ the architect and engineers, and build the plant within the limit of his budget.

3. Decentralization of authority means a faster tempo to the business.

4. Decentralization makes each operating executive feel a greater personal responsibility for the profitability of his company.

5. For us, however, aside from being desirable, decentralization is almost imperative because of the geographical distribution of our Company plus the diverse and complex nature of the different types of businesses in which we operate. For example, a central office located in the Mid-Continent area can not possibly know the details of marketing in the Greater Los Angeles area as well as can the head of a local operating company — a regional chain with offices in Los Angeles.

SOME CENTRALIZED ELEMENTS IN DECENTRALIZATION

The functions that are centrally controlled include: decisions relating to the marketing scope of the operations of the particular operating companies, financial matters, insurance and legal matters, taxes, accounting policies, top management selection, and compensation.

Each operating company has its own officers and board of

directors, and makes its own monthly reports. Most of them pay their own bills and handle their own payroll procedure, but these functions are under the control of the central finance department which furnishes necessary funds as they are needed. The capital budget is made up a year in advance for each operating company; it indicates the amount of needed expenditures for capital assets, and also indicates the size of their accounts receivable and inventories at the end of the fiscal year. These capital budgets are made up two years in advance, and although they are subject to occasional revision, they do form the basis of the financial planning of the Company and therefore must be closely adhered to by the operating companies.

The central, functional staff departments can be grouped in two categories. First are those staff departments which render a service on a controlled basis including finance, accounting, legal matters, insurance, taxes, top management selection, and compensation. These staff departments actually assume the functional responsibility.

The second category would include central, functional staff departments which act on an advisory and counseling basis, such as industrial relations, marketing, administrative services, public relations, research, and other matters of this sort. Here the staff makes recommendations to the operating company but the final decision and the success of the action is the responsibility of the operating company.

* * * * *

A DECENTRALIZED ORGANIZATION PLAN REQUIRES SPECIALIZED TECHNIQUES OF CONTROL

1. Capital charge on capital used. While finances are controlled centrally and through allocated budgets, in order to make each executive more conscious of the necessity of capital control, a capital charge is applied on the amount of capital used. Simplified, this means that interest is charged for that amount of money used at the end of each month to finance inventories, accounts receivable, and fixed assets. We make no charge for any cash balances that may be required for handling that business, nor do we give any credit for accounts payable. This is partly for convenience, but partly also because the central staff is responsible for control of cash, and because we do not want to encourage operating companies to hold down their capital used by leaning on suppliers for long-term dating, consignment of stock, and things of that sort. The capital charge currently is five percent per annum, charged on the capital used each month

on the basis of one-twelfth of five percent per annum. The funds developed by this capital charge are used for central expenses of the Company including central management expense, functional staff expense, interest and legal charges, auditing expense, and other such matters. Each operating company is thus encouraged to hold its capital usage down as much as possible and to get as great a turnover on capital as it can. We figure their profits also in relation to the capital used, feeling that this is a much more important item than that of earnings in relation to sales volume. Getting greater turnover on capital will not only reduce the capital charge of each operating company but will make it possible for it to get greater capital yield. The incentive compensation of each operating executive is computed based on his operating company's capital yield in return to twelve percent par. Each year we publish a list showing these operating executives whose net earnings after taxes exceeded the par of twelve percent of capital used. . . .

2. <u>Forecasting and monthly reports</u>. In order to stimulate responsibility for establishing expected results, each operating company makes a forecast at frequent intervals on expectations of its operation. A forecast is made monthly for the balance of the fiscal year and for the next month along with a comparison with actual results of the previous month and the forecast made at that time. In order to get more accurate forecasts, these are broken down by the significant items having to do with the operating' results of every company so that comparisons can be made to see if reasonable care has been exercised in making a forecast for the subsequent period. Quarterly, a twelve-month forecast is made; the past twelve months are compared with the forecast made at that time. This forecast is both for volume and operating income (which is defined as net earnings before taxes). When an executive makes a forecast he has more or less put himself on record that he expects to accomplish that result. We then expect him to reach that result. Practically speaking, there is a good deal of work yet to be done on forecasts; certain individuals particularly have to be further trained in the proper procedure for making correct forecasts. We believe it is desirable for the top executive in each of the operating companies to see the actual results of his company each month and to know how they are coming out. Since this involves a great many people, some of these reports inevitably are going to leak out to competition. We have found, however, that this does not make a great deal of difference because it is very difficult for any outside company to make accurate comparisons using our figures without knowing a lot more about the classification of accounts, and about various other means that we use for handling our particular reports. . . .

BETTER COMMUNICATIONS THROUGH BROAD COMMITTEE PARTICIPATION IN MANAGEMENT

As a means of maintaining contacts throughout the Company and keeping our organization aggressive and functioning on its toes, we have various groups that meet regularly throughout the Company. The Executive Committee mentioned above meets every Monday to discuss general matters, and usually has as a guest for part of the session one or two heads of operating companies who talk about their particular operations; each talk will be discussed carefully by various members of the Executive Committee so that they may thoroughly familiarize themselves with it. Quarterly we hold a meeting of the Board of Governors of the corporation, which consists of about thirty-five key operating executives. Some heads of larger operating companies, central administrative executives, group executives, and others are included in the Board of Governors. This quarterly meeting analyzes the operation, discusses the forecast for the next twelve months, and then has several papers on various phases of management read and discussed. Though our Company has a Board of Directors for legal purposes, actually the Board of Governors acts as the governing body of the Company in all matters having to do with operation. Our Company also has several other groups that serve as a cross section of our various operating companies.

We have an Advisory Board, consisting of younger junior executives from the various operating companies, which meets every two months to discuss various phases of the operation. We have a Sales-Development Council, consisting primarily of executives who have contact with sales, for study and review of those particular functions. On both a functional and a geographic basis, we have smaller committees also, which meet from time to time to consider various matters. Periodically we hold management clinics; for these, we bring in outside experts to speak to us on different operations. . . .

THE USE OF FINANCIAL INCENTIVES AT GENESCO

Wherever possible, financial incentives of executives are geared to their particular responsibilities. This means that they will have a base salary plus an incentive payment on a formula basis, at least half of which will be geared to the operation with which that particular executive is primarily concerned. These incentives usually relate to the capital yield of the particular operating company, to the growth of the particular operating company, or to a combination of these factors. As a rule, the other half of the incentive compensation will be based on over-all operations of the Company, again on a formula basis. Each management position throughout the Company is classified, evaluated, and established in a particular grade. We have grades ranging from one to twenty-three, with a base salary range for each grade, with a maximum amount which can be established as incentive compensation for that particular grade. All management positions are reviewed every six months; and our budgetary system permits a certain fund to be set up for each operating company for merit increases in their management responsibility.

The plant superintendent of a manufacturing plant may have a base salary of $7200.00 per year. In addition, he might receive additional incentive compensation of $1200.00 based on twelve percent capital yield of the parent company. However, he would also have an incentive-compensation increment of $1200.00 based on twelve percent capital yield in his own operating company.

DEVELOPMENT OF VITALITY IN A DECENTRALIZED ORGANIZATION

One of the most important functions of organization planning is to maintain a vital spirit within the Company. The continuity of this organization depends more, perhaps, on this vital spirit and on policies resulting from it than on anything else. We use several devices to stimulate vitality in the business administration of our Company.

1. We encourage internal competition. By this we mean that we have a number of reports which compare the relative functioning of various functions within those operating companies with each other. We can compare on the basis of capital yield, on the basis of results from previous periods, and on the basis of results compared with standards. . . .

2. For various staff departments we have established standards of operating performances, usually on a mathematical basis, so that they can be measured and reported on from month to month. Even in such departments as Industrial Relations, Finance, Purchasing (see [Table 2]), and various others, we have been able to establish mathematical measures of operating performance.

3. We encourage our executives to travel widely visiting other companies, keeping in touch with customers, visiting within our own organization, attending management conferences, etc., so as to stimulate their imagination and thinking.

4. We have a mandatory retirement age of sixty-five which we feel essential for the vitality of the organization. It is true that some executives are at least as effective or may be more effective after sixty-five, but many others are not. We feel that for proper planning and for developing younger people, it is essential to have a fixed age and to make this mandatory at all levels in the organization. This means that there is a constant upward movement throughout the organization to maintain vitality.

TABLE 2. Monthly Factor Performance Report
Southern Purchasing Group.

February 1, 1961

1. Damaged shoes charged to Purchasing as % of
   Value of Production   0.001%
             Par less than   0.01%

2. Standard Price Index as % of Weekly Bulletin
   Price Index   96.4%
             Par less than   100%

3. (a) Substitution losses as a % of Value of
   Materials Used   0.07%
             Par less than   0.2%

   (b) Low grade Upper Leather substitution — Month   420

             Par $500

4. Obsolescence Loss as % of Materials Used — Month   0.38%

             Par less than   1.0%

5. Raw Materials Inventories as % of Month's
   usage 83M   107.2%
             Par less than   100.0%

6. Department expense as a % of budget —
         Month 119.8   Period 105.3

             Par less than   100%

7. Material shortage by week as %

	Week	%
	1-9	2.6
	1-16	2.5
	1-23	2.0
	1-30	2.0
Par 2.0		2.0
wks. avg.		2.2

(7. ... of total weekly production)

8. Purchase Gain & Loss — 23347   Period 76382

9. Number of job Descriptions & Job Standards
   prepared or improved   2
             Par 5 per month

10. Morale Survey rating   Supervisors   35
             Hourly employee's   36

11. List of projects to develop group image in and outside company
              Par at least —
              2 per month   2

13. Accuracy of Forecast   Percent of difference
             actual to forecast   NA

THE NEED FOR CONSTANT CHANGE IN ORGANIZATION

With economic conditions rapidly changing, with new scientific advances, with the problems of growth and competition, no plan of organization can ever be considered to be fixed and unchangeable. It must be constantly adjusted to changing conditions, and to changing available personnel. For that reason it must be constantly studied, primarily by the chief executive of the business, for proper adjustment so as to keep the structure vital and to attain the purposes of the organization to stimulate and use most effectively the abilities of the people who make up the organization.

34 SPAN OF CONTROL — A METHOD OF EVALUATION

by C. W. Barkdull

Since the original popularization of the term "Span of Control" as an organizational principle, there has been a great amount of thinking and writing on the subject, but unfortunately there has not evolved a common agreement as to what the proper span of control should be, i.e., how many persons should report to a given manager. Graicunas has suggested that a limited span is desirable because of the great increases in interrelationships as the number of persons supervised increases.[1] Considering all levels of supervision in the several companies with which I have had personal experience, limited spans of fewer than 5 or 6 appear to be the general rule. This is confirmed by Healey in his study of 620 firms.[2] In contrast, as one reviews the spans toward the top of many organizations, it is not unusual to find 8, 10, 12, and even more persons reporting to an executive, apparently without undue strain. Dale found great variances in his study of the Presidents' spans in 100 large organizations, with a significant number exceeding 10.[3] Entwisle and Walton found this same phenomenon to a lesser degree in their study of college and smaller company

[1] V. A. Graicunas, "Relationship in Organization," in L. Gulick and L. Urwick (eds.), Papers on the Science of Administration (New York: Columbia University, 1947).

[2] James H. Healey, "Coordination and Control of Executive Functions," Personnel, September, 1956, pages 106-117.

[3] Ernest Dale, Planning and Developing the Company Organization Structure (New York: American Management Association, 1952).

Reprinted by permission from the May, 1963, issue of the Michigan Business Review, published by the Graduate School of Business Administration, The University of Michigan.

presidents.[4] Broad spans are also sometimes found at lower levels, and the subject managers have not appeared to be significantly more overworked or harried than other managers with limited spans.

Why such a divergence of practice and opinion? Suojanen has concluded that span of control is no longer an applicable principle in modern organizations.[5] But it would seem that from the standpoint of logic there must be a limit to the number of persons who can be effectively supervised by another. From the standpoint of business administration, there must be an optimum number under a given set of circumstances. That optimum number, I would like to suggest, is affected by a number of factors which vary between positions, and perhaps vary in time.

One factor which appears quite obviously to affect span of control is the degree to which an executive is assisted in the execution of his duties by staff departments and assistants. This perhaps accounts for the greater spans of some of the presidents studied by Dale, Entwisle, and Walton. Another somewhat obvious factor is that some managers, because of their education, experience, and general competence, just do not require a great amount of supervision.

It was these observations which led to the exploration of the possibility that there was a finite number of factors affecting span, and that these factors might be measured in some way. The objective was to find a means of evaluating logically a given managerial position and of arriving at a fair and supportable conclusion as to what the proper span of control should be.

The rest of this article will describe the case history of the development of an evaluation method of determining proper spans of control.

DESCRIPTION OF THE PROBLEM

A description of the specific organizational problems is significant to an understanding of why the problem of span was undertaken in the first place. The company in question, a division of a larger corporation, had experienced a very rapid growth over a period of five years — from a small handful of scientific personnel to a sizable enterprise of 25,000 employees, consisting of three divisions, each under a general manager, together with several staff and service activities reporting to the president and executive vice president.

---

[4] Doris R. Entwisle and John Walton, "Observations on the Span of Control," Administrative Science Quarterly, March, 1961, page 522.

[5] W. W. Suojanen, "The Span of Control — Fact or Fable," Advanced Management, November, 1955, pages 5-13.

Technically, the company had done an outstanding job, but problems were beginning to emerge from various sources. Employees and supervisors were finding it increasingly difficult to get a job done. Costs were climbing to a point where the management was somewhat alarmed.

In reviewing the organizational structure prior to writing a set of organizational policies, two things became particularly predominant — the frequency with which very limited spans of control occurred (i.e., two and three), and the great many levels of supervision which existed throughout the major components of the company.

The company was to a degree aware that there was a problem, but had attempted to resolve it by establishing certain criteria on supervisory ratios (which is the result of dividing the total non-supervisory personnel by total supervision in a given organizational component). It appeared that these objectives were being met by increasing the number of non-supervisory persons reporting to supervisors at the lowest level.

The span at the director level (the level just below a general manager) ranged from 5 to 10. This was considered to be quite satisfactory. The lowest level of supervision, i.e., the level having only non-supervisory personnel reporting to them, averaged 15 to 18, in the major components. This, too, appeared to be satisfactory. However, the spans of supervision between the directors and first-line supervision (which for this purpose will be termed "middle management") averaged only 3.2 for the company as a whole with little variation between major components.

Great pressure had been exerted by executives and managers all through the development of the company for additional levels of supervision, until in quite a number of cases in the larger of the company's components there were seven levels of supervision up to the directors. This excluded direct line assistants, which if included would have increased the levels in some instances to as many as eleven. The General Managers and the President made two additional levels.

IMPORTANCE OF SPAN OF CONTROL AND LEVELS OF SUPERVISION

Why is the problem of spans of control and levels of supervision important to management?[6] There are several undesirable ramifications of a situation where there are limited spans and too many

---

[6] For an outstanding discussion of a concept of managing and the relation of span of control to managing, see Richard C. Anderson, Management Practices (New York: McGraw-Hill, 1960) pages 5-9 and 79-80.

levels. First, it creates over-supervision. Supervisors tend to spend time reviewing and directing subordinates in much greater detail than necessary. Second, it impedes and lengthens communication. Multiple levels of supervision tend to slow down the flow of information, suggestions, instructions, etc., up and down the chain of command. In many cases, the information may lose its original meaning, intent, and impact. Third, it delays decisions and action because of the many levels of review. Fourth, it decreases initiative and morale. Too many levels often limit delegation of any real authority to the lower levels which in turn interferes with the accomplishment of assigned tasks, and makes the subordinates overly dependent on the superiors. This lack of a sense of accomplishment can lead to low morale. Fifth, it decreases opportunity for responsibility and development. Narrow spans limit the supervision to a few activities and deprive them of the benefit to be derived from supervising a number of related activities. Sixth, it increases costs. Narrow spans and added levels increase the number of supervisors and the attendant extra expenses of secretaries, space, facilities, supplies, and services.

The correction of this kind of situation, then, should improve communication, produce a more responsive organization, stimulate greater initiative, and provide greater opportunity for personnel and supervisory development.

The close relationship between levels of supervision and spans of control is illustrated in Exhibit 1 which shows the effect of varying spans on the number of levels required. In a hypothetical

EXHIBIT 1. Required Supervision & Levels at Varying Spans in a Branch of 3800-4000 Employees

	At Average Span of 3[a]	At Average Span of 4[a]	At Average Span of 6[a]
	6 levels supervisory employees — 302	5 levels supervisory employees — 268	4 levels supervisory employees — 241
	1	1	1
Supervisory	3	4	6
employees	8	13	None
required at	23	None	None
each level	67	50	34
	200	200	200
Non-supervisory employees	3600	3600	3600

[a] Applied to middle management and director levels.

organization having approximately 3600 non-supervisory employees and 200 first-line supervisors, six levels and 302 supervisory employees would be required under an average span of three; five levels and 268 supervisory employees under average spans of four; and only four levels of 241 supervisory employees under average spans of six. (The fact that most organizations do not build up quite this evenly from one level to another because of variations in the sizes of the components, would change the figures somewhat but would not change the effect substantially.)

A vigorous program of increasing spans and decreasing levels was called for, but such a program would have to be based on a logical criteria for determining what the proper spans and levels should be.

THE FACTORS AFFECTING SPANS

The first step was to determine the most significant factors which had a bearing on spans. Literature on the subject contained a number of leads. Experience provided a few more. From these, seven factors were selected and defined:

1. Similarity of functions supervised.
2. Geographic contiguity of functions supervised.
3. Complexity of functions supervised.
4. Direction and control required by the personnel supervised.
5. Coordination required of the supervisor.
6. Planning required of the supervisor.
7. Organizational assistance received by the supervisor.

Another analyst and student of organization principles might very well have selected different factors. It is recognized that other factors have bearing on individual cases. For example, the incumbent of a given supervisory position himself has a bearing on the span. His personal ability, background, experience, and personality may have an important bearing on how many he can supervise effectively. But, as in the establishing of any other standard of measurement, differences in individual abilities should not be worked into the standard.

The definitions of the seven factors were established as follows:

Similarity of Functions: This refers to the degree to which functions performed by the various components or personnel reporting to the supervisor are alike or different — whether they are the same functions (perhaps organized on a geographic basis), or whether they differ in nature (perhaps grouped because of their relation to one another). Its importance is that as the functions increase in the degree of variability the more interrelations to be kept in mind and the fewer number of persons the supervisor can effectively handle.

Geographic Contiguity: This factor refers to the physical locations of the components and personnel reporting to a supervisor. Geographic separation of functions makes for greater difficulty in supervision because of necessity for more formal means of communication, time to get together for necessary discussions, and time to personally visit the separated activities.

Complexity of Functions: This factor refers to the nature of the duties being performed by the majority of non-supervisory personnel, and involves a determination of the degree of difficulty in performing satisfactorily. It is generally considered that the salary and hourly ratings are a reasonably fair reflection of complexity. Hence this factor was related to the job classifications of the more important of the non-supervisory positions in the component. Generally the greater the complexity of the function supervised the smaller the number of persons a supervisor should be expected to handle.

Direction and Control: This factor refers to the nature of the personnel reporting directly to the supervisor and reflects the degree of attention which they require for proper supervision of their actions. High level competent managers with years of background and experience, or highly qualified scientists with Ph.D.'s will require minimum attention except for general administrative and planning matters; while other personnel might require closer supervision, direction, guidance, and training. This also reflects the extent to which responsibility can be delegated to subordinates; the extent to which problems and decisions can be resolved at subordinate levels; the amount of training they require; and the degree to which objective standards can be applied. The greater the degree to which subordinates require direction and control the smaller the span should be of the subject supervisor. (This factor may appear to measure the same thing as complexity, and to some extent they are counter-acting. However, while complexity measures the work of the nonsupervisory personnel, direction and control measures the degree to which subordinates require supervision.)

Coordination: As opposed to the previous factors which mainly relate to the duties and personnel supervised, the factor of coordination (and the next one — planning) reflect the nature of the supervisory position itself. It measures the extent to which the supervisor must exert time and effort (1) in keeping the functions, actions, and output of his components properly correlated, balanced, and going in the same direction to accomplish the goals of the activity, and (2) in keeping his components keyed in with other activities of the division to accomplish divisional plans and programs. Again, the greater the complexity of the coordination functions and the greater the amount of time required to perform them the fewer number of people who should report to him.

Planning: This factor refers to the importance, complexity, and time requirements of one of the primary functions of a manager or supervisor — that of reviewing the objectives and the output requirements in the future, and programming the actions, organization, staff, and budgets necessary to accomplish them. Some distinction must be made in the evaluation of a given position as to how much of these functions are actually performed by others for him, and where planning must be done on a continuing basis or might essentially be accomplished once a year when budgets and programs are proposed and approved. As the importance, complexity, and time required of the supervisor increases, the more prudent it will be to reduce the numbers of persons reporting to him.

Organizational Assistance: This factor considers the assistance received within the organizational component from direct line assistants, assistants to, staff activities or personnel having administrative, planning and control responsibilities, and (at the first-line supervisory level) leadmen.

EVALUATION OF THE FACTORS

An experienced organization analyst could take these factors as identified and develop a "feel" for the numbers of persons who could be supervised effectively in a given situation, based on his experience and on general comparisons. But his thinking process might not be uniform in all cases, thereby leading to some inequities between positions; and probably there would not be uniformity of application between analysts.

Most important, however, it would be difficult to convince an operating manager who was trying to build up his organization unnecessarily the how and why of the answer the analyst came up with, and that he was being evaluated on the same basis as other managers.

This, then, led to the reduction of a thinking process to mathematical weightings and the development of a "Supervisory Index" which represents the relative difficulty of the supervisory job. The approach is similar to job evaluation. Many of the same techniques are used.

Finding the right weightings was not a simple task. A number of different weightings were tried and compared with actual situations before arriving at the final weights described in summary in Exhibit 2. (Detailed descriptions were prepared for each of these weightings in order to provide a basis for uniform applications. They are not included here because of the length.)

Each of the supervisory factors was applied to each supervisory position studied, and the degrees of supervisory burden determined. The sum total of the values represented a comparative measurement of the supervisory burden. This total point value, modified for assistants (described below), was called the "Supervisory Index."

EXHIBIT 2. Degrees of Supervisory Burden Within Span Factors.

Span Factor	Degree of Supervisory Burden				
Similarity of functions	Identical (1)	Essentially alike (2)	Similar (3)	Inherently different (4)	Fundamentally distinct (5)
Geographic contiguity	All together (1)	All one bldg. (2)	Separate bldg's. one plant location (3)	Separate locations one geographic area (4)	Dispersed geographic areas (5)
Complexity of functions	Simple repetitive (2)	Routine (4)	Some complexity (6)	Complexity varied (8)	Highly complex (10)
Direction control	Minimum supervision & training (3)	Limited supervision (6)	Moderate periodic supervision (9)	Frequent continuing supervision (12)	Constant close supervision (15)
Coordination	Minimum relationships with others (2)	Relationships limited to defined courses (4)	Moderate relationships easily controlled (6)	Considerable close relationship (8)	Extensive mutual non-recurring relationships (10)
Planning	Minimum scope complexity (2)	Limited scope complexity (4)	Moderate Scope complexity (6)	Considerable effort required guided only by broad policies (8)	Extensive effort required areas & policies not charted (10)

Equating for organizational assistance in the supervisory index represented a different kind of problem. It was not really a separate factor, such as Similarity of Functions, Planning, etc., and it did not make sense to apply weights in the same manner. Its effect was to <u>reduce</u> the supervisory burden rather than increase it. Therefore, it was decided to apply fractional multiplier values which would reduce the total supervisory index.

This sounded reasonable too from the standpoint that organizational assistance tended to decrease the supervisor's burden in several if not all of the other areas considered. Again, finding the right set of multipliers was somewhat of a trial and error process, until a set of factors was determined which seemed to properly fit the actual circumstances. The multiplier factors for positions with subordinate supervision are as follows:

Adjustment for Assistance

Organizational Assistance Provided	Multiplier Factor
Direct line assistant <u>and</u> staff activities	.60
Direct line assistant (only)	.70
Staff activities (administrative, planning, <u>and</u> control functions)	.75
Staff activities (administrative, planning, <u>or</u> control functions)	.85
Assistant to (limited duties)	.95

Leaders working for first-line supervision were adjusted for as follows:

Number of Leaders	Multiplier
1	.85
2	.70
3	.55
4	.40
5	.25

DETERMINATION OF STANDARD SPANS

A number of positions were evaluated using the weightings developed. Exhibit 3 shows a tabulation of the results of the evaluation in the middle management and director areas. Most of the cases, of course, had actual spans of 2, 3, and 4, and these showed no relationship to the supervisory indices. However, much to our delight, those cases having spans of five and over tended to have a very definite relationship to the index, that is, as the supervisory index decreased indicating less supervisory burden) the spans increased. This was strong indication that there was validity to our supervisory index, and, since these represented actual cases within the company, it was felt that they could be used effectively and justifiably as standards of performance for the rest of the organization.

EXHIBIT 3. Conversion of Supervisory Index into Span of Management.

Supervisory Index	Range of Actual Spans (No. of Cases)[a]										Suggested Standard Spans
	2	3	4	5	6	7	8	9	10	11	
40-42		1	1	1							4-5
37-39	1	1	4	5	4						4-6
34-36	10	9	13		3						4-7
31-33	10	6	12	7	3	1	1				5-8
28-30	12	17	7	3	2	1					6-9
25-27	3	3					1	1			7-10
22-24	1	1	1		1			1	1	1	8-11
Total Cases	37	38	38	16	12	3	2	2	1	1	

[a]Total of 150 cases taken from PMS, SS, Operations, QATS, Research, Finance and Industrial Relations.

The actual standards were developed in the case of middle management and directors by plotting the supervisory index against the actual spans of those five and over, and calculating the regression line (or line of relationship) to fit the sample. A range was then provided to allow for varying circumstances. A number of cases were also evaluated at the first-line supervisory level. A similar relationship developed here, but with broader spans (see Exhibit 4).

The question might be asked why should there have to be different scales for first-line supervision and for supervisors who have other supervisors reporting to them. One might argue that the same factors and weights should apply. Unfortunately, this study did not arrive at an answer to that question. Perhaps there is a greater difference in the amount of planning, coordinat-

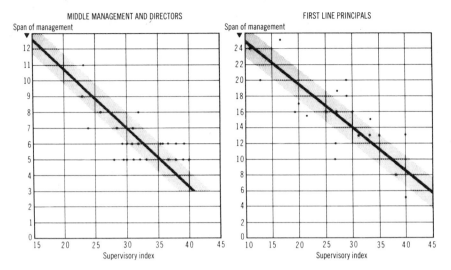

EXHIBIT 4. Proposed Standard Span of Management.

ing, and directing performed between the first-line supervision and higher levels than is reflected in the point values applied. Instead of a straight line relationship, perhaps the line of relationship should be an S curve which would equate for the greater spans of the first-line supervisors. This will have to be a further refinement. The actual situation was that the span for first-line supervision at a given supervisory index was approximately double that of higher supervision with the same index. It appeared proper that the standards should reflect this.

THE PLAN OF IMPLEMENTATION

The feasibility of the end result was readily recognized by management, but getting there was another problem, since it would mean a considerably less requirement for supervision in the middle management areas. To accomplish the job in a short time through a series of rather sweeping reorganizations, would demoralize the organization and negate the improvements in organizational atmosphere for which we were striving. Hence, goals were set to which the various components were to work over a period of time — an average span of six, with a minimum of five; four levels of supervision in the larger components and three in the others. Provision, of course, was made for exceptions.

Each component was then introduced to the program and its background, and requested to prepare a long range organization plan, including a program for accomplishing it over a period of time. Various means were to be taken to arrive at the goals.

Attrition of supervisory personnel (getting jobs outside the company, retirement, etc.) would take care of quite a number of situations. Further expansion of the company would create demands for supervision which would be filled from present supervisory personnel. Careful scrutiny of the supervisory requirements of the other corporate divisions would be made in order to transfer qualified supervisory personnel to open positions there. Some would have to be taken care of through reclassification.

An illustration of how the criteria were used is shown in Exhibit 5. An evaluation of the supervisory burden might indicate that the spans of the managers in the two cases shown could be 5-8. In the case on the left, the possibility of eliminating the middle level of managers would clearly be indicated. In the case on the right, it would indicate that the twelve components on the lower level might be combined into six (or perhaps 5, 7, or 8) which in turn would permit the elimination of the three managers on the second level.

RESULTS OF THE PROGRAM

As of the writing of the article, a number of reorganizations had been effected in several of the company's organizational units. The results were quite gratifying. Although the goals were not yet fully reached, the accomplishment, even in its four months of operation, was significant. Some of the organizations, as was expected, had situations where components just could not be reorganized into logical groupings of more than three or four. In

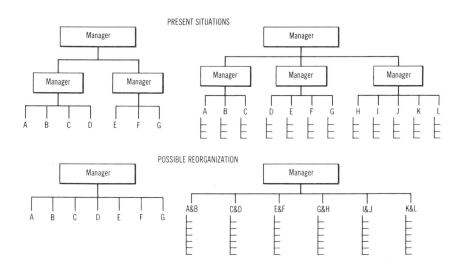

EXHIBIT 5. Examples of Reorganization to Effect Fewer Levels & Greater Spans.

other cases, other important considerations (such as the organization of activities serviced, management emphasis, etc.) dictated something less than the desirable spans.

Many components, however, were able to reach the objectives, in some cases even exceeding the standards; most made significant advances toward the desired goals. Probably the most dramatic of the changes succeeded in cutting out two full levels of supervision (from 7 to 5), increased the average span of middle management from 3.9 to 5.9, reduced supervisory personnel by 7 (mostly in transfers to other expanding activities) and cut supervisory pay roll by the rate of over $70,000 per year.

Although not designed as a cost reduction program, total results in those activities in which the program had been installed amounted to a rate of over $280,000 per year in supervisory payroll. To this saving could be added the cost of the secretarial assistance, fringe benefits, office space, and supplies required by the supervision eliminated.

CONCLUSION

The development of the supervisory indices and the establishment of standard ranges for spans of control was designed as another of the several tools of management and the organization analyst. It was not intended that it be used to the exclusion of the other sound principles of organization. It was not intended to force an organization structure into the standard spans, but rather to use the span of control evaluations in cases where span was a real factor in the determination of the optimum organization.

A study of this nature can point up that, in many areas of an organization, limited spans and many levels have been built up where it has been entirely unnecessary and with an unwarranted build-up of supervisory costs. It can be used to re-establish the organization structure on a sounder basis, and thus contribute importantly not only to reduced costs but to a healthier organizational climate.

35 SPAN OF CONTROL

by John M. Pfiffner and Frank P. Sherwood

I. SPAN OF CONTROL

There is perhaps no more hoary artifact of organization folklore than the notion of span of control. Many a reorganization has taken place almost entirely in terms of the number of people an executive should supervise. Prescriptions as to number abound. Sometimes it is three; seldom does it exceed twenty. In most instances the reduction in numbers of people supervised has been looked upon as good in itself. Thus executives pride themselves that somehow the organization process has been "streamlined" when their span of control has been reduced from twenty to twelve, twelve to seven, or whatever.

Perspectives

Has such emphasis on the idea of span of control been appropriate? Does it deserve a prime place in our thinking? Certainly its dominance as a theme of traditional organization theory is not hard to understand. Its relationship to the hierarchical structure is clear-cut. It has a quantitative aspect which can result in concrete proposals for organization reform. Finally, the span of control notion fitted well with earlier ideas of "principles" for organization behavior.

Nature of attacks. In the past fifteen years, many writers have questioned the usefulness of span of control as an avenue to real understanding of organization processes. Although it was not the first, Herbert Simon's essay in 1946, "The Proverbs of Administration," was particularly successful in bringing these

John M. Pfiffner and Frank P. Sherwood, Administrative Organization. © 1960. Reprinted by permission of Prentice-Hall, Inc., Englewood Cliffs, N.J.

questions to a focus.[1] In the first place, no one really seems to know what the magic number of persons supervised should be. Secondly, it appears that such factors as the personality of the executive, the routine or varied nature of the work, the degree of geographic dispersion, the need for immediate decisions, and the type of program administered, are all factors of prime importance in defining the supervisory relationship. They have much to do with the number of persons who might be included in the executive's span of control. As a consequence there is no quick and sure formula which can be used to determine the appropriate span.

Bias in the concept. The traditional bias in most of the literature on this question is also worth noting. It emphasizes the small span. Seldom even today do executives state publicly and proudly that the number of persons they supervise has been increased from 12 to 20. It must be assumed that the almost unconscious reluctance to broadcast such heresy is based on the traditional theory that the small number permits the executive to obtain more intimate control. Further ambiguity in the concept is added also by the fact that some social scientists would probably argue for a small span but for different reasons. They would likely say that modern teamwork patterns of executive leadership work better with a small group of people interacting.

Relation to hierarchical conformation. The span idea is important not only in terms of executive relationships with subordinates; it is also significant because of its influence on the conformation of the hierarchy. It can do much to determine the number of levels in the organization pyramid, and in doing that it can impose a mushroom-like flatness or a cone-like depth on the structure. Put another way, an organization is in many ways like a rubber ball. If you squeeze it in one place, it bulges somewhere else. Thus, if 20 department heads all report to the president, the organization tends to "flatten." In such a circumstance there are only two levels. If on the other hand only three report to the president and the others report to the three, more levels have been added to the structure. It has "deepened." In the process of deepening, it is assumed that problems of communication become more difficult. In the first instance, everyone talks to the boss. In the second, seventeen talk through someone else, with consequent difficulties of blockage and distortion that inevitably occur.

Research on the Problem

Graicunas. There has been relatively little, if any, empirical study of span of control. Perhaps the most influential paper in

---

[1] Herbert A. Simon, "The Proverbs of Administration," Public Administration Review, VI (Winter, 1946), 53-67.

the past generation was that of Graicunas who carried out a mathematical projection of what would happen to an organization by manipulating the span of control at the top.[2] The general import was that as the span at the top is increased mathematically, the complexity of relationships at subordinate echelons grows geometrically. Along with that of Davis, this study was not based upon empirical observation but rather upon theoretical projection by mathematics. This approach is not to be condemned out of hand: after all, modern nuclear physics is based upon theoretical assumptions and projections. In nuclear physics, however, the assumptions are subsequently tested by experiment. The study of organization is now perhaps approaching a stage of maturity, through the emergence of the behavioral sciences, wherein such theoretical projections will be subjected to experimental, or at least observational, test.

Baker and Davis. An example of an empirical study of this nature is offered by the investigation of Ohio manufacturing companies by Baker and Davis. The inquiry was designed to test Davis' previously expressed "law of functional growth," which maintained that "as line [substantive] personnel increases in arithmetic progression, staff [adjective] personnel tends to increase in geometric progression."[3] The results did not support the validity of this so-called law, because it was found that the number of indirect employees expanded arithmetically, instead of geometrically, at approximately the same rate as direct employees. An incidental result of the study, however, presented data which supported generally-held ideas about span of control.

> These data confirm the contention that there is a unit or span of operative supervision, and that it exists regardless of the industry. These data indicate that the average unit of supervision is 100/6, or 16.7 operatives per supervisor. This is almost exactly in the center of the generally accepted range of units of operative supervision, 10 to 30 employees. These data also confirm the contention that there is a unit

---

[2] V. A. Graicunas, "Relationship and Organization," in Luther Gulick and L. Urwick, eds., Papers on the Science of Administration (New York: Public Administration Service, 1937), pages 183-187. See also Ralph C. Davis, The Influence of the Unit of Supervision and the Span of Executive Control on the Economy of Organization Structure (Columbus: Ohio State University, Bureau of Business Research, 1941).

[3] Alton W. Baker and Ralph C. Davis, Ratios of Staff to Line Employees and Stages of Differentiation of Staff Functions (Columbus: Bureau of Business Research Monograph No. 72, 1954), page 57.

or span of executive supervision. They indicate that the average span of executive supervision is six subordinates, approximately. This is also in the center of the generally accepted range for units of executive supervision of 3 to 8 or 9 subordinate executives.[4]

Relation to decision-making. Other writers, notably Waino W. Soujanen, have emphasized the impact of changes in decision-making practices on the span of control concept.[5] The replacement of the omniscient father figure with the management team has changed the whole system of communication and contact within the organization. Inevitably it has affected attention paid to the way the executive controls in the command sense. As Soujanen has written:

> The most striking feature in the recent development of the large well managed, contemporary American corporation is the variety of decision-making processes that have been incorporated into its structure and philosophy. Hierarchy, or control by leaders, still remains the most significant decision-making process. To an increasing extent, however, other decision-making processes have become important, the price system, or control of and by leaders, is replacing hierarchy at a very rapid pace. Similarly, voting or control by the led, is being increasingly incorporated into the decision-making structure of the progressive organization. Finally, bargaining, or control of leaders by leaders, has shown a phenomenal growth in recent years.[6]

Urwick's reaction. Soujanen's contention that modern social science concepts have seriously modified the traditional underpinnings of the span of control drew a sharp retort from Lyndall F. Urwick.[7] Urwick's article, despite emotional over-

---

4 Ibid., p. 31.

5 See Waino W. Soujanen, "The Span of Control — Fact or Fable?" Advanced Management, XX (November, 1955), 5-13.

6 Waino W. Soujanen, "Leadership, Authority, and the Span of Control," Advanced Management, XXIII (September, 1957), 17.

7 Lyndall F. Urwick, "The Span of Control — Some Facts about the Fables," Advanced Management, XXI (November, 1956), 5-18; Herbert A. Simon, "The Span of Control: A Reply," Advanced Management, XXII (April, 1957), 14.

tones, was more than a mere diatribe because it was exceptionally well-documented. It is not easy to categorize Urwick's points. In general he felt that Soujanen was giving social science credit for a maturity that it had not attained. The claim was made that Soujanen had deliberately distorted Barnard, as well as Dale's study of corporations,[8] in order to support his point.

Urwick also took issue with Herbert Simon. Here he was concerned mainly with Simon's contention that a short span of control at the top must necessarily increase the number of horizontal echelons. Urwick seems to admit that such echelons are created, but he asks, "What of it?" A steep hierarchy with many echelons is not necessarily a bad thing if it offers the opportunity of access to higher authority with key levels where personal leadership stands out. Urwick says that the critics of the short span have failed to make a distinction between "access to" and direct supervision. Span of control applies only to direct supervision and it does not necessarily prohibit "access to" on the part of people not in the formal pattern.

* * * * *

II. SPAN OF CONTROL AND DECENTRALIZATION

Traditional concepts of hierarchy were built upon a philosophy of decision-making which was dominantly characterized by centralization. Decisions were made at or near the top even on matters of minor detail. Today the emergent philosophy of hierarchy emphasizes decentralized decision-making supported by a fabric of group process. Thus two elements are raising a sharp challenge to the standard proposal of a short span: (1) the trend toward decentralization; and (2) the new pattern of leadership evolving from a growing acceptance of group process as a way of life in management institutions.

Hierarchical Flatness as a Means of Forcing Delegation

The most widely publicized arguments in favor of a wider span of control have emanated from the utterances of James C. Worthy, a sociologist who became an executive of Sears, Roebuck and Company.[9] Worthy took a stand against the excessive elaboration of organizational arrangements in general, maintaining

---

[8]Ernest Dale, Planning and Developing the Company Organization Structure (New York: American Management Association, Research Report No. 20, 1952).

[9]He also served as Assistant Secretary of Commerce in the Eisenhower administration.

as one might expect of a person who was sociologically trained that the proper integration or organizations could better be brought about through sociological rather than mechanical approaches.[10] The essence of the "heresy," which attracted widespread attention, was advocacy of a wide span of control at the top and middle echelons, primarily to enforce delegation and decentralization.

Sears, Roebuck. It was alleged that this pattern of organization, often referred to as "flat," was in successful operation at Sears, Roebuck. It grew out of the need to build self-reliance into the retail store manager's job, particularly to protect him against the over-solicitous, clucking-hen type of supervision which previously had been practiced by the area chiefs. In other words, one device for keeping the area offices from exercising too detailed a supervision of the stores was to give them so many stores to look after that they would not have time to devote to inconsequential matters.

> . . . . the company has gone directly counter to one of the favorite tenets of modern management theory, the so-called "span of control," which holds that the number of subordinate executives or supervisors reporting to a single individual should be severely limited to enable that individual to exercise the detailed direction and control which are generally considered necessary. In an organization with as few supervisory levels as Sears, it is obvious that most key executives have so many subordinates reporting to them that they simply cannot exercise too close supervision over their activities. By this means, substantial decentralization of administrative processes is practically guaranteed.[11]

Bank of America. A less publicized but nevertheless noteworthy example is offered by the Bank of America, which has over 600 branches throughout California, each of which reports directly to corporate headquarters at San Francisco. There is no intervening area structure with directive powers over the branch offices.

---

[10]James C. Worthy, "Organizational Structure and Employee Morale," American Sociological Review, XV (April, 1950), 169-179.
[11]James C. Worthy, "Factors Influencing Employee Morale," Harvard Business Review, XXVIII (January, 1950), 61-73.

When officers of the bank are questioned about this seemingly unorthodox setup, their response is that they do not want to risk setting up an echelon that would take authority away from the branch managers. They want them to be self-reliant local business men with a maximum opportunity for making decisions on their own. An intervening layer of district offices would, in their efforts to justify their existence, inevitably invade the sphere of discretion of the branch managers.

The Broad Span and Local Independence

Chain merchandising. As will be pointed out in another place which deals with decentralization per se, there is now a strong movement in the chain merchandising field to alter the role of the local managers. In general the change makes the managers citizens of the local community, rather than puppets manipulated by functional and staff controls from above. This has been partly motivated by a resurgence of competition from locally-owned independent merchandisers who have drawn at least a part of their strength from success in identifying themselves with their communities. Thus the decentralizing forces in chain merchandising have emanated from the felt need to build the local branchmanagers into resourceful and self-reliant entrepreneurs socially integrated into the communities they serve. This has required a change in philosophy away from central attention to detail toward a more general type of supervision by headquarters. The lengthening of the span of control has been one device sometimes utilized to accomplish this purpose.

* * * * *

CONCLUSION

For the present the concept of span of control cannot be relegated to limbo. Rather it is necessary to take the temperate view expressed by Urwick that it may be a valuable diagnostic instrument in certain cases.[12] It seems more realistic to approach the problem by asking how much supervision is needed in each particular situation. By acknowledging that circumstances may differ, and inquiring to ascertain the pertinent variables, an attitude of research will be engendered. Instead of a

---

[12] Lyndall F. Urwick, "The Manager's Span of Control," Harvard Business Review, XXXIV (May-June, 1956), 39, 41.

preconceived formula, people will begin to inquire into the factors which apply in each new supervisory setup. Perhaps after a number of analyses of this kind, empirical evidence will emerge and point to the variables operating. Then it may be possible to begin to establish norms for determining how much supervision is needed.[13]

---

[13] See the section entitled "Criteria for Determining the Span of Control," in Dale, Planning and Developing the Company Organization Structure, page 53.

PART ELEVEN:

COMMITTEES

36 THE NATURE AND USE OF COMMITTEES

by Estill I. Green

Never before have committees had it so good. Now that the psychologists, the social scientists and the managerial mentors have led business safely away from that horrendous thing they refer to as monolithic organization; now that all the blessings of conjoint decision and consultative supervision have been showered upon us; now that we have reached the promised land of milk and honey and group-mindedness, the committee has become a widely used instrument of organization. No longer is the suggestion to appoint a committee greeted with sarcasm, suspicion or distrust. Everybody knows that management committees have made Jersey Standard and DuPont what they are today. Obviously, what's good at the top is good at all levels. So committeeism is rampant. In the vernacular, business has gone whole hog for committees.

To be sure, you do find an occasional skeptic. Herrymon Mauer, for example, tosses in this paragraph in Fortune:[1]

> When the chairman declares the meeting adjourned, the discussion has already gone on for an hour beyond schedule. One member has expressed opposition to the project at hand because he is in the habit of expressing opposition. A second has discussed extraneous issues in detail until finally ruled out of order. A third

---

[1]H. Maurer, "Management by Committee," Fortune, April, 1953, page 145.

Reprinted from Advanced Management — Office Executive, July, 1959, pages 24-28, by permission of the National Office Management Association.

has asked the chairman to explain the project more fully. A fourth has repeated what the chairman has just said. And two members have fallen into an acrimonious dispute, using the project under discussion for display of personal rivalry. In the course of the meeting, one member dozed off; two others lost themselves in doodling; another began writing a memo on a different topic; and the chairman — uncertain at the beginning of the meeting as to the merits of the project — finds himself addled and exhausted at the end of it.

Then, too, you can find an occasional oldtimer who recalls the Kettering innuendo about committees. It appears that Mrs. Kettering was reading the newspaper account of Lindbergh's historic flight to LeBourget. "Isn't it wonderful!" she exclaimed. "And to think he did it all alone!" "Well," remarked the Boss, "it would have been still more wonderful if he had done it with a committee."

But who nowadays would take such detractors seriously? The old saw that a committee keeps minutes and squanders hours is clearly an exaggeration. The fact is that many estimable committees don't keep any minutes. Besides all this, committees have been researched at Harvard. The Laboratory of Social Relations up there, in a bold departure from the mathematical theory of decision-making, has conducted an experimental investigation of the functioning of committees.[2] The result is nothing less than a set of working formulas for the successful conduct of committees.

The Harvard experts have determined the optimum number of members for a committee. And it isn't 7/10 of a man, that delightful if somewhat illusory figure deduced by Bruce Old in his classic treatise, On the Mathematics of Committees, Boards and Panels.[3] Not so, say the Cantabrigians. The optimum number of members is five, and the half-efficiency points lie in the vicinity of 3.8 and 6.9 members, respectively. As to that so-called Old's Law, perhaps better referred to as Old's Hypothesis — which asserts that the work output of a committee is inversely proportional to the organizational level of its members — recent results suggest that the Pentagon environment may have vitiated Old's researches. There appears to be some correlation, but the proportionality factor is not a unity.

---

[2]R. F. Bales, "In Conference," Harvard Business Review, March-April, 1954, page 44.

[3]Bruce Old, "On the Mathematics of Committees, Boards and Panels," Scientific Monthly, August, 1946, page 129.

Neglecting more esoteric details, the conditions prescribed by the Harvard sociologists for most effective committee performance are these: The committee members should be so chosen that their index of participation falls along a gradient — a multistep function ranging, presumably, from proficient members to drones. Fifty per cent of the meeting time should be devoted to information and questions, and 50 per cent to answers and reactions. The reactions are particularly important. There should be precisely two positive reactions for each negative one. A ratio lower than this indicates a divisive and emotional situation, while a higher one indicates inhibition, restraint, and domination by the chairman.

Thus an old art is by way of becoming an exact science. Among the instrumentalities of this new technology we find: high level committees, low level committees, technical committees, task forces, working groups, one-man committees, program committees, community fund committees and eleemosynary committees generally, anniversary luncheon committees, committees ad hoc and committees ad infinitum.

In view of the growing elaboration of committeeism, it appeared that a survey of certain committees existing in the organization with which the author is identified might yield interesting conclusions. Most of these committees were created for the purpose of exercising joint responsibilities where liaison between the staff and the technical departments is essential.

Fig. 1 is a smokestack chart showing the density of committees by numbers of members. Except for the four committees

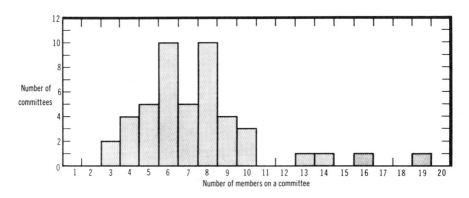

FIG. 1. Density Distribution of Committees.

out on the righthand tail, we find a compact universe ranging in size from three to ten members, with a median, not at five, but at seven, and with two large peaks at six and eight. This might indicate either that committee efficiency falls below the optimum, or that, in the particular circumstances involved, people have learned to work together so harmoniously that the optimum number of members is larger than the Harvard figure.

Another interesting fact is that two-thirds of the committees have an even number of members. This seems to fly in the face of the tradition that the number of members should be odd. It would appear either that deadlocks are not frequent enough to generate a large demand for odd numbers, or that chairmen are quite adept at resolving tense situations.

The next chart (Fig. 2) shows the cumulative distribution curve of committees as a function of number of members. For

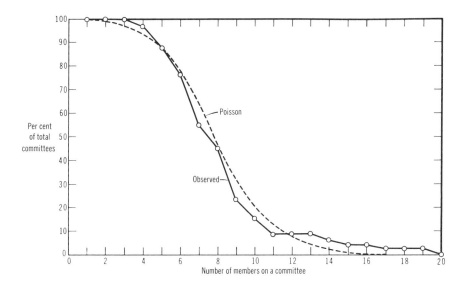

FIG. 2. Cumulative Distribution Curve for Committees.

comparison, a cumulative Poisson distribution curve is shown. The close fit suggests that the committees under consideration are characterized by a high degree of randomness. All this is a long way from fulfilling Lord Kelvin's dictum that you haven't much of a science until you can put numbers on things, but at least there is progress in that direction. So much for quantitative analysis. From here on we shall not need to concern ourselves with anything so tightly disciplined as numbers or facts.

Considering the prevalence of committees, we might, in all seriousness, ask ourselves a few questions about them. Here are some rather obvious ones:

1. What are the advantages of committees?
2. What are their disadvantages?

3. How should they be used?
4. How can successful operation be achieved?

ADVANTAGES

To start with, let's look at advantages. A lot has been written about this. Fig. 3 attempts to list some of the merits of committees, both published and unpublished.

FIG. 3. Merits of Committees.

1. Excellence of Decisions
    (a) Group solution
    (b) Combined judgment
    (c) Continuity
2. Strength of Decisions
    (a) Conjoint decision
    (b) Prestige of committee
3. Development of Personnel
    (a) Broadening
    (b) Teamwork
    (c) Leadership (chairman)
4. Supplement to Line Organization
    (a) Liaison
    (b) Communication

At the top of the list comes excellence of committee decisions. A number of heads contribute to the solution of each problem. There is a pooling of information. Mutual discussion stimulates the flow and interplay of ideas.

Moreover, the solution is objective. The combined judgment of many heads is bound to be better than that of one. Any weak spots in an individual suggestion are likely to be detected. As C. J. Berwitz has pointed out,[4] the final answer should be a realistic synthesis of theory and practice. Also, the committee has a sort of flywheel effect. It can be made a continuing body, with sufficient overlap of personnel assignments to provide continuity of policy.

Next, perhaps, comes strength of committee decisions. Group participation and conjoint decision conduce to good acceptance throughout the organization. Achievement of deserved prestige by the committee can be a further factor toward the same end.

Still another merit of committees is development of personnel. The members profit from friendships in different parts of

---

[4]C. J. Berwitz, "The Work Committee — An Administrative Technique," Harvard Business Review, January-February, 1952, page 110.

the organization. The problems that confront them are different from the day-to-day grist, and frequently much broader. Moreover, the committee members develop a spirit of teamwork and a sense of respect for the ideas of others. And not least important is the practical training that the chairman receives in group leadership.

Finally, a committee which includes in its makeup broad representation from different parts of the organization can be a useful supplement to the line organization. Almost of necessity the committee provides liaison between parts of the organization. Moreover, it can be made a valuable instrument for communication, both communication of its decisions and of the reasoning that underlies them, and also communication of general informational matter.

Some people say that one of the merits of a committee is that it counteracts organizational deficiencies. Another way of saying it might be that crosslinkages of elements make for strength and flexibility in organizations of people just as with molecules.

This is indeed an imposing array of advantages. Clearly committees are not used nearly enough. But before jumping to conclusions, we might inquire whether by chance there may be anything wrong with committees. Drawing in part upon published material, and in part upon experience, another list, this time of shortcomings of committees, has been compiled (Fig. 4).

FIG. 4. Shortcomings of Committees.

1. Inferiority of Decisions
    (a) Compromise
    (b) Domination
    (c) Unqualified members
    (d) Lack of continuity
    (e) Inadequate motivation
    (f) Haste
2. Impotency of Decisions
    (a) Intermittency
    (b) Executive instrumentalities lacking
3. Wastefulness
4. Depreciation of Line Organization

SHORTCOMINGS

In the first place, committee decisions are notoriously inferior. The reasons for this are not far to seek. Committees must operate on an essentially unanimous basis. The members, drawn from different parts of the organization, will have conflicting interests. The net result is a wishy-washy compromise. Unanimity spells mediocrity.

Furthermore, the committee is subject to domination by the chairman. Discussion is therefore denied, creativity is stifled and the members are inhibited. In addition, committee decisions of any importance are subject to political influence. The members are chosen, not for their qualifications, but merely to represent departments.

Because of personnel turnover, committees lack continuity, so that their policies are likely to be erratic. Moreover, committees lack motivation. They are apt to be irresponsible and indifferent. The members can't be held to account for their mistakes. Someone has observed that a committee, like a corporation, "has neither a soul to be damned nor a body to be kicked."

Even worse is haste. As a rule the committee meets very seldom. Hence it has to rush through a crowded agenda, with no time for adequate consideration of anything. Awkward issues are usually placed in cold storage. No wonder the decisions are less than perfect!

Committee decisions likewise lack authority. This is explained in part by factors already mentioned. Furthermore, the committee is by its nature a spasmodic phenomenon, a discontinuous function. Its existence is necessarily limited to the time when it is in session. In between times it is a disembodied spirit. As such it possesses no power to carry out its decisions, and cannot handle subsidiary problems as they arise.

To go on with the list, committee operation is wasteful. Travel to and fro, tardiness, and outside interruptions during meetings, these are all spendthrifts of time. The committee operates at the speed of the least informed member. Hours are consumed in coming to grips with a problem. High-priced time is frittered away on irrelevancies and non-essential details. Moreover, old committees never die. After all, you can't expect them to commit hara-kiri. The best you can hope for is that an astute committee, when it has accomplished what it set out to do, will enter into a state of suspended animation. All in all, committees are an expensive luxury. As a final drawback, any committee setup detracts from the effectiveness of the line organization, and obscures the chain of command.

So now where are we? Just a short while ago we seemed to have found the foot of the rainbow. Now the sun's gone dim and the moon's turned black. We begin to suspect that the truth lies somewhere in between. But just where? Perhaps we can best get the answer by asking when and for what purposes a committee is useful.

USES OF COMMITTEES

The next chart (Fig. 5) lists some of the purposes more commonly served by committees, and over on the side a characterization of the effectiveness of each. To some extent these

FIG. 5.   Uses of Committees.

Function	Value
For operational decisions	Special situations only
For facilitating acceptance	Fair
For implementing decisions	Poor
For advising management	Excellent
For creative technology	Fair to Poor
For unifying points of view	Good
As educational agency	Fair
As training agency	Fair

characterizations stem from published sources,[5] but in all cases they represent the opinions of the author.

For handling regular administrative decisions, a committee is not very effective. For the most part such use should be limited to special situations. In facilitating acceptance of decisions, a well-chosen committee can play a useful part. It would, however, be inadvisable to place exclusive reliance on a committee to exercise this function. When it comes to implementing decisions, it is extremely difficult to clothe a committee with adequate authority. In general, such use of committees should be avoided like the plague.

On the other hand, committees can be of extremely high utility in the area of advice to management. For such purposes as defining policies, formulating objectives and recommending plans, they are often nearly indispensable. Even in matters of less importance, the power of a committee in reflecting different points of view should not be underestimated. And consensuses, though seldom soul-stirring, are none the less valuable.

As to the question of whether a committee can contribute effectively to creative solution of technical problems, this is merely one phase of the broad questions of group creativity, which has been the subject of extensive discussion and limited investigation. To some extent the answer depends on semantics. Obviously neither a committee nor any other group can, as an entity, create ideas. Only individuals can do this. Individuals meeting as a group may, however, stimulate one another to create ideas, as in the rather overadvertised technique of "brain-storming." In most situations, a committee is likely to be less original and less efficient in producing ideas than its members acting separately.

---

[5]W. R. Spriegel and J. K. Bailey, "Functions of the Committee," Advanced Management, December, 1953, page 12.

On the other hand, a committee confronted with the type of problem that requires a combination of creativity and judgment can usually reach a better solution than any one member could achieve.

Not only can committees reflect different points of view; they can on occasion go a long way toward reconciling differences. More broadly, a committee sometimes can be used to advantage as an educational agency. If this is a serious aim, then the committee members should have adequate individual time to devote to it.

Finally, the broadening and development that members and chairman receive through service on a committee is a real and valuable by-product. We should not forget, however, that the curve of individual benefit vs. time flattens off quite rapidly.

MANAGEMENT RESPONSIBILITIES

Comes now the fourth question: how can successful committee operation be achieved? Anything that can be said about this will sound obvious. Even so, a few things may be worth saying. After all, neglect of the obvious probably causes more trouble in this world than failure to fathom the obscure.

Suppose now for simplification we phrase the question this way: How can management, members and chairman contribute to committee success? Management, being the creator of committees, naturally comes first.

A few suggestions as to the usual obligations of management toward its committee offspring are ventured in Fig. 6. It needs

FIG. 6.   Obligations of Management Toward Committees.

1. Sound Charter
2. Qualified Members
3. Right Size
4. Turnover
5. Reports
6. Follow up Decisions
7. Discharge

no sage to tell us that management should start the committee off with a sound charter. More specifically, management should assign real problems, make the objectives clear and clothe the committee with adequate authority. In most cases the purpose and composition of the committee should be announced in writing.

Next, management has the responsibility of choosing qualified members. Actually, the desired characteristics are not too different from those we look for in the usual team approach to creative technology. Committee members should have broad vision, should be well-informed, creative, analytical, objective and cooperative. They should be good workers, good listeners and so forth. Rarely is it possible to find all the desired qualities in a single person. The members should therefore be chosen so that their characteristics supplement one another. Also, the members should usually be representative of different parts of the organization, with good balance as to points of view. At most, there should be only one peculiar member, or so-called "odd ball".

Of course, the magic figure of five committee members is not mandatory. However, the matter of committee size deserves careful attention.

There seems to be general agreement that for any continuing committee there are advantages to be had through turnover of membership. If left to the chairman or members this can lead to embarrassment. Accordingly, management should make definite arrangements for planned rotation or staggered terms.

Management has still other obligations. If a committee is worth having, it is worth at least occasional recognition. Management should know what its progeny are doing. Periodic reports, either oral or written, should be required. Any decisions reached by the committee should, to whatever extent necessary, be followed up by management. When at last the committee has fulfilled its purpose, it should not be left to linger on the vine. Let it be discharged with grateful appreciation.

RESPONSIBILITIES OF MEMBERS

Now what about the responsibilities of committee members? A few are noted in Fig. 7. First is advance preparation. The

FIG. 7. Responsibilities of Committee Members.

1. Advance Preparation
2. Regularity and Punctuality
3. Intelligent Participation

members have an obligation to familiarize themselves with any material circulated before the meeting. If they are assigned specific tasks to be done between meetings, they are obligated to complete these on time, or to inform the chairman that they cannot do so. In attendance the members should be regular and punctual.

But most important, the members should participate intelligently in the proceedings. This means that they should be willing to work, that they should apply to the committee problems as much of scientific analysis and ingenuity as possible, that they should submerge bias, respect the integrity of other members, avoid irrelevant discussion and contribute to the collective decision.

Now we come to the key figure in the whole business — the committee chairman. It's easy enough to write a set of specifications. The chairman must be able to encourage, cajole, soothe or inhibit. He must be calm, alert, aggressive. He must at once use and restrain the genius. He must embolden the timid, stimulate the indifferent, convince the stubborn, make the superficial think.

Such demigods are hard to come by. Fortunately, an inexperienced chairman does not have to learn solely in the rugged school of experience. He can find a lot of published material to help him do his job. Enough has been written about successful committee operation to establish certain essentials. Some that should concern the chairman are listed in Fig. 8.

FIG. 8.   Responsibilities of Committee Chairman.

1. Advance Planning
2. Business-like Procedure
3. High Participation
4. Familiarity with Published Material

Few things are more important to committee success than advance planning. A prepared agenda, normally circulated in advance, is a great help toward economy of committee time. A good secretary can relieve the chairman of a lot of work of this kind between meetings.

No one but the chairman can hold the committee to business-like procedure. He should first state and define each problem. Next he should solicit discussion, usually by asking questions. Only then should he invite solutions. The chairman should talk to the whole group, and show interest in the reactions of each member. In difficult situations, he should discover and exploit all areas of agreement. The meeting should proceed with neither undue haste nor waste time.

One key to success is a high rate of participation by the members. On any important matter, the chairman should obtain at least some verbal comment from each member. A high rate of suggestion, if it can be had, is even more valuable. In most cases, the accomplishments of the committee can be greatly enhanced by assigning in-between-meeting tasks to different members.

As already suggested, the chairman should make it his business to get acquainted with some of the available literature on committee or conference leadership, committee operation, group decision-making and the like. True, some of the socio-psychological studies go beyond the limits of practical application. Anyone who wades in very deep should be politely skeptical. Nevertheless, there is in the published material a good deal of direct value to any practitioner in the field of committee operation.

CONCLUSION

In summary, committees are here to stay. We can't do without them, and we can't do with them all that we might wish. Let us make the best of them. For advising management on how to do this, recourse might be had to a Committee on Committees.

37 ROLE OF COMMITTEES IN PLANNING PROCEDURE

by Preston P. LeBreton and Dale A. Henning

In the discussion that follows, we recognize full well the dangers of generalization. There are doubtless many exceptions to the general rules. Nonetheless, we think the tendencies indicated below are sufficiently forceful to warrant generalized statements about the applicability of group or individual effort in the several steps of the planning process. Here, as elsewhere throughout this book, we invite research to prove or disprove the generalizations laid down.

Committees, as planning devices, cannot be classifed as being either effective or ineffective. Planning is not single activity but rather involves a series of steps or phases that was pointed out [earlier]. Committees operate with varying degrees of effectiveness in these several phases of the planning process. Slightly modified from their [earlier] presentation. . . these phases are as follows:

1. Determination of the need for a plan.
2. Gaining approval to undertake the planning.
3. Obtaining the necessary information.
4. Evaluating the information.
5. Formulating conclusions or alternative conclusions.
6. Preparation of final plan of action.
7. Gaining approval of the plan.

NEED DETERMINATION

The first step most often arises from some individual need. An operator finds that materials are not on hand when required; a statistical analyst finds that quality tolerances will soon be ex-

---

ceeded, or a sales manager finds that sales quotas are not being met. In some cases, committees, in their deliberations, will come upon some problems that will call for the drawing up of new plans, but by and large the initiative, the determination that plans are needed, is found in an individual rather than in a group. The need for plans becomes most obvious to those who are carrying on the operations of the firm, who are directing, controlling, and executing. Such individuals may very well refer their ideas to a committee, but the original impulse is most likely to occur in individuals rather than among groups.

Where committees are performing a control function, they are particularly likely to discover need. If a given committee has as its responsibility the observation of performance and the relating of performance to a predetermined standard, it will see deviations from the standard as requiring revised or new plans. But the majority of committees do not have control as a primary function. The direction and control that is part of the execution of plans is most often assigned to individuals and these individuals in turn discover need for new planning.

APPROVAL TO UNDERTAKE PLANNING

The second step, approval to undertake planning, in most cases will be performed more effectively by individuals. Where the plans are minor in character, no approval is necessary. But where the planning will involve substantial amounts of time, manpower, and finances, approval is necessary. Planning sometimes involves considerable expenditures of time and effort, but it does not ordinarily involve a great deal of risk. Generally, vast funds are not invested in planning, and decisions involved in the planning process (as distinguished from approval of the final plans) are not usually of a life-or-death nature for the enterprise. Decisions to undertake planning have the characteristic that they are reversible — planning can be stopped, usually without too much in the way of wasted resources. The decision to undertake planning, then, is a relatively minor decision when compared with other kinds of decisions the executive is called upon to make. Generally, it does not warrant the time and attention of a group of men. One man is capable of judging whether or not the problem is worthy of study and whether a plan is necessary to meet the problem. Committees, given as they are to indecision, compromise, and time consumption, are not the best medium through which to approve the undertaking of planning activities. There are, of course, some exceptions to this general rule. Sometimes the decision to undertake planning can irrevocably commit funds, men, and facilities, but this is not ordinarily the case.

If this step is viewed from the standpoint of the planner, that is obtaining approval from someone else, it still is more appropriately performed by an individual. The individual sees the need, draws up a proposal to develop a plan, and presents it to the superior authority for approval. Committee action in presenting the proposal is usually unnecessary.

DATA GATHERING

Obtaining the necessary information also is a task for individuals. Committees may be useful for this purpose if the information is of a sort that can be brought together quickly by members of the committee — fingertip information, so to speak. But where research and intensive fact gathering are involved, they must be done essentially by single persons, working in concert, perhaps, but not as a committee. Fact gathering involves locating sources, interviewing, searching through files, sifting data, interpreting charts, taking surveys, and other activities that do not lend themselves to group effort. Committees, especially committees of higher executives, are notoriously poor as research units. It is better to provide the committees with staff manpower who will perform the necessary fact-gathering duties. An important exception to this general rule is the use of committees in data gathering by means of interviewing.

EVALUATING THE DATA

Evaluating the information is best done by a group. Evaluation has in it a judicial element. "Judging" is always a precarious art. Different people use different standards and values in making their judgments. This is why we have major judicial decisions made by groups rather than individuals; by juries rather than individual judges, and by multimembered courts at the judicial levels. Judgment is used in evaluating the information gathered in the planning process, and several judges are usually better than one — provided, of course, they can overcome their proclivities for indecision and ineffective compromise. Evaluation is justly a group activity.

FORMULATING CONCLUSIONS

Step five, formulating conclusions after weighing alternatives, also is a relatively profitable group activity. It arises directly from the evaluation of the data. Conclusions are usually better thought out after the discussion and give-and-take that occurs in committee meetings. More aspects of the alternatives are likely to be aired in a group than by an individual who draws up the alternatives and formulates conclusions. Even if the individual executive informally consults with his colleagues on an individual basis, a thorough exploration of the virtues and shortcomings of alternatives will much more likely take place in a meeting where ideas and one alternative points up another.

PREPARING FINAL PLAN

Preparation of the final plan of action (Step 6) will most logically be accomplished by the committee that evaluated the data and drew tentative conclusions. Of course, the routine task of recording on paper the results of the committee's deliberations will be done by a single person who has attended the meetings, but this is a relatively minor part of the "preparation of final plan" stage in the planning process. The committee, of course, can merely cite the alternatives, their merits and demerits, and send this information to a superior executive for whatever use he chooses to make of it. This is not a very effective use of staff, however, whether it be in the form of committees or not. Since the group has expended time and effort in evaluating the information gathered and drawing up alternatives, and since this group probably knows more about the subject than any other persons in the company, it is only logical that its recommendations be sought.

FINAL APPROVAL OF PLAN

Final approval of a plan (Step 7) is often held to be a line-executive decision-making responsibility. The American Management Association survey previously cited showed that committees were at their weakest in decision-making. This is typically the view of practicing administrators, who are impressed with committee proclivities for procrastination and compromise, slowness and divided responsibility. Theorists and some practitioners, on the other hand, point out that really effective carrying out of the decision is a function of the implementer's participation in the decision-making. (Committee action is one form of participation, but there are others.) Proponents of the former view hold that committees are very useful in analyzing and evaluating information and in preparation of the proposals, but they generally fall short of the mark when acting to assign final approval or disapproval to their proposals or the proposals of subordinate persons or groups.

Practitioners join theoreticians, however, in granting that group decision-making can be appropriate at the company's top level. Company-wide policy making generally is fruitful ground for the "plural executive" type of decision-making. On unprogrammed, long-range, slowly deliberated, company-wide planning, the need for several minds becomes evident. Although such groups often merely advise the president, in many other instances they are given the right to make binding decisions. Among the more publicised of the latter type is the du Pont Company's executive committee.[1] This is a body composed of the president and nine vice-presidents who are also members of the full board of directors. The executive committee has direct operating responsibility over 10 manufacturing and 12 staff divisions. The division directors are appointed by and responsible to the executive committee. The committee approves all major plans of both manufacturing and staff divisions. It is in shorter term, less inclusive operating decisions that committees manifest their greatest shortcomings. They leave much to be desired, for example, in deciding whether to approve plans for the relocation of the shipping department or changing salesmen's quotas. In spite of these shortcomings, there has been a greatly increased dependence upon group decisions even at the middle and lower management levels. These may not be group decisions in the extreme jury sense where there is no superior to veto the decision, but, as one scholar has put it, "all that is left of the old entirely unilateral decision is the official skeleton of individual responsibility." In theory, the executive has made the decision and must be held responsible for it, but in practice the decision is often made by a group.

Where does this leave us? Generalizations are difficult, but we have indicated that high-level plan approval — including the final approval of the plans — probably is most effectively done by groups. At lower levels and on shorter-term plans of lesser significance, the speed, decisiveness, and pinpoint responsibility of individual judgment often outweighs the advantages of group decision-making. Participation is likely to enhance the success of the decision's execution, but participation may take many forms and need not include approval of the final plan.

---

[1]See William H. Mylander, "Management by Executive Committee," Harvard Business Review, May-June, 1955, page 51.

PART TWELVE:

DEPARTMENTS

38 THEORIES OF DEPARTMENTALIZATION

by James G. March and Herbert A. Simon

Although an explicit theory of departmentalization can be traced back to Aristotle (Politics, Book IV, Chap. 15), we will consider the theory here in its contemporary form in the well-known essay by Luther Gulick (Gulick and Urwick, 1937). To have a short name for this line of development, we label it the "administrative management theory." Among the prominent exponents of the theory, in addition to Gulick, have been Haldane (1923), Fayol (1930), Mooney and Reiley (1939), and Urwick (1943).

Although there was considerable communication and overlap between the students of organization we have assigned to "scientific management" or "physiological organization theory" and those we are now labelling "administrative management theorists," the two bodies of doctrine are conceptually rather distinct. They share, particularly in their more formal versions, a preoccupation with the simpler neurophysiological properties of humans and the simpler kinds of tasks that are handled in organizations. As we shall see, however, the administrative management theorists tended to carry their analysis, at least at the level of wisdom and insight, beyond the boundaries set by their formal models.

Since the formal body of theory is somewhat more limited in scope than the area considered in a less formal way, we will begin our analysis with the formal structure, and later supplement it with comments on the broader ramifications.

The general problem to which the formal theory addresses itself is the following: Given a general purpose for an organization, we can identify the unit tasks necessary to achieve that purpose. These tasks will normally include basic productive activities, service activities, coordinative activities, supervisory

Reprinted from Organizations (New York: John Wiley & Sons, Inc., 1958), pages 22-29, by permission of the publisher.

activities, etc. The problem is to group these tasks into individual jobs, to group the jobs into administrative units, to group the units into larger units, and finally to establish the top level departments — and to make these groupings in such a way as to minimize the total cost of carrying out all the activities. In the organizing process each department is viewed as a definite collection of tasks to be allocated among, and performed by, the employees of the department. To understand the formal theory, it is important to recognize that the total set of tasks is regarded as given in advance.

DEPARTMENTALIZATION AS AN ASSIGNMENT PROBLEM

The problem of allocating a given set of activities efficiently among a number of persons has received some attention from mathematicians and game theorists, who refer to it as the optimal assignment problem. The form of the problem that has usually been considered is a little different from that treated here. The usual statement (Kuhn and Tucker, 1953, p. 5) is:

> Given $\underline{n}$ persons and $\underline{n}$ jobs, and a set of real numbers a_{ij}, each representing the value of the $\underline{i}$th person on the $\underline{j}$th job, what assignments of persons to jobs will yield the maximum total value?

A brute-force solution to the assignment problem involves testing all possible permutations of persons among jobs. Since the number of possible arrangements is $\underline{n}!$, this becomes obviously infeasible if $\underline{n}$ is more than a very small number. Several efforts have been made to reduce the computational task to manageable dimensions, with some measure of success (Kuhn, 1955). What has emerged has not been general propositions about optimal assignment, but computational routines that when combined with the power of modern digital computers, give promise of providing numerical solutions for the problem in individual cases.

The form of the assignment problem that is particularly relevant to the theory of departmentalization is somewhat different from that described above, and has received little attention in the literature. With any possible set, $\underline{S}$, of activities, we associate a number, $\underline{t(S)}$, that measures the time required for a person to perform this set of activities. By $(\underline{S_1} + \underline{S_2})$ we mean the set of activities obtained by adding the activities $\underline{S_1}$ to the activities $\underline{S_2}$. In general, the time required to perform the sum of the two sets of activities will not be equal to the sum of the times required for each set alone: $\underline{t(S_1 + S_2)} \neq \underline{t(S_1)} + \underline{t(S_2)}$.

A set of activities, $\underline{S}$, is a <u>task</u> if it can be performed by a person in a certain specified time, $\underline{T}$ (say 8 hours): $\underline{t(S)} \geq \underline{T}$. To determine the total number of persons required to perform the whole set of activities, we partition it into subsets, each of which is a task. There are many such partitionings, and the number of tasks will vary from one partitioning to another. We define an <u>efficient</u> partitioning as one that minimizes the number of <u>tasks</u> — and consequently, the number of persons and number of man-hours.

The complication in finding an efficient partitioning lies in the nonadditivity in times required to perform sets of activities. The rationale of this, as applied to first-level jobs, is that most activities involve initial "setup" costs of various kinds, and that these costs often can be economized by combining activities that have them in common. There are short-run costs of this kind associated with changeover from one activity to another; there are longer-run costs associated with various kinds of training and information-gathering. Because there are numerous and important complementarities of these kinds, there are great differences in the economy of performance of tasks with different groupings (Simon, Smithburg, and Thompson, 1950, pp. 137-145).

Some propositions can be deduced from the formalization of the assignment problem that are equivalent to standard propositions in the literature on departmentalization, but the formalization does not appear to give much that is new, except to contribute precision to the statements.

In an organization that has the usual pyramidal structure, a single task must include only activities related to a single department: the department to which the employee performing that task is assigned. Further, if for reasons of economy in the use of personnel, a single task must be limited to a range of activities requiring only a restricted number of skills and processes (e.g., clerical skills and processes), then the task partitioning must be a subpartitioning of <u>both</u> the departmental and process partitionings. It may well happen that the most efficient task partitioning that satisfies these two constraints is not by any means the most efficient of all possible task partitionings. That is to say, it might be more efficient, if it were only feasible, to combine stenographic activities from one department with those from another into a single task; or it might be efficient to define a task requiring skill in both medicine and legal analysis. The constraints forbid combinations of these sorts.

The constraints on combining activities into tasks are likely to be most significant when the total number of activities is small relative to the range of different purposes and processes, for then it will be impossible to group activities into full-time tasks preserving similarity of both purpose and process. Hence, in small organizations, purpose departmentalization, by interfering with process specialization, can lead to serious inefficiencies; while in large organizations it may be possible to introduce process specializations as subdivisions of the purpose departmentalization, and hence to preserve the important complementarities.

These propositions have been made in common-sense terms by Gulick (Gulick & Urwick, 1937) and others:

> First [organization by major process] . . . by bringing together in a single office a large amount of each kind of work (technologically measured), makes it possible in each case to make use of the most effective divisions of work and specialization.
>
> Second, it makes possible also the economies of the maximum use of labor saving machinery and mass production. These economies arise not from the total mass of the work to be performed, not from the fact that the work performed serves the same general purpose but from the fact that the work is performed with the same machine, with the same technique, with the same motions (p. 23).
>
> . . . there is danger that an organization erected on the basis of purpose will fail to make use of the most up-to-date technical devices and specialists because . . . there may not be enough work of a given technical sort to permit efficient subdivision (p. 22).
>
> Is there any advantage in placing specialized services like private secretaries or filing in [process departments]? In a very small organization, yes; in a large organization, no. In a small organization, where there is not a full-time job on some days for each secretary, it is better to have a central secretarial pool than to have a private secretary for each man. In a large organization, the reverse is true (p. 20).

A study of the mathematical structure of the assignment problem suggests that there is little to be hoped for in the way of global generalizations beyond the propositions, just stated, that are already to be found in the nonmathematical literature on the subject. Task allocations will be efficient to the extent that they are based upon similarities in activities that are recognized as yielding important complementarities in task performance. These are what we generally mean by "process" similarities.

A serious limitation of the theory is that there is apparently no way of recognizing process similarities in general, except through the complementarities associated with them. Hence, propositions like "with low work volume, organization by process is efficient" are largely tautological. At best, they instruct us to search for possible complementarities of activities as a basis for grouping.

Beyond this point, solution of the assignment problem requires specific empirical knowledge of the specific empirical complementarities that exist — e.g., the structure of human skills and machine capacities — an obvious point that is not always made clear in the discussion of recommendations for organizational structure.

GENERALIZATION: COORDINATION PROBLEMS

One peculiar characteristic of the assignment problem, and of all the formalizations of the departmentalization problem in classical organization theory, is that, if taken literally, problems of coordination are eliminated. Since the whole set of activities to be performed is specified in advance, once these are allocated to organization units and individuals the organization problem posed by these formal theories is solved.

Of course, writers on organization theory are aware that coordination is a highly significant problem. Our point is simply that this problem is absent from the formal models, and hence that the formal models depart widely from what is asserted in a common-sense way about organizations. As is often the case, common sense appears to be more relevant to the real-world phenomena than do the models. To fill this gap between formal theory and wisdom, we need a framework that recognizes that the set of activities to be performed is not given in advance, except in a most general way — that one of the very important processes in organizations is the elaboration of this set of activities, and the determination of which precise activities are to be performed at which precise times and places.

We will introduce this generalization in two stages: only the first of the two will be examined in any detail [here]. The first generalization is that the activities of the organization may belong to well-defined, highly routine types, but the occasion for the performance of any particular activity may depend on environmental stimuli — "instructions," "information," and what not. Thus, automobiles are produced on the assembly line in an exceptionally routine way, yet there are all sorts of contingencies to be settled in each case, such as body style, color, and motor type.

The second generalization, to be considered at length [elsewhere,] recognizes that often not even the contingent program of activities is given in advance; that, in fact, one of the important activities that goes on in organizations is the development of programs for new activities that need to be routinized for day-to-day performance.

Let us return to the first stage of generalization. Behavior in the organization is not determined in advance and once for all by a detailed blueprint and schedule. Even if it is highly routinized, the routine has the character of a strategy rather than a fixed program. Specific activities are performed in response to signals and stimuli of one sort or another. Moreover, the appropriateness of particular activities is invariably dependent, frequently to a very important extent, upon the time of performance. There may be a standard job ticket giving detailed specifications for producing a particular product in a factory, but this job ticket becomes a program for human (and machine) behavior only when an order is received for that product and when the order has been scheduled for production.

We can describe such a routinized organization in a static way in terms of the kinds of activities that are performed from time to time, but this is very different from describing the actual set of activities, with the time subscripts attached. It is because activities are conditional, and not fixed in advance, that problems of organization, over and above the assignment problem, arise. For convenience, we may make the following specifications, without interpreting them too strictly:

1. The times of occurrence of activities may be conditional on events external to the organization or events internal to the organization.
2. The appropriateness of a particular activity may be conditional on what other activities are being performed in various parts of the organization.
3. An activity elaborated in response to one particular function or goal may have consequences for other functions or goals.

As far as we are aware, no one has constructed a formal model of the departmentalization problem that takes account of the contingent character of activities. Let us sketch out briefly what such a model would look like, and then return to the common-sense propositions about organization that are related to this model.

In the revised model of departmentalization, the roster of kinds of activities (i.e., the whole set of job specifications, formulas, blueprints of standard products, standard operating procedures, etc.) is given in advance, together with a large number of conditional statements that specify the conditions under which each activity will be performed.

If all the conditions on which activity is contingent refer to the external environment, then we return to the assignment problem in a new form. In this case, specific activities are not assigned to departments, but conditional responsibilities for performance. Tasks are described either in terms of these conditional statements, or in terms of the probability distributions of activities that will in fact occur. The condition in the assignment problem that a task should represent not more than a day's work becomes a condition that the expected average amount of time required, or the time required at most, in any given period, should not exceed a day's work. These concepts of average load or maximum load again permit us to define a time function on each possible set of activities, and to go through with the solution of the assignment problem.

If some activities are conditional on other activities, the situation becomes more complicated. To handle this complication, we must introduce as variables various determinants of the ease and accuracy of communication (e.g., communication is easy within a professional group, difficult across professional lines; communication is easy along lines of the formal hierarchy, difficult across such lines, etc.). Ease and accuracy of communication may depend upon both motivational and cognitive factors.

The problem of arranging the signalling system for interdependent conditional activities is the coordination problem. Here is a simple example: If hiring is done by the personnel department, then this department must be informed when there is a vacancy, and what kinds of skills are required for the position. Its hiring activities will vary accordingly. (Of course, if the roster of activities is sufficiently detailed, the "what kind" can always be turned into a "when.")

When two organizational plans — two allocations of tasks — are compared in terms of this model, one of the central variables is the degree of self-containment of the several organization units (Simon, Smithburg, and Thompson, 1950, pp. 266-267). A unit is self-contained to the extent and degree that the conditions for carrying out its activities are independent of what is done in the other organization units. If there are time costs associated with the coordination, then these costs must be balanced against the time costs associated with lack of complete process specialization. This proposition has often been made in the classical literature, as the following passages from Gulick (Gulick and Urwick, 1937) indicate:

> The advantages of organization by purpose are three: first, it makes more certain the accomplishment of any given broad purpose or project by bringing the whole job under a single director with immediate control of all the experts, agencies and services which are required in the performance of the work. No one can interfere. The director does not have to wait for others, nor negotiate for their help and co-operation; nor appeal to the chief executive to untangle a conflict. He can devote all his energies to getting on with the job (p. 22).
>
> These are the major advantages of organization on the basis of process. There are, of course, offsetting difficulties (p. 24). . . .
>
> And, finally, the necessity of effective coordination is greatly increased. Purpose de-

partments must be co-ordinated so that they will not conflict but will work shoulder to shoulder. But whether they do or do not, the individual major purposes will be accomplished to a considerable extent and a failure in any service is limited in its effect to that service. Process departments must be co-ordinated not only to prevent conflict, but also to guarantee positive co-operation. They work hand in hand. They must also time their work so that it will fit together, a factor of lesser significance in the purpose departments. A failure in one process affects the whole enterprise, and a failure to co-ordinate one process division, may destroy the effectiveness of all the work that is being done (p. 24).

The significance of self-containment as an organizational variable has been examined by Ely Devons (1950) in the context of British wartime administration, and by Marschak and Radner (1954) and Marschak (1955) in a formal model of optimal decision-making in teams.

The problem of departmentalization that emerges out of this section and the previous one centers on two variables: self-containment (or, alternatively, coordination requirements), and skill specialization. Its central proposition is that the forms of departmentalization that are advantageous in terms of one of these outcomes are often costly in terms of the other: Process departmentalization generally takes greater advantage of the potentialities for economy through specialization than does purpose departmentalization; purpose departmentalization leads to greater self-containment and lower coordination costs than does process departmentalization. As size of organization increases, the marginal advantages accruing to process organization from the first source become smaller, while the coordination costs become larger. Hence, the balance of net efficiency shifts from process to purpose organization as the size of organization increases.

In conclusion, we repeat that the schemes we have described in this section and the previous one leave out of account the dynamics of program elaboration — the processes of developing new activities and programs of activities where these have not existed before. The more general model that encompasses these factors takes us pretty much beyond the limits of classical organization theory, at least insofar as that theory has been formalized.

References

E. Devons, Planning in Practice (Cambridge, England, 1950).
H. Fayol, Industrial and General Administration (London, 1930).

L. H. Gulick and L. Urwick (eds.), Papers on the Science of Administration (New York, 1937).

R. B. H. Haldane, Report of the Machinery of Government Committee (London, 1923).

H. W. Kuhn, "The Hungarian Method for the Assignment Method," Naval Research Logistics Quarterly, I (1955), 83-97.

H. W. Kuhn and A. Tucker (eds.), Contributions to the Theory of Games, Vol. II (Princeton, 1953).

J. Marschak, "Elements for a Theory of Teams," Management Science, I (1955), 127-137.

J. Marschak and R. Radner, "The Firm as a Team" (Abstract), Econometrica, XXII (1954), 523.

J. D. Mooney and A. C. Reiley, The Principles of Organization (New York, 1939).

H. A. Simon, D. W. Smithburg, and V. A. Thompson, Public Administration (New York, 1950).

L. Urwick, The Elements of Administration (New York, 1943).

39 COMMON WAYS OF GROUPING ACTIVITIES

by William H. Newman

Departmentation is the process of grouping activities into units for purposes of administration. This process takes place at all levels in an enterprise. The president groups activities into major divisions under the senior executives who report directly to him; the sales manager may divide his work among an advertising department, customer service department, market research department, and three or four sales districts; the credit manager, who directs one of the groups under the treasurer, may divide his work among a group of credit men, each of whom handles a specific group of customers; the shop superintendent appoints foremen to look after each step in the production process; and the activities in the bookkeeping office are grouped into jobs for individual bookkeepers. The common question faced by all executives from the president down to the first-line supervisor is, "How should duties be combined into jobs so as to promote the most effective results?" The administrative units created may be called divisions, bureaus, branches, units, offices, or some other name; whatever the name of the unit created, this process of partitioning is generally called departmentation.

TYPICAL PATTERNS USED IN DEPARTMENTATION

Several typical patterns are found in the departmentation of many enterprises, and an administrator will find it useful to be thoroughly familiar with these different alternatives. In business enterprises the patterns most commonly found are groupings by products, territories, time, customers, and functions. In government enterprises Gulick has found similar groupings, which he

William H. Newman, Administrative Action: The Techniques of Organization and Management, 2nd. ©1963. Reprinted by permission of Prentice-Hall, Inc., Englewood Cliffs, N.J.

designates as purpose, place, person or thing, and process. Other students of organization have reported a somewhat similar list of patterns. A few very brief examples will illustrate the meaning of these terms and call attention to the benefits often secured by using the particular pattern.

Grouping by Products or Services

Activities directly associated with a product (or service) are often combined. Thus, the corner grocery store may have divisions for meat, groceries, and fresh produce. On a grander scale we find in General Motors separate divisions for Chevrolet, Buick, Cadillac, Frigidaire, Diesel engines, and other major product lines. Sometimes this product division occurs only within a department; for example, the work of the purchasing department may be divided according to different types of products to be secured. Such grouping by product takes advantage of specialized product knowledge, promotes coordination of the various activities connected with the product (purchase, production, storage, sales, and the like), and often makes it easier to place responsibility for the results achieved.

Grouping by Locations

When activities are widely dispersed, it is frequently desirable to provide local administration. Instances of this arrangement are found in the territorial sales divisions of a company distributing its products in several states, and in the self-contained operations of branch plants. Even within a building we may find a department store floorwalker assigned to a particular floor or the maintenance man to a given section of the building. Among the advantages of this form of departmentation is the more intimate knowledge executives should have regarding local conditions. This permits adaptation to local needs and also helps in getting prompt action. Likewise, the activities within the area are more easily coordinated, and it is often possible to exercise more direct and immediate control.

Grouping by Time

When operations during a day or week extend far beyond the normal work period of an individual, a "second shift" is often added. Public utilities, restaurants, continuous-process industries, and many other enterprises have divisions distinguished on the basis of time as a normal arrangement. Other companies wishing to provide quick deliveries or obtain greater output from limited facilities may use this device. Typically, the "second shift" performs operations that are very similar to those done in the normal working hours, but at least first-line supervisors are needed to provide adequate supervision and control. The more difficult organizational questions are how fully serviced and self-contained each shift should be, and what relationships should be set up between specialized executives who work only normal hours and the men who perform similar duties during the off hours.

Grouping by Customers

This pattern, which is naturally found most often in sales operations, is sometimes reflected throughout the enterprise. The bargain basements of department stores, for example, often cater to a different group of customers than those served by the upstairs store, call for different buying and service activities, and may follow somewhat different personnel policies. Customer grouping is sometimes a dominant factor in the organization of brokerage houses. In government operations we find separate bureaus for immigrants, veterans, Indians, children, farmers, and small business. Again, the advantages of such grouping are to be found in the use of specialized and detailed knowledge, the coordination of activities related to the customers, and, by no means unimportant here, the assurance of adequate attention.

Grouping by Processes

Under some circumstances it is desirable to place all or most of the people using a given kind of equipment in one department; for example, stenographers, painters, or operators of heat-treating furnaces. In other cases, notably in manufacturing, the division may be based on clearly defined steps in a sequence of operations. Thus, a sweater mill may have separate units for knitting, steaming, cutting, sewing, trimming, pressing, inspection, and boxing and shipping. Among the advantages of such departmentation are the expertness that comes with concentration on the single process, a tendency to avoid investment in duplicate facilities, and, when the process is performed in one place, the possible improvement in supervision.

Grouping by Functions

With the growing complexity of administration of almost all types of enterprises — business, government, military, and elee-mosynary — functional departmentation has become increasingly popular. Just what is recognized as a function, however, differs greatly in actual practice. Some functional departments deal with a particular aspect of management, such as scheduling or inspection. Others are built around a similarity in work, as in a clerical department; or they may be based on a similarity in ability required to supervise them, as in the case of research. In other instances, the distinguishing characteristic of a functional division is its singleness of purpose or objective. The public relations department is a fairly recent example of this type, while the time-honored separation of sales, production, and finance has made functional grouping one of the dominant patterns in business enterprise. The chief characteristic and benefit of such grouping is specialization. By concentrating on some single phase or similar group of activities, specialized knowledge and skill can be fully utilized. Functional divisions are also established to assure that adequate attention is given to the activities concerned.

A familiarity with these typical ways of grouping activities is important background for the executive who is designing or modifying an organization. They are significant, not so much as patterns to be copied, but more as suggestive approaches in the development of an organization structure adapted to the specific needs of the enterprise.

INADEQUACY OF PATTERNS

Difficult Questions Not Answered

Unfortunately, an executive cannot settle his departmentation questions simply by casting a vote for some one of the typical patterns just discussed. Even if a decision is made to follow, say, a product pattern, numerous questions will remain of just what activities belong in each division. For example, a retail store may decide to adopt a product pattern, but this still leaves unanswered the question of whether each department is free to do its own credit work, whether delivery will be centralized, what kind of accounting records should be maintained and who will keep them, and so forth.

Likewise, the decision to establish branch sales offices does not determine who will do the advertising, the extent to which personnel activities will be performed by the home office, or the matter of local storage of merchandise. A decision to establish a controller's division does not provide automatic answers as to who should be responsible for corporate and real estate taxes, insurance, cost accounting, economic forecasting, and market research, nor does it answer the even more fundamental question of whether the controller is expected really to control or merely to provide data and analyses that will be helpful to operating executives in controlling their respective departments.

In other words, these so-called patterns of departmentation at best emphasize the dominant characteristic of a division or department. Important as this characteristic may be, it provides no formula for determining just what is to be included in a particular department — be it functional, customer, territorial, process, or product. And these questions of content and border line are often the most troublesome to resolve.

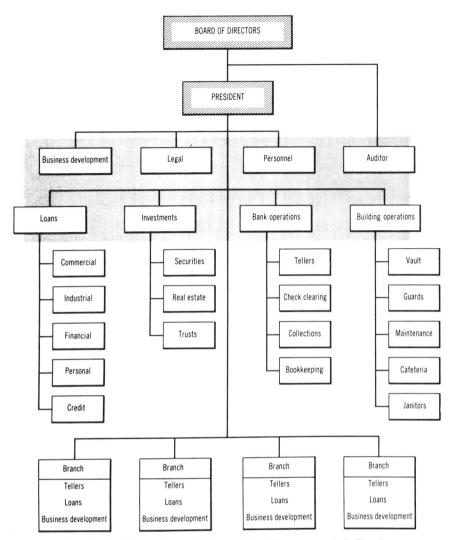

FIG. 1. Departmentation of a Commercial Bank.

Most Organizations Are Composite

We should also note that very few organizations follow any one pattern of grouping. From the point of view of structure the subdivisions under any single executive should be based on a single pattern, and where similar activities are performed in several different locations a parallel form of organization should be followed. Even this is not essential, however, and there certainly is no need to follow, say, a territorial pattern at all levels in the organization just because it is the dominant characteristic of the major departments.

The use of several different patterns is illustrated in the

chart of departmentation of a commercial bank, shown in Figure 1. While the organization of this, and most other commercial banks, is predominantly functional, the branches have been established on a territorial basis and the loaning activity, except for a centralized credit department, is divided according to types of customers. The detailed organization within the check-clearing department (not shown in the chart) is on a process basis.

The departmentation of a manufacturing concern, indicated in Figure 2, again shows that several different patterns were

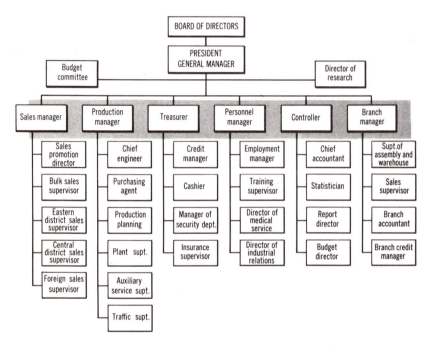

FIG. 2. Organization of a Manufacturing Concern.

used. The predominantly functional pattern was modified to provide for a branch manager because of the difference in location of the branch plant. Also, the subdivision under the sales manager is primarily on a territorial basis. Both the commercial bank and the manufacturing concern have relatively simple organization structure, and yet no single pattern would have been adequate for the grouping of their activities.

BASIC FACTORS IN GROUPING ACTIVITIES

What activities should be included within a department, section, or other organizational unit? Where is it practical to draw a dividing line between the responsibilities of two closely related sections? What relationships between organizational units should be formalized, and what delegations of authority should be made?

Clarification of points such as these is essential if the organization is to function smoothly. In actual operations, the administrator will face questions of clarification and refinement of his organization many more times than he will have occasions to consider changes in major characteristics of the organization structure. Shifts in volume or in operating conditions are occurring all the time, and minor organization adjustments to these changes are often necessary. For practical purposes, then, we need some guidance, not only in deciding on the basic organization pattern, but also for spelling out that pattern and resolving borderline issues.

The effective answers to these questions, unfortunately, are not simple. Experience demonstrates that no formula or mechanical application of rules provides a satisfactory answer. Instead, the particular arrangement will be influenced by the purpose of the enterprise, its size, people involved, stability and maturity, technology employed, major obstacles faced, and similar factors.

A practical way to design such an individualistic organization is to identify the vital operational factors and then make combinations of activities that give optimum results in terms of these factors. Thus, the firm that seeks to give prompt delivery to distinctive customers may find that coordination is a dominant factor; whereas, the company emphasizing mass production at low cost may stress economies from functional specialization.

A number of guiding considerations operate in almost every departmentation problem. Although their relative importance varies from one situation to another, they are prevalent enough to warrant the administrator's at least considering them when shifting and grouping activities. In most situations appropriate attention to these factors will be all that is necessary to secure a sound and workable arrangement of activities. These key considerations in departmentation are:

1. Take advantage of specialization.
2. Facilitate control.
3. Aid in coordination.
4. Secure adequate attention.
5. Recognize local conditions.
6. Reduce expense.

Because of the significance of these considerations, it will be helpful to examine in more detail typical situations to which they apply.

40 "ASSISTANT ——" AND "ASSISTANT TO ——" POSITIONS ARE INCONSISTENT WITH GOOD ORGANIZATIONAL PLANNING

In the discusion of Organization Structure up to this time, it is noteworthy that provision has not been made for positions with such titles as "Assistant ——" or "Assistant to ——."

There are two classes of reasons for this fact. First, there are better kinds of positions for getting work done, which are designed in accordance with important principles of delegation and of organization structuring. Second, there are better kinds of positions for stimulating the self-development of the incumbents.

To examine the first set of reasons in more detail, reference is made to the chart on Delegation [which shows that a] responsibility (duty) cannot be shared by two or more individuals. One either has a responsibility, or he does not. If the assistant has the responsibility for helping his manager by doing bits and pieces of work which that manager asks him to do, he is simply being a clerk, a messenger or "leg man." If, on the other hand, the manager has truly delegated to a so-called "assistant" a piece of work which is his and his alone to do, then he is not acting as an assistant but as a direct individual contributor just the same as other persons who report to the manager in that capacity.

If the assistant is not given specific work to do for which he and he alone is accountable, then it is inferred from his title that he has some unknown share of his manager's total responsibility. Confusion reigns unless this uncertainty is cleared up by specific assignment of responsibilities, because neither the individual himself nor others who report to the same manager know what work the assistant is supposed to do or for what he is accountable. Even worse, the other men reporting to this manager do not know with assurance the relationships between themselves and

Reprinted from Professional Management in General Electric, Book II: General Electric's Organization (General Electric Company, 1955), pages 189-197, by permission of the publisher.

the assistant, or between themselves and their manager if the assistant in any sense becomes, or tries to become, the manager's deputy or "alter ego."

The general notion of assistantships inherently violates another principle of delegation, in that responsibilities are not clearly defined and assigned to only one individual for performance. Because of this fuzziness of work assignment and of commensurate accountability, an assistant may often not receive full credit for some work of his which was well done, and even worse, he may be blamed for poor work when he was not at fault.

Assistants are often tempted to violate another principle of delegation in relations between themselves and others who report to the same manager. If they act as though they were in the line of responsibility, this is equivalent to adding an additional managerial level with attendant disadvantages in lengthened lines of communication in both directions. Other men cannot be accountable both to a manager and also to his assistant in any clear-cut manner since the assistant position as such carries with it no line authority and cannot be considered to be in the line of managerial responsibility.

The above reasoning leads to the principle, in General Electric's organizational approach, that positions with such content or titles as "Assistant ————" or "Assistant to ————" have major disadvantages, in that they violate fundamental principles of delegation. . . .

The second set of disadvantages inherent in "Assistant" positions is that the incumbents do not get the best opportunities for personal development in terms of learning how to be good managers, to wit:

1. Men who are acting as errand boys for their managers may gather much information by observation; but they do not have the stimulating opportunities to "learn by doing" as far as making their own decisions are concerned, coupled with the sometimes painful mind- and judgment-sharpening experience of having to live personally with the results of those decisions.

2. Men who get in the habit of gathering information requested by their manager so that he can make better decisions, run the risk of also getting in the habit of letting him do the thinking as well as the deciding. They get out of the habit of thinking things through themselves. Thus, there is a real danger that such experience will weaken rather than strengthen potential leadership abilities, and therefore will be a hindrance rather than a help to a man who is trying to develop himself for managerial — or for that matter, for significant individual contributor — work.

3. The best men will not let themselves get stuck for long in "assistant" positions, because they are not satisfied unless they are responsible and accountable for work which is uniquely their own. Both intuitively and by logical reasoning, they recognize that

"assistantships" are likely to be weak positions and not conducive to rapid growth and recognition, unless misused for unusual personal, political, or publicity purposes. They have confidence in their own ability to think things through and to make wise decisions, and they are anxious to stand on their own feet so as to reap the personal satisfactions and benefits from their own performance.

4. Experience has shown that men develop their managerial abilities and their self-confidence and belief in themselves faster and more surely if they have complete personal responsibility and accountability for a particular piece of work, even though it be small, than they do when they have some unknown and necessarily fractional part of their manager's larger responsibilities.

The above conclusions are frankly presented here, and in General Electric generally, even though such positions as "Assistant ——" and "Assistant to ——" are still used commonly in the existing organization structures of other American businesses. A few situations in which "assistantships" have been used in the past are therefore examined below so as to show how straightforward, "in line" delegation of work is better.

SITUATIONS WHERE ASSISTANTSHIPS HAVE
BEEN USED IN THE PAST

A. Suppose the Objective in Creating the Position Is to "Relieve Excessive Load on the Manager."

The manager who seeks such relief will get that relief better if he thoroughly organizes the total job to be done in accordance with patterns which previous experience has validated; if he keeps only work which he needs to do personally and can do in his own available hours; if he truly delegates operating decision-making to those who report to him; and if he helps them learn voluntarily to assume such responsibility and holds them accountable for performance.

When a manager asks for an assistant instead of thus delegating work to those who report to him, it means one of two things. Either he wants to hang on to detail decision-making because of the fancied personal satisfactions which he derives therefrom and because of self-assurance from past accomplishments; or he does not have sufficient confidence in the men reporting to him — he is doubtful about their ability to perform and therefore hesitant about delegating responsibility to them.

In either case, the manager will obtain lasting relief from overload faster and better if he will truly delegate work to such men, help them perform it well, and, if they do not do so after fair trial, get some new men who can and will. This is better for him and better for the men who report to him.

B. Suppose the Objective Is to "Help a Man Broaden His Experience in Preparation for a Bigger Job."

Since the sure way to solid learning is finally by doing, the best way to give a man a chance to learn is by giving him a job to do for which he is definitely responsible and accountable, which in its performance will require that the man broaden himself, his knowledge, his interests, his comprehension and understanding. There are many ways to do this which are completely consistent with principles of good organizing. For example:

1. Make sure that staff meetings are run so that each man knows both his own immediate work to be done and also so that each man has a chance to explain his own broad objectives, plans, activities, schedules, and problems, and to learn about those of the associates with whom he works and of the larger component of which their component is a part. Broadening takes place automatically as he learns to think from the point of view of the boss one and two steps "up the line."

2. In addition to a man's regular work, give him an assignment on a component-wide or a Company-wide part-time Services project or Study team; so that he learns to face up realistically to finding solutions to complex problems which are broader, deeper, and longer-range than would be encountered otherwise in connection with his regular job.

3. As a promotion from his present job, give him an opportunity to move to a more important job of greater scope and consequence in the same function, or to a corresponding job in another function or in another geographic area or another product line. Any one of these moves automatically affords a man an opportunity to grow in ability, in leadership qualities, in self-confidence, and in "worth to the Company," with attendant personal satisfaction and financial compensation.

4. As a promotion from his present job, give the man an opportunity to participate full time for, say, a one- to three-year period in the Company-wide activities of one of the Services. The problems being studied and the work being done by these divisions afford an excellent opportunity for learning and for broadening. Furthermore, because of the very nature of Services work, a man in such work learns to lead by persuasion, suggestion, and example, and by the authority of knowledge, through carefully collected, thoroughly analyzed, and skillfully presented facts. Such experience is especially valuable for men preparing themselves for and becoming competent later to fill Operating manager and general manager positions.

C. Suppose the Objective Is to "Reward a Man for Good Work by Giving Him Recognition and Status."

The best recognition is an increase in pay or a move to a more responsible job having greater opportunity, or both. The best indication of increasing status is specifically designated full responsibility and accountability for positions of successively greater "worth to the Company."

The soundly thinking man, with justified confidence in himself and his potential, would rather have full responsibility for a sub-component for which he is personally accountable and on whose performance his reputation stands or falls, than to be merely "assistant to" a higher level manager.

In the past, having one or more assistants in itself has at times been considered one form of achieving "status and prestige." This is poor for the manager, because it indicates that he hasn't yet learned to delegate clearly. It is poor for the assistant, in that he tends to become dependent and subservient rather than independent, thorough, and confident in his own judgments.

Such a condition is also bad for the Company, in that it tends toward having several people doing the work of one, with small spans of responsibility and many layers in the organization structure; with the ridiculous net effect of looking as though General Electric people needed some form of supervision for every 2 or 3 workers. This is organizationally unsound and unnecessary. In fact, it is competitively impossible in the long run because of attendant cumbersomeness, high managerial overhead costs, and the complete assurance that smart competitors will not have such unnecessary costs, so that they could only come out of profits rather than sales prices if allowed to persist.

D. Suppose the Objective Is to "Provide an Understudy for the Boss, One Who Is Capable of Taking His Position If He Should Be Promoted or Leave for Any Reason."

The leaders of the General Electric Company believe, from long experience, that it is not wise to single out so-called "crown princes" who are thus known to be scheduled for specific promotion. On the contrary, everyone is eligible for consideration for promotion, as is made crystal clear in the Company Policy on "Promotion or Transfer of Personnel to Manager, or Equivalent Professional or Technical, Position. . . ."

From this point of view, all men now reporting to a particular manager should be logical candidates for his position if it should become vacant for any reason; as should able and eligible men in other parts of the Company. Such men are likewise themselves eligible as opportunities for promotion open up in other components on a company-wide basis.

If each man knows the facts, is thinking "up-stream" as he performs his present work assignment, is consciously striving to develop himself so as to be worthy of promotion, and is being encouraged by his manager in so doing, the best possible managerial climate exists for the competitive and constructive development of managerial talent.

By such means all men are stimulated toward excellent performance of their own present work, as well as of the total work of the component. Furthermore, the designation of a "crown prince," or an "understudy," is unnecessary and the disadvantages attendant upon so doing can be avoided.

This means that promotions are based upon excellence of job performance and evidences of potential for further growth, not upon social or political favoritism, proximity, or failure to realize the availability of all qualified candidates.

If the boss is away for a period, any one of his men can be designated to act for him while he is away and can carry his own part of the work at the same time; or it may afford an excellent chance for the boss's own manager to get familiar firsthand with the boss's own work — and the men reporting to him. Conditions revert to normal automatically when the boss returns.

E. Suppose the Objective Is to "Break In an Announced Successor Who Is Openly Being Prepared to Take Over a Particular Job."

This is the only situation in which the designation of an "assistant" is justified, and even here it is only a temporary situation, rarely of more than a few months' duration.

During this break-in-period, the "assistant" should really get into all phases of the boss's job and act as his general deputy while learning the ropes. In this special case, the boss and his successor — temporarily called "assistant" — should not divide the total job between themselves, but rather they should act in each other's company as much as possible and should keep each other so well posted that men reporting to this position can treat them interchangeably, as one, while the transition period lasts. Better yet, in many cases, the incoming man can be put directly on the job, and the outgoing man — especially if he is to retire, rather than himself go on to new responsibilities — can stand by as an adviser and backstop until his successor is ready to carry on under his own power.

As a result of many considerations such as those cited above, and as a direct result of concentrated analysis in the premises, leaders of the General Electric Company have come to the definite conclusion that positions such as "Assistant ———" or "Assistant to ———" do not represent the most efficient way to subdivide and assign the total work to be done. Nor do they provide the best self-development opportunities for men who are striving to improve their ability as managers. Therefore, such positions are not normally to be incorporated, or retained, in the Company's Organization Structure.

41 THE APPROPRIATE ROLE OF STAFF

by Douglas McGregor

The appropriate role of any major staff group (excluding a few, like an economic forecasting department, whose relationships are relatively limited) is that of providing professional help to all levels of management. In some cases, such as engineering, the help is provided primarily to one or two functions, e.g., manufacturing and sales. In other cases, such as accounting and personnel, the help is provided to all other functions.

The hierarchical nature of the organization has tended to focus attention on help given to the level at which the staff group reports. Rewards and punishments for staff members come from there. Moreover, prestige and status are greater the higher the level of "attachment." In large companies, where there are both headquarters and field staff groups, it is particularly important that the headquarters groups recognize and accept their responsibilities for providing help to all levels of management.

The provision of professional help is a subtle and complex process. Perhaps the most critical point — and the one hardest to keep clearly in mind — is that help is always defined by the recipient. Taking an action with respect to someone because "it is best for him," or because "it is for the good of the organization," may be influencing him, but it is not providing help unless he so perceives it. Headquarters staff groups tend to rationalize the effects of many of their activities on the field organization in a paternalistic manner and, as a consequence, fail to see that they are relying on inappropriate methods of control. When the influence is unsuccessful, the usual reaction occurs: The recipients of the "help" are seen as resistant, stupid, indifferent to organizational needs, etc. The provision of help, like any other form of control of influence, requires selective adaptation to natural law. One important characteristic of "natural law" in this case is that help is defined by the recipient.

The concept of management by direction and control carries the implication that staff groups reporting to a given manager will do what he tells them to. If he assigns a responsibility to a staff group which provides help to him, but at the same time hampers the effective performance of lower levels of management, this is his prerogative. If he places a staff group in the untenable position of being both policemen and "helpers," this is his affair. The duty of the staff group is to follow his orders.

This presents a difficult problem. An independent professional — be he lawyer, doctor, or industrial consultant — faced with such demands would raise the point of conflicting obligations. His professional ethics will not permit him to undertake to help one client at the expense of another. Moreover, his clients usually recognize the potentiality of negative consequences for themselves and agree.

An internal professional staff specialist faces the necessity of persuading those to whom he reports that they will defeat their own purposes if they do not abstain from creating conflicting obligations. The problem is not an ethical one alone. As we saw in connection with the problem of managerial controls in the previous chapter, it is a problem of ineffective as opposed to effective methods of achieving objectives. In this respect, staff groups face the necessity of undertaking an educational role relative to their superiors — a somewhat unusual but not unheard of relationship! In fact, this role is a major one for staff in a number of respects.

Let us examine briefly four kinds of help which the typical staff group will find itself called upon to provide. With respect to all of them, a primary consideration is that help is defined by the recipient.

1. Help in Strategy Planning. The specialized knowledge and skill in the use of the techniques of problem analysis and research possessed by staff groups are increasingly utilized by management, particularly at upper levels, in planning. Often the research and knowledge of a staff group will be the major determinant of organization policy or of managerial strategy.

> The role of the staff in providing such help may be compared to the role of an architect in helping a client plan a new home. (The analogy cannot be pressed too far because the architect's role during actual construction is typically not comparable to the staff role after a managerial strategy has been decided.) The client has ideas concerning the kind of house he wants, and lots of experience in living. The

architect has professional knowledge which can help the client to end up with a house which will better serve his needs than one which he might design for himself. The problem faced by the architect is to bring about an integration of his own and his client's ideas which will satisfy the client and at the same time utilize his own professional competence.

The client's original idea of the house he wants may be quite naive, perhaps impractical, sometimes unnecessarily expensive. However, if the architect takes a condescending, or an authoritarian, position with respect to the client's ideas, he may find himself out of a job (unless his prestige is so high that the client will accept him on any terms). On the other hand, if the architect simply accepts the client's initial ideas, regardless of their merit, he is not serving the purpose for which he was hired. Given a relationship of mutual confidence, and skill in the consultant role as well as professional knowledge on the part of the architect, the necessary integration may be achieved.

Staff groups helping management in strategy planning have a similar role to occupy. If they are not sensitive to management's needs — expressed and unexpressed — their professional knowledge will not be utilized. On the other hand, if they attempt slavishly to give management what it requests, without bringing to bear their own professional knowledge, they are not fulfilling their responsibilities either to management or to the organization as a whole.

A colleague in the personnel department of a manufacturing company was approached by several middle managers of a technical department who wanted a rapid reading course provided for their subordinates. Their diagnosis: The subordinates could not cope with the materials that piled up on their desks because they had insufficient reading skill. My colleague persuaded these managers to discuss the problem further with him. In the course of the discussion, they decided that it would be worth while to undertake a more detailed analysis of the situation, and they carried it out with his help. The findings: The heart of the problem lay, not in reading skill, but in job assignments,

erroneous beliefs of the subordinates about
what was expected of them, and other aspects
of the relationship between these managers and
their subordinates. Reading skill was a trivial
factor.

The "clients" not only abandoned their original diagnosis and prescription; they involved my
colleague as a helper in a rather complete reorganization of their department and a program
focused on improving their own managerial
competence.

While some staff groups — an economics department is a good
example — devote their primary effort to strategy planning with
upper-level management, others provide much less of this kind of
professional help than they might. Many staff groups, for example, become so preoccupied with administering plans and programs and "putting out fires" that they do not fulfill this particular responsibility adequately. Others are unwilling to take the
risks involved in attempting to persuade management that its
diagnoses and prescriptions, in the absence of professional staff
help, are often inadequate. Actually, much can be accomplished
in top management education through competent professional help
in strategy planning. Here the architect-client analogy is particularly relevant. Some of the recent talk, for example, about
the "bankruptcy" of personnel administration may be significant
in just this respect.

2. Help in Problem Solving. This form of professional help
is not unlike that involved in strategy planning except that (1) it is
likely to be concerned with more immediate and specific problems, and (2) it is provided to all levels of the organization. Exactly the same role is called for.

The danger with respect to this kind of professional help (in
contrast to strategy planning with top management) is that staff
groups too easily forget in their dealings with middle and lower
management that help is defined by the recipient. It is one of the
favorite pastimes of headquarters groups to decide from within
their professional ivory tower what help the field organization
needs and to design and develop programs for meeting these
"needs." Then it becomes necessary to get field management to
accept the help provided, and a different role is taken by the
staff: that of persuading middle and lower management to utilize
the programs. The term "selling" is often used to describe this
process, but the power of headquarters staff groups (by virtue of
their direct access to top management) is such that field management usually perceives the process as one of "buy or else."
Field visits of headquarters staff members are often devoted almost exclusively to such selling of headquarters-designed programs or to checking up to see whether the field is using them.

This kind of help is one reason why the term "burden" is so often applied to staff groups. It is why my young friend referred to earlier feared that the staff would help him to death. It is why many staff-conceived programs which are "bought" by top management achieve indifferent success in the field.

If the staff is genuinely concerned with providing professional help to all levels of management it will devote a great deal of time to exploring "client" needs directly, and to helping the client find solutions which satisfy him. Often the most effective strategy for this purpose is one in which the client develops his own solution with professional help. As indicated by the rapid reading example in the previous section, helping the client diagnose his problem may often be a critical step in this strategy.

Problem-solving help to all levels of management, competently and sensitively provided, is _the_ way to develop line confidence in the staff. The needed skills and the understanding of what is involved in providing this kind of help are all too rare among staff specialists today. Professional education in some fields is beginning to include training along these lines, but the need appears not even to be recognized in most engineering schools or schools of business.

In providing this kind of help, the professional specialist will sometimes face the problem of conflicting interests.

A personnel staff member, for example, may be asked by management to give a judgment on the qualifications or performance of a "client" at some lower level of the organization. Or he may, in the course of his professional work, become persuaded that a particular manager is doing substantial harm to the organization through lack of qualifications for his job.

He will destroy the possibility of providing professional help to all levels of management if he permits himself to be used as a source of information or judgment in such situations as these. In the latter case, direct discussion with the individual himself may be called for. However, if the staff man fulfills his responsibility to the organization by revealing his judgments about members of management to their superiors, he will soon preclude the possibility of fulfilling his responsibility for providing help to all levels of management. He cannot help one member of management at the expense of another, nor can he occupy successfully both the role of judge and the role of professional vis-à-vis his "clients."

There probably are cases where the staff member must compromise with respect to such conflicting obligations, but these will be extremely rare. The problem today, all too often, is that no consideration is given to this crucial aspect of the helping role. The consequences for the climate of staff-line relations are readily observable.

3. Help with Respect to Managerial Controls. This form of help has already been considered at some length, and it is perhaps now clear why conventional practice creates so many and such difficult problems. As indicated earlier, the principle of self-control requires that a staff group should never be asked to provide any manager with information to be used for the control of others. Granted that this is a theoretical requirement to which certain practical adjustments must be made, its significance should be very clearly understood by the staff. Otherwise, staff "help" will compound the problems discussed above.

The same principle — that staff provides help for self-control only — applies to what is usually called "coordination," but which means policing the organization with respect to policy and procedures. Help can consist in informing an individual that he is out of line, or that a contemplated action would be in violation of policy — but with the full understanding by both parties that the staff member will not report his knowledge or opinion to anyone else.

The helping role and the role of policeman are absolutely incompatible roles. To place an individual in the latter is to destroy the possibility of his occupying the former one successfully.

One further consideration with respect to the staff and controls deserves mention, and that is that maximum standardization is not necessarily accompanied by maximum efficiency. These two variables are less highly correlated than many professional specialists believe. In fact, there is a good deal to be said for establishing the goal of the minimum standardization of human behavior consistent with the ability to operate the organization. This idea quickly runs afoul of the aims and practices of those working in the data processing field in particular. The essential point, however, is that the decision which achieves organizational objectives must be both (1) technically and scientifically sound and (2) carried out by people. If we lose sight of the second of these requirements, or if we assume naively that people can be made to carry out whatever decisions are technically sound, we run a genuine risk of decreasing rather than increasing the effectiveness of the organization.

Top management in a large, geographically decentralized company became concerned over the size of their permanent inventory of replacement parts. The dollar figure was staggering. Accordingly, a consulting firm was hired to design and install an efficient purchase and inventory control system. The desired objective was to cut the investment in parts inventory in half.

The system designed by this firm was a marvel of efficiency. It included several volumes of coded parts listings and procedures, and a sizable staff to administer the program. A year after it was installed, the inventory investment had been reduced to the desired figure.

During a series of discussions with middle- and lower-level field management about this time, I was simply overwhelmed by the vehement condemnation of this system and of the way it was being administered. Examples, literally by the dozens, were cited of sizable but unnecessary costs to the organization which were resulting. Gross inefficiencies of many kinds were made necessary by rules and procedures which took too little account of local conditions and which provided almost no opportunity for the exercise of managerial judgment.

Of course, many of these managers disliked the curtailment of their freedom and the tightening up of free and easy practices. But the kinds of examples that were cited made it clear that much more than this was involved. The attitude was frequently expressed that "if top management doesn't care any more about waste and inefficiency than this, why should we." Many competent, sincere men said, in one form or another, "We have been wasteful sometimes, but we sure had an interest in the company's welfare. We could have shown them many ways to reduce the parts inventory that would still have permitted us to operate efficiently. But now we are completely hemmed in, and we find we can't do anything to change these unworkable rules. The headquarters staff won't listen. So we live with the rules, and we find ways — sometimes costly — to get around them. <u>And we're beginning not to give a damn whether the company loses or gains.</u>"

When I reported these field reactions to top management, they were dismissed as "typical gripes of guys whose sloppy practices have been corrected." The system of control had been designed by a good company; it cost a lot of money to install; the results in terms of the inventory figure were just what had been desired. And that was that.

4. Help in Administering Services. A fourth activity of staff groups is essentially a line operating function. It consists of administering certain services: equipment maintenance, plant security, payroll administration, eating facilities, activities made necessary by legislation, data processing facilities, benefit plans, etc. Often these require more in the way of managerial than specialized professional skill, but they fall logically within the fields of competence of given staff groups, so they are left there to be administered.

There are no particular problems of staff-line relationships involved in this form of help except (1) poor administration when it occurs and (2) the problem just mentioned of the staff tendency to equate degree of standardization of practice with efficiency.

There is a danger, as previously indicated, that staff groups may become so preoccupied with these administrative responsibilities that they fail to provide the degree and kind of professional help that the organization requires. If the incumbents of staff jobs are former line managers, or technically but not professionally trained specialists, they are likely to find these activities highly congenial. If, however, staff departments include a preponderance of trained and sophisticated professional specialists, there is little danger that the administrative tasks will have priority over genuinely professional activities — unless line management establishes such a priority by its assignment of responsibilities to the staff.

42 THE MAYTAG COMPANY

* * * * *

In establishing our organization we have determined that, basically, the organization shall be upon a functional basis. Logic impels us to conclude that all of the aspects relating directly to the manufacture of the product ought to become the responsibility of one major corporate officer. Similarly, we have lumped other broad functions under corporate officers, so that, basically, our organization is comprised of six major divisions, each headed by a corporate officer and devoted, as the names suggest, to the following six functions:

1. Manufacturing
2. Marketing
3. Research and Development
4. Finance
5. Personnel
6. Legal

It might be argued that organization on a product-line basis or organization by geographical distribution would be quite as effective as this organization on a broad functional basis. In many companies organizations of these types had proved most effective. Since, presumably, the organization form for any company ought to be tailored to that individual group, it may be argued that the organization form which serves admirably for Company A may not be at all acceptable for Company B. If our product line were as large and varied as those of several of our major competitors,

---

Excerpt, reprinted from E. F. Scoutten, "Application at the Maytag Company," in Mason Haire (ed.), Organization Theory in Industrial Practice (New York: John Wiley & Sons, Inc., 1962), pages 78-84, by permission of the Foundation for Research on Human Behavior.

it might be quite desirable to modify our organization form to reflect this complexity of product. Since this is not the case, it seems equally obvious that to imitate our competitors would, in this instance, be foolish.

Superimposed upon these six major divisions is a subsequent organization which is required by the geographical factor. In the Manufacturing Division, this aspect of organization is evident in the several plant organizations; in the Marketing Division, this is illustrated by the several branch organizations. Finally, there is a further organization which is warranted by the nature of the product involved. Within both the Manufacturing and the Marketing Divisions, our organizational units are devoted to a single product. The product organization is subservient always to the geographical organization which, in turn, is subservient to the basic functional organization.

The basic nature of our organization, as described above, requires, of course, no unusual or penetrating analysis or insight. We have adopted it because it seems to be not only a logical and defensible organization, but, most important, a successful one. It seems obvious that the function of geographical organization, as well as that of production organization, should be determined to a considerable degree by the extent of the geographical distribution of the several segments of the Company. Since all three of our manufacturing plants are in the State of Iowa, it becomes relatively simple to ignore the geographical aspect within the manufacturing function. In our sales function, however, with ten sales branches and six wholly owned sales subsidiaries distributed from coast to coast, the geographical factor becomes much more significant.

The final test of the effectiveness and, therefore, of the desirability of any organization form, it seems to us, is whether or not the organization succeeds in attainment of the group goals. A scholar in this field may argue that this is not a defensible criterion, since many differing organization forms have proved effective and successful. I submit that this is not a legitimate criticism of this criterion. The scholar's habitual concern over form and consistency often finds itself at odds with the businessman's concern over results. The fact that one organization form produces the desired results in one situation, while another organization form produces equally effective results in another situation, even when these contrasting situations exist within a single company, should be of no particular concern to anyone. No better analogy of this approach can be had than by comparing it with the game of golf. This sport is full of examples in which individual participants who violate many of the generalized "principles" of good golfing form are, nevertheless, most effective and successful golfers. It may be true, in general, that driving a golf ball from the tee is best accomplished by observing certain distilled rules. The obvious fact remains, however, that the ultimate test of a successful and satisfactory drive from the tee is the distance and direction which the ball travels. I submit that, in the area of business organization, the ultimate test consists solely of the results obtained.

Over and beyond the establishment of this simple, skeletal structure, we have attempted to implement it in the selection of our personnel and in the creation of our operating procedures by acting upon several basic assumptions.

We believe that the only truly effective authority which one man asserts over others springs from competence. We believe that mere rank, as such, carries essentially no intrinsic authority. Finally, we believe that authority is granted by the subordinates to the superior, and that such granting of authority comes only because of demonstrated competence on the part of the superior. It should be understood that, in the use of the term "authority," we refer specifically to real, effective, result-getting authority, and not to the kind of "authority" which is presumed to exist by virtue of the position of a man's name on a formalized organizational chart. The authority which is formally assumed to reside within a department head, by virtue of his assigned responsibilities, may or may not, in fact, be present. The traditional use of the word assumes that authority is a commodity which, basically and originally, is in the exclusive possession of the chief executive of the company. Furthermore, it is assumed that the several layers of subordinates acquire a portion of this commodity only as the chief executive chooses to distribute it among them. Companies will point for verification of this assumption to position descriptions, which set forth solemnly, in black and white, the amount of this commodity which has been allocated to them by their superiors. Such position descriptions are replete with notations such as: "Has authority to approve purchase of new equipment, up to a maximum cost of $5,000." This type of "authority" is sterile and meaningless; it is roughly comparable to issuing a key to the executives' restroom. This is not the vital authority with which we are concerned at this point.

Vital authority, as we use the term, is descriptive of the real power which a leader exerts in determining the conduct and performance of his subordinates. This is the authority which cannot be allocated by any superior, but which, in reverse, is permitted by the subordinates. Without this vital authority, no amount of "delegated" authority can possibly produce an effective leader or an effective organization.

We believe that delegation of responsibility must obviously carry with it both the delegation of the sterile-type authority mentioned above and the requirement of a corresponding accountability on the part of the delegatee. Finally, we believe that there are obvious and very real limits upon delegation, and that to exceed these limits results not only in the proliferation of jobs and personnel but, more importantly, in real confusion.

The delegation of the sterile authority ought, normally, to include the delegation of "the right to acquire and exercise vital authority, provided that the delegatee is capable of acquiring and holding such vital authority." Many formalized statements of delegation presume that the delegation of this vital authority comes from their superior. Our only criticism of this formalized presumption is that it may so insinuate itself into the thinking of the delegatee that he fails to recognize the true source of real authority and, consequently, finds himself in real trouble when his subordinates choose to withdraw the authority which they have permitted him.

It seems hardly necessary to belabor the reader with the necessity of delegating both sterile authority and the right to acquire vital authority in measures necessary to permit the delegatee to exercise the responsibility which he has, in fact, been assigned. This basic truism has long since been pounded home in the minds of all those who have been subjected to courses, lectures, or articles dealing with the area of organization structures.

There is a third element which, in any proper organization form, ought to accompany both the responsibility and authority which are involved in the structure. This is the element of accountability. Every man in every organization, regardless of his level, scope, or responsibility, ought to be required and expected to make periodic and regular accounting of the manner in which he has discharged his responsibility. Without the requirement of accountability, the organization loses at least two essential elements to any successful administration: determination and measurement of results and adequate motivation with the resulting quality performance on the part of the delegatee.

We believe that committees should not be entrusted with the making of decisions. We believe that conferences, discussions, and even advisory committees have a perfectly legitimate role in the management of our corporation; but we believe that the taking of a decision, regardless of its significance or the level of the organization at which the decision is taken, must ultimately and invariably be done by a single individual. We, therefore, reject all forms of joint management, multiple management, or other similar devices of which some of our friends have become so enamored.

We believe, in our Company, that there are essentially only two basic functions: Manufacturing and Marketing. These two Divisions, therefore, we believe are and should be line organizations. We believe that they must accept the responsibility for making all decisions involved in their function, and that they should never under any circumstances delegate any portion of responsibility to any staff organization.

Correspondingly, we believe that all other organization units in our Company should serve in a true staff capacity, with the sole objective of contributing to the increased efficiency and effectiveness of both Manufacturing and Marketing Divisions. We believe that the staff function is that of the expert consultant who will advise, in any proper fashion, the line organization so that, in making any decision, the line organization may have the benefit of specialized staff knowledge, experience, and advice.

Finally, we believe that, other things being constant, the organization is strengthened — and its effectiveness increased — in inverse ratio to the number of organization levels existing between the worker and the president. We, therefore, are constantly striving to eliminate organizational groups and levels, and have, for this reason alone (although there are additional valid reasons), endeavored to eliminate all positions of "Assistant ————" or "Assistant to ————." We have, upon occasion, been criticized because such a policy fails to establish any clear-cut path of executive succession. We regard this criticism as a distinct compliment.

With respect to the line and staff functions mentioned above, especially as they relate to the use of authority, both sterile and vital, it would appear desirable to add a word of clarification. In our Company, the staff divisions exist originally at the corporate level. In their responsibility, they maintain and administer staff services at all levels of the line organization, ranging from the level of the first-line supervisor up to and including that of the Vice-President. Within the staff division, therefore, there is a line function in that the subordinates within the staff division are subject to the same basic principle of delegation as applies in the line division itself.

Within both line divisions (Manufacturing and Marketing) there are numerous functions attached at appropriate levels of the line organization, but eventually within the control of a line executive. In the Manufacturing Division, for example, the industrial-engineering function, the production-engineering function, and the inspection function are staff areas, all of which report, ultimately, to the same Vice-President who heads the entire Manufacturing Division. In the Marketing Division there are staff functions, such as Market Research, Advertising, Field Education, and Market Planning, all of which report to the Vice-President in charge of the Marketing Division. Just as the primary function of the Manufacturing Division is to produce the product, so the primary function of the Marketing Division is to sell it. The central core, therefore, of each of these divisions is, respectively, the production organization and the sales organization. The real ultimate and final line organizations, therefore, are Production and Sales. Within the purview of Manufacturing and Marketing, however, exist these captive staff functions which serve to aid the line core.

Regardless of whether the staff function comprises an entire and independent division, such as Industrial Relations, or is a captive staff, such as Industrial Engineering, the staff personnel operate under conditions which are somewhat different from

those of line personnel. The question of responsibility, accountability, and authority of staff functions frequently appears to bother
many students in this area. Apparently, it is difficult for some
observers to reconcile what they regard as irreconcilable
principles:

1. That staff personnel are accountable for the discharge of
    their responsibilities, and
2. That staff personnel may advise only, and that line personnel
    must invariably make the ultimate decision.

Some persons illustrate their concern by noting that the Labor-
Relations staff — charged with the responsibility of administering the Labor Agreement and of maintaining a satisfactory Company-Union relationship — is prohibited from dictating decisions
to the Manufacturing personnel. Those who become concerned
about this dilemma argue that if staff personnel are excluded
from dictating decisions, then it is illogical to hold staff personnel accountable for the results of such decisions as may be taken
by line personnel. Two aspects of this seeming dilemma seem
perfectly evident to us and seem to make it quite obvious that
there is, in fact, no such dilemma.

Consider first, if you will, the results which would occur, and
do occur, whenever line personnel accept and follow the advice of
staff without exception and without qualification. Under such conditions, staff is obviously saddled with complete responsibility
and accountability for the results which accrue from decisions
suggested and accepted. If the results are acceptable and desirable, staff may bask in the approval of all concerned. If the results are unsatisfactory, staff has no legitimate alternative other
than to confess that its advice was faulty. (In a practical situation, it should be noted, staff has a tendency in such an event to
disclaim total responsibility by adverting to any number of various justifications, including the allegation that, although the line
group accepted the staff advice, they failed to execute the resulting decisions wholeheartedly and with enthusiasm.)

In actual practice, of course, the vast majority of decisions
are taken as a combination of staff advice, modified by line experience and judgment. The results which accrue are frequently
not directly attributable either to staff or line as an exclusive
responsibility, but to the combined group as a group. Within reason, this is a desirable situation. Staff and line, ultimately, are
teammates, not competitors.

Then there is the matter of vital authority which, in the staff
function particularly, is spotlighted and serves to demonstrate
the true nature of authority. The Labor-Relations consultant, in a
staff function, is successful in imposing his concepts and programs upon the line organization only to the degree that the line
organization accords him authority in such areas. This is the

vital authority which is earned by demonstrated competence on the part of the staff man. The Labor-Relations man who advises the line man in the preparation of an answer to a formal grievance will be accorded the reception by the line man directly ascribable to the quality of prior suggestions which the staff man has made. If former suggestions have resulted in calamitous results, the line man will tend to discount and probably ignore entirely the advice of the staff. If earlier suggestions have almost invariably produced the desired results, the line man will come close to accepting staff suggestions without even the slightest modification.

Is it wrong for the chief executive to insist that his Vice-President for Labor Relations earn the vital authority which he seeks over the line personnel? Is it wrong for the president of a corporation to hold this vice-president accountable for the Company-Union relationship which exists? Is it wrong for the president to replace such a vice-president who is unable to win acceptance for his program from the line organization? Is it wrong for the president to remove such a vice-president who succeeds in imposing his program, only to find that the net results are calamitous? We suggest that the real authority of the staff is identical with the real authority of the line: It must be, and is, earned. It seems evident, therefore, that the accountability of staff personnel should be no different than accountability on the part of line personnel. Staff may allege that line refused to cooperate, but one level of line may allege also that a subordinate level failed to cooperate. In the end both are, and should be, completely accountable.

43 ELEMENTS OF ORGANIZATION PLANNING

by K. K. White

*   *   *   *   *

When it comes to deciding which components of a business are line and which are staff, the distinction cannot be so clearly drawn [as it is, for instance, in the military.] Basically, all the specialized units which carry out the main operating activity of the company are line, and all the units which act in a service relation to the line are staff. A manufacturing business, for instance, will certainly consider each of its production facilities a line unit, and nearly always it will classify its accounting department as a staff unit. The reasoning here, of course, is that the accounting department has no part in the physical construction of the company's product, therefore it must be staff. In most manufacturing businesses the same is true of the entire finance department, personnel, the corporate secretary's unit, and all others not directly engaged in manufacturing or in supervising the manufacturing unit (or units). In a company which has only one product and one factory, the factory manager may be the only line subordinate of the company president. All other managers head staff departments.

But let us suppose that the business is not engaged in manufacturing. The line function in this case cannot be the manufacture of products, and the factory manager is nonexistent. In a freight-forwarding firm, transportation is a line unit, since its work is the chief activity of the company. In a large department store, the purchasing activity is most often regarded as part of the line. In most manufacturing firms, however, the contrary is

Excerpts, reprinted from Understanding the Company Organization Chart, Research Study, No. 56 (New York: American Management Association, 1963), pages 33-36, by permission of the publisher.

true: purchasing is regarded as a staff service. Purchasing's principal function in a manufacturing corporation is to make raw materials and semi-finished products available for further elaboration by the manufacturing units.

The personnel function is almost invariably regarded as a staff specialization, no matter what the main activity of the business may be. Here we find perhaps the clearest representation of what a pure staff department or executive should be. (In the first place, every manager, whether line or staff, is obliged to practice the arts of personnel administration. A factory foreman, for instance, certainly assesses the capabilities of the employees under him. He is frequently the one who ultimately determines when performance is unsatisfactory and gives the word when he has decided that retraining or "involuntary separation" is to take place. He will discipline an employee who comes in late every morning. In short, personnel administration or the work of employee relations makes up part of the duties of every supervisory and managerial employee in a business.)

The need for staff services in this area comes about when the line managers realize that there is simply too much work to be done or that they are in need of competent advice or service. After all, a factory manager has something else to do besides keeping the employment records which are included in the regular and necessary work of personnel administration. If it occurs to him (or to some other manager in the organization) that — for example — an investigation of pre-employment aptitude testing seems to be needed, he has little time to do it and will seek the advice of a trained expert. If, finally, it is decided to install a battery of tests to determine whether or not applicants for jobs are likely to succeed in them, the factory manager will certainly not administer them himself and score the results. The personnel unit grows out of the need for advice, service, and assistance. All other staff specializations are born and develop out of similar needs and, in well-ordered corporations, are confined to these ancillary or auxiliary types of activity.

As previously stated, although the main ongoing activity of the business is always the line operation, the distinction is sometimes difficult and, particularly to an outsider, frequently mistaken. In the abstract, for instance, only manufacturing units might be expected to be line units in a manufacturing business; yet many of he manufacturers in the case-study section of this report regard other specializations as part of the line, in addition to their manufacturing divisions. The other unit most commonly considered to be line in a manufacturing corporation is marketing or sales.

The Koppers Company, a very large manufacturing firm, has engineering and construction as part of its line operation. Ordinarily, engineering and construction in a manufacturing corporation are staff services. Engineers either design products or act as service personnel in plants, and the construction unit builds new factories and other facilities as needed by the line production activity. At Koppers, however, engineers and construction personnel actually build new plants and facilities for customers.

American Cyanamid states that its research organization is part of the line, simply because of the speed at which the chemical industry moves ahead. As told in its case study in Part Three of this report, Cyanamid has placed its research department in the line operation because of the recognized fact that the company would soon be out of business if it did not produce a steady stream of new products. It follows that research in this corporation exists to carry on the part of the main ongoing activity without which the firm would cease to exist. More often, manufacturing firms consider research and development of new products as a service, and therefore a staff activity.

And so, as we have seen, there is valid reason for confusion in distinguishing between line and staff in many businesses. One example of the variations that come readily to mind is that the line activity in a firm of attorneys is, obviously, the practice of law, whereas in almost every other business the general counsel is a staff executive.

Why is this seemingly abstract matter of definition important in business, it may be asked. Why can't business managers simply ignore the whole question and go on working as they do from one day to another?

Let us imagine a rather large business which has several product divisions, each headed by a vice president. Product Division A manufactures plastic appliances, Product Division B makes metal implements, and Product Division C makes wood products. On the corporate staff are a personnel man, a marketing man, a vice president of finance, a corporate counsel, and a public relations executive.

The product divisions are responsible for making their various products at a reasonable cost, allowing the firm to make a profit in a competitive market. Each product division has its own sales force, self-contained and completely responsible for maintaining adequate sales. The marketing man at a corporate headquarters works in a staff capacity. His work is to give advice, service, and assistance. The reason is that the product divisions are so busily engaged in making and selling that they do not have time to carry out research, to investigate new techniques, to explore the potential of overseas sales — in fact, to fulfill any function other than their primary ones of production and sales. All staff executives of the corporation work in the same way, or are supposed to do so.

In such a corporation the differentiation between line and staff is simple to make: the product divisions, which are ultimately accountable for profits, are line, and the departments at corporate headquarters are staff.

The staff executives of this corporation are active, capable men and wish to see the company excel in every way. But suppose the personnel staff man, for example, has become enamored of a whole battery of new personnel techniques. He wishes to install pre-employment tests, periodic merit reviews, on-the-job training to improve skills, and the use of several committees at the plant level to exchange views among middle managers so that operations will go on more smoothly. He also feels that it is important to regain "management prerogatives," and wants to come into the various product divisions and install a campaign of hard bargaining against the various production-worker unions.

Being brash as well as active, this personnel man next outlines his complete new program and takes it to the heads of the product divisions. All of them realize that what he proposes to do would be very expensive. They feel that, no matter how the money would be allocated, the expenditure of such sums would eventually cut the profit margin so severely that the firm, far from making a profit, could barely "hold its own." After mature consideration they reject the whole program, stating in regard to its industrial-relations aspects that they believe it to be the wrong time to engage in combat with the production-worker unions in the shop, and that furthermore they have little confidence in the personnel man's proposed methods of dealing with the unions.

Far from being deterred by this cool reception of his plans, the personnel head returns to the corporate offices and writes clear and distinct orders announcing that his program will go into effect immediately and that it will be directed by the corporate personnel department.

Here we have an extreme example of a staff man who does not know what he is doing, for when such "orders" are received by product division heads in the line, they are never obeyed. In such a case there would be an immediate appeal to the company's chief executive, and one would suppose that he would side with his product division heads. The personnel man's program would be rejected.

In our extreme example lies the whole kernel of the necessity for the differentiation between line and staff units in the modern corporation: this personnel staff man is trying to arrogate to himself the power of determining the success or failure of the line units. On his own authority he has ordered extensive alterations in the methods of operation of the line units — changes which, although they might improve operations, might, on the other hand, cause disaster. He simply cannot be allowed to do so. Remember too that there are four other corporate staff executives (marketing, finance, legal counsel, and public relations). If all these men were allowed to go ahead with their own plans, the product division managers would have five sets of orders flowing from five separate men. In effect they would have five bosses, and the nature of human beings is such that complete agreement among all five is unlikely. The legal counsel of the firm, for instance, would be highly querulous about "hard bargaining" with well-established production unions. Such activity might, in fact, amount to unfair labor practice, particularly if the personnel man were so outspoken as to announce that the company intended to "de-unionize" the plants. The counsel might well issue a "cease and desist" order of his own. The product division managers would then face contradictory orders and, of course, to tolerate such a situation is impossible.

Now, this is admittedly an extreme case and would almost never be brought about by anyone except a personnel man completely uninformed in business methods. But there are real, less clear-cut cases. Occasionally, a staff man hits upon an idea for improving operations, an idea which is entirely feasible but involves some risk. The line man may not wish to take the risk. Without rancor, and after considerable thoughtful discussion, he decides that he simply cannot agree. The dispute then goes to a higher executive — possibly the chief executive — who decides what is to be done. If the proposed program is accepted, it goes ahead because the company's chief executive has ordered it after the dispute was brought to his attention.

*　*　*　*　*

44 LINE-STAFF IS OBSOLETE

by Gerald G. Fisch

Since we have grown up under the line-staff concept, we rarely question it. As an organizational scheme it has become something of a sacred cow. No matter how much it gets in the way of our progress at times, no one seems to dare even to suggest that it ought to be pushed out of the way.

What do companies do when they find themselves dissatisfied with the "form" of their organizations? They experiment — sometimes on the grand scale. Since World War II, such experiments have included:

1. Decentralization versus centralization.
2. Functional organization versus product organization.
3. Committee management versus individual authority.

Why then has no one conducted an experiment on an equally grand scale to discover alternatives to the line-staff concept. This is hard to understand, since line-staff may well be the cause of much of the administrative confusion from which many companies suffer.

Accordingly, it will be my purpose in this article (1) to question the wisdom of a slavish adherence to the line-staff concept; (2) to explore the possibility of its being the root of many of our postwar organizational problems; and (3) to offer, tentatively, an alternative organizational scheme (which has never yet appeared full-blown as I shall present it, but has persistently cropped up in bits and pieces throughout industry). Whether or not readers agree with any of my conclusions and suggestions, surely they must begin to examine this fundamental concept in the light of the needs of our time as long as we are dissatisfied with aspects of present organizational performance.

Excerpts, reprinted from Harvard Business Review, September-October, 1961, pages 67-79, by permission of the publisher.

Before I go ahead, however, let me readily admit that the line-staff organization serves, and has served, some companies well. The concept is useful when a company's product lines are simple and not subject to frequent changes over the years. It is the larger company whose products are in constant flux that has the serious problems with the line-staff concept (L-S).

EVOLUTION OF L-S

* * * * *

Contrasting Eras

The line-staff concept was first applied on a grand scale to American industry in a period when product lines were relatively stable, when companies manufactured a comparatively homogeneous product line, and when the factory was the center of operation. In those days steel makers made steel and later steel products, and textile manufacturers made cotton or wool yarn or cloth. Then the chief factor in a company's growth was the technical improvement it could make in manufacturing methods and processing techniques. This was true for textiles, for steel, and for most of the early industries that arose during the beginning of the Industrial Revolution in the United States.

As companies became larger, the general L-S concept was applied to all the functions of the corporate enterprise. A contributing reason for this extension of L-S was that most of the early heads of these companies received their basic training in manufacturing where line-staff division had first taken root. The result has been the indiscriminate application of the concept, which I believe, as I said, to be the cause of many of the organizational problems faced by modern U. S. industry.

Whereas the hub of corporate life used to be in the one simple factory, today it is in the product and service mix. Product lines are so complex that an industrial classification is at best a tenuous exercise in semantics. Packing houses have gone into the chemical business; one flour mill has gone into the electronics business; steel mills sell plastics and nonferrous alloy products; and brass companies have gone into the aluminum business. Many of the larger companies like General Motors, Union Carbide, and Olin Industries are so highly diversified that they cannot be stated to be in any one industry at all. Indeed, the only way in which any good-size American company may be understood is through a complete and thorough examination of its total product line.

The product line, of course, is created by research, development, and engineering, or by acquisitions or mergers that are studied by the finance department. These functions have become the very core of profit or loss opportunity for most large companies in the United States. But research, development, engineering, and finance, under the line-staff concept, are classified as staff or advisory functions.

Surely there must be something wrong with a concept which treats as advisory or support groups those functions that create the hub of today's manufacturing enterprises.

*   *   *   *   *

Span of Control

*   *   *   *   *

Improved communications has strengthened the hand of the chief executive in terms of his ability to centralize authority. The power of decision making by subordinate line managers, on the other hand, has been reduced in many situations. For them, better communications means that their job is one of obtaining coordination and cooperation between departments in response to orders from above. And, conversely, since the traditional staff functions can now report directly to the chief executive or his delegates, their influence has been expanded.

RESULTING PROBLEM

These are the facts about the changes that have taken place. But when some companies fail to recognize these changes and adhere, formally, to the L-S concept, problems are likely to arise. Let us consider some of them in the areas to which they apply.

In Finance

I am sure you can find in your company many instances where, if the controller had more authority to initiate action to remedy inefficiency in both manufacturing and sales, substantial savings could be achieved faster than under the pure L-S system where the controller may only function as an adviser. Indeed, the controller's role in industry today is undergoing a revolution, and perhaps rigid adherence to the line-staff system (where it occurs) is one of the last remaining obstacles to his full utilization. It is perhaps no accident that the former president of Ford Motor Company (now U. S. Secretary of Defense) came out of finance, and that the current vice president of administration of Chrysler Corporation was formerly a partner in Touche, Ross, Bailey & Smart, a certified public accounting firm.

The fact is that financial departments have become the nerve centers of many large modern corporations. Frequently, they

-364-

alone have the knowledge and control of the basic communications network of the corporation in terms that count — namely dollars. As a result they, more than anyone else, are in a position to suggest sound decisions in certain crucial areas. To imply that this control of the nerve center is under today's conditions merely a staff and advisory function, and subordinate to manufacturing and sales, is already recognized by some companies to be unrealistic. As a case in point, the senior financial executive of Du Pont does not report to the president exclusively, but reports independently to the corporate finance committee.

In Purchasing

When companies accept the line-staff definition of purchasing as a staff function, problems arise, too. Let us see what happened to the purchasing function when one large company decentralized its operations:

> Pursuant to doing a market study on a product which was being purchased by a large company (that had recently decentralized its operation), I found, within an area of less than three square miles, eight purchasing agents of eight decentralized divisions, each purchasing the identical item on divisional requisitions. As for the inventories of the item which I was researching, I estimated them to be five times as large as were necessary for the company in the region. But, of course, under the L-S concept the condition described was probably a foregone conclusion.
>
> None of the purchasing agents in question, with the exception of two, had been in his job for more than six months and my estimates of the inefficiency in the total purchasing operation, quite apart from excessive inventories, defy description. All but one of the eight agents lacked a knowledge of supply sources, of pricing, and even of the division's own long-range requirements. Furthermore, none of the eight purchasing agents, even though they all worked for the same company — within an area of three square miles — had ever met for a coordination meeting to consider how they might pool their purchases for the benefit of the company as a whole. After all, they really had no authority to buy, except on requisition, for their own division and certainly had not been charged with attempting any coordination.

* * * * *

In Manufacturing

The line-staff concept affects manufacturing in two ways:

1. In the relationship of manufacturing with staff departments which, at least on the organization chart, are of equal or higher status than is manufacturing.
2. In the relationship between manufacturing and those staff departments which are subordinate to the head of manufacturing.

In most companies, the cohesion between product planning, purchasing, plant personnel departments, and the line operating departments is reasonably satisfactory. But questions still arise. If production planning is a staff or advisory department to the operating departments which are charged with turning out goods, do its instructions have to be followed? Does the production schedule really have to be met, or is it established merely as a piece of advice on production? Should the personnel department hire any additional labor required, as it does in some companies, or should foremen do the hiring, as they do in many other companies?

* * * * *

Further problems occur between the engineering development group and the production group. Special products, of course, cannot be manufactured until production drawings are available; nor can raw materials be ordered until material specifications have been established. Here, too, large amounts of money are lost under the L-S concept. Since the engineering department is a staff group, and since production planning rarely schedules engineering time (as perhaps it should in a central corporate scheduling department), delivery schedules are often delayed and customer dissatisfaction incurred.

In Sales

The mandate of the sales department is clear. It has the authority and the responsibility for getting orders. In some companies it is also charged with the distribution of the product from warehousing to customer delivery, as well as with credit, collection, and distribution financing. Thus, the company's finished goods inventories are sometimes under the control of at least two departments — manufacturing and sales.

Frequently, excessive inventories need to be maintained for any given level of customer service because the line-staff concept does not permit smooth coordination between sales and production. An analogous situation has forced a company like U. S. Rubber to set up a separate and costly sales production coordination department for its tire division. Indeed, one of the key reasons for stating that the L-S concept is obsolete is the age-old wrangle between sales and production in a situation where each one has unilateral authority over its own function and each manager is a line boss, and coordination is supposed to be accomplished by some staff scheduling group.

* * * * *

In Product Lines

Problems arise with product lines when research, development, and engineering are considered staff functions. This is especially true in the area of new product development. For example:

> Take the case of a 100-year-old family business which, as its history revealed, practically went bankrupt every 25 years. During each 25-year span, it made a relatively homogeneous product whose market shrank toward the end of the period. No one in the company with line authority was charged with developing new products. Thus, toward the end of the 25-year cycle, there was invariably a mad scramble for new products, and, as luck would have it, three times in a row a new product was found which sustained the company for another 25 years.
>
> Recently, the company found itself in the same dire straits and the recommendation was made to add a product-line manager, that is, a man responsible for searching out, developing, and introducing new products into both manufacture and profitable sales. Since the addition of product-line management as a line function five years ago, this company has quadrupled its sales and serious losses have changed into substantial profits.

Perhaps a more dramatic example of the kind of problems with product-line decisions which arise under the L-S concept is afforded by recent troubles in the automobile industry:

> It is common knowledge that in the automotive industry the management of product lines has been carefully decentralized — an action, as

we have seen, that often intensifies line-staff problems. Further, in these companies, product-line management, research, development, and engineering have been allowed to remain staff departments. This has had the effect, in my opinion, of leaving the automotive product line of any given automobile manufacturer at least partially without proper total executive control from a corporate point of view. This may be responsible for some of the key problems that have been encountered in this industry during the last few years — namely, the extensive overlapping of price lines and the loss of brand differentiation which have so confused consumers that they have virtually refused to buy some models altogether.

* * * * *

TOWARD A NEW CONCEPT

* * * * *

My experience with a great variety of companies in the United States, Canada, and elsewhere has led me to notice a trend which is occurring in the way many companies are conceptualizing their organizational framework. This trend, which I will attempt to put into words, I call the functional-teamwork concept, or F-T (in contrast to L-S).

But, first, let me offer a few words of caution. Regardless of the conceptual approach that a company takes to organization, any new organizational scheme must include all the functions performed under the old form of operations — only it must perform them better.

Then, too, since the basic difference between one concept and another lies in how the organization is perceived and in how power and responsibility are assigned to each group of functions, the goal of any organizational scheme is to achieve a type of grouping that not only permits the highest level of corporate efficiency but will suit realities of the present and foreseeable future. Hopefully, too, my concept meets this test and, in the bargain, fits people better than do silly notions about the line-staff characteristics of executives.

* * * * *

COMMON DENOMINATORS

I have just finished claiming that the success of the F-T concept depends on placing proper emphasis and balance on the truly important functions of any enterprise. But just what are the basic functions of a business in today's complex world? We can, perhaps, define these essential functions best if we reduce all the activities of a business to their simplest common denominators — specifically to business functions that can be grouped around time, resources, and human interrelations.

Process Functions

Functions that must be controlled on a time basis I call process functions. By this, I refer to those business activities which are like a 100-yard dash — although there is a beginning and an end, the race must be won over and over again, day after day, or week after week. A partial list of these would include:

1. Product design — from idea to tested prototype.
2. Purchasing — from requisition to receipt of materials.
3. Manufacturing — from production drawings to finished product.
4. Advertising — from marketing plan to an appropriate advertisement appearing in the right medium at the right time.
5. Physical distribution — from customer order to final receipt at the ultimate point of sale.
6. Billing — from shipping notification to mailing the invoice.

Two process functions which have been recognized from the beginning are, of course, manufacturing and sales, but others such as those just listed have not been so recognized in the L-S system. In industry today the true line functions are essentially process functions.

Resources Control

Functions which involve the acquisition, disposal, and husbanding of a wide variety of resources — tangible and intangible, human and physical — I call simply resources-control functions. Thus, in its business, any company uses a wide range of resources, which are the tools by which it generates products and profits. These include:

1. Money obtained from shareholders, banks, and insurance companies.
2. The diverse skills of people.
3. The facilities required.
4. Necessary patents and inventions.

Surely the industry tools in this sample have this characteristic in common: if a company acquires the wrong resources, it will surely fail, but if it acquires the right combination, quantity, and quality of resources — and uses them well — surely then it has a good chance of being successful. Thus, the functions which control resources are the watchdogs of the corporation, concerned with the input, output, and most efficient utilization of all the company's resources, and serve as an independent check and balance control on the process functions.

Relations Function

The function which directs the company's communications effort as it affects the behavior of people inside and outside the company — within the framework of the company's legitimate objectives — I call the relations function.

Today a large company must communicate effectively with many diverse groups of people. The timing, effectiveness, and cohesion of all corporate communications are major factors in company success or failure. Thus the corporate image is created — to customers, to government, to stockholders, to the general public — indeed, to any group inside or out of the company which is even remotely interested in the company's affairs.

Let us face it: most companies, like most individuals, are poor communicators, and the L-S approach to corporate communications does not help things.

In most companies, there is little coordination of the complex relations within and outside, except at the level of the chief executive — he of course has many other duties. Labor relations, stockholder relations, public relations, community relations, government relations, and customer relations are often managed at variance with one another, thus reducing the success of the diverse efforts of the corporation. Indeed, when one deals with the various staff and line groups charged with relations responsibilities in most corporations, the corporation appears to be a multiheaded monster without cohesiveness of direction or any consistency in its objectives, and without the means of expressing these objectives.

The relations function seeks to remedy this confusion by coordinating all communications so that they will achieve desirable end results for the corporation. It concerns itself not with what is to be communicated, but with the how and when of communications, and thinks constantly of the effect that communications will have on the recipient.

General Management

Under the F-T concept, general management, having delegated effective control over process, resources, and relations functions, is freed from piddling day-to-day responsibilities and enabled to concentrate on seeing to it that teamwork between the functions takes place. Under the L-S concept, on the other hand, where effective checks and balances do not usually exist, many presidents spend most of their days fighting one fire after another, fires which would never occur or certainly never reach their desks if their companies were properly organized. Thus, in a way, the F-T concept forces general management to concentrate its efforts on the following functions:

1. Establishing corporate philosophy.
2. Setting corporate objectives and targets.
3. Developing and approving plans and programs for the achievement of objectives.
4. Developing and adjusting the organization.
5. Offering specific leadership to the people in the company.
6. Exercising total managerial control of the enterprise.

HOW IT WORKS

Now, let us observe in action how the concept of organization that I call F-T recognizes the fact that the people called "staff" in some businesses are really just as vitally and crucially concerned with what we arbitrarily call line decisions as are the "line" executives. It also recognizes that, no matter what the traditional organization chart shows, in actual work situations people do coordinate their efforts and do work together in ways that cut across functional lines. Judge for yourself whether, in the case of Jones Jams, the F-T concept will take into account these facts of modern business practice.

The Case of Jones Jams

Suppose that the Jones Company, a manufacturer of food products, is organized according to the F-T concept as shown in Exhibits I and II. Let us also imagine that the company has been having difficulty in keeping costs down to a competitive level on a certain line of jams. The director of manufacturing (see Exhibit I) believes that his cost problems can be solved by the purchase of some very expensive, automated equipment that will turn out jams in a limited line of jar shapes and sizes. However, it will enable costs to be cut only because a significant number of workers and supervisors can be eliminated.

The director of sales and distribution, on the other hand, believes that he would have increased difficulty selling jams in the limited range of jars produced by the automatic equipment. A large variety of shapes and sizes, he argues, are a vital necessity to his salesmen, in order for them to meet competition. He also fears that this new equipment will make it more difficult to produce for private labeling, since the various distributors have a stake in maintaining the size and shape of jar associated with their brand.

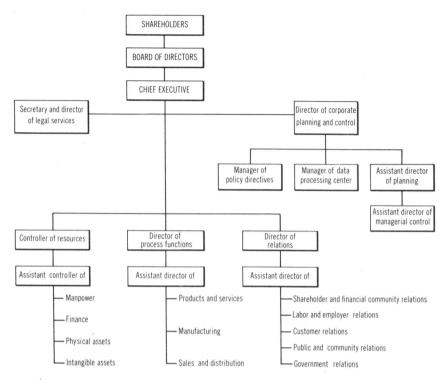

EXHIBIT I. How a Company Might Be Organized
Under the Functional-Teamwork Concept.

Under the F-T concept, this difference of opinion would never arise because the specific responsibility for deciding the company's jam line would be assigned to the product manager. It would not be left to haphazard adaptation as a result of the compromise settlement of arguments between sales and manufacturing. Teamwork is involved because manufacturing, sales, resources, and relations people are, of course, consulted as to the future product line — but the decision is not theirs. Once general management has approved the corporate commitment and consequences inherent in the product plan, the rest of the organization smoothly goes into action.

The assistant director of manufacturing determines his production schedule on the basis of sales estimates which form a part of the new jam product plan. Working with the manufacturing department, the assistant director of physical assets checks machinery requirements and proceeds to acquire the new equipment and to dispose of the obsolete equipment. (The decision to buy and sell equipment is his; but, of course, his effectiveness is measured by how well he meets production schedule requirements,

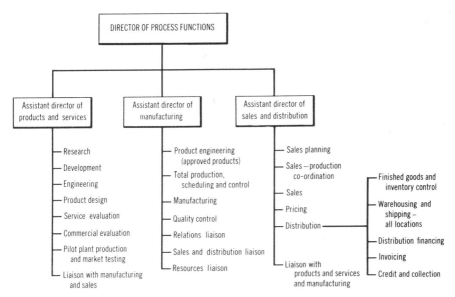

EXHIBIT II. How Process Functions Might Be Organized.

and quality and efficiency needs over both the short and long range.)

The assistant controller of manpower sees whether the displaced workers can be absorbed elsewhere in the company; and in the event that there must be some layoffs, functional lines are once more crossed, and the relations people consider what effect, if any, the laying off of some workers will have on worker morale and on community relations.

As a result of this team effort, the directors of the process, resources, and relations functions strike a balanced solution based on the facts — a solution, moreover, that has every possibility of benefiting the company as a whole. Thus, we see that the key concepts of F-T as practiced in Jones Jams are these:

1. All the functions, whether they be process, resources, or relations, have authority and decision-making power in their own functional area.

2. There is a logical sequence of decisions. The first decision is the product-line decision. Once that is fixed, then the other decision-making functions can smoothly take hold of their areas, dovetailing where necessary, and can build essentially around this product planning. Thus, the first decision relates to the product and service mix; and once that is made, then manpower planning makes decisions about manpower, size of the staff, composition; finance makes decisions about financial requirements; manufacturing makes decisions as to production schedules; marketing makes decisions as to its sales effort to

achieve the called-for sales results; and so on.

3. There is teamwork, but only to the extent that the decisions of one function impinge upon the operating efficiency of another.

It is for these reasons that we call this concept a functional-teamwork concept, or one where each function has its appropriate role and the authority to accomplish its tasks. There is, moreover, a fundamental recognition that teamwork between the functions is a fact of life in the modern corporation.

This, of course, has been just one example. Readers referring to the F-T charts in Exhibits I and II can readily determine how other typical examples can be handled expeditiously in their own companies.

* * * * *

CONCLUSION

* * * * *

Perhaps one of the more important suggestions presented in this article is the argument that research, development, and engineering can surely no longer be considered as staff departments — that they are of equal importance, and hence require equal authority with manufacturing and sales. This fact has long been recognized by the highly successful Du Pont company, which perhaps more than any other large corporation has had early and long experience in operating in an environment of a rapidly changing and complex product line.

A strong plea has been made for placing more power in the hands of people who are classified here as resources controllers — financial controllers, manpower controllers, and purchasing agents — so that corporate assets can be husbanded more effectively than they are now. If such power is given, the acquisition, disposal, and management of all corporate assets (including people) can become doubly important as a strong check and balance on the command authority of the process functions. And an equally strong plea has been made for recognition of the need for centralized control over corporate relations and communications as a second check and balance on the effective operation of the entire company.

And, finally, . . . successful companies have moved in bits and pieces toward the functional-teamwork concept as soon as they have found themselves in stress situations. In this article, I have wondered whether this tendency is not a good and inevitable thing in all business situations. For if key people cannot do their best living and working under a conceptually confused and contradictory organizational system such as L-S, perhaps they could be relieved of considerable strain and anxiety and made more efficient and productive if the L-S concept were discarded entirely. If something like the functional-teamwork concept were adopted, executives and employees in general might be better enabled to work more efficiently and harmoniously toward total success, which is the ultimate goal of any corporation.

45 THE HEADQUARTERS STAFF MAN IN THE ROLE OF A CONSULTANT

by Harry D. Kolb

Theories of organization underlying the American business corporation are not static. Fortunately, continuing process of change is at work. Thus, we find new concepts evolving while old, established ones are challenged and sometimes must give way.

Such is the nature of the subject of this paper. It deals with a changing idea as to what type of relationship should prevail between the staff man in a corporate headquarters and the various key managers he serves. It includes a change in role with respect to the corporate headquarters managers, but even more specifically a change in role with respect to the field organizations. It is in this arena that the internal (or "captive") consultant represents an emerging concept.

An example may illustrate the need. Consider a group of managers from a variety of field units meeting under the auspices of a headquarters staff department. If given an assignment to discuss what types of help they want from the headquarters staff group, the resulting discussion tends to be cautious and unenthusiastic. It is not difficult to imagine why. The headquarters staff man is normally seen as being in a controlling role rather than a consulting one. He sits in judgment. He has an inherent power of recommendation and communication to the headquarters line management. He has often failed to measure up to the expectations of those in the field who may have looked to him for help.

Reprinted from Mason Haire (ed.), Organization Theory in Industrial Practice (John Wiley & Sons, Inc., 1962), pages 143-152, by permission of the Foundation for Research on Human Behavior.

Even if the headquarters staff man should seek to operate in a new role, he still must deal with the experiences of the past. There have been a variety of roles taken by staff men. These include:

1. The auditor or inspector, who is concerned with enforcement, procedural compliance, faultfinding, and data collection for communication back to the headquarters.
2. The advisor or "helper" who offers unnecessary help and is less than fully responsible for the consequences of his advice.
3. The promoter or experimenter, whose interests are self-centered rather than designed for real problems in the field unit.
4. The technician who, though competent, is too rigid to be adaptable.

And now, the concept of "consultant" is being added as a new type of staff man from headquarters. In the past, field-unit managers have learned to recognize these various types of staff men and have built up their own procedures for dealing with them. The intent here is not to belittle the fundamental usefulness of all these activities; rather, it is to point out that when a new role is created, some light needs to be shed on what is intended and how this new type of staff man should be dealt with.

Field organizations have held certain stereotypes regarding the headquarters staff man. These are inherited and must be examined if a different type of relationship is intended. One of these stereotypes is that headquarters line managers rely on their staff men to provide information to them in order that the line managers can exercise their function of control. This type of staff behavior has to be changed under the consulting relationship that is intended. But, in order to accept this change, headquarters managers must first re-examine their own philosophy which says they need information from their staff people in order to exercise control. Fortunately, the newer consultant concept is an outgrowth of central managers relinquishing control to their field units. Thus, an implementation of true decentralization of control has both permitted and promoted the growth of the concept of the headquarters consultant. It is believed that the use of consultants will grow in proportion to the amount of progress a multi-plant corporation makes in this type of decentralization.

By decentralization is meant the transfer of latitude to the local field unit, particularly in terms of the methods, procedures, and emphasis used to motivate and communicate and strengthen its own internal organization. It includes the way in which the organization develops its people, the philosophies that underlie its training efforts for its organization, and, in general, its latitude in deciding how to utilize resources in order to accomplish its assigned mission.

When headquarters grants real latitude in these directions, it then faces a dilemma as to the amount and kind of staff help and direction which it should furnish, in order to avoid over-controlling the activities of field managers. Some staff help is intended, since the philosophy of decentralization does not mean abandonment. In addition, headquarters should provide staff help, first because of its responsibility for the business and, second, because of the inherent potential here for profit improvement.

Let us separate here certain types of staff service essential for financial procedures, for quality control, and for research and technical support. These are not usually areas in which there is as much doubt regarding appropriate staff behavior. More frequently, the question of the staff consulting role comes up in connection with headquarters departments in the fields of employee relations, public relations, organization planning, management development, and various advisory services. The following comments refer to staff work of these latter types of groups in which the focus is on human behavior.

The tradition of using a consulting role for such a staff man is not yet well developed. As a result, the staff man frequently falls into the pitfall of using inappropriate means in order to enhance his status and influence. This may constitute telling the local managers what they may or should not do. It involves utilizing the influence of headquarters management in order to constitute pressure on field units to get them to do what the staff man feels they should do.

The many types of inappropriate behavior are fairly clearly known. Although they may be regarded as inappropriate, even by those who indulge in them, what is not too clear is what alternative behavior is necessary first to be effective and, second, to be acceptable, both in the field and at headquarters.

The headquarters manager has his own concerns about what he should expect of the staff man. On the one hand, he feels the need for furnishing only such central services as can be really justified. On the other hand, he wants to rely on his staff to keep him informed wherever problem areas exist in the field, so that he can then be in a position of protecting the company's interests. This presupposes, therefore, that the staff group renders frequent and critical reports to the headquarters management. Yet doing so prevents growth of the type of consultant who is welcome in the field on the basis of being able to provide professional help, while at the same time maintaining a confidential relationship with his client. It is on this paradox of help to the headquarters manager and a confidential client relationship in the field that the problem is centered.

Herbert Shepard of Case Institute has commented in this direction as follows:

Staff groups often try to enhance their influence by identifying themselves with groups that have formal authority in the organization. Thus some staff groups may be regarded as spies serving higher levels, as agents of headquarters authority, or as mechanisms for the prevention of decentralization.

Sometimes this reputation is gained through indiscreet use of privileged communication, sometimes by the explicit operating principles of the staff man, as when he identifies himself as being responsible to a higher level.

The temptation may be strong to use privileged communication or observations made in the field to build the staff's influence and reputation in the home office. Related to this is the tendency of the staff man, if he is unable to influence lower levels in the direction he thinks best, to try to get someone at higher level to lend his authority. This procedure may be momentarily effective, but turns the staff man into a threat rather than a resource for the future.

Professor Shepard goes on to point out that any indiscretion on the part of the consultant can very quickly render him of little further use. Therefore he concludes that:

If the staff man thinks certain kinds of information should be shared between groups or levels, his job is to help the parties communicate, rather than to communicate for them.

Headquarters management has to make up its mind whether or not it can rely on its field managers as the source of upward communication regarding problems, needs, and developments. The use of the staff system as a substitute for reliance upon direct upward communication has in the past subverted this more logical and appropriate direct upward channel.

Therefore, one of the essential conditions for an effective consultant role is this confidential relationship between the headquarters staff man and the field unit. The information which he gains regarding the operation of the field unit is not to be communicated by him within the headquarters. When he is in the field unit, he is serving the local manager in the same manner that an outside consultant would; he has a status of independence and, yet, he is working for the local manager.

Until the local unit accepts the fact that the consultant is not going to relay punitive information back to the headquarters, the consultant will not really gain access to reliable sources of information. If, however, this type of trust can be developed, then the staff man can be immensely more valuable to the local manager because he will be in a position to facilitate communication within the organization he is serving. His independence and freedom from immersion in the local organization's channels makes him a powerful mechanism for aiding the organization to surmount blockages that have been built up in its communication network.

If a headquarters management can accept the idea that its specialized consulting staffs do not make reports in the home office, how can it determine that such centralized services are justified or properly being used? The consultant has to rely upon the field management to communicate upward its own evaluation of his worth. This is, of course, risky and perhaps uncomfortable for the staff man. He is frequently by nature one who feels the lack of power in his position and, therefore, tends to want to draw attention to the usefulness of his work in order to enhance his own reputation. To the extent to which he develops a true consultant role, however, he will find less appropriate opportunity for doing this. Yet this can benefit the organization. If line management has to rely on appraisal of the effectiveness of staff work as judged by the clients (rather than as reported by the consultant), there can be a lifting of standards of performance. Certain kinds of staff support which have been covered up, despite inadequacies in their quality, might by this system be revealed for what they are.

Thus far, we have dealt with the three-party relationship between the staff man, the local manager, and the headquarters manager. Considerably more is to be learned regarding the two-party relationship of the consultant with the local manager. Here is a man free from the bonds of organization channels and, therefore, free to approach the local manager directly. Does this mean that he concentrates his efforts at this spot in the organization, rather than working with lower echelons and rather than working with some counterpart local staff? The answer is not simple or clear-cut since all three types of concentration may be appropriate at different times.

There is no doubt that many an outside consultant has come to the conclusion that his effectiveness depends upon being able to communicate directly with the top man. However, this may be merely a question of strategy in order to get some initial commitment to a study or an undertaking. If the internal consultant is going to be useful, he needs to be able to bridge the gap between local staff and the local manager and to be a communication catalyst and link. Also, if the kinds of activities he is to engage in are those which rightly involve the total organization, he would be ill-advised to confine his contracts to just the top manager. A potential competitiveness exists between the consultant and any counterpart local staff. The effective consultant can recognize this, not be channel-bound because of it, and yet be supportive rather than destructive in order to enhance the position of the local staff man.

Another difficulty can arise when the consultant finds a local situation which is alarming, and yet sees his recommendations for improvement being ignored. What can he do? We have already seen that it would be inappropriate for him to communicate this to headquarters, and yet he is hardly so disinterested as to be able to ignore the situation. Few men are in the position that a famous outside consultant was in once when he rendered a report to a prominent American corporation regarding their labor-relations problems. With his report went his invoice for a substantial fee. Subsequently the president of the corporation called him in and said: "Here's the check for your fee, but we don't plan to do a damn thing about any of the recommendations in your report." Whereupon the consultant said, "If that's the way you feel, we don't need your check." Whereupon he tore up the check in front of the man and left.

This independence is commendable — and rare. Subsequent events proved the consultant right, and the firm recalled him and started to rely on his advice. Perhaps this does suggest that the internal consultant can only rely upon patience, while at the same time trying to maintain his independence and the integrity of his ideas. One of the continual worries is that the internal consultant will tend to sacrifice his own values as a result of pressure to conform, or to fit the requirements of a local situation. If this were to happen, in time the consultant's values would become synonymous with those of his client — frequently with the result that they would have become less valid and less useful to the company.

Another area of considerable interest is the extent to which the consultant should assume the role of an expert. If we are talking about a technician who is brought in to solve a problem of design, methods, or materials, it is normal to expect this staff man to come up with an expert's answer. But the problem changes with problems or changes affecting relationships, motivation, or organization behavior.

What happens if the consultant assumes the role of an expert in these situations? He may prescribe well, and yet accomplish little. The reason for this is clear. The matters we are dealing with here require more clarity and accuracy of analysis in order for them to be accomplished. Any change affecting these organizational relationships, systems, climate, and standards of behavior will come about only when certain conditions prevail. Not just one person but all the participants themselves need to accept both the need for change and the desirability of a certain type of remedial action. The effectiveness of the change intended is dependent upon involvement of the total group affected. Thus, the consultant's job is more to accomplish this recognition and involvement than to prescribe the solution to the problem. One description of how the consultant should perform has been offered by Chris Argyris of Yale University in a privately published report on the consultant role. Professor Argyris offers the following thoughts:

> The aim of the consultant is to help the participants become more aware of the blocks and barriers that prevent them from achieving their objectives. He also attempts to help the participants develop new diagnostic skills and take concrete actions to resolve their problems.
>
> The consultant strives hard to facilitate effective problem-solving without becoming the center of attention or the control mechanism for change. He attempts to help people by encouraging them to verbalize and clarify their views, to express their feelings, to become more open about their attitudes and beliefs.
>
> The consultant resists making the diagnosis, making alternative recommendations or taking the lead to plan further action. His objective is not to solve a particular problem for the managers. He realizes that the more problems he solves, the more dependent the organization can become upon him. . . . The more the consultant analyzes, recommends and suggests, the more he behaves in ways which are not consonant with self-diagnosis, self-growth, self-responsibility for action.

It is a rather disturbing thought to extend this idea to its logical conclusion. It states that the field unit which invites the consultant of this type in in order to get his help, finds that he is spending his efforts on getting them to solve their own problem rather than offering them a professional opinion or expert solution. Immediately, this creates some confusion. The consultant is brought in because of his superior knowledge, and yet submerges his own opinion in order to concentrate on a developmental job within the group. Obviously, this suggests the real difference here is that the consultant is looked upon as a trainer (or should be) rather than as a man who has a ready prescription.

It is difficult to know how consistently one could follow Argyris' definition. Field managers are in need of help. They are busy. They seek expert advice. They might well become annoyed or disinterested if instead of advice they get suggestions for involvement of their people in self-analysis work. No doubt frequently some compromise will have to occur. The consultant may find that, to stimulate action, he must take some initiative and provide a direction. At the same time, so long as he is concerned with human-behavior problems, he cannot escape the fact that solution to these problems requires a constructive process rather than a prescription. To this extent, as Argyris points out, "A consultant who is interested in helping the organization must give attention to the processes by which plans are developed, introduced, and made a part of the organization." This differs from many consulting relationships, where the ends are considered more important than the means.

Argyris believes that the effective consultant will tend to invite a greater degree of participation on the part of the members of the organization he is working with. He states:

> At the core of his relationships are such factors as openness, authenticity, the capacity to create minimal defensiveness, listening with minimum distortion, etc. Thus we find that even a consultant who provides help on such "hardware" tasks as incentive systems, cost reduction, and production problems may have to concern himself with authenticity and other interpersonal and group issues. Obviously the consultant whose objective is to provide help in the human factors area has no choice but to focus on creating authentic client-consultant relationships. In order to succeed in their work such consultants must be interested in the processes or means, as well as the ends.

What can be set forth as the objective of the consultant on problems involving human relationships? He must be a capable expert in his field, yet his expertness in this sense should also be related to his being able to develop the organization in its capacity to solve its own problems. Thus, the consultant could be said to have achieved his ultimate objective only when the following conditions prevail:

1. The organization has found an appropriate way to handle the problems which were of initial concern;
2. The organization has developed good procedures for identifying future problems;
3. The organization has recognized the benefits from periodic evaluation of its own effectiveness;
4. The organization has learned procedures which will help it maintain a healthy state of adaptability.

The development of internal consultants who meet this description represents a worthwhile objective for management. There is a potential here for effective help and service from a headquarters organization, in contrast with many of the presently acknowledged shortcomings of today's systems for central staff support. More specifically, there is potential for real development of field organizations toward greater self-sufficiency. Therefore, this represents a new and useful form of management development.

Certain specific steps by top management will be essential to its growth. There needs to be, for example, a clear understanding of the latitude available to field managers to use or not to use consultants on their own initiative. Likewise, local managers need to have full latitude with regard to the routes they pick for study, diagnosis, and involvement of their organization in activities of a developmental nature. Likewise, local units clearly need to have the latitude to collect data and yet not be forced to use it in ways amounting to self-incrimination. In place of this, there should be a clear understanding that the organization is judged on the basis of performance criteria rather than symptomatic data collected in its own work in problem diagnosis.

Management should anticipate paying a high premium for real skill and competence in the consultant function — and yet not settle for less in staffing this type of service. In view of apparent shortage of competent men at the present time, attention should be given to the selection and training of candidates with the range of skills needed.

An additional point to bear in mind deals with the importance of keeping the consultant group intact as a centralized staff. One might ask why, in view of a policy of decentralization, a consultant staff should not also be scattered and spotted in the various field units where it might be of help. One reason, of course, is the fact that there is an intermittent need for such help in the field, and therefore economy dictates some centralization. In addition, the highly skilled type of person that is needed further suggests that he be placed so that he can be utilized fully in a variety of locations.

But there are additional important reasons for not having the consultant located full-time and on a continuing basis in the field unit he is serving. To do so is running the risk that he will be absorbed into the unit, bound by organization channels and unable to exercise the independence of comment and judgment essential to a high-quality job. In fact, even when located in the headquarters, it takes special attention to maintain an attitude of true independence. There are the countervening influences of concern about status, reward, promotion into other lines of work, and pressure toward conformity. Is it really possible to accomplish true independence with internal consultants in a modern industrial organization? It is still too early to know. Meanwhile, hope is bright because the bits of experience to date have been encouraging — and the potential benefits are great.

46 CENTRAL STAFF AS A CONTROL AGENCY

by Daniel L. Kurshan

*   *   *   *   *

Line and Staff

Another of our communications pitfalls is the phase "line and staff." We all recognize the semantic bear traps involved in the use of these words.

To try to stay as much out of trouble as possible, I will use the word "line" to mean the operating side of the business. In a utility or other service company, this would include the units providing service to the customers. In a manufacturing company the operating units would be the manufacturing, sales, or product divisions. In my own organization, The Port of New York Authority, it would be the groups responsible for operating our airports, seaports, tunnels and bridges, and inland terminals.

So much for "line." Any other unit can be called a staff unit. This would include finance, public relations, purchasing, management analysis, industrial relations, or what have you.

These so-called staff units are intimately involved in the problem of central control. The way "staff" is used by headquarters determines whether control will be tight or loose and, therefore, the degree of decentralization.

Consider, for example, the field of industrial relations. Top management may be concerned about the quality of personnel recruited, about nepotism, about salaries being too high or too low. One way of "controlling" the problem is to give the vice-president for industrial relations complete authority over hiring and wage rates. While this might insure a good recruitment and

Excerpts, reprinted from Management Record, April, 1960, pages 10-18, by permission of the National Industrial Conference Board.

pay system, what would it do to the ability of the divisional manager to get results through people if he has no control over their selection or how much they get paid?

What other methods are available for the use of headquarters staff? Actually, the available alternatives range from exclusive authority in headquarters on the one hand to no authority on the other.

For example, the headquarters staff unit may set standards of recruitment and pay, leaving the divisions with authority to hire and promote only within these standards.

Or the divisions may be given authority themselves to set standards for jobs and for pay, subject to prior approval by headquarters.

Or headquarters may later review and possibly veto the standards that the divisions have promulgated.

Or the divisions may have authority to move the whole way with no prior approval, no subsequent approval, subject only to reporting what they have done. Then the staff unit is free to audit if it chooses.

Such audits may be on the initiative of the president at the instance of the staff unit itself, or perhaps only on invitation of the division concerned. Or the audit may be proposed by the staff unit, and the operating division may refuse to have the audit. In this case, staff in turn could appeal the division's refusal to the next higher echelon.

The result of an audit may be reported to top management only or to the division only, or to both. The responsibility for correcting difficulties shown by the audit may rest with the headquarters staff or with the division.

The responsibility for follow-up may also be set up in different ways. And the cost of the service of the staff unit may be spread over the whole company as undistributed overhead, or it may be charged directly to the division served, or it may be charged only if the service was sought by the division affected. How it's done depends on the needs of the company, the management philosophy of the company, and its organization policies.

Now let's come back to that concept of centralization-decentralization. Delegating comparatively great authority to division managers predetermines to a considerable extent the dimensions of line-staff. Top management, having relinquished a good deal of active supervision through the act of delegating authority, will have more need for central control units to assure that the company is on course.

Now let's look at a contrast between the product-type organization and the function-type organization from the viewpoint of line and staff. I already stated that: (1) the top executive of a company organized by product tends, as a result of that type of organization, to free himself from the responsibility of coordinating functions; and (2) the man on the No. 3 level (that's me and my pizzas) tends to make the final decision on the functional questions relating to that product.

However, both these generalizations have to be modified by the impact of line and staff. For example, if a product-type organization chooses to build up a group of strong staff headquarters units with effective control authority, this could negate some of the advantages cited earlier.

Specifically, if my division vice-president in charge of pizzas, Bill Machaver, can be overridden by the headquarters financial vice-president on matters of financial judgment regarding the product; if our division sales manager must get final approval on his marketing plans from the headquarters marketing vice-president and not his product boss; if Berry, as head of the corporate manufacturing staff, tells me how long to leave the oven on, then many of the advantages of a product-type organization have been lost.

What's more, that splendid insularity of the top executive, who we thought would be contemplating plans and objectives for twenty years ahead, becomes lost in trying to resolve conflicts between the headquarters staff and the product division chiefs.

CENTRAL STAFF AS A CONTROL

So the question is: How can we maintain adequate central control in a company that has delegated great authority to its divisions, particularly where these divisions have been organized on a product basis? Must it be in the direction of considering recentralization?

My answer is emphatically no. I believe that the central staff, when used in accordance with modern management principles, can actually strengthen product divisions as well as the lower echelons to which authority has been delegated. At the same time, it can assure central management that performance is adequate and proper. And it can do these things without involving top management in a continuous refereeship of squabbles between the headquarters staff and the operating divisions.

Prerequisites for Effective Control

What are the requirements for effective use of central staff as a control agency? To begin with, we must have tangible and measurable objectives, policies, programs, goals, standards, and budgets so that we have something to control against.

Central staff may have an important job in helping the chief executive know that these objectives have been well thought out, are consistent, and in harmony with top management thinking. But you can't control if you haven't thought through these fundamentals, because there just isn't anything to control against.

Next, it is important to have an organization structure that will permit effective control. Authority and responsibility must be pinpointed, relationships must be soundly established to prevent undesirable duplication and overlapping, and decision making must be delegated to that level of the organization most likely to produce the best answers.

These are all familiar management fundamentals; but if we haven't poured a solid footing, the control structure is likely to teeter.

Finally and, of course, most important, it is necessary to have the right people in central staff spots. If we are to be assured that staff will not command but will merely assist the other units and top management in maintaining uniformity of policies, adequacy of standards, and evaluation of results, we will need a special breed of temperament for these posts. What we have to find are people who are technically qualified, yet have a broad, company-wide, industry-wide outlook, an ability to harmonize conflicting viewpoints — and that includes being patient, discreet, and a good listener — and an ability to subordinate their own egos.

Philosophy of Sound Line-Staff Relations

In order for the central staff agency to assure top management that the company is under effective control, there are certain general principles that should govern the dealings between units.

In our organization we have adopted some eight of these principles (see the accompanying [Table]). In general, they are designed to create mutual trust and mutual respect for each other's contribution. Let's take a look at a few of them.

A test of a department's sincerity is the extent to which it communicates with other departments on pertinent matters. In other words, if a line division plays it close to its chest and doesn't give the interested staff divisions a crack at its plans until it is too late for them to make a contribution, well that just isn't playing the game.

Staff departments are urged to seek acceptance through persuasion, building informal relationships, and demonstrating a realistic understanding of the problems of the other divisions. They are urged to shun emphasis on jurisdictional rights. In the situation I just mentioned, for example, the staff division doesn't achieve results by tossing a crackling memorandum to the offending division — making sure that copies go to the heads of the other divisions. Where were the staff department's intelligence agents? If they were doing their job and were close to the line division where they belong, they would have known of the plan in time and tactfully assured themselves a crack at it.

We direct attention to the nature and quality of negotiations between divisions. These we feel should be dominated by a sense

INTERDEPARTMENTAL RELATIONSHIPS – PRINCIPLES ADOPTED BY THE PORT OF NEW YORK AUTHORITY

Underlying all formal assignments of authority are certain general principles that apply to all departments and to their dealings with each other.

1. The relationships among departments must be characterized by mutual trust and mutual respect for the contribution that each group can make to the solution of the common problem. One basic test of a department's sincerity in this respect is the extent to which it communicates with other departments – i.e., how well it keeps them informed of significant developments which directly or indirectly affect their work, the accuracy and timeliness of the information and the courtesy or consideration with which their views are solicited.

2. The staff departments should not place excessive emphasis on jurisdictional rights, but should undertake to obtain acceptance by persuasion, building informal relationships, performing high quality work within agreed time limits, and especially by demonstrating a realistic understanding of the problems and point of view of the other departments. (This is commonly referred to as using the "authority of knowledge" rather than the "authority of rank.")

3. The line (as well as staff) should not become inbred, inflexible, or shortsighted; it should welcome new and fresh ideas, improvements in methods, and attention to long-range needs.

4. Negotiations should be dominated by a sense of practicality, by a recognition of what makes sense in the situation, even when this collides with consistency.

5. Negotiations should be characterized by informality, face-to-face contacts and good-humored attempts to resolve differences. But if a fundamental principle is involved and there is no other way, the issue must be thrashed out at higher levels and not allowed to fester inside the organization.

6. As a primary condition of organizational effectiveness, it must be taken for granted by all departments that the responsible department (whether line or staff) will adopt the recommendations of another department if they are sound and will reject them only for compelling reasons. If the other department is unable to persuade the responsible department, and a basic principle or policy issue is involved tying back to its own responsibility, the other department should appeal the matter to the executive director.

7. When a department has made a recommendation or given advice which is not accepted or when its advice or concurrence should have been sought and was not, the responsible department must answer to the executive director for any inadequacy of performance resulting from such decisions or such omissions.

8. When standards have been developed for Port Authority-wide application (more than one department) and have been incorporated in official statements of policy, such as the PAI manual, or where the executive director has made it clear through other media or methods that certain standards are to be observed, the role of the staff department is no longer advisory but becomes one of inspection and reporting.

of practicality, even at the expense of consistency: "Sure, we did it the other way last time. Granted, a solution isn't in the books, but if it looks promising and may save dollars, why not give it a try."

Negotiations should be characterized by informality, face-to-face contacts, and good-humored attempts to resolve differences. A long exchange of correspondence may satisfy the frustrated hopes of embryonic literary lights, but it is not likely to improve the margin of profit. On the other hand, if a fundamental principle is involved and there just is no other way, the issue has to be thrashed out at a higher level and not allowed to fester inside the organization.

* * * * *

QUESTIONS AND ANSWERS
BY VARIOUS PANEL MEMBERS

Question: In an organization decentralized on either product or geographic lines, there may be some staff functions performed on the scene and others in the home office. What is the relationship between these corporate and division functions?

Take accounting, for example. If you have accounting in Houston, Texas and the home office in New York, is the accounting department in Houston working for New York or is it working for Houston? Who hires the accountant in Houston, for instance; who sets the policies for the local accounting department; and who oversees the accounting operation there?

Mr. Fish: I think we would agree that if you were relying on the Houston management to operate effectively, it should have the tools to do the job.

Accounting is an important arm; it provides the facts and figures a manager has to have readily available to know where his unit is going and what he should do next.

Now obviously, the manager in Houston would recognize, as a good member of the total team, that a uniform system of accounting is necessary for the smooth operation of the company as a whole. I have never seen an operating manager who disagreed with that principle.

The division manager is usually willing to recognize that the headquarters comptroller should establish the standards for accounting throughout the company. And the division's accountant should conform to these standards, while at the same time serving his local superior.

I think it is most important, in the case that you raised, that the local accounting manager feel that he is working for the head of the Houston organization and is a member of the Houston team.

But I don't feel that this is incompatible with recognizing that he has to conform to general systems and patterns of accounting that are established for the entire company.

In the matter of selection or removal of the local accountant, we might all agree that there are two people who have to be satisfied.

Since the corporate comptroller bears the responsibility of reassuring the president or the financial vice-president that the company's accounting system is functioning smoothly, he has to be satisfied with the division accountant's performance in the over-all system and his professional competence. And the division manager who is served has to be satisfied that the fellow fits into the team, works effectively, and is really assisting him in the management process.

Either could block a promotion or initiate a change if, in his judgment, it was necessary. The final decision would probably be made at headquarters where both points of view could be taken into account.

As a footnote, I might add that one of the largest companies in the United States has its accounting setup reporting directly to the over-all accounting management at headquarters. Because of this, the heads of the various operating divisions just don't take the accountants into their confidence. Thus, the accountants are not effective members of the local team. I think that is a natural reaction and one of the obvious disadvantages of that type of organization.

Question: In some companies, decentralization accompanied by a reorganization on product lines has created tremendous conflict between line and staff. The chief executive is often put in the position of the referee. This raises the following question.

Mr. Kurshan indicated that under a decentralized setup the control function of the staff could be affected through the process of appraisal and evaluation.

Yet, if you have local autonomy on a product basis, and someone from the corporate group comes in to appraise, normally there is likely to be resistance to being appraised and evaluated, particularly when that appraisal is going to go upstairs to somebody.

If corporate staff has no authority, the local decentralized operating groups are going to do everything they can to withhold information from the staff groups and, in effect, try to seriously limit their activity. Hasn't this been your experience?

Mr. Kurshan: It surely has, and that is why we have worked so hard to try to establish acceptable standards of performance and sound working relationships to minimize undesirable conflict and friction.

Of course, I challenge the assumption that all has to be sweetness and light in an organization. I can't think of anything more deadening than to have everybody agree with each other. It makes for a very sodden kind of environment. We get some of our best ideas in the heat of conflict, in staff discussions, and in the legitimate and wholesome rivalries that are generated by productive people with imagainative ideas.

Mr. Lucking: The key phrase in your question is "this is go-ing upstairs." Do the audits necessarily always have to go up-stairs? I don't agree with this. If we have individuals who can handle their own jobs in a decentralized operation, shouldn't they be in a position to ask for their own audits so they can do a better job? Shouldn't these audits first go to the people who have been audited so they have an opportunity to see what kind of a job they've been doing? I refer again to the human relations aspect of the process. Is the man being controlled, or is he being allowed to do the best job he can? Is he allowed to make a mistake, if that is what he has to make, in order to do a better job?

Mr. Fish: If the staff advice is any good, if the staff people really know more about certain aspects of the business than the people they are advising — and unless they do, they are not worth their keep — then they ought to have something to sell that the man in operations, who is held accountable on a profit-and-loss basis, can't afford not to take advantage of.

If staff is there trying to help that man in operations do an even better job, instead of making him look offbase to his supe-riors, staff will usually get a lot of cooperation and appreciation.

Mr. Kurshan: The real problem is not in the area of aids to profitability. Anybody would be a fool not to accept advice on how to do better. The real problem occurs when the staff control agency seeks to carry out top management's attempt to assure uniformity in corporate standards — such as uniform standards of accounting, uniform personnel standards, and things of that sort. These may not help profitability at all for a particular product manager. Here I think is where we have our most acute friction between staff agencies and the line.

Mr. Fish: I agree that "profitability" is too narrow a term.

Let's assume that all of the members of management in each of our companies are measured and gauged in terms of a half-dozen main things that you expect them to accomplish. To my mind, the staff people are there primarily to help line manage-ment do even better on those five or six things. On that basis there is usually a very good ground for acceptance.

47 ORGANIZATION GROWING PAINS

by Eugene J. Benge

In foundry practice the design of the mold frequently determines the strength of the casting. Similarly the structure of the organization frequently determines the strength of the company.

Business organizations, like people, grow from childhood through adolescence to adulthood — successful business organizations, that is. Some pass away in childhood through frailty, some never get through adolescence because they don't know they're growing up, and of course some die of senility because they can no longer adapt to change.

Of the 1909 100 largest corporations in our own country, only 31 were in this class fifty years later.

The National Industrial Conference Board studied 150 well known companies to discover the underlying laws of growth. Two important findings:

1. One man management has characterized the childhood of virtually all successful companies, but in order to get beyond the shortpants stage these companies had to change to team management.
2. It is important that each company realize when it is outgrowing the existing organization pattern.

A shop or department, as well as an entire company, can likewise suffer from a need to change the organization structure. Exhibit 1 shows the evolution of supervision in a machine shop.

Reprinted from Advanced Management — Office Executive, October, 1960, pages 4-7, by permission of the publisher.

MACHINE SHOP

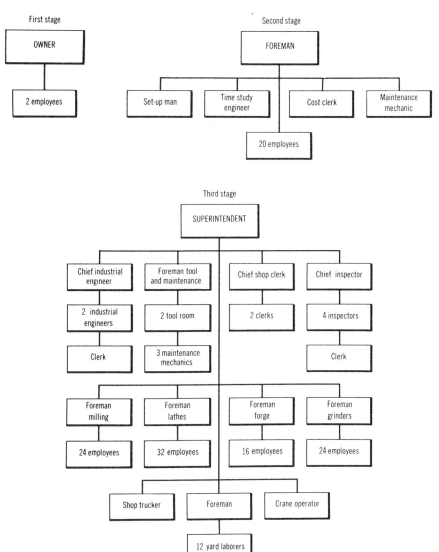

First stage

OWNER

2 employees

Second stage

FOREMAN

Set-up man | Time study engineer | Cost clerk | Maintenance mechanic

20 employees

Third stage

SUPERINTENDENT

Chief industrial engineer | Foreman tool and maintenance | Chief shop clerk | Chief inspector

2 industrial engineers | 2 tool room | 2 clerks | 4 inspectors

Clerk | 3 maintenance mechanics | | Clerk

Foreman milling | Foreman lathes | Foreman forge | Foreman grinders

24 employees | 32 employees | 16 employees | 24 employees

Shop trucker | Foreman | Crane operator

12 yard laborers

EXHIBIT 1. The Characteristic of This Type of Organization Is That the Executives in Charge of the Principal Functions, Both Line and Staff, Report Directly to the President or Executive Vice-President.

	Total number of employees	Number reporting directly to the boss
Stage 1	3	2
Stage 2	25	24
Stage 3	135	11

Neither State 2 nor Stage 3 was properly organized. The reader can, if he so desires, sketch the organization chart he would propose for this group and compare it with the actual solution shown at the end of this article, as Exhibit 4. The actual solution will not necessarily be better than one developed by the reader.

Generally it is easier to understand organization principles for the company as a whole than for a given shop or department. Once the principles are grasped, applications to specific situations can more readily be made.

FUNCTIONAL ORGANIZATION
(see Exhibit 2-A)

As a business grows beyond the scope and energy of one man, it begins to functionalize. As various functions become burdensome, specialists are employed to supervise them. Perhaps the owner hires someone to supervise production. Later he may hire a sales manager.

The chart shows four functions only but others will usually be found.

Characteristic of this type of organization is that the executives in charge of the principal functions, both line and staff, report directly to the president or executive vice-president.

Organization growth merely consists of adding personnel to the basic skeleton. Occasionally an "assistant" or "assistant to" is designated to lighten the load on the head of the function. Likewise, at lower levels foremen, subforemen, technicians, chief clerks, section heads and branch managers are appointed. These additions do not, however, change the basic reporting structure.

DIVISIONAL ORGANIZATION — GEOGRAPHIC
(see Exhibit 2-B)

If a company is widely dispersed, a geographic divisional organization may be indicated. Dispersion, or the desirability of dispersion, results from far-flung selling effort, from widely scattered sources of raw materials, from high costs of hauling raw materials or finished goods.

In one kind of divisionalization, branch plants are established

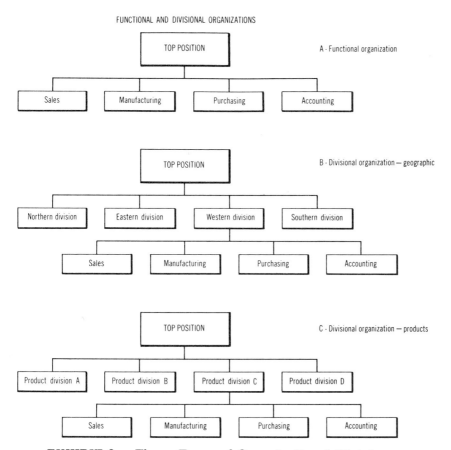

FUNCTIONAL AND DIVISIONAL ORGANIZATIONS

A - Functional organization

B - Divisional organization — geographic

C - Divisional organization — products

EXHIBIT 2.   Three Types of Organizational Division.

at various geographic locations. Each one is virtually autonomous as to manufacturing, selling, purchasing, accounting, etc.

Sometimes all manufacturing is done at one plant location, but sales effort is organized on a divisional, geographic basis. In this situation, top management needs to realize that policies and practices which operate well in manufacturing (with probably a functional organization) may not be applicable in marketing (with a divisional, geographic organization).

DIVISIONAL ORGANIZATION — PRODUCTS
(see Exhibit 2-C)

In some instances, the problems of manufacturing varied products are so different that it pays to set up special manufacturing units. In this event, the organization pattern is likely to be that shown in the chart. It reveals four product divisions, each one virtually autonomous as to manufacturing, selling, purchasing, accounting, etc. Frequently a vice-president heads up each division.

It is usually feasible for manufacturing to be done on a product division basis, with a unified selling organization organized on a geographic division basis.

It is difficult to change a manufacturing organization to either a product division or geographic division basis because of the heavy plant investment involved and the upheaval to the existing organization.

In any proposed reorganization, the reporting lines and the authorities of staff departments, groups and individuals are likely to present difficult problems for decision.

STAFF DEPARTMENTS

Staff departments can be attached to line departments, or to other staff units, at any organization level.

There can be general corporate staff at headquarters only, serving the entire organization. There can be divisional staff only, serving the respective divisions, or there can be both.

Staff can be used for advice only or it can be used for advice and control.

In the accompanying (illustrative) advice and control chart, Exhibit 3, the four staff vice-presidents report directly to the president. The four staff managers in manufacturing and the four in sales report directly to the vice-presidents of manufacturing and sales respectively, but the dotted lines (3-A) reveal that the general staff vice-presidents additionally exercise a control over their staff counterparts in manufacturing and selling. This control normally consists of plans, policies, procedures and appraisals of results — seldom is it supervisory direction.

The vice-president of personnel, for example, lays down policies and procedures to be followed by the personnel managers in manufacturing and sales. The vice-president of finance and other general staff officers exercise a similar control over their staff counterparts in line departments.

Of course, they also serve as staff advisers to their immediate superiors.

Staff advice and control are likely to be found in organizations which are decentralized, i.e., either divisional, geographic or divisional, product. Usually, management denies that the staff groups have any control power, despite the obvious fact.

The personality and prestige of the staff head can help or hinder his success in the control aspect of his work. Likewise the attitude of the chief line executive can enter into the relationship between a staff head and his staff counterpart, directly responsible to the line executive for conduct. For instance, in some life

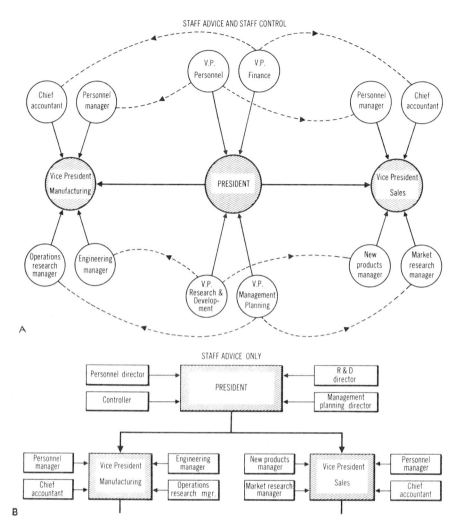

EXHIBIT 3. The Additional Control Exerted by the Staff Vice-
President Consists of Plans, Policies, Procedures and Appraisals of Results, Seldom Supervisory.

insurance companies the branch cashier is directly responsible
to the head cashier at the home office.

STAFF ADVICE ONLY
(see 3-B)

In contrast, note the simple relationships where the staff is
used for advice only: information, consultation, research and
perhaps training. In this situation the staff exists principally to
advise a line executive as to its area of specialized knowledge.

If it wishes to establish policies and procedures for staff counterparts at decentralized points it must work only through the line authority.

SOME STORM WARNINGS

When companies or departments are expanding rapidly, management is likely to become conscious of a need to change the organization structure, but many static companies and departments are already suffering from incorrect organization. Like an old man with gout, they have lived with the disease so long that they endure it as a necessary evil. Stages 2 and 3 in our machine shop example, Exhibit 1, exemplify such a situation.

Following are some signs which suggest need for a searching analysis of relationships existing within the present organization pattern. The presence of one or two of these "growing pains" may not be significant but the intrusion of a great many of them almost certainly indicates the need for change.

TWELVE "GROWING PAINS"

1. There are more than two organization levels between the first line foremen and deciding authority. The foreman asks for a decision from the assistant superintendent, who asks the superintendent, who asks the plant manager. This situation can mean that the superintendent has not been granted sufficient power to decide or hasn't been told what power he does or does not have.

2. A high level executive has various "assistants" and "assistants to." This condition usually signifies centralization of authority in a situation where decentralization is indicated. Generally, too many key men report directly to the top executive.

3. Conflict between high level line and high level staff executives. It takes careful analysis to distinguish which staff functions should be divisionalized, i.e., should be detached from corporate or headquarters staff and attached to divisionalized line executives.

4. Conflict between corporate and division staff men. Fault here may lie with the personalities of the men involved; with lack of understanding of authority, duties and accountability; with the reporting lines dictated by the organization chart.

5. Shortage of executives. Sometimes a company grows sales dollars faster than executives. Ill health, death and resignations can cause shortages in managerial talent. Even when these conditions do not exist, a company may suffer executive shortage because the organization simply does not encourage the development of executives. Usually such a company is the highly centralized, functional type.

6. Methods are radically changed. These may be in manufacturing, marketing or administration and may involve new equipment as well as methods.

7. Top level policies are altered. These may apply in a number of directions: finance, ownership, markets, products, labor relations, governmental relations, etc.

8. Little lateral communication. Functional lines are drawn so sharp that it is difficult for a middle management executive in one function to work with his peers in other functions. Contacts between the two functions must be made through their respective chiefs.

9. Too many committees. Committees can be useful for information, participation, complaint drainage or gathering of viewpoints but majority votes of committee members can rarely be substituted for executive decision making.

10. New plants, scattered geographically. Geographic decentralization is likely to force authority decentralization. Until this is brought about, long distance phone bills, and long distance frustration, are likely to be excessive.

11. Product diversification. The manufacture or sale of widely different products may not be economical through existing production or marketing facilities.

12. Competitors divisionalize. If a competitor changes from a functional to a divisional organization, you can be sure he gave it a lot of study first. Maybe it's time to consider your situation too.

REORGANIZATION OF MACHINE SHOP

Reverting to the machine shop organization problem outlined at the beginning of this article, Exhibit 4 shows the recommended organization chart. Two assistant superintendencies have been created, one to handle production, the other office detail and cost control. The foreman of tool room and maintenance reports to the assistant superintendent of production. Three persons, instead of eleven, now report directly to the superintendent, freeing him for better planning and control. Despite the increase in supervisors from ten to fourteen, the total number in the department has been reduced from 135 to 129.

RECENTRALIZATION

Neither centralization nor decentralization is, in itself, a good or bad thing. The effects, or probable effects, must be studied.

In some companies, factors are at work which lead to re-centralization of authority. Principally these factors are:

1. Top management disappointment over the results of decentralization. Due to insufficient experience, lack of conceptual ability, inadequate information or narrow viewpoints toward profits, some divisionalized executives have failed to live up to the much-heralded benefits of decentralization.

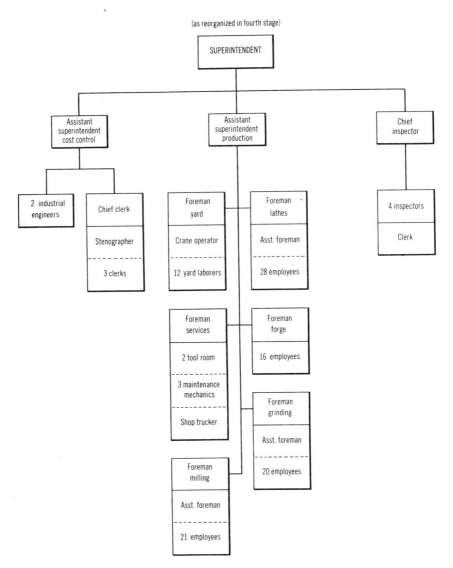

SUPERINTENDENT

Assistant superintendent cost control

Assistant superintendent production

Chief inspector

2 industrial engineers

Chief clerk

Stenographer
- - - - - - - - - -
3 clerks

Foreman yard

Crane operator
- - - - - - - - - -
12 yard laborers

Foreman lathes

Asst. foreman
- - - - - - - - - -
28 employees

4 inspectors

Clerk

Foreman services

2 tool room
- - - - - - - - - -
3 maintenance mechanics
- - - - - - - - - -
Shop trucker

Foreman forge

16 employees

Foreman grinding

Asst. foreman
- - - - - - - - - -
20 employees

Foreman milling

Asst. foreman
- - - - - - - - - -
21 employees

EXHIBIT 4. Two Assistant Superintendencies Have Been Created, One to Handle Production, the Other Office Detail and Cost Control.

2. Introduction of electronic computers. By centralizing the collection and interpretation of factual data, top management feels able to make important decisions better than hunch-following division managers. Similarly, operations research, with its application of complex mathematical concepts, must necessarily rest in the hands of a few staff advisers to high level management.

3. Automation and numerical control. Normally these features involve such radical changes in manufacturing and such large capital investments that decisions must be made at the very top level.

Economists tell us that normal organization growth follows a typical cumulative (s-shaped) curve: a period of struggling for existence, a rapid rise, a slowing to maturity. Some companies achieve their growth in twenty years, some in fifty, some never get out of short pants. Management understanding as to the necessity of changing the organization pattern permits the growth to occur.

48 U.S. STEEL GOES FUNCTIONAL

The United States Steel Corp. was born 62 years ago as a Morgan-Carnegie financial coup. It assembled 65% of American steel capacity, most of its iron ore and much of the world's finest coal into one of the earliest trusts. Twice in two decades, it survived a challenge under the antitrust laws.

Those probes — plus energetic, irreverent competition by such individualists as Eugene Grace (Bethlehem), Ernest Weir (National), and George Verity (Armco) — reduced Big Steel to manageable competitive proportions. By 1936, it had only 38% of American capacity, 34% of shipments, and a philosophy that induced its chairman to lament that it was hard to "find men who will leave private business and devote themselves to the affairs of the corporation."

By then — and with such an attitude — USS was locked-in on many of today's problems. Formed from 10 companies, it grew up with a savagely divisionalized management. It was making steel in at least 25 plants — of which 15 remain today. Most of that capacity was in the Pittsburgh-Youngstown, Chicago, or Birmingham districts, but the rest was as far flung as Massachusetts, Minnesota, Utah, and California. And it had coal, ore, cement, and transport properties almost everywhere.

Such diversity — advantageous in booms — also had disadvantages. Markets had to be served, even when declining. Public and government relations problems were many and diverse. Overhead costs were staggering. So USS moved slower than some when steel's future was born late in the 1920s with the invention of the continuous hot wide strip mill. Such nimble competitors as Armco and National rode that mill from obscurity to commanding market positions during the Depression. USS, meanwhile, strove

---

to hold its share of a changing market, maintain its plants, support its capitalization, and live with a militant new union. It became a byword that you didn't have to be good to make money in steel — you merely had to produce it a little cheaper than USS, which didn't make steel very inexpensively at all.

USS got a hard, unedifying look at itself in the mid-30s when it commissioned a study by the engineering firm of Ford, Bacon & Davis. Thereupon, under Chmn. Myron Taylor, it set out to become the world's most efficient steelmaker. The change — delayed by war and postwar shortage — was massive, the effort tremendous. The results were gratifying.

I. TURNING A GIANT AROUND

Last week, USS embarked at last on perhaps the most shattering step of all — a hard-boiled, fundamental management reorganization. . . .

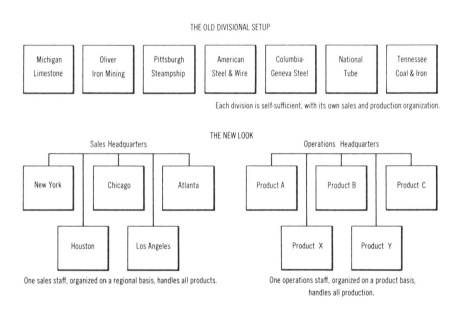

FIG. 1.   How U. S. Steel Is Reshaping Itself.

Effective Jan. 1, [1964,] USS Chmn. Roger M. Blough . . . announced, operating and sales functions of seven USS divisions will be consolidated with its Central Operations Div. — which by itself is the world's largest steelmaker. Seven other nonsteelmaking divisions will retain their identity and present form.

"The objective," says one insider, "is to get the maximum amount of administration from the fewest people. It'll take a long time to make all the changes. But when it's all done, literally thousands of job descriptions will have been affected."

The Changes

Other USS executives deny so drastic an upheaval. They pin great faith on attrition as the means of cutting back on management employment.

However it's described, there's unprecedented change ahead in that jam-packed management layer between general superintendent and executive vice-president.

USS alone, including Central Operations, lists 54 vice-presidents. Last week's reorganization plan creates seven more. Each of the seven doomed divisions — American Steel & Wire, Columbia-Geneva Steel, Michigan Limestone, National Tube, Oliver Iron Mining, Pittsburgh Steamship, and Tennessee Coal & Iron — had an organization quite similar to that of the corporation and its Central Operations Div. So it's evident that USS is hip-deep in management people — 24,000 altogether — even though it has fewer than it did a couple of years ago.

In January all steelmaking and domestic raw materials production will be pulled together in one unit. Immediately, seven division presidents will face reassignment. Manuals containing the new assignments at the top levels have been distributed, but remain pretty closely guarded. Still, even the clerks know that the president of National Tube, Henry J. Wallace, will become an administrative vice-president-sales, handling distribution, while Bennett S. Chapple, Jr., and Marcus J. Aurelius, both of whom have been administrative vice-presidents-sales for some time, will keep their titles and handle marketing and solicitation respectively.

Five New VPs

The revised sales organization will report through these five new regional vice-presidents:

In New York City, J. Michael Curto, now district manager for Central Operations, in Chicago, Howard J. Mullin, presently a sales vice-president in Pittsburgh, in Atlanta, David A. Challis, Jr., presently sales vice-president of TC&I, in Houston, William C. French, now sales vice-president of National Tube, and in Los Angeles, Ralph W. Seeley, now sales vice-president of Columbia-Geneva.

All Great Lakes shipping will be consolidated under Charles R. Khoury, now president of Pittsburgh Steamship.

Arthur V. Weibel, president of TC&I, whose headquarters is at Birmingham, is expected to join the staff of Executive Vice-Pres. Stephen M. Jenks, who handles engineering and research.

Van H. Leichliter, president of American Steel & Wire, is calculated to become one of four officers who will supervise product breakdowns.

Two new vice-presidencies will be added to the staff of USS Pres. Leslie B. Worthington, joining similar vice-presidents who have functioned for years in Chicago and Washington.

Attrition among the top men in the divisions is not expected to be severe. Somewhere, though, as you go down that long list of line and staff jobs to the general superintendent level, quite a few — probably most of them staff, but line executives also — will prove unneeded.

*   *   *   *   *

49 KAISER ALUMINUM'S PROBLEM IN ORGANIZATION

by Scott Nicholson

Back in 1957, the Kaiser Aluminum & Chemical Corp. set out to answer a simple question and ended up in a maze of confusion. An offshoot of the Kaiser Corp., the $796.6-million (gross property) company had ordered a 30-million-pound stretcher, the machine that draws and rates aluminum as it is being extruded. But two months had gone by, and the company had not yet decided on the specification for the machine.

Angered and determined to discover who had delayed the job, Kaiser's then-President Donald A. ("Dusty") Rhoades and Thomas J. Ready Jr., now its president, summoned all managers with a hand in drawing up the specifications. To the amazement of the two executives, no less than 100 men turned up, from departments as diverse as sales and metallurgy, process control and research.

As confusing as the experience was (the meeting had to be moved to Oakland's Leamington Hotel just to get room for the men), it made one point frighteningly clear. It showed why Kaiser, with rising sales, had seen its profits drop by $16 million in a single year. It also partially explained why, with over-capacity then rampant in aluminum, Kaiser had kept proliferating in people.

For as the two Kaiser executives realized, any organization in which 100 men decide on the specifications for one machine is wrongly organized. In large measure, then, the company's cost-price squeeze problems were home-grown. Too many people doing too many things, with no way for the upper levels of management to keep an eye on them.

As more and more companies are discovering even now, Kaiser has not been the only company to manufacture its own

---

Reprinted from Dun's Review & Modern Industry, June, 1963, pages 43-44, 68, 72, by permission of the publisher.

cost-price squeeze. And in more than one of these cases, management has discovered the same truth as Kaiser about the organization chart. No staid, lifeless thing suitable only for hanging on executive suite walls, the chart represents a very direct line to profits. Indeed, a host of companies ranging from Union Oil Co. of California to Genesco, Consolidated Freightways to ITT, have gone through the same experience in recent years.

Nevertheless, the problem of developing a profitable, suitable organization is not one that is easily solved. The man who draws up the most simple chart possible, seemingly a case of reducing complicated subjects to infallible black and white, may find out he has really added to the complications [see Fig. 1].

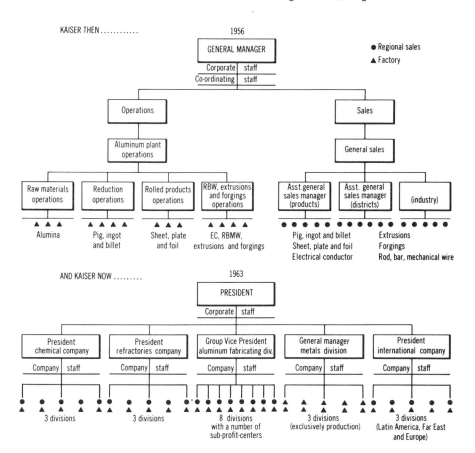

FIG. 1.   Which Is the More Efficient Company?

Things are not always black and white on an organization chart, though they sometimes appear that way. The two charts, showing the organization of Kaiser in 1956 and today [1963], appear equally complicated. They are not. The lower chart has resulted in a far more efficient organization.

Kaiser itself discovered that, as Tom Ready admits today. Ostensibly, the company already was set up in the only way possible. Aluminum is made by a single-line process of baux-ite-to-alumina-to-sheet and extrusions. So it seemed clear that Kaiser's production had to be organized functionally, following the steps of the highly integrated aluminum process.

Again, it appeared that marketing followed the only logical line of organization. Here, too, functional was the style. Yet a regional grouping meant more compact sales territories, and nothing could seem to be simpler or more efficient.

Yet something was wrong at Kaiser. Lines of command drawn on a chart crisscrossed in a maze of production, central purchasing, product sales and other responsibilities. Kaiser's central scheduling office, certainly not a corporate function that could add to profits, had been born and grown to 77 persons in less than five years. And a disproportionate 20,000 employees were in nonprofit staff positions, the budgets to support them growing by 10% to 15% a year.

Executives themselves added to the confusion. Middle managers were finding it increasingly difficult to pinpoint responsibility, measure performance or get prompt action on their decisions. And Ready realized what was wrong with even higher executives. "They were not thinking," he says today, "about the over-all picture."

WRONG, BUT WHERE?

Realizing Kaiser was wrong, but not knowing where, Ready and Rhoades decided to start off with a set of goals and then find an organization to fit them. And these aims became a perfect blueprint of modern management: "I want us to be organized," Rhoades said, "so that we can turn to just one person when there's a question on any product or market. Furthermore, I want more people to get experienced in making the same types of decision I have to make — that is, broad business decisions."

That was a starter. "The organization structure," Ready went on, "should not only make growth possible but actually compel it. Each manager must get a responsibility for a complete segment of the business — a segment large enough to challenge him to the fullest but small enough to get his arms around."

The man chosen for the job of literally bringing order out of chaos was Carlos A. Efferson, Kaiser's director of organization and planning. Efferson immediately set out on a four-month journey to companies large and small. He probed into such questions as what managerial abilities can be measured and controlled, what structure best brings out ideas and abilities from below, the most natural units in a corporation and what system allows a company to grow with the least strain. He also read heavily, particularly in the justly lauded works of Louis A. Allen.

One way or another, Efferson came upon Kaiser's weakness.

Its functional structure gave responsibility to nobody but the president. "You can't hold manufacturing responsible for profit," Efferson noted, "if it controls only one element of the profit picture. And you can't hold sales responsible if it controls only one element."

But how can you give the maximum number of people control over profits without creating complete corporate chaos?

The solution: divisionalization, with the entire company grouped around product lines. Now being used by many companies, but still unclear and an object of suspicion to a large number of others, divisionalization actually becomes a necessity for many corporations — even though they often do not realize it until nearly too late.

That happens when they become prone to the workings of what management planners call "the rule of three." The state (which Kaiser had already passed): when a company sells to three wholly different markets, distributes in three national regions and has a sales volume of $300 million or more.

While many companies delay such a move — and even fight it, because of its broad ramifications within the corporate structure — Kaiser's executives found that the evolution from functional structure to one grouped by product lines often is inevitable. Looking at the organization charts of du Pont at four different states of growth (ranging from 1902 to 1956), for example, they found that the charts resembled the structures of four totally different companies.

But how could Kaiser organize by product lines when it had 23 or more of them? The answer, of course, was that the products had to be grouped. But how? Arranged by manufacturing, Kaiser's structure would feature a finished-products division, a pig-and-ingot division, a rolled-products division, a forgings division and an extrusions division. By marketing, the organization would fall into divisions of sheet and plate (serving such a tidy grouping of customers as truck, train, ship, plane and trailer makers), foil and containers (another neat grouping of bakeries, food processors and packagers), electrical wire (utilities) and so on.

Kaiser opted for the latter choice as the one that held the highest profit potential. Its organization was split into five independent companies for aluminum, refractories, chemicals and international. The aluminum company was further subdivided into eight divisions: sheet and plate, extrusions and forgings, industrial foils and containers, household foil, highway products, building products, electrical products and ingot and billet. To each of these newly formed entities went its own factories, sales organizations and staff.

This way, each market-centered group is entirely independent, self-sufficient and in full control of all the elements affecting its total profit. And where one division depends on the raw materials or technical aid of another, "transfer prices" controlled by a corporate office make the interchange. With this "profit-centered" approach, moreover, responsibilities can be easily pinpointed and performances measured fairly far down the line. (As Kaiser uses the term, a profit center is the unit where an individual controls substantially all the elements of profit. Formerly, only the company president controlled them all. The production manager governed only part, the sales manager the other part, a system under which neither branch could be measured for profit.)

The new structure soon made itself felt in the very highest echelons of Kaiser Aluminum. Responsible for all decisions on sales, manufacturing and products, Tom Ready had never been able before to develop enough time to give to planning and development. Since the divisionalization, Ready has been able to concentrate on such massive tasks as developing a chemical company in the U.S. and spreading Kaiser's international operations across fourteen countries.

DIVERSIFICATION AND ENTHUSIASM

And that is not the only change in Kaiser. Under the old system, a new product aggravated problems in sales and production to the point where managers lacked enthusiasm for any diversification at all. Today the managers realize that new products and ideas bolster their profit picture, and they are taken up enthusiastically. So receptive has Kaiser become to new ideas, in fact, that when two managers, M. E. Seimers and A. P. Girior, had the idea to reduce paperwork by attaching a signed blank check to Kaiser's purchase orders, Kaiser management actually approved the plan — which most other companies would have thrown out as preposterous. Since then, the plan has become a resounding success ("Purchasing: From Rags to Riches," Dun's Review, May).

The one aspect of the charge that particularly delights Tom Ready, however, is the way it is developing new leaders at Kaiser. General managers, for example, now must think about their problems from the point of view of over-all profit, in the same fashion as the president of a small company. Thus the manager of the electrical products group has complete profit responsibility for this segment of Kaiser's operations, tying together production, sales, product development and research. Not surprisingly, this division last year recorded a 400% increase in net income over 1959.

"Being held accountable," notes Carlos Efferson, "is the key to management development. You can tell a production manager for years that he should view matters a certain way, and make no headway. But when you put him in charge of a division, you have concentrated education because his desk becomes the place where the buck stops." Adds Efferson: "This sobers and develops a man."

But the major benefits of the new plan undoubtedly accrued to Kaiser's marketing. "Which is as it should be," says Ready, "in an industry that is suffering from overcapacity."

By substituting a market-centered structure for the earlier geographical breakdown, the new plan simplifies marketing's job immeasurably. Where each salesman handled the entire Kaiser line of 23 clusters of products and knew more of them thoroughly, each is now a specialist for one market, which he knows exclusively. As Tom Ready puts it: "He lives and breathes one group of closely related products."

This makes for a decided advantage in Kaiser's marketing. No longer a mere order taker, with the creative parts of selling handled by specialists, the salesman today knows his market and his product thoroughly. In a profit-centered structure that means he must also be an all-round man, bringing the art of profit-making to bear on his small product line. Observes Carlos Efferson: "If your business is at all large or complicated, and you want to be most efficient, you should break the work of the business so that each person, even at lower levels, gets as much authority and responsibility as he can handle."

An added advantage: speed and simplicity for making field decisions on sales. Where the Kaiser salesman had to appeal through six levels of hierarchy before he could win a change of specifications, settle a claim, gain a price adjustment or get agreement to develop a new product, today he needs to appeal at the most two levels up to get a quick decision. Another advantage: being the company's only expert on his product for his region, the salesman takes more interest in his work.

True enough, his territory has grown in area, in some cases enlarged by thousands of square miles. But the Kaiser salesmen have found that servicing the greatly enlarged area does not require very much more travel than before. Once they have established themselves with the customer and gained an intimate knowledge of his facilities and technical problems, they find that many questions can be answered by letters and phone calls.

As in any such change on so vast a scale, Kaiser experienced some transitional problems. But most of the objections to the organization change proved illusory. A major fear, for example, was that it would be foolish to strip the best salesmen of their wide product lines; theoretically, this potential would be divided. As it turned out, though, a good salesman giving eight hours a day to his product brings in more income than when he spreads and dilutes his time over several dozen products.

Just as illusory were the objections of regional managers who felt that their jobs were being made smaller. In almost every case they have acquired greatly increased responsibilities.

Again, the problem of coordination seemed a major one. Aluminum production being an integrated process, the divisions would inevitably be dependent on supplies from the ingot and billet division and need technical help from one another. It was anticipated that a host of knotty problems would arise and many coordinating staff groups would need to be superimposed over the organization to keep the communication lines open between the divisions.

The contrary was the case. The change made possible the elimination of some staff departments. Central scheduling, analysis and product offices to backstop the sales and engineering efforts became dispensable. And transfer prices enabled divisions to purchase supplies and technical help from one another.

The biggest change of all, however, has come in the over-all picture at Kaiser. Though industry-wide conditions have slowed it up in recent months, the company last year raised sales to a record-breaking $444 million, profits to a comfortable $31.2 million.

What is more, even those impressive figures do not tell the full story. During those years Kaiser was building eight factories, developing two bauxite mines in Jamaica and Australia and branching out in fourteen foreign countries. But at the same time, Kaiser was reducing its administrative force by 16% and its sales force by 20%.

Proof that Kaiser has reached the ultimate in ideal organization? "Certainly not," snaps Tom Ready. "We will always continue experimenting." Ready, however, adds an afterthought: "But I feel that in view of our gains from pushing responsibilities on our people, the changes we make will be in line with our growing confidence in every man's ability to make decisions properly."

50 PATTERNS IN ORGANIZATIONAL STRUCTURING

by Harold Stieglitz

1. GREATER DIVISIONALIZATION ACCOMPANIED BY DECENTRALIZATION

As companies move into new fields of operations occasioned by expanded product lines or wider sales regions, they are confronted by new problems of competition, new technological problems, and new marketing problems. For example, a company historically identified with the production and sale of glass containers meets a whole new field of competitors when it expands its product line to include metal and paper containers. A service company operating in one region meets a new field of competitors when it expands its services to new regions.

The functional-type organization so well fitted to the single-product company or the company operating in one socio-economic region has difficulties in adequately coping with the new problems. For example, it is difficult for a single head of manufacturing to deal with all the different manufacturing problems associated with a variety of different products; or for a single head of sales to give adequate attention to the sale of different products to different customers in different regions. More importantly, it is hazardous to leave the over-all coordination of the production, engineering, and sale of a variety of products serving a variety of regions and customers to one man. But that is the case in a strictly functional type of organization: one man, the chief executive or his deputy, coordinates all line elements.

For several reasons — adequate emphasis on different product lines, easier identification of profitability, greater flexibility of operations, and increased ability to compete in a variety of

---

Reprinted from Corporate Organization Structures, Studies in Personnel Policy, No. 183 (New York: National Industrial Conference Board, 1961), pages 12-15, by permission of the publisher.

markets — more companies have grouped functions on a product basis and delegated responsibility for their coordination to the head of a product division. This divisionalization, almost by definition, has brought with it a greater degree of decentralization. For, in a divisionalized organization, the authority to make decisions involving the coordination of the activities relating to one product and accountability for profits occurs at a level lower in the organization than the president or the executive vice-president.

Of course, divisionalization may proceed from two different directions. Most often it occurs in a company previously organized along functional lines. But it may also proceed from a totally different direction: for example, where wholly-owned subsidiaries are more closely integrated into the operations of the parent company; or where merged or acquired companies operate as divisions of the over-all company. In the process of becoming a division, the subsidiary, merged, or acquired unit loses some of its autonomy.

It has been argued that this loss of autonomy amounts to recentralization rather than decentralization. But from the point of view of the parent or over-all company, it is still decentralization. (Because there are other aspects to this point, it will be touched on later.)

Among the companies participating in this report, the tendency to divisionalize operations is noticeable. For some, the move began after World War II and has continued; for many others, it is more recent. It is most noticeable, naturally, among those diversified manufacturing companies whose operations lend themselves readily to grouping of activities on the basis of product. But even companies engaged in businesses whose production processes historically have lent themselves to a functional organization (steel, for example), or those who have a common market for a variety of products (foods, for example), have adopted divisionalized organizational structures.

The move to divisionalize has not been without its problems. One is that as more specialized product groupings are attempted, it becomes increasingly difficult to meet the three basic criteria for optimum divisionalization along product lines: differing production technology, differing markets, and sufficient demands for the product. As a result, some companies have regrouped production (but more often sales) of previously established product units. Instead of having ten different product units, for example, they may regroup to eight, with one unit handling sales of the products that have the same customers.

A second problem arises, in establishing product or regional divisions, over the allocation of staff or service units to the product divisions. Need a division have a full staff complement in accounting, personnel, public relations, and research? Judging from the charts and manuals of the participating companies, economics, tempered by considerations of decentralization, seems to provide the answer. If the requirements of the division are such as to require a full-time staff component in any of the mentioned fields of specialization, the unit is set up. But if the services can be more economically provided by a central unit or a unit serving several divisions or a group of divisions, the staff service is not placed within the division.

However, as mentioned above, this purely economic consideration is tempered by the nature of delegated authority. If the division head or other unit head is held accountable for results, he may require or feel that he requires certain staff units at his elbow.

The companies participating in this report show a variety of staff arrangements so far as their divisions are concerned. In companies whose divisions are virtually major operations, or whose divisions are geographically dispersed, a full staff complement often exists within the division and/or units of the division. More often, when the company is smaller or not so widely dispersed, the product divisions may have less staff or none at all. The head of the product division in such a situation can avail himself of central staff services or, depending upon the degree of decentralization, hire outside consultants to furnish his requirements.

2. ELABORATION AND CHANGING ROLE
OF CORPORATE STAFF

As a company grows, staff also grows. Part of this growth in staff is a natural consequence of the need for more services of the same type: it takes a larger accounting department to service a company with $1 million in sales and 1,000 employees than to service one with $500,000 in sales and 400 employees. Part results from companies setting up units to carry on activities previously bought on a contract basis: the company may have grown to the point where it needs a full-time staff department to provide services that were formerly provided by an outside public relations firm or legal counsel on a part-time basis.

Another reason for the growth of corporate staff is evident in the charts of participating companies: many of them are finding a need for types of service that had not been of concern previously. Thus, in some companies certain staff components are now appearing at the corporate level for the first time. Some examples of the "newer" staff functions are: community relations, government relations, stockholder relations, computer technology or electronic data processing, research, product development, marketing and market research, manufacturing, executive development, organization planning, long-range planning, organization development, management services, and control.

Some of these functions arise from the changed competitive environment the business operates in; research, product development, and market research are prime examples, and government and community relations might also come under this heading. Some are more directly attributable to the move to divisionalized operations; for example, organization planning, executive development, and the emergence of marketing and manufacturing as corporate staff activities. And some are consequences of both; for example, electronic data processing, long-range planning, organization development, and management services.

Although the types of staff activity at the corporate level have been increasing, it is not accurate to say that the number of personnel engaged in corporate staff work has also increased. For much of the service-type work with which staff is identified is carried on by staff personnel within the divisions, leaving a smaller but more specialized, versatile, and highly skilled staff at corporate headquarters.

This fact points up another aspect of the elaboration of corporate staff: the general shift of emphasis from its role as primarily a service agency to its role as an agency assisting in planning and control. This change in emphasis is partly apparent in the titles of the emerging corporate staff units. But it is far more apparent in the organization manuals and position guides that detail the responsibilities of corporate staff. The shift is especially common in companies that have moved to divisionalized organization. For in a divisionalized company that practices decentralization, corporate staff takes on the major job of assisting in the formulation of over-all corporate objectives and policies. And it acts as the agent of the chief executive in measuring and appraising performance within functional specialties relative to the established objectives and policies.

Possibly the change in the role of corporate staff in a divisionalized and decentralized company might be more easily viewed from the perspective of the chief executive. In a functional type of organization he (or his deputy, the executive vice-president) has responsibility for coordinating the line elements — production and sales.

But, in a divisionalized organization, the chief executive delegates responsibility for coordination of what amounts to separate businesses to two, five, or more division heads. However, if his aim is decentralization rather than fragmentation, he attempts to set up objectives and policies that act as a cohesive and unifying force. Thus, the chief executive concentrates on those responsibilities that affect the organization and its future as a total entity: determination of objectives and long-range plans, policy formulation, surveillance, and control. As the business becomes more complex, the exercise of these reserved responsibilities calls for more and better information. Corporate staff has been characterized as the lobes of the brain that make it possible for the chief executive to carry out these essential responsibilities.

The emergence of corporate staff as a major force in the planning and control of corporate objectives and policies has been characterized as "recentralization" — as a reaction to too much decentralization.[1] Upon analysis, it can be seen that his claim contains some truth. But it can also be seen that other factors may contribute to what has been loosely termed recentralization.

First, some companies attempted to set up "divisionalized, decentralized" operations without first establishing over-all corporate objectives, objectives for each of their divisions, and corporate policies. After the effects of such disorganization became evident, the companies sought to establish those unifying elements that had been lacking. In such situations, organization analysts argue, the company was not decentralized in the first instance; it was atomized.

Second, some companies that have decentralized find that over a period of time there are changes in the three factors affecting the degree of decentralization.

1. Competence. The demonstrated competence of a position incumbent may fall short of the requirements of the job, or a new replacement may lack the competence required. In either case, the position may be redefined with less authority.

2. Information. The information required at a given level of decision making may not be available at that level. Authority is moved up to the level at which it is available.

3. Scope of impact. Because of a change in circumstances, certain decisions made by lower level heads may be found to have a widening scope of impact. Authority to make such decisions is moved up to the level at which all affected units are coordinated. Or where the company decides that a uniform course of action is necessary, the authority to make separate decisions is withdrawn.

In all three of the situations above, there is less decentralization than before; "recentralization" has occurred.

The use of these terms serves to emphasize a basic point: decentralization is a matter of degree. It varies from one company to another; it varies within a given company when, for example, certain organizational units may exercise a higher degree of delegated authority than others.

Other problems confront companies as a result of the elaboration and changing role of corporate staff. One is determining the types of controls the company can use and still maintain a decentralized organization. It is possible for central staff, in the name of control, to set up detailed audits and reporting procedures that amount to a constant check on the division heads. The alternative

---

[1] See, for example, "Top Management Tightens Control," Dun's Review and Modern Industry, July, 1959.

stressed by organization planners is control or appraisal of performance on the basis of established objectives and accountability for results.

Another problem arises from the fact that, in a divisionalized organization, corporate staff heads tend to be less involved in servicing operations than under a functional type of organization. Also, former heads of such traditionally line functions as manufacturing and sales may now find themselves heading a corporate staff manufacturing or marketing unit. In both cases, changes in relationships and methods of operation are called for. Reports from companies indicate that not all executives find it easy to make this adjustment.

3. EMERGENCE OF GROUP EXECUTIVES

As divisionalized companies increase the number of product divisions, effective coordination of the separate divisions becomes a greater problem. A fairly common organizational device many companies have used, and still use, is the setting up of an executive vice-president to ease the load of the president. In some companies, the executive vice-president coordinates staff activities. Far more often he coordinates the operating units or divisions, and the president retains direct supervision of the corporate staff units vital to his over-all planning and control responsibilities.

However, with the proliferation of product divisions and corporate staff units, some companies are finding that even an executive vice-president cannot adequately provide the required direction. So they have added general executives accountable for the performance of two or more product divisions that are somewhat related in terms of production technology or markets served. Most often, these executives carry the title of group vice-president or group executive. In some companies, they constitute an additional level between an executive vice-president and product divisions; in others, they are apparently in lieu of the executive vice-president.

The emergence of group executives is not confined to the giants among the companies in this report.

In a few companies, a position somewhat similar to that of group executives also appears at the corporate staff level. Two, three, or more corporate staff units may be grouped together under a senior vice-president or a position titled vice-president, administration.

Cutting down on the chief executive's span of control is the reason most often given for the increased number of group executives. The factors that seem most relevant to the determination to set up a group executive are:

1. Increased demand on the chief executive's time: when the extent of the chief executive's external relations and over-all

responsibilities rises so that the time remaining for him to furnish personal contact with major unit heads is inadequate, the new level is created to act in lieu of the chief executive.

2. Increased interaction between divisions: when the objectives or plans of several divisions begin to have greater effect on each other, possibly by virtue of overlapping markets, closer coordination is provided by means of a group executive.

For many practical purposes the group executive, like the executive vice-president, may be likened to an assistant president (rather than assistant to the president) as far as the divisions reporting to him are concerned. And as is often the case with assistants, the responsibilities and authority of the group executive, and their impact on the degree of responsibility and authority of those reporting to him, are not always clearly defined. It certainly cannot be found in the charts of companies where this position exists. But judging from position guides and organization analyses, some companies attempt to have it clearly understood that the division head's accountability for profitable performance, and his attendant authority, are in no way diminished by the insertion of a group executive; the group executive in these companies exercises some of the authority formerly reserved to the president relative to divisional operations. However, it is recognized that in such cases, although there is no lessening of the formal authority of the division head, he may feel he has less "authority" (in a prestige sense) because he is one level removed, or one level further removed, from the president.

4. ELABORATION OF THE CHIEF EXECUTIVE'S OFFICE

The elements so far discussed can be viewed as means used by the chief executive to manage a growing and far more complex business; all three allow him to devote more of his time to those responsibilities uniquely reserved to him.

Some of the unique responsibilities of the chief executive have already been mentioned, or at least implied, in the preceding discussion. Analyses of organization indicate that the following are the hard core of the chief executive's reserved responsibilities:[2]

1. External relations — The chief executive is the company as far as external relations with the public, stockholders, government, and business associates are concerned.

2. Objectives and long-range planning — The chief executive determines the appropriate long-range and short-range objectives and plans for their accomplishment.

---

[2] For a fuller discussion of these reserved responsibilities and some of the organizational device structures used by the chief executive, see "Organization of the Chief Executive's Job," Management Record, February, 1961.

3. <u>Over-all policy formulation</u> — The chief executive sets the code of ethical conduct that the company will adhere to in pursuit of its objectives.

4. <u>Surveillance and control</u> — The chief executive sees to it that all components of the organization are moving in the direction of established objectives and are conforming with corporate policies.

5. <u>Development of a successor</u> — The chief executive assures the continued survival and perpetuation of a company by developing the next chief executive.

There seems to be little question that the nature of these reserved responsibilities is the same for a chief executive of a small company, a medium-sized company, or a large or very large company. But as the company grows in size and complexity, the scope of these reserved responsibilities grows to such an extent that they are beyond the capabilities of one man. External relations alone may so preoccupy the chief executive of a giant enterprise as to leave inadequate time for proper attention to the other responsibilities. Or, at different stages of development, the other responsibilities may demand the full attention of the chief executive.

Not only does the scope of the reserved responsibilities grow beyond the capabilities of one man; but also, the abilities required for their performance become so increasingly varied that one individual cannot supply them.

It is evident from the organization structures in this study that companies — or more particularly, chief executives — are using several methods to cope with the expansion of the reserved responsibilities of the chief executive. All the methods elaborate the office of the chief executive so that these reserved responsibilities — the "chief executive function" — are being performed by more than one man. Accountability still rests with the chief executive officer alone, but the function, it might be said, is "decentralized."

One fairly widespread method, by no means new, is the use of personal staff assistants. In some companies, their responsibilities are rather general. They carry out whatever jobs of a temporary or a continuing nature the chief executive may assign to them. In others, the assistants specialize in fields of interest that the chief executive has chosen to reserve to himself; possibly, organization planning, technical development, and market development.

The distinction between these more specialized staff assistants and corporate staff units is not always sharp. Often they provide functional assistance to other units of the organization. Their major emphasis, however, appears to be on studies or plans, sometimes of a confidential nature, that fall within the reserved responsibilities of the chief executive.

Another method that appears quite frequently among the participating companies amounts to an upgrading of the president-executive vice-president relationship. An increasing number of companies are allocating the chief executive function to a chairman of the board designated "chief executive officer." The president in these companies is sometimes designated "chief operating officer," or sometimes "chief administrative officer." In some companies there is a definite split in responsibility of the two men, but quite often they "share the same box" and share responsibilities.

In a very few of the participating companies, not just two but three (a chairman, president, and an executive vice-president) and even four men (a chairman, president, and two executive vice-presidents) share this top box and the duties of the chief executive.

Still another method of coping with the increased complexity of the chief executive function calls for the creation of a council of top executives to carry out this chief executive function. The concept involved here cannot be adequately depicted on any chart. But a few companies use a special charting device to emphasize the idea. One box labeled "executive office" or "executive management" or "office of the president" appears at the top of the chart. It includes not only the chief executive and the executive vice-president(s) but also those group executives and general staff executives accountable for coordinating the operating and corporate staff components of the business.

In effect, the group executives and general staff executives making up this top council wear two hats. As group or general staff executives they are accountable for the performance of the units reporting to them. But, as members of the executive office, they lose their identities as line or staff men and become, to quote one company:

> "A group of executives free of detailed administrative and operating matters to assist the president in policy development and the over-all leadership and coordination of the company's business and management."

Having men with specified areas of functional and business responsibilities and with complementary abilities in this "office of the president" is viewed as assuring more adequate consideration of all factors that bear on any over-all decision. And, the chief executive function, instead of being the sole responsibility of the chief executive officer, becomes the responsibility of a composite personality, the chief executive office. The chief executive officer under this concept has the job of coordinating the component parts of his office and gives direction and purpose to their work so the company can reach the objectives for which he is accountable.

REDWOOD CITY, Calif. — It is the summer of 1960. You are a securities analyst and your assignment is to forecast the year's results for a company which in the previous 10 years has shown a spectacular growth in annual sales from less than $1 million to more than $73 million and in earnings from $115,000 to nearly $4 million.

You decide there is nothing to indicate the company will not continue to grow at a brisk rate and you make your forecast accordingly. When the results are posted months later, it turns out you were dead wrong. The company not only reports a decline in sales to $70 million, but it also shows a jarring net loss of $3.9 million.

This is no hypothetical case. The company in question is Ampex Corp. and more than one securities analyst was caught by surprise when the electronics firm took a sudden nosedive after a decade of steady advances, technological as well as financial. In Ampex's case, the stunning reversal did not prove to be long-lived. The company bounced back in its next fiscal year, ended last April 30, to report sales of $84.1 million and profits of $3.2 million. So far this fiscal year, sales and earnings are at record levels.

PROBLEMS OF GROWTH

In somewhat extreme form, Ampex's experience provides a vivid study of the problems that can build up almost without notice during periods of great corporate growth. It was not until Ampex's sales began to falter in the 1960-61 recession that the

Reprinted from Norman C. Miller, Jr., "Drastic Changes Help Solve Big Headaches of Fast Corporate Growth," The Wall Street Journal, September 17, 1962, page 1, by permission of the publisher.

true extent of the company's troubles became apparent. Then it became clear to the company's board that management needed help and a consulting firm was called in. Before it was over, the consultants actually were running the company.

As one source close to the company puts it, Ampex's former management "was intelligent and well educated, but simply lacked the experience necessary to control" the company's rapid development.

Now that Ampex appears to have weathered its big storm, a look back at what went wrong — and at what was done to correct it — might provide valuable lessons for other young enterprises. The case also points up why all-around management ability is assuming increasing importance in the electronics industry, an industry in which technological innovation once almost guaranteed success.

Few companies in any business have achieved more rapid growth than Ampex. The company was founded here on the San Francisco peninsula in May 1946 by Alexander M. Poniatoff, a Russian emigre. Mr. Poniatoff and a small group of engineers had hardly more than an idea for a product: A magnetic tape recorder. No commercial models were then available of this type of recorder, which records pictures, sounds and anything else that can be converted into electrical impulses. Today magnetic tape recorders are widely used to record television programs and shows and to record and store information from computers and scientific instruments.

EARLY SALES DISAPPOINTING

For the first four years of Ampex's corporate life, Mr. Poniatoff and his engineers made considerable technical progress but the company's sales were disappointing. However, the firm did pick up financial backing from a private group of investors. Mr. Poniatoff, who today as Ampex chairman still spends most of his time in the laboratory, was glad to turn over management chores to his financial backers. Among these men was George I. Long, Jr., who in 1950 left his job as assistant vice president in a large bank to become Ampex's treasurer and five years later moved up to its presidency.

In 1951 Ampex's sales more than doubled from the year before to $958,000 and in five years annual volume reached $11 million. In 1956 Ampex brought out the first tape recorder for television — the company received more than 100 orders for the $45,000 recorder within three days — and it was this product that spurred Ampex's sales growth to $73.4 million in the fiscal year ended in April 1960.

Ampex geared itself for growth. As the company got bigger, executives worried that it would become cumbersome. So in 1959 it decentralized completely on the theory that small units would build sales fast. The company set up five almost autonomous divisions, each with its own manufacturing, engineering, development, accounting and sales departments.

It was an organizational structure that stressed initiative but paid little attention to efficiency, according to some present executives. One top officer of Ampex estimates the decentralization move added several million dollars to overhead in one year. Not all members of the company's board of directors were sold on the plan. One director recalls that in 1959 he warned Mr. Long, in a friendly fashion, that if decentralization failed, it would cost him his job as president. As it turned out it did.

"LEARNING ON THE JOB"

Another problem was management talent. "The company decentralized on the basis of establishing good, local management of operations," one source at Ampex says. "But the top executives did not have the management strength below them that is necessary for a decentralized operation. Like many other young companies, Ampex was — and is — full of green managers who are learning on the job."

So long as sales continued to rise, the new organizational structure did no apparent harm. "When your sales are growing constantly you can afford to operate on a high-cost level," declares an Ampex officer. But when the 1960-61 recession hit, the story became altogether different.

As one executive relates what happened, Ampex officials simply couldn't believe it when in mid-1960, at the beginning of a new fiscal year, demand for magnetic tape recorders began to ease. "In its 15-year history the company had been able to withstand business recessions with absolutely no downturn in sales or profits," this source says. "Though a recession had been predicted by some economists for 1960, Ampex's management had assumed they would be able to withstand one and had set expense levels to accommodate a very substantial increase in sales. Even after the order trend clearly had turned down, management didn't recognize it soon enough and didn't cut back expenses."

Because the company failed to cut production when sales fell short of goals, inventories of finished goods swelled. This situation was worsened later when the company, finally alarmed by the sales downturn, began tinkering with its products in an effort to make them more attractive to potential buyers. "Engineering change orders were coming through on some products at the rate of one a day," an official recalls. The hasty design changes had the effect of making some unsold products and unused parts obsolete. In all, Ampex was forced to write off $4.3 million in "obsolete and excess" inventory in its 1960-1961 fiscal year.

A former top engineer at Ampex describes the situation within the company in mid-1960 as "chaotic." He contends that in pressing for sales volume "the company started to sell equipment before it was designed." Ampex admits to one example: It guaranteed a computer manufacturer it could deliver a tape transport mechanism that would match the speed of the manufacturer's computers. The computer required a mechanism that would move tape at 100 feet a second. But the Ampex unit was not designed for such a high speed. When the Ampex unit failed in service, the company was forced to "re-engineer" it.

RAPID PERSONNEL SHIFTS

As Ampex's troubles mounted, personnel changes came rapidly. The former Ampex engineer says "the going joke was that when you went to work it was safest to wear a visitor's badge so you wouldn't be fired. At first, there was a constant reshuffling of lower management. Then when the consulting firm was called in, their men started their own house cleaning."

The consulting firm, Cresap McCormick and Paget, was called in late in the summer of 1960 when, according to one director, Ampex's board, after making its own study of the company's operations, lost confidence in the old management. (Mr. Long, Ampex's former president, was the only member of the former management to sit on the nine-member board.) During the last half of the company's 1960-1961 fiscal year, the board in effect transferred responsibility for the company's operation from the top officers to the consultants. In June 1961, after reporting Ampex's $3.9 million loss, Mr. Long resigned.

During the time leading up to the reporting of this loan, Ampex took care to smooth over its problems in public. Even after reporting a $1.8 million loss in its fiscal quarter ended in January 1961 the company predicted its fourth quarter would show "considerable improvement." But instead it showed a $2.6 million net loss, bringing the deficit for the year to $3.9 million after taking into account profits made in the first half.

In their efforts to revitalize Ampex, the consultants began a search for a new chief executive who had a reputation as an administrator. The hunt led to William E. Roberts, then executive vice president of Bell & Howell Co. Mr. Roberts, then 46, had been with Bell & Howell for 25 years. Five years senior to Bell & Howell's president, he felt blocked in his ambition to become a chief executive and was casting about for a top spot in a "growth" company. When he came to the West Coast to talk with Ampex directors, he recalls, he telephoned his wife to tell her "this is it" even before receiving an offer of $90,000 a year in salary, plus an initial stock option for 35,000 shares.

A 12-HOUR WORKING DAY

The soft-spoken Mr. Roberts is not an executive who leads by sheer force of personality or brilliance of specialized knowledge.

He regards a working day of 12 hours as "normal" and he packs a briefcase when he leaves the office. Says an aide: "He's one of those guys who likes to get detailed reports at 5 o'clock Friday so he can read them over the weekend."

When Mr. Roberts took over, he faced a demanding task. He was expected to restore Ampex's sales momentum and get its costs under control. The record shows that during the fiscal year ended in April 1962 Ampex's sales shot up $14 million and administrative expenses decreased $4.6 million.

Mr. Roberts began cutting costs quickly. Duplicate division staffs were wiped out; central corporate offices were established to supervise accounting, legal work, industrial relations, marketing, research and advanced development. Nearly 200 jobs were eliminated.

A single ad agency replaced five agencies serving the divisions; the ad budget was cut from $2 million to $1.4 million. One of two accounting firms employed by the company was dropped. Four Los Angeles sales offices were combined into one as were three sales offices in New York. The video and instrumentation divisions, whose products were similar, were combined. Products were dropped if it was found they weren't contributing to profits.

In one area, however, Mr. Roberts raised expenses: Research and development. "We can't afford to risk sacrificing our technical position for short-term profits," the new president said. He promptly raised the research and development budget to $7.5 million from $6.3 million and added some 200 scientists and engineers to the technical staff.

Mr. Roberts brought two former colleagues with him from Bell & Howell as controller and financial vice president. He ordered "position descriptions" drawn up for each supervisory job, defining the area of authority, budgetary responsibility and relationships with other supervisors. Mr. Roberts credits this move with bolstering the confidence of lower management. "We began to get decisions made again."

Mr. Roberts also credits reorganization moves with giving sales a lift. The 175 salesmen employed by divisions were placed under corporate control. By having each salesman represent the full Ampex product line instead of just one division's wares, duplicate customer calls were eliminated. "In effect we increased our sales force three or four times," says Mr. Roberts.

Perhaps the most important element in Ampex's sales recovery, however, was an upturn in demand for tape recorders. By the end of the company's disastrous 1960-1961 fiscal year, several months before Mr. Roberts assumed his job, the company's order backlog was at a record high of $41.2 million.

WHAT DOES THE FUTURE HOLD?

Where does Ampex go from here? As Mr. Roberts analyzes it, four of the five types of products the company makes are in a "dynamic growth" phase. These are computer memory products, television recorders, magnetic tape for recorders and "instrumentation" recorders for military, scientific and commercial uses. Only sound recorders for the broadcasting and consumer markets are in a slowly expanding market, he believes. The company intends to introduce 25 or more new products by next April. One example: An improved tape transport system for use in computers. Mr. Roberts expects this $18,000 unit to generate "over $25 million in sales" over the next three years.

Mr. Roberts is particularly interested in pushing foreign sales. "We have a tremendous opportunity overseas," he says. "Our products have just barely scratched the surface there." The company plans to expand its manufacturing facility at Reading, England, and is considering building a Plant in Germany. In its last fiscal year sales of Ampex International in Switzerland were about $13 million.

Mr. Roberts is taking care that his earnings predictions do not go awry. At present, the company's forecast of a better than 10% gain in its current fiscal year does not include some $2 million from pre-tax earnings that is being channeled into a general contingency fund. This is being done as a precaution because Mr. Roberts is not satisfied that he has "adequate controls on all aspects of the business." Among other things, he wants to improve inventory control by using computers and to set up an improved system of work standards for production workers. If these measures work out as expected, Mr. Roberts says it is likely that most of the $2 million will be released from the contingency reserve and treated as profit this year.

52 GENERAL MOTORS' PLANNING

In Paris last spring, General Motors vice-presidents James E. Goodman and Edward N. Cole stood for two and a half hours on a busy corner watching the cars stream by.

They weren't idling: They were studying what kind of autos Parisians were driving. GM makes a fetish of learning what people think about cars and why they buy them. The executives were trying to pick up one more tiny piece of information to fill out the vast jigsaw puzzle that is GM's product planning. This planning is the envy and despair of the auto industry, and in the 1963 model year brought GM 3.9-million passenger car sales, almost 55% of the American-made cars sold in the U.S. As the new models went on display last week, there were signs that 1964 might turn out to be even better than this year.

Nothing is too small or too big to fit into the GM jigsaw. Some bits are supplied by the famous committees, mainly Distribution and Engineering Policy, others by consumer research, division engineering, sales, and corporation staff. All major executives make their contributions. Even Chmn. Frederic G. Donner and Pres. John F. Gordon are intimately connected with product planning.

No Specialists

About the only thing GM doesn't have is the specialized product planners on whom Ford and Chrysler lean heavily. The corporation wants no part of such specialists.

In the last analysis, it is the general managers of divisions who make the final decision on what products they will sell. The five men who make these decisions . . . are Semon E. Knudsen

---

of Chevrolet, E.M. Estes of Pontiac, Jack F. Wolfram of Oldsmobile, Edward D. Rollert of Buick, and Harold G. Warner of
Cadillac.

The decisions are theirs, but so precise is the picture that
emerges from the completed jigsaw that in a sense the decision
is ready made for them to see.

Cost of Goofing

The decisions had better be good. In the auto industry a mistake is measured in hundreds of millions of dollars. The problem
is made more complex by long lead times; [GM's five managers]
are deciding now what the 1967 models will be like — and by that
time the consumer can have changed his tastes twice over. There
just isn't any way to test market the product, though GM comes
close when one division tries out something, and the others tag
along if it succeeds.

Mistakes cost more than money. In 1958, Buick came out
with a barred rear window that the public wanted no part of. Sales
fell steeply; the division manager lost his job a year later.

Roughly, the corporation has assigned each division a portion
of the market. Thus Chevrolet has the low-priced field, Cadillac
the luxury. But the areas overlap. Buick, Oldsmobile, and Pontiac
sell cars that compete with Chevrolet's Impala. Cadillac feels
competition from Buick's Electra 225 and the Oldsmobile 98.
Buick competes car for car with Oldsmobile.

What's more the intra-family competition is intense — and the
corporation wants it that way. Asked if the corporation were
worried by the Buick-Oldsmobile invasion of Pontiac's 1964 Catalina market, V-P Goodman said: "Nobody will call them off —
in fact, they'll be encouraged. Pontiac will fight back. That's
where our real strength comes from."

I. RIVALRY AND COOPERATION

To understand how GM's product planning really works, you
have to grasp the curious mixture of competition and cooperation
between the corporation and its divisions. It's an elusive eel to
grasp, especially because GM prides itself on having no system,
and apparently never using the same procedure twice. Speaking
of product planning, Buick's Rollert says: "Sometimes we follow
a plan and sometimes we don't."

Persuasion

Of course, corporation management has some influence on the
final product say exercised by the division manager. Goodman
calls it "coordinated" control, rather than centralized, with the
corporation showing the division chief such an array of facts and
figures that he reaches the desired conclusion on his own.

That doesn't mean that the corporation and its committees always talk the division manager out of everything. Cole remembers when the committees cast skeptical eyes on the rear engine concept of the Corvair, but yielded to his array of answers.

Cole, whose domain is the Car & Truck Group, says that changing specific products and features "is a gradual process of watching trends." The watching takes in market research, things like the annual bouquet-and-brickbat study of what auto buyers think, dealer reports, even the intuitive knowledge of GM's huge and immensely experienced pool of executives.

Seeing Eye

Whatever the method, it has been uncanny in spotting turns in the market. In 1954, it recognized that a single type of car no longer satisfied a rapidly segmenting market. So each division began to add lines within the brands, such as the Bel Air and Biscayne series at Chevrolet.

In 1960, it concluded that the stripped down compact wasn't what most customers wanted. So the 1962 models — it took two years to incorporate the changes — had luxury interiors, sporty options, and powered accessories.

For 1964, GM thinks it has detected another trend. It is serving up a new line of longer "compacts," built on a 115-in. wheelbase. Every division except Cadillac will have a car with this "A-body." (The A-body is common to all the compacts, except the Chevy II, as the B-body is to the standard-size cars, and the C-body to the luxury types.)

Hundreds of people spent months of study and analysis to reach the simple decision that people wanted a longer car and more trunk space. And the A-body is probably the most radical change in the '64 model year.

The Steps

The process began in the autumn of 1959 when GM introduced its 112-in. wheelbase compacts, and customers began to complain they were too small. GM also noted that standard-size cars were holding their volume despite the vogue of compacts. For example, Chevrolet's expensive standard-size Impala has jumped from 19% of '58 Chevy sales to 40% last year.

The Chevrolet owner relations people, who have held 300 meetings with owners in the past four years, noted that at each meeting, at least one customer said the "1956 Chevrolet was the ideal size." (Outside dimensions of the new Chevelle are almost identical to the '56 Chevy.)

Corporation Executive V-P Goodman added the intuitive note: "People like to improve themselves, to move up to a bigger car."

Meanwhile, GM's central engineering staff coordinated complaints and decided that at least two were valid: (1) The compacts had a poorer ride than standard-size cars because they were lighter and had a shorter wheelbase, and (2) it was difficult to get into the backseat of GM compacts because the rear wheelwell blocked the way.

To solve these two problems, the engineers picked a 115-in. wheelbase. The ride was smoother, space could be used more efficiently, and the extra inches were just enough to get the rear wheelwell out of the way.

Different Roads

There are all sorts of examples of GM's ever-changing methods. Sometimes the corporation sets the parameters — height, width, weight, and wheelbase — for a new car, with the divisions merely concurring, as it did with the '64 line of longer compacts. Sometimes a division develops a product entirely on its own, with the corporation merely assenting, as Buick did with the 1963 Riviera and Pontiac did with the Grand Prix.

The same thing goes for individual features, which are sometimes developed and jealously guarded by a division on its own. Thus Pontiac is the developer and sole user of the transaxle, a rear-positioned transmission. But the corporation's Detroit transmission division teamed up with two car divisions to develop a new automatic transmission for Buick and Cadillac this year.

The powerful Engineering Policy Committee used economic arguments to line up four divisions to adopt the A-body. The committee pointed out that a lot of parts could be used by all, saving tool costs, and that the four divisions working in concert could do a better job of selling the new concept.

Styling

As Cole points out, this did not mean that there was one corporation car. Each division did its own styling of the basic package.

Styling at GM is typical of its mixed methods. All styling is concentrated at the corporation's technical center at Warren, Mich., but each division has its own stylist who keeps his work secret from the others. Not even Pres. Gordon has a key to the styling offices.

At Buick, Rollert explains his philosophy of styling. "We give the stylist free rein to do anything he wants in preliminary design. We let him go way out. Then we bring him back gradually to the mainstream of contemporary design. That way we may get a few 'way out' features — like the centurion grilled fenders on the Buick Rivera — on a car that is styled conservatively."

All GM cars do have a family resemblance, resulting from shared stampings and sheet metal tooling. Once in a while this backfires on everybody, as it did with the batwing rear end designed in 1959 by the corporation's advanced styling group. The consumers said no.

II. FAMILIES OF INDIVIDUALS

Usually, the divisions do a fine job of maintaining individuality. A frustrated competitor remarked of the new small cars . . . "All of them are the same, but the customers will never realize it."

Actually, each new compact has at least one distinctive feature. The Tempest has the split grille dear to Pontiac. The Buick Special carries the trademark portholes.

GM spends a lot of money every year to maintain individuality. It cost Oldsmobile nearly $12-million to tool up for a special concave rear window when it planned the Starfire to compete in the individualized car field.

In the new compacts, each also has a personality of its own. Says Cole: "Each division has its own rideability, steerability, and engine and transmission performance."

Helping Sales

Personality makes it easier to sell such competing cars. L.A. Averill, sales manager of Chevrolet, says: "There are Chevrolet families, Pontiac families, Buick families, Oldsmobile families, and Cadillac families. They like one division's cars, get used to the way they drive and ride, and they'll stay with them forever." To this, Cole adds: "Because of the loyalty, you can't jump around and make too drastic a change in a car."

The A-body cars won't be the only intra-GM competition this year. For at least two years, Buick and Oldsmobile have watched the surge of Pontiac, which expects to set a division record of 600,000 sales this year, solidifying its grasp on third place in the industry by 100,000 units.

Noting that Pontiac's low-priced Catalina series made the biggest gain, Buick and Oldsmobile have drawn a bead on its market for 1964. . . . Oldsmobile is introducing a slimmed down Jetstar 88 line, that will cost $60 less than the Dynamic 88. Buick omitted the new series, merely slimming down the LeSabre and chipping $30 off the price.

Common Engine

Interestingly, the Oldsmobile will install a Buick engine and transmission — one more example of the cooperation that economy breeds. In the GM family, only Chevrolet has the volume to go it alone. Thus Cole confides: "GM would like a volume of 1-million units for each transmission design to make its manufacturing tools efficient."

Cole believes that continued good sales for both GM and the industry as a whole depend on keeping costs down. That's why executives like Goodman and Cole try to show division managers why they should help other divisions by sharing tooling costs.

Rule of Profit

The argument that works best is profit, for that's what the division manager is judged on. And in the last analysis, GM never does anything that might damage a division's market position, no matter how great the saving might be. As Goodman puts it: "We try for as broad a usage of our tools as we can, but we always give each division something to merchandise." He adds that no matter what happens, "We will not take advantage of any cost reduction to ruin the individuality of a division."

Rollert at Buick echoes the importance of profit: "I can do anything I can afford." At Cadillac, Warner adds: "I could be as radical as I want with my products, but a lot of people would try to talk me out of it.

Conservatism

The profit angle, indeed, may account for GM's generally conservative product tastes. Rivals often accuse the company of waiting for others to lead — and make mistakes. Ford testily points out it was first with 115-in. wheelbases, in 1961, with the Ford Fairlane and Mercury Meteor. But sure enough, the Meteor flopped last year and was dropped for 1964.

GM did learn from the Ford pioneering; it noted that the bigger Fairlane devoured a lot of Falcon sales. So, when it came out this year with the bigger Chevelle, it eliminated five models of the Chevy II, just leaving enough for the owner who wants the least expensive transportation. The man who wants a bit more can upgrade to the Chevelle and then to the standard-size Chevrolet.

GM isn't always conservative. After all, its rear engine Corvair was probably the biggest innovation of the last decade in autos. And the Corvette, often called the only true U.S. sports car, is another industry innovation.

53 TOWARD A THEORY OF DIVISIONAL INCOME MEASUREMENT

by Gordon Shillinglaw

Accounting theory traditionally has been restricted to the twin problems of valuation and income measurement for an economic entity, usually the private business firm, with emphasis on an institutionally determined accounting period, usually one year. There is no reason, however, why theory cannot or should not be extended to cover any aspect of accounting. Indeed, theory has been applied to accounting for governmental units and non-profit organizations and there is evidence of increasing interest in these branches of accounting. Two gaps in accounting theory remain relatively untouched, however: (1) interim measurements of enterprise income for public reporting; and (2) internal income measurements for segments of the enterprise, segments that correspond to major organizational subdivisions of the corporate entity. This paper is directed to the second of these neglected areas, the measurement of divisional income.[1] More specifically, the object of this paper is to take the first steps toward

---

[1]Throughout, the term "division" will be used to refer to a major organizational subdivision of a company although it may take the legal form of an incorporated subsidiary or bear some other name such as "department," "product-business," or "profit center." The wholly-owned subsidiary is of course a special case, but the objectives of measurement are the same and these, as this paper will try to demonstrate, govern the establishment of measurement principles. The partially-owned subsidiary is, for external reporting, subject to enterprise accounting standards; for internal reporting, it should be treated in the same manner as other divisions.

Reprinted from The Accounting Review, April, 1962, pages 208-216, by permission of the American Accounting Association.

a theory of divisional income determination, employing a structure similar to that used for the theory of enterprise annual financial reporting.

THE NEED FOR A THEORY

Why is such a theory needed? To answer this question, it is perhaps wise to consider briefly why it has been necessary to construct a theory for enterprise accounting. The reason is not hard to find. Enterprise financial statements are prepared primarily for the information and guidance of outsiders, many of whom have in the past or may in the future invest in the enterprise. Lacking access to the company's internal records, the outsider needs some way of learning and defining what the published statements purport to show; he also wants assurance that measurement rules consistent with these definitions have been followed. Theory is designed to supply the first of these; it also provides the auditor with a basis for satisfying the outsider on the second count, through the mechanism of the independent audit and the auditor's certificate. In addition, the accountant himself needs a theory for another reason, to furnish him with directives as to what is to be measured and how to measure it.

In divisional income determination the purpose of theory is certainly not to provide the basis for annual auditors' certificates. There is no distant public that needs this kind of periodic reassurance that the rules of the game are being followed. Rather the objective of theory is to provide a basis for designing the measurement systems in the first place, and then for revising them as conditions change. Without a theory, this is likely to be a haphazard process, yielding systems notable mainly for their lack of consistency, the measurements of income clouded in ambiguity. Furthermore, without a good theory divisional income measurements are more likely to mislead than to inform.

ELEMENTS OF DIVISIONAL ACCOUNTING THEORY

The elements of an accounting theory for divisional income determination, and indeed of any accounting theory, are:

1. A set of basic concepts and definitions.
2. A set of postulates, or axioms, including a statement of the assumed objectives of the divisional units.
3. A set of objectives of accounting measurement, derived by deductive reasoning from the postulates.
4. A set of measurement standards or principles that, if followed, will produce division financial statements that meet the measurement objectives. These standards provide a basis for testing the acceptability of proposed rules of measurement.

Most of the concepts and definitions to be used in the theory are part of the professional vocabulary and need not be repeated here. A few of the more important concepts will be spelled out as the argument proceeds, but in the main this paper will be concerned with outlining a tentative set of postulates, measurement objectives and measurement standards. Specific rules of measurement will not be discussed, except to illustrate how a particular standard might be applied.

BASIC POSTULATES

As used in accounting, the term "postulate means a statement that is assumed to be true for purposes of theory construction. The theory, therefore, is valid only if the postulate is true. In scientific disciplines, the truth of a set of postulates may be inferred from comparisons of observed data with those predicted with the aid of the theory based on the set of postulates, but in accounting, the validity of the postulates must be tested by other means. The purpose of accounting theory is to provide a basis for generating data and not for predicting the consequences of specified actions, predictions that can be compared with actual results.

The theory of divisional income measurement proposed in this paper is based on the following set of postulates:

Postulate 1:   The firm is expected to yield income for the suppliers of long-term capital funds.

Postulate 2:   The division is an organizational segment of the firm, operated by division management as a semi-independent company, its independence of action subject only to the restrictions imposed by general company policies.[2]

Postulate 3:   The management of the division is expected to employ the resources of the division in such a way as to produce income for the company.

Postulate 4:   The division is a going concern which is expected to continue operations for an indefinite period of time that is long relative to the length of a single accounting period.

Postulate 5:   Division management has at least partial control over some but not all of the elements that determine the amount of income generated by the division's operations.

Some of these postulates are largely definitional and may be acceptable without further proof; others, the third postulate in particular, are advanced here without empirical proof, even though an empirical test would be possible. Supplying such proof

---

[2] It should be noted that this postulate is often invalid in that many divisions lack the requisite degree of independence. Most functional divisions (e.g., manufacturing) fall into this category.

would be a worthwhile research project, but in this paper the validity of the postulates will be unquestioned. At the same time, it should be recognized that this is not the only set of postulates that might be advanced. If there is reason to believe that another set of postulates is truer or more universal, then a theory could and should be constructed on that alternate basis. For example, the going concern postulate might be replaced by one stating that each division is at all times regarded as an active candidate for liquidation, which would lead to an entirely different set of measurement objectives and standards from those that follow from acceptance of the going concern postulate.

MEASUREMENT OBJECTIVES

Given these postulates, the next step is to determine the appropriate measurement objectives. The objective of any measurement, of course, is utility. As Kircher has said, the only useful measure of performance is one that indicates progress toward the goals of the recipient of the measure.[3] These goals are indicated by the nature and objectives of the business unit, in the present instance the corporate division. Once these fundamentals have been established, preferably by empirical research but by assumption if need be, then and only then is it possible to proceed with the next step, the identification of the objectives of measurement.

The nature and objectives of the division are embodied in the first four postulates. First, the company as a whole is assumed to have an income objective. Second, the division is a segment of the company, operating in many respects as an independent business unit, with the company as its primary and in most cases the only supplier of ownership capital, and formed with an income objective. Third, the managers of any business unit are always accountable to the suppliers of capital and in particular to the suppliers of ownership capital, in this case to company management. In view of the postulated income objective, this accountability must be regarded as primarily accountability as to the amount of income produced. Therefore, the primary measurement objective is to provide both company and division management with a basis for evaluation of division management's use of company resources to produce income. Measurements of wealth enter in only insofar as they have a bearing on the effectiveness of division management's utilization of resources in producing income.

---

[3]Paul Kircher, "Theory and Research in Management Accounting," The Accounting Review, XXXVI, 1 (January, 1961), 43-39.

The goal, therefore, is to provide a measure of income produced by division management. There is a second measurement objective, however: to provide top management with a measure of the profitability of the resources invested in the division. This also follows from the postulate that management expects resources to be utilized to produce income. If divisional income is inadequate to meet management's objectives and efforts to increase income are unavailing, then presumably resources will be diverted to other uses. It follows that top management needs some means of identifying unprofitable resource utilization for guidance in these future resource allocation decisions. The second income measurement objective, therefore, is to provide such a guide, an index of the level and trend of divisional resource profitability.

Unfortunately, it is not possible to satisfy this second objective precisely without abandoning one of the other basic postulates. The period income of the division can never be measured in absolute terms as long as the going concern postulate is accepted. Common costs and revenue interdependence among divisions create problems that can never be solved uniquely in the going concern. Only if the going concern assumption is dropped does the notion of absolute divisional income have operational meaning. Then the measurement objective becomes the determination of the income that would have been lost had the division been liquidated. This can be measured, or at least estimated, uniquely, but only by introducing drastic changes in accounting procedures. For example, it would be necessary to credit more than one division for all the revenue from a given sale if the sale would have been lost if either division had not been in existence.

To put this another way, abandonment of the going concern postulate means that each division must be regarded continuously as a candidate for liquidation. To accomplish this, its wealth must be defined to include all those resources and only those resources that could be set free by liquidation, and this wealth must be measured at liquidation prices. Division revenue becomes company revenue that would have been forfeited by liquidation, and division expense becomes company outlays that could have been avoided by liquidation, adjusted for any changes in net asset liquidation values during the period.

Fortunately, acceptance of the going concern postulate not only makes it impossible to measure division income uniquely — it also makes it unnecessary. If the division is regarded as a going concern, then liquidation is not an active possibility. And with liquidation not a recognized alternative, evaluation of the desirability of discontinuing the division's activities is not a proper measurement objective. The problem, therefore, is to devise income measures consistent with the going concern postulate that will be adequate to serve the objective of providing a rough measure of resource profitability, recognizing that absolute accuracy can never be achieved.

With these objectives as a guide, it is now possible to specify a set of accounting standards or principles that must be met by a system of divisional income measurement. The following eight measurement standards should be both necessary and sufficient to complete the theory presented in this paper:

1. Objectivity.
2. Co-variability.
3. Independence.
4. Comparability.
5. Controllability.
6. Service potential expiration.
7. Realization.
8. Revenue-expense matching.

Objectivity

First, the standard of objectivity. This pillar of enterprise accounting is no less essential in divisional accounting. Divisional income measurements are to be used by management in appraising managerial performance. The measurements, therefore, must be free from personal bias. This is all that objectivity means – it neither requires nor rejects the historical cost basis of valuation. Neither does the objectivity standard necessarily presume verifiability to the extent necessary in enterprise reporting. Verifiability merely means the ability to determine the true facts about a transaction.[4] When there is room for dispute as to the truth, more than one interpretation may be objective, and for this reason in enterprise accounting it is often necessary to postulate that one interpretation is verifiable to the exclusion of others. For example, the postulate of a constant value of money means that price index adjustments are not verifiable even though they may be objective. In divisional accounting, in contrast, there is no need to specify the minimum degree of verifiability that will be acceptable. If a given procedure is objective and meets the other measurement standards as well, then it can be regarded as adequately verifiable.

Co-Variability.

The standard of covariability requires that the income measured for the division respond in direction and if possible in amount to

---

[4] For example, see William A. Paton and A. C. Littleton, <u>An Introduction to Corporate Accounting Standards</u> (Urbana, Ill.: American Accounting Assocation, 1940), page 20.

changes in the division's contribution to real company income. Division income is unimportant in itself; its importance stems from its relationship to overall company income. This follows from the third basic postulate, that division management is expected to utilize a portion of the company's resources to generate income for the company. Top management is not interested in spurious income, produced by inappropriate accounting procedures or conventions. If the management of a division has taken actions that have increased company income, the division's income statement should reflect this increase.

This standard is most likely to be violated by unsound intracompany transfer prices or allocations of costs common to two or more divisions, but it is an important test to apply to other income-determining elements as well. It should be noted that although division profit contribution as a measure of divisional income is wholly consistent with the standard of co-variability, the standard does not require that divisional income be defined in terms of contribution. The division income figure must, however, reflect changes in the division's profit contribution and the safest way to accomplish this may be to accept a profit contribution definition of income.

Independence

Closely related to the standard of co-variability is the standard of independence. The second postulate states that each division is to be operated as a semi-independent unit. Its independence, however, is both contrived and restricted, and the artificial nature of the independence should be clearly recognized in income measurement. To accomplish this, each division's reported income should be independent of performance in other divisions. This follows primarily from the managerial performance measurement objective, an unstated postulate being that the effects of actions that are not subject to an executive's control are irrelevant in evaluating his performance. Variations in executive performance in other divisions are controllable, if at all, only by the management of those divisions. Therefore, such variations should be excluded from the measure of divisional income.

It should be acknowledged immediately that neither the firm nor the division is independent of its environment, and any attempt to eliminate all the effects of interdependence would lead to a sterile income measure. For example, one division's income may be influenced by reductions in the sales volume of the divisions that are its internal customers. If the division were a completely independent company it would experience a similar effect, however, and it is not proposed that the results of this kind of interdependence be eliminated. Instead, the measurement standard of independence refers to the elimination of effects that result solely from the fact that the division operates within a larger company framework and that its in-dependence in its relationships with other units of the company is synthetic and incomplete. To illustrate, this standard is violated by any cost redistribution procedure that permits sales volume in one division to influence the amount of administrative expense to be assigned to another division.

Comparability

Fourth, the measure of divisional income must be comparable in all respects with the income objective that is to serve as the bench mark for appraisal. This standard has no immediate counterpart in enterprise accounting, although it might be argued that the latter embodies an implicit comparability standard in the standard of universality.

In enterprise financial reporting, the income objective is typically multi-valued, a value being supplied, often implicitly, by each investor. Furthermore, it is by no means certain how each investor would measure income if he had unlimited access to company data. For this reason the accounting profession has supplied a basic definition of income to be used universally for all companies. Each investor then must either phrase his income objective in comparable terms or must make whatever adjustments to reported income he deems appropriate to render it comparable with the statement of his objective.

In divisional accounting, in contrast, the income objective is expressed explicitly by a specified group of recipients. The standard of universality in defining income is unimportant and unnecessary. Income can be defined in any way that makes for a sensible and useful definition of the income objective. This flexibility is most disturbing to those who seek a universal definition of divisional income, but it is unavoidable. The truth is that no single definition of income follows from the basic postulates. Only by introducing additional postulates, such as constancy of purchasing power or the homogeneity of costs, is it possible to derive a unique definition of income.[5]

---

[5] Paton and Littleton, for example, denied the validity in enterprise reporting of any but a net income definition, based on the postulate that costs are homogeneous, differing only in the difficulty of assignment. Op. cit., pages 67-69. Similar reasoning presumably was behind the conclusion in the 1957 revision of the concepts and standards statement that "the omission (from product cost) of any element of manufacturing cost is not ac-ceptable." American Accounting Association," Accounting and Reporting Standards for Corporate Financial Statements — 1957 Revision," The Accounting Review, XXXII, 4 (October 1957), page 539.

Just what does the standard of comparability require, then? First, for management performance appraisal the income objective should be stated explicitly and should be agreed upon beforehand as a reasonably attainable goal, given the expected environmental conditions of the period; in other words, it should be budgeted income rather than a uniform company-wide percentage return-on-investment objective. This conclusion is inescapable so long as divisional income is to be used as a basis for appraisal of division management. Appraisal of personal performance requires the measurement of differences between attainable objectives and achievements; if the objectives are not attainable, then the differences are not valid measures of performance.[6]

Second, for meeting the objective of providing a rough measure of resource profitability the income objective should consider the amount of resources committed to a division; company-wide, minimum acceptable return-on-investment ratios provide one means of accomplishing this. This does not necessarily mean, however, that divisional income must be net income, after deducting charges for a share of noncontrollable common expenses, as well as expenses traceable to the division but not controllable by division management. Although there is little objection to making such deductions from divisional income so long as they do not reduce the comparability of reported and budgeted income for management appraisal, these allocations are in fact unnecessary. Instead of reducing reported income, it is sufficient to inflate the return-on-investment objective by an equivalent amount to allow for unallocated or unreported expenses. A similar adjustment can also be made to allow for undistributed investments. Such adjustments can be quite crude because they are to be used only in preliminary evaluation of resource profitability; examination of any apparent problem areas will require more careful analysis based on different postulates. All that is required is that the periodic income measurements and the income objectives be stated in comparable terms.

Controllability

Closely allied with the independence and comparability standards is the standard of controllability. Division management should be charged for the use of all those resources over which it has control, and any variances between the income objective

---

[6] This is based on an unstated postulate that performance standards that are unattainably high will provide an unfair basis for personal appraisal. This assumption should be distinguished clearly from the assumption that unduly tight standards do not stimulate performance, an assumption that is neither used nor rejected in this paper.

and income achieved should result from factors that are at least partially subject to division management's control. This is based on the fifth postulate, that division management has only partial control over the division's destiny and no control at all over some of the income-determining elements. Given that income measures are to be used in management appraisal, then the influences of any noncontrollable elements should be eliminated from reported income or else neutralized in the appraisal of income. For example, if materials purchasing is not under the control of the operating divisions, then purchase price variances should not be shown on the divisional income statements that are used in management appraisal. Observance of the independence standard will insure comparability in this regard in most instances, but if noncontrollable variances are allowed to appear they should at least be neutralized by means of equivalent adjustments of the income objective.

Although this standard requires that divisional income reflect all controllable resource consumption, it does not mean that the division should not be charged for any consumption of resources, whether controllable or not. In fact, for the appraisal of resource profitability, the more complete the statement of resource use the better. For managerial appraisal, however, the fifth standard requires only that controllable elements be reported and that noncontrollable variances be eliminated; it is possible to record other income-determining elements in divisional accounts and then either to suppress such elements in managerial performance reports or to neutralize any variances arising from these elements, as suggested above.

Expiration of Service Potentials

The three final standards are more familiar. The sixth standard is the standard of service potential expiration. A useful and valid carry-over from enterprise accounting, this standard requires that expenses be measured in terms of the expiration of service potential. Once again this is derivable from the basic postulates. Division management is entrusted with certain re-sources. These resources may be tangible or intangible, but in any event they may without further proof be regarded as re-positories of given quantities of potential services which may decline or expire with use or age. Inasmuch as division manage-ment is answerable for its use of the division's resources, it follows that any service potential that expires as a result of the use of these resources should be deducted from the division's revenues.

It should be noticed once again that this standard does not state how service potential should be measured. If historical outlay cost satisfies all the other standards in a particular case, then decline in service potential should be, or at least can be, measured in terms of historical cost. But if one of the standards, such as the standard of controllability, is violated by historical cost measurements, then some other measure such as standard cost should be substituted.

Nothing in this should be intrepreted as implying that depreciation on long-life assets must be charged against division revenues. In measuring resource profitability such charges presumably should be made. For management performance reports, on the other hand, it is well to recognize that depreciation is seldom controllable in any significant sense and a comparison of actual with budgeted depreciation adds little if anything to the evaluation of the performance of division management. Control over division management's exercise of its limited authority to make capital expenditures can be achieved better by other means, such as required pre-outlay justification procedures and routine performance audits. Whenever resource utilization meets the controllability standard, however, the expense charge should reflect the expiration of service potential in whatever terms are most appropriate to the particular situation.

Revenue Realization

The next standard is the realization standard, or realization criterion, which states that divisional revenue should be recognized at that moment when realization is deemed to take place. But what is "realization?" A useful statement of the concept is the following: Realization occurs at that point in the transfer of an asset or a service to a party outside the division (including another division of the same company) when the amount of cash or its equivalent ultimately obtainable from the transfer becomes predictable with an acceptably high degree of accuracy.

Although the concept is not customarily described in these exact terms, this definition not only fits practice very well but also makes sense. The postulate that management's performance is to be appraised in part on the basis of its reported income leads to the conclusion that income should be recognized when the results of management's efforts are statistically determinable at an acceptable level of probability. Myers would phrase this differently, as a recognition of revenue at the time of the "critical event" in the process of asset transfers, but the result is essentially the same.[7]

_____

[7] John H. Myers, "The Critical Event and Recognition of Net Profit," The Accounting Review, XXXIV, 4 (October, 1959), 528-532.

Finally, there is the standard of revenue-expense matching. Expenses of a given period must include the monetary equivalent of those service potentials consumed specifically to produce the revenues of that period, provided that such expense recognition does not violate any of the other measurement standards. This also follows from the evaluation objective, in that income will be an inappropriate measure of performance if some service potentials consumed to produce current revenues have been charged off in prior periods or are deferred to future periods. This standard does not, however, preclude charges to expense covering service potentials that have expired during the period but that have had neither a direct connection with current revenues nor have created a significant benefit for future periods. Whether and how individual divisions are to be charged for such additional items will depend on the objective of measurement and on whether the charges meet the standards of controllability, comparability and independence. Inventory obsolescence, for example, is likely to be a valid charge against division management, even though it results not from use but from non-use of resources. As such, it should be shown on the management performance report and on the division resource profitability statement. For other expiring service potentials that do not meet the controllability test, however, the only justification for charging the division is to meet the resource profitability measurement objective.

CONCLUSIONS

To summarize briefly, there is a need for an accounting theory that will provide valid standards for measures of divisional income. Such a theory needs to be based on postulates as to the nature of the firm and of the division and their objectives. These postulates should be tested empirically, if possible. The postulates that I have proposed lead to a set of standards which, briefly stated, require that divisional income be determined objectively, be independent of performance in other divisions, co-variable with the division's contribution to company profit, and strictly comparable with income objectives attainable in the current period, deviations from budget being restricted to those currently controllable by division management. Such income measures may be supplemented, but not replaced, by measures giving rough approximations to the profitability of the division's resources, but the main emphasis should be on division income as a reflection of management performance.

Objections undoubtedly will be raised that this paper has not explored such questions as the use of variable costing, the validity of the profit contribution definition of income or the appropriateness of various methods of dealing with price level fluctuations. It will even be objected that income measurement standards that do not include a unique definition of income present a contradiction in terms. The second of these objections can only be answered with the observation that for management appraisal it is not important that all companies measure divisional income in the same terms; what is important is that performance be appraised in terms that make sense in each individual case.

In reply to the other objection, that this paper has overlooked many important topics, it must be observed that measurement rules are subordinate to measurement standards, and in internal accounting the use of replacement cost or of variable costing are questions of measurement rules rather than of standards. If standards can be agreed upon, the validity of measurement rules can be tested, but in the absence of standards the discussion of rules must necessarily take place in a vacuum.

54 DIVISIONAL PROFIT CALCULATION – NOTES ON THE "TRANSFER PRICE" PROBLEM

by Howard C. Greer

Management of complex industrial enterprises often involves efforts to calculate profits and return on investment for each of a number of product divisions. Such calculations are believed to be useful in evaluating performance, planning future investments, and maximizing overall results.

Where the several divisions are completely independent of one another, such measurements serve an important purpose. Where the divisions are closely interrelated, producing substantial quantities of goods for one another, the case is much less clear. When the stated results are heavily influenced by the prices at which goods are transferred from one division to another, weaknesses and defects in the transfer-price mechanism frequently invalidate the conclusions which the divisional profit figures might seem to suggest.

In such cases, the figures may not merely fail to motivate the right management decisions, they may actively encourage the wrong ones. This danger is not just the accidental result of unsound philosophy or careless application, it is inherent in the nature of the accounting process involved. In essence, the divisional profit calculation is based on the presumption that the results of two closely interrelated processes can be separated and independently evaluated; in the realities of a complex business activity, this just isn't so.

Through use of arbitrary standards and procedures, inter-

Reprinted from Howard C. Greer, "Divisional Profit Calculation – Notes on the 'Transfer Price' Problem," National Association of Accountants Bulletin, July, 1962, pages 5-12, by permission of the National Association of Accountants.

divisional profit allocations are possible, and for certain purposes (later noted) these are plainly indispensable. If, however, they are permitted to become the yardsticks for evaluating performance by division managers, and the motivating force in the decisions and efforts of those managers, they may lead not to better returns for the entire company but to the exact opposite.

The meat-packing industry provides a classic example of interrelated divisional operations, in which products of most departments may be either (1) sold in their existing semi-finished state, or (2) transferred to some other department for further processing — with most companies convinced that results for each department can be (must be) separately evaluated, for all management purposes. A quarter-century of intensive study of this problem by the writer has led to the conclusion that (1) there is no satisfactory basis for such evaluations, (2) the use of such data as may be developed, at the department manager level, leads to wrong decisions as often as to right ones.

The reasons are quite simple. If a manager is to be judged by the reported profitableness of his division, pressure is on him to do two things:

1. Take whatever steps seem indicated to maximize the profits of his division, regardless of their effect on other divisions, or on the company as a whole.
2. Apply himself to manipulating the profit-measurement procedures to his individual advantage, at the expense of other division heads less concerned or less influential.

It may be properly said, of course, that the division manager should be "broad enough" in his outlook to put company advantage ahead of division advantage but, if that is expected of him, it is unjust and ineffective to set up a measure of performance which has precisely the opposite bias.

While interdivision overhead allocations (possibly involving such elements as research, administration, advertising, public relations, etc.) are often a subject of controversy, they are normally minor influences on divisional profits. The crux of the problem usually is the establishment of interdivisional transfer prices, and that becomes the focus of the attention of all concerned. Factors and alternatives involved are sketched in the following sections.

The three principal bases for establishing interdepartment transfer prices may be designated briefly as (1) cost, (2) market, (3) negotiation. Each may be judged: first, in terms of the mechanics of its application; and second, in terms of its usefulness for purposes of (1) performance evaluation, (2) investment planning, and (3) managerial motivation.

The term, as here used, embraces all transfer prices in which cost to the producing department is the primary determinant of the charge to the receiving department. The cost figure adopted may be "standard" or "actual," overall or incremental, "full-apportioned" or "direct charge" only, etc. It may well include an allowance for "profit" (return on investment), or any other arbitrary factor deemed appropriate.

The outstanding advantage of this criterion is its integrity, its understandability, and its convenience. The "cost" (or "cost-plus") figure employed may be a pure accounting convention, but once the principle is established the calculations can be made precisely and easily, and all concerned can readily apprehend just what has been done and just what it signifies.

The obvious weakness of the method is its almost complete lack of utility in the fields of evaluation, planning, and motivation. Each primary and intermediate processing department is "guaranteed" the recovery of its cost (or cost plus profit) on each product transferred to another department — no less, no more. If, in the producing department, costs are high (poor location, poor facilities, poor management), it suffers no penalty — the burden is passed on to the receiving department. If, in the producing department, costs are low (fortunate position, efficient operation) it derives no advantage — the saving is ultimately reflected in the profit of the department doing the final processing and selling.

Furthermore, the assigned "cost" may be heavily influenced by varying conditions within the producing department — e.g., the current and changing "product mix" in that department. If Product A is made for outside sale and Product B for transfer to another department (same facilities employed), fluctuating quantities of Product A sold to others may affect the costs chargeable to Product B, in turn distorting the results of departments receiving that product, through wholly unrelated operating factors.

Worse yet, if there are several joint-products, or by-products, involved in the calculations, the philosophy of inter-product cost assignment may become a controlling, if entirely irrelevant, determinant of transfer prices. How much of the combined cost of joint products A, B, C, D, and E should be assigned to Product B, when input, output, yield, raw material cost, available sales prices, and facility usage are continually fluctuating in a radical and unpredictable manner? As long as reference is made solely to supposed "costs," the problem becomes insoluble, except in terms so arbitrary as to become managerially meaningless.

Consider the stated result as a motivating influence. Assume that alternative available processes will increase or decrease the relative yield of Product B from the raw materials and facilities available. If large returns are currently obtainable on outside sales or other joint products, the pressure is toward re- duction of output of Product B, no matter how badly it may be needed by a receiving department, which may employ it even more profitably. Conversely, if other products are losing money, while B returns a satisfying "cost-plus" price, the influence is toward pushing receiving departments into accepting more of the product — even expanding their own facilities to utilize it. Thus, overall company policy may become infected with purely divi- sional influences, with a resulting confusion of objectives, aris- ing from circumstances both fortuitous and transitory.

The unrealistic and illusory nature of reports and decisions, reflecting assumed "cost" elements only, eventually pushes al- most every enterprise affected into complete or partial use of one of the other available transfer price bases, of which so-called "market" pricing clearly has the greatest theoretical justification.

MARKET BASIS

The theory of this measurement procedure is that transfers should be priced at whatever would be realized or paid in an "arm's-length" transaction occurring in an "open market." This is to say that each producing department should charge, and each receiving department should pay, a price which the product would command if sold to, or bought from, outside customers or sup- pliers.

From the philosophical viewpoint, this procedure almost fully satisfies the requirements of evaluation, planning, and motiva- tion. Granted the premise — that there is a free, open, and vir- tually limitless market for the product, at an established, known price — the appropriateness of the measure is virtually unchal- lengeable. Each division becomes, in effect, a business of its own, with completely free choice as to selling outlets and pur- chase sources. Its achievements, its potentials, and its adminis- tration are well measured and guided by reports made on this basis.

Unhappily, the applicability of the method is severely limited by the absence of dependable market price quotations on a majority of industrial products. An item may be unique, or at least peculiar, and trading may be quite restricted, mostly on a contract or sale- by-sale price basis. Actual transactions, even if published, do not necessarily establish a dependable "open market" value.

Furthermore, the quantities involved may radically alter the apparent position. The fact that 100 X units sold yesterday at a certain price does not insure that 100,000 X units can be sold (or bought) tomorrow at an identical figure. Major expansion (or contraction) of a market supply may lead to much lower (or higher) prices. Quotations are often "nominal" even when avail- able: they may reflect the "last previous sale" of some months ago, or a contract which could not be renewed under present conditions.

Moreover, reported price quotations are (regrettably) not always free from purposeful manipulation. Distress sales, at cheap prices, may be cloaked with the anonymity of "private terms." A propped-up price, at an artificially high level, may reflect only a price agreed on between affiliated enterprises. A well regularized set of transactions may involve a price schedule that would not apply to a "spot" sale, or the erratic occasional dumping or grabbing of a quantity outside the limits of normal marketing conditions.

When prices change, what weight should be given to the old and the new price, as applied to transfers occurring at about the time of the change? What recognition should be given to quantity discounts, area and trade channel differentials, transportation and delivery allowances, service factors, etc? And if (as often happens), what one must accept to make a sale differs from what one must pay to effect a purchase, should the figure selected for bookkeeping purposes be one which will benefit the producing to the receiving department?

These and many other questions are difficult to resolve in a manner which all concerned will recognize as "fair." Sometimes the decision is left wholly to an impartial referee, with the parties stripped of any influence on the outcome. The alternative may be a requirement that the department heads concerned shall "agree" on what constitutes a "fair" price. This automatically transfers the subject into the realm of "negotiation" — the third of the suggested bases for transfer pricing, discussed in the following section.

NEGOTIATED BASIS

There is often a feeling that "trading," between the division managers concerned, will establish a more realistic price than is likely to be arrived at by reference to a cost-plus formula or a published market price. Each manager is presumed to understand the economics of his own situation and the importance of "making a trade" at some specific price. If free to offer the same buying or selling opportunity to outsiders, he can bargain intelligently for his output or his requirements, closing the deal (internal) or accepting an alternative (external) as conditions warrant.

The trouble with this appealing alternative is that it diverts the efforts of key personnel from activities promoting company welfare to those affecting divisional results only. Where the price in question is a major determinant of divisional results, the bargaining may be protracted and bitter. Some managers, pressured by unfavorable influences in their outside dealings, attempt to bolster their position by out-trading their fellow-executives in other divisions. Some become experts in persuasion and cajolery (to say nothing of deceit and bribery) as a means of achieving their profit objectives.

This sort of activity is not merely a time-waster and dissension-breeder; it may lead also to confusing top management as to the facts of a situation. A complaisant or inattentive manager in one department may accept an artificially high or low price on an item which is of minor importance to him, thereby inflating the results of another department in which the item is a major factor. From such misstatement, top management may derive a completely false impression as to managerial performance and profit opportunities. Result, at worst, may be expanded capital investment in facilities unlikely to yield a genuine return under normal competitive conditions.

CONCLUSION — AND A PROPOSAL

Reference was made earlier to the writer's long experience with this problem in an industry which has probably studied it more intensively than any other. This experience was partly as an accounting and marketing expert for the industry trade association (having intimate contact with top management in every major company), and partly as general manager of one of the larger companies (having responsibility for establishing policies, procedures, and controls within that company). The net result of years of study and experimentation in this field was a painful and grudging recognition of the fact that he could neither (1) evolve a method which served the desired purposes in his own company, nor (2) discover such a method which was giving satisfaction in any other. This provides some excuse for a conclusion that the problem is inherently insoluble.

This does not mean, however, that the practice of assigning transfer prices to interdivision product movements can be abandoned. Some value must be placed on each element of input and output, or the whole structure of intradepartment analysis and control will fall to pieces. It is merely necessary to recognize that no available transer-price scheme is likely to serve all possible purposes equally well, and that the results of any method employed must be interpreted with a clear conception of its limitations (as a device for performance evaluation, policy determination, and managerial motivation).

The writer's considered judgment is that a method will be most useful if it has these characteristics: (1) is uniform, consistent, and invariable; (2) utilizes only specific criteria, objectively determined and impartially applied; (3) can be easily administered, with a minimum of delay, research, and negotiation. It is his further opinion that review and interpretation of the resulting computations should be restricted to those who are, by training, experience, and position (1) fully cognizant of the precise and limited significance of the data, and (2) solely responsible for company-wide (not divisional) achievements.

This means abandonment of the demonstrably fallacious idea that in an integrated, multiproduct, sequential-processing enterprise, the activities of any segment can be either evaluated or motivated by its calculated individual profitableness. The division exists not to earn a profit of its own, but to contribute to the profit of the entire business. The manager should be stimulated to make, not the most for himself, but the most for the company. Saying that he will be judged on his individual results, but must also take a "broad view" of company-wide needs and interests, involves a contradiction in both terms and objectives. To paraphrase: What's good for General Motors isn't necessarily good for the country, and no purpose is served by ignoring the fact.

The preferable course would seem to be: (1) let judgments on profitableness be made, and implemented, exclusively by top management (with aid from experts in analysis and interpretation); (2) develop other criteria for evaluating and motivating divisional management performance.

The latter is by no means difficult. The division manager may be encouraged to concentrate on such problems as improving volume, maximizing yields, minimizing costs, utilizing facilities to best advantage, evaluating capital investment programs in terms of their potential additions to company-wide return on investment, etc. When his responsibilities include developing and maintaining sales to outsiders, his results naturally must be measured in part by the profitableness of such business, if its contribution can be successfully segregated from that arising from production for (or purchases from) other company divisions.

Use of a cost (or cost-plus) valuation on transferred output may best serve to remove (or at least normalize) the influence of interdivision production from profit calculations of a producing unit (though a market or market-related price must necessarily be employed for by-products which cannot be independently costed). On the other hand, assessing all previously accumulated "other-division" costs to a receiving unit on transferred input may so penalize (or inflate) its results as to give a false impression of its real profit contributions and potentialities.

A partial solution, in some instances, might be found in a combination procedure, under which (1) the producing unit is credited with cost (plus) or market, whichever is higher, and (2) the receiving unit is charged with cost (plus) or market, whichever is lower. The difference (if determinable) is then identifiable as the cost to the company of compelling two divisions to do business with each other, instead of utilizing independent outlets or sources. Such a figure could be studied and interpreted by top management, for purposes of company-wide policy decisions, without infecting divisional results evaluation or interdivision political relationships.

This is no cure-all, and it is not applicable in all situations. It does, however, permit each manager to state his own results on a basis which puts them in the most favorable light, leaving appraisal of their validity, from an overall viewpoint, where such appraisal belongs, as a function of top management. The essential is to free divisional managers of what are not divisional responsibilities.

How useful this method would be in practice, the writer is unable to say with any great confidence (never saw it tried). It might work well in some cases and not in others (would depend on circumstances). It appears, however, to be well worth trying out in any enterprise where the problem is major and the difficulty acute.

It should be fairly simple to develop measurements of this type, through statistical calculations collateral to the basic accounting records, and to expose them to a selected executive group, with carefully prepared explanations and interpretations. If initial reactions are favorable, the method might next be applied, experimentally, to one or more selected operations, in areas where the greatest uncertainty, controversy, and dissatisfaction exist. Outcome of the experiment might well suggest whether such a plan, or some adaptation or modification of it, might lead to better operations and/or sounder policy-making procedures.

Whatever the program, it should be developed with due regard for the following conclusions, each well-supported by both reason and experience:

1. Data most useful for motivation purposes are commonly least suited for pragmatic analysis and realistic forecasting, and vice versa (e.g., sales quotas established as goals for selling achievements are seldom acceptable as the foundation of dependable production or financial budgets).

2. Conclusions and decisions stemming from reports on "results" should be reached only by those well-schooled in the correct interpretation of the figures and responsible only for the results of the business as a whole (not just some one of its parts).

Establishment of a practical and productive transfer-price policy will depend on full recognition of these inescapable realities of business experience.

PART FIFTEEN:

EXECUTIVES' COMPENSATION

55 DEFERRED COMPENSATION

by Richard C. Smyth

Most people want the money they earn as soon as they can get it. In fact most employees, even most management employees, live from payday to payday. However, in some cases there are advantages in deferring the payment of current income until some future date, for the tax impact on high-paid executives can be reduced in only two basic ways. One is by converting part of compensation into capital gains for tax purposes. The other is by deferring part of compensation to a time when income and tax brackets will be lower.

When an executive's ordinary income tax rate approaches 50 per cent, the deferral of the payment of a portion of the income may ultimately provide significant tax savings for the individual. Also, as will be seen, in some cases the company can benefit by deferring part of the compensation of a high-level employee and thus assure the continued services of the individual to the organization and the denial of his services to a competitor.

Deferred compensation arrangements are being increasingly used, primarily because of our confiscatory ordinary income tax rates. Thus, a recent survey[1] of over six hundred large companies showed that in 1957 one-third used some form of deferred com-

---

[1]Arch Patton, "Annual Report on Executive Compensation," Harvard Business Review, XXXVI, 5 (September-October, 1958), 131; Dean H. Rosensteel, "Executive Compensation: Developing a Balanced Program," The Management Review, American Management Association, XLV, 5 (May, 1956), page 396.

pensation in paying top-level executives, while as recently as 1955 only about 17 per cent of the companies used this form of compensation.

TAX ASPECTS OF QUALIFIED DEFERRED COMPENSATION PLANS

Under any deferred compensation plan the essential considerations are how and when the benefits received by the employee will be taxed and how and when the employer will be able to take a deduction for the cost to him.

If the plan is a qualified plan, that is, if the plan meets certain detailed regulations of the U.S. Treasury Department, the employee is taxed only as and when he receives the benefits provided for under the plan, even though he had previously acquired a nonforfeitable right to them. Also, if the benefits are paid in a lump sum, they may be treated as a long-term capital gain subject to a maximum tax of 25 per cent. Likewise, under a qualified plan the employer can take a deduction each year for the amounts paid out that year to finance the plan.

However, in order to qualify, a plan must be either a pension, profit-sharing, or stock bonus plan. These terms are not defined in the Internal Revenue Code. Nevertheless, the Treasury Department regulations define a pension plan as one that is established and maintained primarily to provide for the payment of definitely determinable benefits over a period of years after retirement. The benefits must not be dependent upon the employer's profits.

A profit-sharing plan is defined as one which is established and maintained by an employer to provide for the participation in his profits by his employees or their beneficiaries. The plan must contain a definite predetermined formula for allocating employer contributions among participants and for distributing funds based on the happening of some future event.

A stock bonus plan is defined as one which is established and maintained to provide benefits similar to those of a profit-sharing plan, except that contributions by the employer are not necessarily dependent upon the profits of the organization and the benefits are distributed in the form of stock in the company.

There are other requirements for qualification, one of the most important of which is the requirement that the plan must not discriminate in favor of officers, stockholders, supervisors, or highly compensated employees, either as to their eligibility for benefits or as to the amount of benefits they may receive under the plan.

The most common application of a qualified plan is either the pension or retirement plan, which is found in nine out of ten companies today and which covers the great majority of employees, or the profit-sharing trust. One of the best-known examples of a qualified profit-sharing trust is the Sears, Roebuck and Co. plan, which, incidentally, now owns over 25 per cent of the outstanding capital stock of the company.[2,3]

Certainly, from a tax viewpoint the qualified deferred compensation plans are the most advantageous to both the employer and the employee. Nevertheless, plans which fail to qualify have definite advantages in certain specific situations even though the tax picture is less advantageous and less clearcut.

TAX ASPECTS OF NONQUALIFIED DEFERRED COMPENSATION PLANS

Because of the wide employee coverage which is mandatory under a qualified plan it is usually necessary to turn to the nonqualified plan where the intent is to defer a portion of the income of higher-management personnel. However, here the tax picture becomes somewhat confusing.

In essence the nonqualified plan is a promise, either absolute or conditional, by the employer to pay certain compensation to an employee, in future years, as part of the consideration for current services. The employer claims a deduction when the payment is made. The employee is taxed when the income is received, if the doctrine of constructive receipt and the theory of economic benefit can be avoided.

The doctrine of constructive receipt is fairly simple. It was designed and is written into the interpretive regulations of the Treasury Department to prevent a taxpayer from determining the year in which he will report his income by a simple refusal to accept accrued income. Where a taxpayer has the unqualified right to draw upon available funds, he will be taxed to the extent of such right in the year in which the right accrues, even though he does not exercise it during that year.

In order to withstand the constructive receipt challenge, the right to receive the deferred compensation must not be absolute but must be made contingent upon the continued perform-

---

[2] Stock Ownership Plans for Employees, New York Stock Exchange, December, 1956, page 88.

[3] Because qualified plans are so widely used in business and industry and are so thoroughly described elsewhere in the management literature, no attempt has been made to cover them in this book. Those interested in such plans should see Pensions and Profit Sharing, (2d ed.; Washington, D.C.: BNA Incorporated, 1956); A Study of Industrial Retirement Plans (New York: Bankers Trust Company, 1956); and Pension and Profit-Sharing Plans and Clauses (Chicago: Commerce Clearing House, Inc., 1957).

ance of future conditions, the breach of which would cause a forfeiture.

The theory of economic benefit is more complex.[4]

> It is judicial doctrine, and there is nothing in any of the Treasury Department rulings or regulations which explains the extent to which the Treasury Department may attempt to apply it. This theory may be said to be the expression of the view that an employee should be taxed not only upon his monetary compensation but also upon the value of any property rights irrevocably granted to him as compensation which have a monetary value — particularly if the property rights are of a kind (for example, an annuity contract) that the employee himself might purchase. It has undoubtedly been developed by the courts in large part to nullify attempts to minimize the tax burden upon executives by the use of non-cash media of compensation. The theory has been applied even though the employee cannot immediately utilize or sell the property rights granted to him.

Aside from the qualified pension, profit-sharing, and stock bonus plans there are three principal nonqualified ways of deferring management compensation. These are (1) individual contracts deferring income for specific executives; (2) "phantom stock" plans; and (3) deferred incentive bonus payments.

INDIVIDUAL CONTRACTS DEFERRING COMPENSATION

If a fifty-five-year-old married executive is receiving a salary of $50,000 a year and is given a $10,000-a-year raise, the raise will amount to $100,000 of additional income during the ten-year

---

[4] Louis Schreiber, "Tax Aspects of Employee Compensation Plans," Management and Taxes: Building a Tax Conscious Organization, Special Report, No. 10 (New York: American Management Association, 1956), pages 61-74.

See also Laurence F. Casey, "Deferred-compensation Plans Today: Their Status, Their Forms, and Their Uses," The Journal of Taxation, VI, 4 (April, 1957) pages 216-218; J. K. Lasser and V. Henry Rothschild, "Deferred Compensation for Executives," Harvard Business Review, XXXIII, 1 (January-February, 1955), pages 89-102; George Thomas Washington and V. Henry Rothschild, Compensating the Corporate Executive (New York: The Ronald Press Company, 1951), pages 168-185.

period prior to his retirement at age sixty-five. Under current tax laws the Federal government would take $61,400 of the $100,000. However, if the raise were deferred and paid to the executive over the ten years following his retirement, the government would take only $22,000. Thus, the executive would retain over twice as much of the raise after taxes, or an additional $39,400.[5]

This example points up the appeal of deferred compensation for high-paid executives. Such deferral of compensation is achieved through an individual written contract between the company and the individual. One famous deferred compensation contract was executed some years ago between the National Broadcasting Company and Milton Berle. As reported, under the terms of this agreement Berle receives $50,000 a year for thirty years. He is required to work for twenty years but receives the same salary for an additional ten years.[6]

In business and industry the typical deferred pay contract provides payments to the executive for ten years after termination of active employment. Also, typically the payments amount to from 20 to 50 per cent of the salary the executive was receiving at the time the commitment was made.[7]

For example, under an amended employment agreement dated December 23, 1955, the president of the Copperweld Steel Company receives $50,000 annually until December 31, 1959, for full-time services and $20,000 annually thereafter for serving in an advisory capacity after his full-time employment ceases. In case he dies before receiving 120 monthly payments for advisory services, the remaining payments will be made to his beneficiaries.[8]

Another example is that of the American Bosch Arma Corporation. Under the employment agreement between the corporation and its president, the president is employed at a salary of $110,000 a year for a five-year period ending April 30, 1959. At the expiration or termination of his executive employment he is entitled to receive, for advisory and consultative services, compensation at the rate of $20,000 a year for a period equal to two months for each month after April 30, 1954, in which he served as an executive of the corporation.[9]

---

[5] Assumes that current income tax rates are continued and that other income equals deductions and exemptions in the years before and after retirement.

[6] William J. Casey and J. K. Lasser, Executive Pay Plans (New York: Business Reports Incorporated, July, 1951), page 35.

[7] Lasser and Rothschild, op. cit., page 101.

[8] Copperweld Steel Company Proxy Statement for Special Meeting of Shareholders Held November 8, 1957.

[9] American Bosch Arma Corporation Proxy Statement for Annual Meeting of Stockholders Held April 25, 1957.

The Wheeling Steel Corporation pays its president an annual salary of $125,000. An agreement between the company and the president provides, in substance, that commencing May 1, 1959 (or May 1 of the subsequent year in which his full-time employment terminates) the corporation will pay him for services in a consulting and advisory capacity for five years at an annual rate equal to 50 per cent of the annual salary being paid to him at the time of such termination, provided, among other things, that he does not engage, directly or indirectly, in the operation or management of a competing business. Payments under the agreement will be made in the event of death or total disability.[10]

To withstand the doctrine of constructive receipt and to help protect against possible stockholder suits, agreements deferring executive compensation should provide for a period of active employment before any deferred payments are made. Also, the payment of the deferred compensation should be contingent upon the employee's meeting a series of conditions such as the following:

1. The employee's services during the period of active employment must be satisfactory.
2. After the conclusion of the period of active employment the employee agrees:
   a. Not to work for any competitive organization;
   b. Not to take any action which is detrimental to the interests of the company;
   c. To act in a consulting or advisory capacity as requested by the company.

The agreement should also provide that if the employee fails to meet any of the specified conditions all future payments are forfeited.

ADVANTAGES OF INDIVIDUAL CONTRACTS DEFERRING COMPENSATION

The individual contract deferring compensation is a selective device with a fairly limited application. It is of interest primarily to the older and highly paid executive who is relatively close to retirement.

The principal advantage to the individual is the deferral of part of current income to a time, not too far off, when the tax impact will be reduced. Also, he is assured of substantial income during retirement and is better able to accumulate capital for his own security and that of his family.

---

[10] Wheeling Steel Corporation Proxy Statement for Annual Meeting of Stockholders Held April 30, 1958.

From the point of view of the company there are also certain definite advantages in specific cases. A company may not be able to pay enough current income to attract an executive who is already highly paid by another company. The problem is still more difficult to handle if the executive has accrued nonvested pension rights or a deferred compensation contract with his present employer. Under these circumstances deferred pay may be the only method of compensating an executive for the risk and disturbance involved in changing jobs. Also, paradoxically, deferred compensation contracts tend to keep the company's own top executives from moving to other companies.

In some cases older executives, who may have slowed down, are reluctant to retire either because there is no pension plan or because the pension payments they would receive are inadequate owing to inflation or to the fact that they have not had sufficient length of service with the company. Frequently, they feel they must continue in office to maintain their standard of living. Of course, this tends to delay the promotion of younger and perhaps even more capable executives. In such situations deferred compensation contracts may provide a realistic solution.

Finally, the deferred compensation contract provides a way in which the company can secure the consultative and advisory services of its mature and experienced top executives after their retirement from active employment, while at the same time assuring that their talents and knowledge will not strengthen a competitor.

DISADVANTAGES OF INDIVIDUAL CONTRACTS
DEFERRING COMPENSATION

The great majority of younger executives, who are apt to be in somewhat lower income brackets, prefer current income to deferred compensation. The executive forty-five to fifty years of age must wait approximately twenty to fifteen years before the deferred income is received. This means he will have to pay the ordinary income tax rate in effect at that time on the deferred income. Not only is it uncertain as to what this tax rate may be, but Congress or the Treasury Department may change the tax laws or regulations with the result that current tax advantages may not only disappear but tax penalties may be imposed.

Even if the tax laws and regulations remain unchanged, in some cases the future tax advantage may prove to be an illusion, particularly where the executive will receive large pension payments and will have sizable income from other sources.

From the point of view of the company the principal disadvantage to using deferred compensation contracts is that such contracts usually produce only slight effects in providing incentives and stimulating the efficiency of the executives involved. The incentive aspect of deferred compensation is limited by the long span of years between the effort that produced the reward and the receipt of the reward.

In at least one extreme case a company agreed to pay its president very substantial annual payments for as long as he lived, beginning whenever his employment was terminated. Certainly, an agreement of this sort would not motivate an executive to build the company into a more profitable or larger enterprise.

Deferred compensation should bear some relation to the performance of the individual. For example, there is no reason why the amount of deferred compensation or even the existence of deferred compensation could not be related to the performance of the individual or to the profit or sales performance of the company during the executive's period of active employment.

A sound business purpose is the key to a successful deferred compensation plan. The company should think in terms of attracting, holding, and motivating an experienced and capable executive. The individual should think of providing for his current needs and for the financial security of himself and his family when he will have to retire.

56 PROFIT SHARING FOR RETIREMENT INCOME

by Mitchell Meyer and Harland Fox

The concept and practice of sharing company profits with employees has had a persistent, if somewhat checkered, role in the American enterprise system for nearly a century now. The first plan for which there is a definite record was installed by the Bay State Shoe and Leather Company of Worcester, Massachusetts in 1867. Although it is not recorded how long this plan remained in effect, the subsequent history of profit sharing indicates that if it was typical, it may not have had a long life. For profit-sharing plans have been particularly susceptible to the ups and downs of the business cycle: each upswing has resulted in a rash of new plans, and each downturn has brought abrupt terminations.[1]

As might be expected, then, the postwar economy has had its share of new profit-sharing plans. But there has been a basic shift in the objectives and the structure of these new plans. In the Forties the typical profit-sharing plan was of the type now called "current distribution"; that is, the share of company profits earned by employees in any year was distributed to them in cash at the time. Thus, the result was a current wage supplement.[2]

But the quest for economic security that has characterized the postwar years has changed this emphasis on supplementing

---

[1]See, for example, "Profit Sharing and Other Supplementary Compensation Plans Covering Wage Earners," Studies in Personnel Policy, No. 2, 1937.

[2]In one sense, this still is the most "important"form of profit sharing, for it underlies almost all executive extra-compensation systems, whether of the "year-end" bonus variety or the formalized executive bonus plan.

Reprinted from Management Record, May, 1960, pages 2-6, by permission of the National Industrial Conference Board.

take-home pay. The characteristic profit-sharing plan being in-stalled today is <u>deferred</u> profit sharing; that is, payment of the share of profits earned in any year is deferred until termina-tion of employment, with the emphasis on providing retirement income.[3]

This article summarizes basic statistical data on this new role of profit sharing in company employee benefit structures.

THE GROWTH OF COMPANY RETIREMENT PLANS

The accompanying chart illustrates the growth of retirement-income plans during the last two decades. The data are from statistics released by the Internal Revenue Service on the num-ber of plans approved under Section 401 of the Internal Revenue

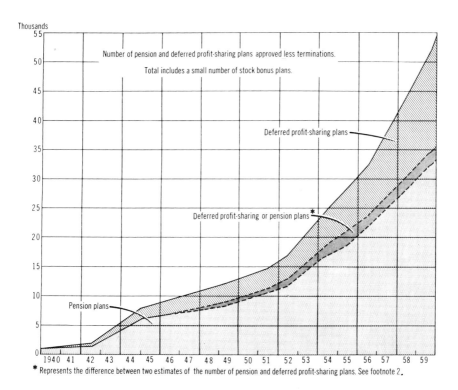

FIG. 1. Qualified Retirement Plans, 1940-1959.

(<u>Source:</u> Internal Revenue Service.)

---

[3]For a recent analysis of profit-sharing plans for rank-and-file employees, see "Sharing Profits with Employees," <u>Studies in Personnel Policy</u>, No. 162.

Code. For the most part, these are either pension plans or deferred profit-sharing plans.[4]

An analysis of all the qualified plans indicates the following three distinct growth periods, each with its own pattern.

1. A relatively rapid growth of qualified plans during the war years. Although the number of qualified plans increased sixfold in the decade prior to 1940, five years later, as the end of the war approached, almost eleven times as many retirement plans had been added (Table 1). The increase in these plans is particularly noticeable between September, 1942 and the end of 1944; some 5,800 plans were qualified during this period alone. A key to this growth, of course, was the wartime wage controls; in order to attract and hold a work force, management looked to the fringe items. And high corporate tax rates meant that a significant part of the cost of these fringe benefits could be financed with dollars that might otherwise have gone into taxes. In this context, the special tax treatment accorded approved deferred plans assured the growth of retirement-income plans as a wartime fringe.

2. A continued growth, but at a reduced rate, of qualified plans in the immediate postwar years. Although about 1,000 qualified plans per year were installed from 1945 through 1951, this yearly growth was only about half that of the war years (see Table 1). While favorable corporate tax rates and the special rax rule on these deferred plans continued as a positive growth factor, there is little doubt that the ending of wage and salary controls reduced the intense wartime interest in fringes. The rate of growth of qualified plans in this period reflects, perhaps, the more "normal" interest of management in retirement-income provisions in a society becoming more and more security conscious.

3. A tremendous increase in the rate of growth during the Fifties. In the early 1950's new momentum to the growth of retirement plans was provided by organized labor's drive to bargain pension plans for their members; thus, the number of plans qualified in fiscal 1952 was almost double the number for each of the two preceding years (Table 1). And by the end of the decade, the rate for new plans was 6,500 a year. This figure undoubtedly is the product of a number of factors, including continued union pressures, all merging to keep the installation of new retirement plans at their peak. Not the least important of these factors is the role of deferred profit sharing.

---

[4]The number of plans is a net figure: approved terminations in each period were subtracted from initially approved plans. The continuity of the data on approved terminations is broken briefly in 1955; therefore terminations during the first half of 1955 are estimated. The data also include some 100 stock-bonus plans.

TABLE 1. Qualified Retirement Plans, 1930-1959[a].

	All Retirement Plans[b]		Pension Plans		Deferred Profit-Sharing Plans		
	Number Added	Annual Rate	Number Added	Annual Rate	Number Added	Annual Rate	% of All Retirement Plans
Before 1930	110	—	105	—	5	—	5%
1/1/30-12/31/39	549	55	517	52	32	3	6
1/1/40- 9/ 1/42	1,288	483	843	316	445	167	35
9/2/42-12/31/44	5,839	2,502	4,208	1,803	1,631	699	28
1/1/45- 8/31/46	1,584	950	1,189	713	395	237	25
9/1/46- 6/30/48	1,888	1,030	—	—	—	—	—
7/1/48- 6/30 49	896	896	—	—	—	—	—
7/1/49- 6/30/51	2,517	1,259	—	—	—	—	—
7/1/51- 6/30/52	2,347	2,347	—	—	—	—	—
7/1/52- 6/30/53	3,657	3,657	—	—	—	—	—
7/1/53- 6/30/54	4,204	4,204	—	—	—	—	—
7/1/54- 6/30/55	3,291	3,291	—	—	—	—	—
7/1/55- 6/30/56	4,141	4,141	2,658	2,658	1,466	1,466	35
7/1/56- 6/30/57	5,734	5,734	3,302	3,302	2,423	2,423	42
7/1/57- 6/30/58	6,484	6,484	3,543	3,543	2,926	2,926	45
7/1/58- 6/30/59	6,496	6,496	3,581	3,581	2,893	2,893	45
7/1/59-12/31/59	3,275	—	1,618	—	1,633	—	—

[a]Plans initially qualified by Internal Revenue Service less terminations approved during the period.
[b]Includes a small number of stock bonus plans.

Until 1955, the Internal Revenue Service did not differentiate between pension plans and deferred profit-sharing plans in issuing statistics on the number of plans approved. However, in 1947 the agency released an analysis of the types of plans qualified prior to August, 1946. Despite this ten-year gap in the data on deferred profit-sharing plans, it is apparent, as can be seen in Table 1, that the growth of both pension and deferred profit-sharing plans has followed the patterns already described: a sharp upturn during the war years; reduced activity immediately after the war; and a big jump in the early Fifties, with the upswing continuing so that at the end of the decade, new plans were being added at a rate considerably above the war years.

However, of much more significance is the fact that an increasing proportion of the plans approved each year have been the deferred profit-sharing type. Prior to 1940, only 6% of new retirement plans were based on profit sharing. This jumped to 35% during 1940-42, dropped first to 28% in 1942-44, and then to 25% during 1945-46. When the series begins again in 1955, deferred profit sharing accounts for 35% of all new plans. By the end of the decade, 45% of the retirement plans approved during a year are deferred profit-sharing plans.

The chart illustrates in graphic form the growing importance of deferred profit sharing over the twenty years since 1940. By the end of the Fifties, some 54,000 retirement plans had been approved by the Internal Revenue Service.[5] Somewhere between 19,000 and 21,000 of these plans are deferred profit sharing, accounting for 32% to 38% of the total plans approved over the years.[6]

THE ROLE OF DEFERRED PROFIT SHARING

In the usual type of pension plan, a company determines the level of retirement benefit that it will provide and then each year sets aside the amount that it is actuarially necessary to support these benefits. Thus, the company has taken on a cost that, in general, will not vary in terms of its ability to pay.

---

[5]52,646 by September 30, 1959. This is a net figure; approved terminations have been subtracted.

[6]If it is assumed that 25% of the plans approved between September, 1946 and July, 1955 (the years in which specific data are not available) are deferred profit sharing, then the total number of deferred profit-sharing plans shown in Table 1 is approximately 18,600. If it is assumed that 36% of the plans approved during that period were deferred profit sharing, the total is 20,600.

The basic attraction of deferred profit sharing as a retirement-income device, however, is the direct relationship between company expenditure for employee retirement protection and the profit level of the company. The company merely promises to contribute — for those years in which a profit is recorded — a specified share of these profits. Of course, from the employee's point of view, there is a basic disadvantage in this arrangement. He cannot know what his retirement benefit will be, as it will depend primarily on the profitability of the company during his working years.

However, despite this drawback, deferred profit sharing, as would be expected, is particularly appealing to small companies. Many of these small firms, trying to operate a security-conscious environment which encourages retirement-income benefits, must face the primary consideration of whether they can afford a retirement-benefit program. Profit sharing assures that company funds will be spent for this purpose only when earnings are sufficient for the task.

That deferred profit sharing as a retirement-income device has in fact been essentially a small-company phenomenon is indicated in Table 2, which shows the average number of employees in companies installing new deferred profit-sharing plans approved by the Internal Revenue Service. In the 1940-46 period

TABLE 2. Average Number of Employees in Companies
Initiating Pension and Deferred Profit-Sharing Plans,
1930-1959[a].

Period	Profit Sharing Plans		Pension Plans	
	Employees per Company	Number of Companies	Employees per Company	Number of Companies
Before 1930	23,826	5	17,086	105
1/30-12/39	806	32	2,529	517
1/40- 8/42	571	445	2,558	843
9/42-12/44	487	1,631	851	4,208
1/45- 8/46	301	395	695	1,189
7/55- 6/56	160	1,579	487	2,824
7/56- 6/57	382	2,549	419	3,483
7/57- 6/58	218	3,100	372	3,757
7/58- 6/59	117	2,396	272	3,834
7/59-12/59	124	1,728	233	1,746

[a]Plans initially qualified by Internal Revenue Service.

the average number of employees in companies installing new plans was 472; for the period 1955-59, the average was 245 employees.[7]

It should be noted, too, that the average size of the profit-sharing companies has steadily decreased at the same time that deferred profit-sharing plans have become an increasing proportion of all new retirement plans. It is also apparent that in each period the average company installing deferred profit sharing is consistently smaller than the average company installing a pension plan. For example, average employment of companies installing pensions in 1940-46 was 1,052 (compared with 472 in profit-sharing companies) and for the 1955-59 period, 366 (compared with 245 in profit-sharing companies). It will be noted that average size of the pension companies has also steadily decreased over the period, but, in contrast to profit sharing, pension plans have become a decreasing proportion of all new retirement plans.

These data accent the role of deferred profit sharing in the small company as a substitute for a pension plan. But in the larger companies, deferred profit sharing may be attractive as a supplement for a basic pension plan. For example, a company may not be able to afford the substantial commitments required for a pension plan with liberal benefits; therefore, the company may install a pension plan with a small basic retirement income and depend on the profit-sharing plan to provide more adequate benefits. Similarly, the profit-sharing plan might be used so that benefits from the basic plan do not have to be continually revised upward in a prolonged period of inflation.[8] Finally, deferred profit-sharing benefits, paid as a lump sum at retirement or in substantial installments, may allow an employee to make an easier adjustment to his lower-income level after retirement.

But despite its use as a supplement in some companies, deferred profit sharing appears to be used most often as a substitute for a pension plan. For example, in a recent Conference Board study of 141 companies with a deferred profit-sharing plan, only 40% also had a pension plan.[9] However, the larger companies

---

[7]A study of employee benefit funds administered by banks located in New York State in September, 1954 found that the average number of employees covered by some 588 deferred profit-sharing funds was 290. See "Pension and Other Employee Welfare Plans" (New York: New York State Department of Banking, 1954), page 1.

[8]A few companies have invested the profit-sharing fund entirely in common stock and use this equity fund to provide a variable annuity as a supplement to the fixed benefit from the pension plan.

[9]"Share Profits with Employees," op. cit., page 73.

with deferred profit sharing were much more likely to also have a pension plan than the smaller companies with deferred profit sharing, as shown below.

Size of Company	Total Profit-Sharing Companies	With Pension Plan	
		No.	%
Less than 250 employees	17	3	18
250-999	49	14	29
1,000-4,999	51	24	47
5,000 and over	24	16	67
Total	141	57	40

The above data do not, of course, indicate how common deferred profit sharing is generally, either in conjunction with a pension plan or as the sole retirement-income plan. However, a recent Board survey of companies on the New York and American Stock Exchanges revealed the prevalence of deferred profit sharing in the following industries.[10]

Industry	Total Companies	With Deferred Profit Sharing	
		No.	%
Manufacturing	400	75	19
Finance[a]	13	8	62
Retail trade	25	14	56
Mining	13	3	23
Transportation	35	2	6
Gas & electric utilities	74	0	0

[a]Excludes banks and insurance companies.

Of course, the percentages above, especially in the nonmanufacturing industries, are merely suggestive and do not present a precise picture of the prevalence of deferred profit sharing in these industries. The number of companies involved is quite small, and these companies, by and large, are the largest in each industry. For example, only forty-eight of the 400 manufacturing

---

[10]"Compensation of Top Executives," Studies in Personnel Policy, No. 173, 1959.

companies in the sample has less than 1,000 employees. It might be noted that among the 352 companies with more than 1,000 employees, there is no apparent relationship between the size of the company and the prevalence of deferred profit-sharing plans. But, among these large companies sixty-one of the sixty-eight that have deferred profit sharing also have a regular pension plan. In other words, as was suggested earlier, deferred profit sharing is being used in these larger companies primarily to supplement the retirement income provided by a fixed-benefit pension plan.